OCT '05

Smith, Ron.
The big book of tin toy cars
R 745.162 9221 SMI

D1788182

**REFERENCE
DO NOT CIRCULATE**

50
AS

The Big Book of
TIN TOY CARS
Commercial and Racing Vehicles

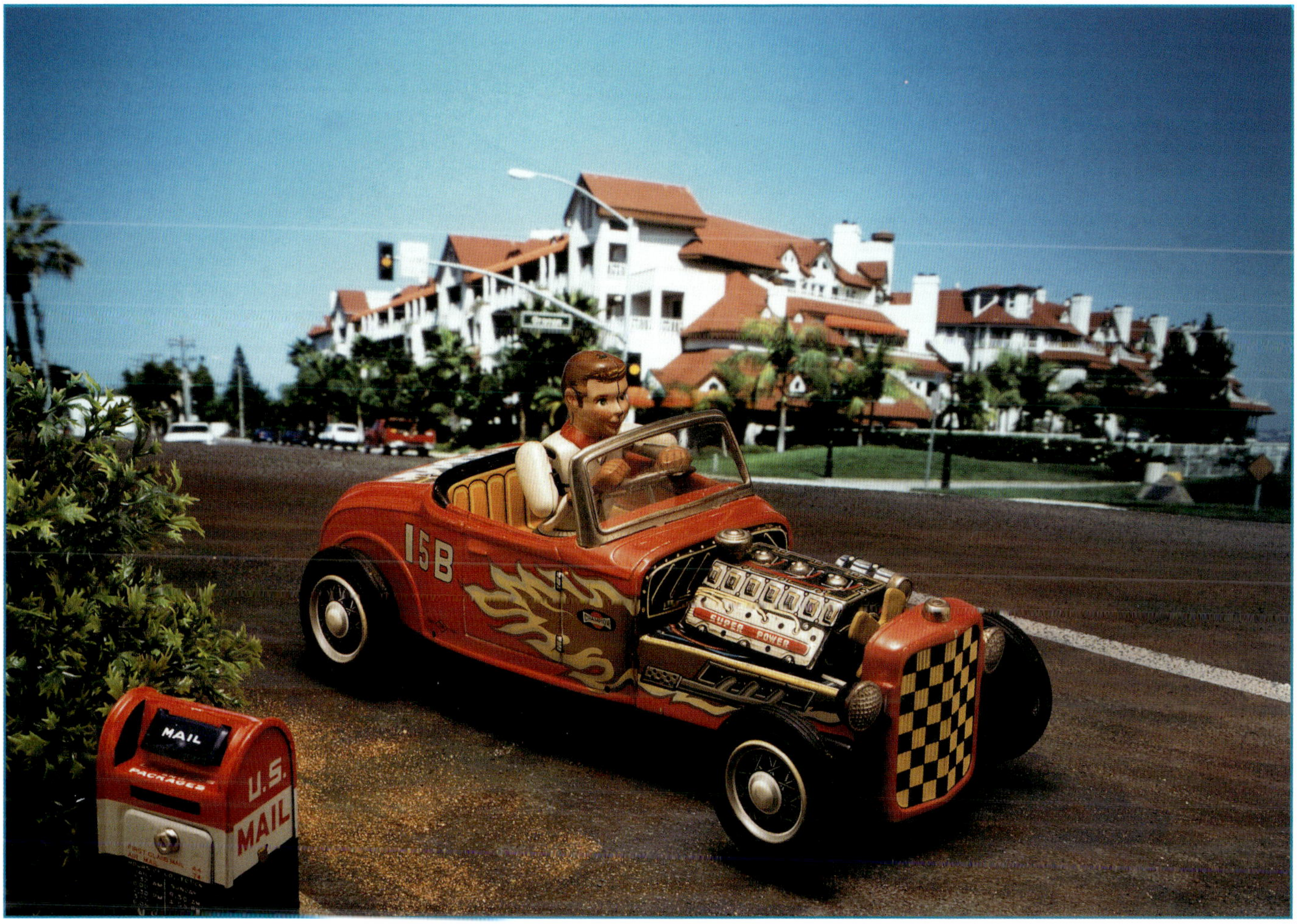

Ron Smith and William C. Gallagher

4880 Lower Valley Road, Atglen, PA 19310 USA

Photo by Rodney Abensur

Disclaimer

Most of the toys shown in this book and the prototypes from which they were derived may be covered by various copyrights, trademarks, and logotypes. Their use herein is for identification purposes only. All rights are reserved by their respective owners.

The text and items pictured in this book are from the collections of the authors or other various collectors and collections. This book is not sponsored, endorsed, or otherwise affiliated with any of the companies whose products are represented herein. This book is derived from the authors' independent research.

Copyright © 2004 by Ron Smith and William C. Gallagher
Library of Congress Control Number: 2003112760

All rights reserved. No part of this work may be reproduced or used in any form or by any means—graphic, electronic, or mechanical, including photocopying or information storage and retrieval systems—without written permission from the publisher.

The scanning, uploading and distribution of this book or any part thereof via the Internet or via any other means without the permission of the publisher is illegal and punishable by law. Please purchase only authorized editions and do not participate in or encourage the electronic piracy of copyrighted materials.

"Schiffer," "Schiffer Publishing Ltd. & Design," and the "Design of pen and ink well" are registered trademarks of Schiffer Publishing Ltd.

Designed by John P. Cheek
Cover design by Bruce Waters
Cover photography by William C. Gallagher
Title page photograph by Tosh Wakabayashi
Contents page photograph by Rodney Abensur

Type set in Americana XBd BT/Humanist 521 BT

ISBN: 0-7643-1949-3
Printed in China
1 2 3 4

Published by Schiffer Publishing Ltd.
4880 Lower Valley Road
Atglen, PA 19310
Phone: (610) 593-1777; Fax: (610) 593-2002
E-mail: Info@schifferbooks.com
Please visit our web site catalog at
www.schifferbooks.com
We are always looking for people to write books on new and related subjects. If you have an idea for a book, please contact us at the above address.

This book may be purchased from the publisher.
Include $3.95 for shipping.
Please try your bookstore first.
You may write for a free catalog.

In Europe, Schiffer books are distributed by
Bushwood Books
6 Marksbury Avenue
Kew Gardens
Surrey TW9 4JF England
Phone: 44 (0) 20 8392 8585
Fax: 44 (0) 20 8392 9876
E-mail: Bushwd@aol.com
Free postage in the UK. Europe: air mail at cost.

Contents

Acknowledgments	4
Introduction	6
Determining Toy Car Values	9
Commercial Delivery Vehicles (By Make, Year, Size, and Toy Maker)	11
Public Service Vehicles (By Make, Year, Size, and Toy Maker)	40
Airline Service	40
Ambulances	42
Fire	53
Military Service	72
Police	78
Postal Service	133
Road Service	134
Taxis, Limousines, and Transportation	137
Television and Broadcasting	148
Hot Rods and Jalopies (By Year, Size, and Toy Maker)	153
Race Cars	161
Dragsters (By Year, Size, and Toy Maker)	161
Speed Record (By Size and Toy Maker)	163
Rally and Stock Cars (By Make, Year, Size, and Toy Maker)	166
Single Seat Racers (By Car Number, Size, and Toy Maker)	190
The Toy Companies and Their Marks	218
Bibliography	232

Acknowledgments

To include so many toys in this reference work could not have been done without help and lots of it!

First, we were able to include photographs from some of the world's major tin toy car collectors including **Rodney Abensur, Rich Finney, Sonny Glasbrenner, Dr. Wolfgang Gutmann, Barry Skelley, Bruce Sterling** who are pictured here, and co-author **Ron Smith**. The photographs from these important collections became the foundation of the listings included in this two-volume set.

Rodney Abensur

Sonny Glasbrenner

Rich Finney

Dr. Wolfgang Gutmann

Acknowledgments 5

Barry Skelley

Bruce Sterling

Many other individuals contributed photographs beyond this foundation and helped provide information and assistance that made this book possible. From identifying toys, the real cars, trademarks, historical information, and language translation, each of these individuals contributed to making this book an encyclopedia-like reference guide for toy car collectors and historians:

Tom Allen, Tom Anstey, Rex and Kathy Barrett, Ron Cenowa, Dan Crossman, Fran Daher, John Dailey, Noriaki Enoki, Lionel and Annie Fournier, Jim Freeman, Eric Genemans, Jerry Gilpen, Mara Glasbrenner, Chihoko Goto (Hakone Toy Museum), Carl Gruber, Steve Hayes, Jack Herbert, Ayako Honda, Don Hultzman, Masamichi Inoue, Eiji Kaminaga, Dale Kelley, Doug Kelly, John Kopeckey, Marty and Debbie Krim, Mikio Machii, Moktar, Kinya and Takashi Morita, Shigeru Mozuka, Noburo Nakajima, Tsuneaki Niikura, Richard O'Brien, Ike Ogawa, Jack Pocher, Jean Roche, Hank Saito, Harumasa Saito, Rumi Sakamoto, Mike Sarvas, Herb and Barb Smith, Sumihiko Takasawa, Toyoji Takayama, Yoku Tanaka, Yoshio Udagawa, Kikuo and Kazuyo Uno, Don Wagner, Kozo Wakabayashi, Tosh Wakabayashi, Bill and Stevie Weart, Jim Whitaker, Sumihiro Yamashita, Hiromi Yoshikawa.

In addition to thanking our editor, **Donna Baker**, and our publisher, we want to thank all of the staff of **Jim's Open Kitchen** in Solon, Ohio: **Jim, Carol, Chris, Squid, Rich, Heather, Janice** and **Petra**, who inspired us to work through the daily tedious details of this book to be rewarded with good food and fun.

Jim's Open Kitchen

Introduction

The Vehicles In Our Lives

In the Introduction to our companion volume for this book, we discussed how the toy car industry mirrored our fascination with real cars. It is not surprising then that the variety of uses for motorized vehicles would also be reflected in the toys of the times. Many of the same car models we drove as private vehicles were used as police cars, fire chief cars, taxis, or delivery station wagons. Hot rods and jalopies were modified or old passenger vehicles. People raced their cars, and modifications plus a fancy paint job helped turn them into racing cars. Rally and stock cars too, were derivatives of standard sports or passenger vehicles.

Toy makers recognized this and realized that they could reuse much of their tooling and create a new toy release by converting their toy car models into police, fire, or other public service vehicles or race cars. For children playing with the toy cars, these variations added to the play value and imagination possibilities. You could create scenes and situations with these different purpose cars that simulated real life.

From passenger to police cars with added features.

Porsche 911 Rally

The variations from the toy companies proliferated. Any vehicle could be turned into a police vehicle. Not only did we see vehicles typical of what a police department might use, we also began to see luxury cars outfitted as police vehicles. Luxury brands such Cadillac, Lincoln Continental, Bentley, Nissan President, and Mercedes Benz were produced as public service vehicles. Sports cars like Porsche, Corvette, and Aston Martin were turned into police cars. Of course, everything that could be a police car could also become the fire chief's car. Great fun, even if it was not practical for the local police or fire department.

Old Fords became hot rods. Cars and station wagons became TV vehicles, airport vehicles, taxis, and ambulances. With the addition of commercial graphics they also became commercial delivery vehicles.

All of these colorful variations have become great collectibles since they cover so many different collecting categories. You can collect a certain model of car regardless of the category. You can collect only police cars or fire cars or ambulances. You can collect cars with advertising logos. You can collect cars designed for racing. In fact, the quest for racing speed was reflected in many types of toys. Toy companies produced tin dragsters, models of famous speed record racers, and an amazing number of single seat and open wheel race cars patterned after Grand Prix, Indy or Formula racing. This side of collecting offers so many possibilities to the collector that the list goes on and on.

During the 1950s and 1960s, Japanese toy makers produced more tin toy car models than any other country—just as we saw with the passenger vehicles covered in our companion volume. Accordingly, there are more toys listed from Japanese makers than from makers in other parts of the world. European tin toy carmakers were again second in production quantities.

Just Like the Real Thing

As with passenger vehicles, toy makers made a major effort to add realism to their toys. In addition to body style, the toy actions were enhanced. Clockwork and inertia powered friction motors, popular before the war, continued during this postwar period, but features like mechanical remote control and battery-powered headlights added another touch of realism. Battery powered electric motors were added in the early 1950s. Not only did this provide power to the wheels, but flashing and rotating lights and sirens also gave added realistic features to emergency vehicles.

Just as with passenger vehicles, the yearly changing designs of real carmakers and the introduction of new models presented a challenge to the toy maker. Requests for new toys often came from the importers, who would ask the toy makers to produce a specific new or popular car model. The process of studying the prototype design, hand building samples for approval, developing the final tooling required to stamp the tin parts of the toy, gathering new orders, and producing quantities for sale was a long one. Many retailers purchased their merchandise for the entire year at one time. If this total cycle overlapped a model year change, toy makers found themselves with toy designs that were already outdated. While this is understandable, it does explain the often seen inaccuracies found in toy cars. We find toy cars with the body of one model year and the trim of another. We find the front of the car corresponding to one model year and the rear of the car corresponding to the previous model year. And we often see box art that depicts a specific model, only to find a different model inside the box. Such were the complexities of keeping up with the rapidly growing automotive industry. However, even these variations and inaccuracies do not detract from the charm and appeal of the tin toy cars produced.

Oldsmobile pictured on the box, Lincoln inside the box.

There were many international toy companies who designed and marketed tin toy cars; the names of these companies are included later in this book. As mentioned above, some toy cars were much more detailed than others, but these toys provided an opportunity for a child (or an adult) to own and play with a toy car that looked just like the real thing. In spite of often seen inaccuracies in the toy cars, this realism is probably the one key feature that endears them to collectors and the primary reason that tin toy cars have remained one of the most popular and desirable of all toy collectibles.

While the Japanese produced the most tin car toys after the war, traditional toy companies in Europe and other parts of the world also continued to make tin toy cars. Even though these toys were often more expensive, they were and remain popular with collectors. Virtually every industrialized country had a maker of tin toys. Toys from the following countries are referenced in this book and its companion volume: Argentina, Brazil, Canada, China, France, Germany, Great Britain, Greece, India, Italy, Japan, Korea, Mexico, Spain, Sweden, Taiwan, USA, and USSR.

Tin remained one of the most popular mediums for toys from the early 1900s up through the 1970s before being replaced by plastic. The look and feel of tin gave a toy car the substance and appearance of the real thing, the excitement of chrome trim, and the heft of a toy that could be played with. Collectors of an age to remember those big, powerful, and highly styled cars of the 1950s and 1960s, the commercial adaptations, and the speedy racecars, find these toys an ideal way to recapture those hopeful memories from the past.

What's in This Book?

With so many tin toy vehicles having been produced, it would be difficult to document and impractical to include every toy vehicle produced in one publication. Our goal, however, was to create the most comprehensive tin toy car reference listing that would appeal to both general and specialized collectors and aid them in enjoying their hobby. We wanted to be as thorough as possible in order to provide a legitimate reference guide and hopefully document enough detail that readers may learn something new about tin toy car collecting. Accordingly, we have assembled photographs from some of the largest tin toy car collections in the world into a two volume work as the most complete and comprehensive listing of tin toy cars published to date.

Each car listing contains the following: make, model, model year, body style, size, graphic markings, description, producing company, country of origin, trademarks found on toy and box, a scarcity rating, and value ratings based on condition.

Generally, the toy cars listed in this book were produced close to the year of the prototype car the toy makers were trying to model. The exceptions to this occurred where toy makers modeled older cars for their antique car series or for hot rods and jalopies. Also, some 1950s cars have again been produced (or reproduced) in tin in recent years, primarily from developing countries. If a car was produced at a different time than the model represented, we have tried to note this in the listings.

To establish some general guidelines, we decided to limit the scope of this book by concentrating on:

1) Vehicles that were intended to be realistic toy representations of the actual vehicle. You should be able to look at the toy vehicle and determine what it was patterned after.

2) Toy vehicles that were 7 inches (18cm) in length or larger.

3) Toy vehicles that were primarily modeled after vehicles produced in the 1950s and 1960s.

4) Toy vehicles produced by the major tin toy manufacturers, which were in Japan and Europe.

5) Commercial (including public service and delivery vehicles) and racing vehicles in this volume; passenger cars, sports cars, and concept vehicles in the companion volume.

The majority of the vehicles included in this two-volume reference fall within these guidelines, but there are exceptions within each book. These exceptions generally were included because of their importance or interest to the tin toy car collector.

The prototypes for most of these cars came from the leading real car manufacturers in the US, Europe, and Japan. The importance of these countries to developing the global automotive industry is reflected in the choice toy makers made to replicate them.

Photo by Rodney Abensur

Determining Toy Car Values

Estimated current values for each toy are shown with the individual toy identification. Establishing value ranges is by no means an exact science due to the many variables and the subjectivity involved. In the end, the market will determine the price realized at a sale, so this guide should be viewed as just that—a guide! The values published in this book represent a compilation of known sales at auction houses, from Internet auctions, and from sales at antique and specialized toy shows. In most cases, they correspond to rarity of the toy and the market demand. The prices represent primarily North American values and should be considered in light of the following influences and the comments regarding interest and prices in other major geographic markets such as Japan and Europe.

Value Influences: Scarcity

Value is directly related to scarcity, with scarcity being determined by the *rarity* of the toy, *demand* for the toy, and finally, the *condition* of the toy. Each toy in this book contains a scarcity rating on a scale of 1 to 10, with 10 being the scarcest. Scarcity takes into account not only how many of the toys were produced but also how much of a demand exists among collectors. A rare toy with low production quantities can exist without much demand, just as a more plentiful toy can be in high demand and thus relatively more scarce.

Value Influences: Rarity

Rarity is influenced primarily by how many toys were produced, how many survived, and in what part of the world they were marketed. To the manufacturer, the success of a toy was measured by sales. Poor selling toys were a financial disappointment to the manufacturer, but because of low supply and high demand, they result in higher prices for the collector today. Also, those individuals who had these toys as children, and their parents, did not realize they would become so collectible and valuable someday. Accordingly, toys were given away, thrown away, or often abandoned.

Color variations impact rarity. Most toy makers produced their toy cars in assorted colors, but sometimes only one or two colors were used. Years later, it is difficult to know how many colors were produced and in what quantity. However, there is no question that some colors are harder to find than others. Collectors who seek out these hard-to-find variations will find that because of their rarity, prices will be higher.

Toys move easily around the world today, but where the toys were marketed in earlier years impacts where they are today. The result is that toys made primarily for the North American market are harder to find in other parts of the world, causing the prices realized for those toys to be higher than that of North America. Conversely, toys made for the Japanese market are not often found in North America and toys made for the European market are also not as common in North America. This makes these toys more rare in North America, with the prices higher accordingly. And finally, some toys were only produced as samples that were taken by the trading companies to show importers what was available. Importers may have taken a sample but never placed an order, thus the toy never went into higher volume production.

Value Influences: Demand

The next major influence on values is demand. Some toys are just more popular than others, based on the interests of collectors. Logic follows that toys sought by more collectors end up in more collections, making those toys harder to find.

Value Influences: Condition

Toys have survived in all stages of condition, from junk parts to near mint and in the original box. While the grading scale of C-1 to C-10 is widely utilized, there is certainly little consistency on how individuals grade their toys against this scale. If C-10 is truly mint (just as it came from the factory) and C-1 is for parts, most collectors will search out toys in the C-6 to C-10 range. There is minimal interest among collectors for toys below C-6 (fine) condition. Accordingly, value estimates have been shown only for C-6 to C-8 and C-10 toys, **all without boxes**.

C-6: *Fine*. Complete with no missing or broken parts. Nice condition with some evidence of aging and wear, but not played with hard.
C-7: *Very Fine*. Very minimal scratching and wear, but still bright.
C-8: *Excellent*. Very light general wear and appears close to new.

10 Determining Toy Car Values

C-9: *Near Mint*. Looks like new, but upon close examination is not truly mint.

C-10: *Mint*. As it originally came from the factory with no defects; however, factory touch-up is acceptable.

Finding toys that are in factory mint condition is very difficult and these toys are uncommon! The best chance for this is when someone finds old unused store stock.

This is not a C-10!!

Value Influences: Boxes

Boxes were often discarded, as the focus was on the toy car. Also, because these toy boxes were not very strong, they were very susceptible to tearing and bending with handling. The toy protrusions often would poke a hole in the box. Moisture would cause the box staples to rust and children would write on the boxes. Still, the box art on many of the toys is very colorful and pictorial, making the boxes a significant item to the collector and very desirable in their own right. Sometimes boxes pictured the real car that the toy was modeled after, making identification easier.

We have *not* included boxes in our value listing. However, boxes should be graded separately to accurately describe the condition of the toy and box and to better determine the approximate value of the toy and its box together. The C-1 to C-10 scale is appropriate for box grading.

Having the original box greatly enhances the value of the toy car. Some rare C-10 boxes can double the value of a toy and some may add only 20% to the value. Be aware that reproduction boxes now exist for many toys and are generally worth maybe $10 to $25. Reputable dealers will identify when the box is a reproduction.

Commercial toy car boxes.

Commercial Delivery Vehicles

(By Make, Year, Size, and Toy Maker)

Ford Ice Cream truck, Coronado, California. *Photo by Tosh Wakabayashi*

Ford Standard Coffee Panel Delivery. *Photo by Rodney Abensur*

12 Commercial Delivery Vehicles

(Not pictured) **1958 Buick 2-door pick up**. **6 in** (15 cm). **Friction**. Known colors: Assorted. Maker: **Bandai**, Japan. Toy marks: Bandai. Box marks: Bandai. Box text: *Model Auto Series Buick*.
Scarcity: 3. Fine to Excellent (C6-C8): $75-$100, Mint (C10): $150

(Not pictured) **1960 Buick 2-door pick up**. **12 in** (30 cm). **Friction**. Known colors: Assorted. Maker: **Gorgo**, Argentina. Toy marks: Gorgo. Box marks: Gorgo.
Scarcity: 8. Fine to Excellent (C6-C8): $150-$250, Mint (C10): $350

1954 Chevrolet 2-door delivery dump truck with driver, opening door, and dump action. **11 in** (28 cm). **Battery operated**. Known colors: Red, white, and blue. Graphics: Multi Action Dump Truck. Maker: **Yonezawa**, Japan. Toy marks: Y (Yonezawa).
Scarcity: 7. Fine to Excellent (C6-C8): $350-$550, Mint (C10): $850

1954 Chevrolet 2-door delivery dump truck with lever action dump. **12 in** (30 cm). **Friction**. Known colors: Red and black. Maker: **Yonezawa**, Japan. Toy marks: Y (Yonezawa). Box marks: Y (Yonezawa), SKK (Shinsei). Box text: *Chevrolet Dump Truck*.
Scarcity: 6. Fine to Excellent (C6-C8): $300-$500, Mint (C10): $775

1955 Chevrolet 2-door delivery fuel truck. **13.5 in** (34 cm). **Friction**. Known colors: Red, white, and blue. Graphics: Gasoline. Maker: **Marusan**, Japan. Toy marks: SAN (Marusan). Box marks: SAN (Marusan), Okuma. Box text: *Gasoline Tanker*.
Scarcity: 5. Fine to Excellent (C6-C8): $300-$450, Mint (C10): $600

1956 Chevrolet 2-door sedan delivery. **9.75 in** (25 cm). **Friction**. Known colors: Black. Graphics: Newspaper Delivery. Maker: **Bandai**, Japan. Toy marks: Bandai. Box marks: Bandai. Box text: *Newspaper Delivery Wagon*. Notes: Box illustrates 1957 Chevrolet.
Scarcity: 6. Fine to Excellent (C6-C8): $200-$400, Mint (C10): $600

1956 Chevrolet 2-door pick up. **9.75 in** (25 cm). **Friction**. Known colors: Assorted two tone. Maker: **Bandai**, Japan. Toy marks: Bandai. Box marks: Bandai. Box text: *Chevrolet Pickup #547*.
Notes: Box illustrates Chevrolet Apache pickup.
Scarcity: 4. Fine to Excellent (C6-C8): $150-$225, Mint (C10): $300

Commercial Delivery Vehicles 13

1958 Chevrolet 2-door pick up. 8 in (20 cm). **Friction.** Known colors: Assorted. Maker: **Bandai**, Japan. Toy marks: Bandai. Box marks: Bandai.
Scarcity: 3. Fine to Excellent (C6-C8): $75-$125, Mint (C10): $200

(Not pictured) **1958 Chevrolet Cameo 2-door pick up. 8 in** (20 cm). **Friction.** Known colors: Assorted. Maker: **Shioji**, Japan. Toy marks: none. Box marks: SSS (Shioji).
Scarcity: 5. Fine to Excellent (C6-C8): $175-$250, Mint (C10): $400

1958 Chevrolet Apache 2-door pick up. 8 in (20 cm). **Friction.** Known colors: Assorted tri tone. Graphics: Chevrolet Apache. Maker: **Shioji**, Japan. Toy marks: none. Box marks: SSS (Shioji).
Scarcity: 5. Fine to Excellent (C6-C8): $175-$350, Mint (C10): $500

(Not pictured) **1960 Chevrolet 2-door Ice Cream delivery** with driver, bell, and sliding canopy. **10 in** (25 cm). **Friction.** Known colors: White. Graphics: Delicious Ice Cream - Caution Watch Children. Maker: **Nomura**, Japan. Toy marks: TN (Nomura). Box marks: TN (Nomura).
Scarcity: 5. Fine to Excellent (C6-C8): $250-$400, Mint (C10): $500

(Not pictured) **1960 Chevrolet 2-door Ice Cream delivery** with driver, bell, and sliding canopy. **10 in** (25 cm). **Friction.** Known colors: White. Graphics: Good Humor Ice Cream - Caution Watch Children. Maker: **Nomura**, Japan. Toy marks: TN (Nomura). Box marks: TN (Nomura).
Scarcity: 6. Fine to Excellent (C6-C8): $350-$450, Mint (C10): $550

1960s Chevrolet 2-door pick up. 8 in (20 cm). **Friction.** Known colors: Assorted two tone. Maker: **Ichimura**, Japan. Toy marks: none. Box marks: Ichimura. Box text: *Chevrolet Pick-up Truck*.
Scarcity: 2. Fine to Excellent (C6-C8): $15-$25, Mint (C10): $35

1965 Chevrolet 2-door delivery with fender mirrors, Japanese roof sign, and cardboard container in truck bed. **11 in** (28 cm). **Friction.** Known colors: Yellow. Graphics: (Japanese). Maker: **Masudaya**, Japan. Toy marks: MT (Masudaya). Box marks: MT (Masudaya).
Scarcity: 8. Fine to Excellent (C6-C8): $600-$900, Mint (C10): $1,200

1970s Chevrolet van with bump and go action, lighted picture panel on roof, lithographed occupants, and dinosaur graphics. **8 in** (20 cm). **Battery operated.** Known colors: Blue, red, and white. Graphics: Sports Van. License: 4666. Maker: **Masudaya**, Japan. Toy marks: MT (Masudaya). Box marks: MT (Masudaya). Box text: *Sports Van*.
Scarcity: 5. Fine to Excellent (C6-C8): $200-$300, Mint (C10): $400

14 Commercial Delivery Vehicles

1970s Chevrolet 2-door delivery fuel truck 13.5 in (34 cm). **Friction.** Known colors: Red and white. Graphics: Esso Extra Gasolin - Esso Standard Petroleum. Maker: **Yoshiya**, Japan. Toy marks: KO (Yoshiya). Box marks: KO (Yoshiya), ST (Safe Toy). Box text: *Chevrolet Gasoline Truck*.
Scarcity: 4. Fine to Excellent (C6-C8): $150-$250, Mint (C10): $350

1961 Chevrolet Corvair 95, 2-door sports wagon, panel truck, and pickup. 8 in (20 cm). **Friction.** Known colors: Assorted. License: 1069. Maker: **Tatsuya**, Japan. Toy marks: KTS (Tatsuya). Box marks: KTS (Tatsuya), Frankonia.
Scarcity: 5. Fine to Excellent (C6-C8): $125-$185, Mint (C10): $275

1961 Chevrolet Corvair 95, 2-door pick up. 8 in (20 cm). **Friction.** Known colors: white and silver. Graphics: AA, ABC Rescue Truck, 24 Hour Service, 1069 license. Maker: **Tatsuya**, Japan. Toy marks: KTS (Tatsuya). Box marks: KTS (Tatsuya), Frankonia.
Notes: Also produced with Coca-Cola graphics (+$100).
Scarcity: 5. Fine to Excellent (C6-C8): $100-$150, Mint (C10): $200

1961 Chevrolet Corvair 95, 2-door panel van. 8 in (20 cm). **Friction.** Known colors: Green and silver. Graphics: Air Express, Air Express Out Delivers Them All, or REA Express. Maker: **Tatsuya**, Japan. Toy marks: KTS (Tatsuya). Box marks: KTS (Tatsuya), Frankonia. Box text: *REA Priority Air Express*.
Scarcity: 5. Fine to Excellent (C6-C8): $75-$125, Mint (C10): $160

(Not pictured) **1961 Chevrolet Corvair 95, 2-door panel van,** promotional toy for Meyers Arnold. 8 in (20 cm). **Friction.** Known colors: White. Graphics: Corvair - Meyers Arnold - For Pleasant Shopping - 232-6411. License: South Carolina. Maker: **Tatsuya**, Japan. Toy marks: KTS (Tatsuya).
Scarcity: 9. Fine to Excellent (C6-C8): $100-$200, Mint (C10): $300

1961 Chevrolet Corvair 95, 2-door panel van. 8 in (20 cm). **Friction.** Known colors: Yellow and black. Graphics: School Bus. Maker: **Tatsuya**, Japan. Toy marks: KTS (Tatsuya). Box marks: KTS (Tatsuya), Frankonia.
Scarcity: 5. Fine to Excellent (C6-C8): $95-$150, Mint (C10): $195

1961 Chevrolet Corvair 95, 2-door panel van. 8 in (20 cm). **Friction.** Known colors: Assorted. Graphics: various liveries. Maker: **Tatsuya**, Japan. Toy marks: KTS (Tatsuya). Box marks: KTS (Tatsuya), Frankonia.
Scarcity: 5. Fine to Excellent (C6-C8): $125-$185, Mint (C10): $275

Commercial Delivery Vehicles 15

1961 Chevrolet Corvair 2-door panel van. 9 in (23 cm). **Friction.** Known colors: Orange and white. Graphics: Bakery Fruit Cake - Milk or Flowers. Maker: **Toyo Plaything**, Japan. Toy marks: A1 (Toyo). Box marks: A1 (Toyo). Box text: *Commercial Van Truck.*
Scarcity: 5. Fine to Excellent (C6-C8): $100-$150, Mint (C10): $250

1961 Chevrolet Corvair 2-door panel van. 9 in (23 cm). **Friction.** Known colors: Blue and white. Graphics: Fresh Fruits. Maker: **Toyo Plaything**, Japan. Toy marks: A1 (Toyo). Box marks: A1 (Toyo). Box text: *Commercial Van Truck.*
Scarcity: 5. Fine to Excellent (C6-C8): $100-$150, Mint (C10): $250

1961 Chevrolet Corvair 2-door panel van. 9 in (23 cm). **Friction.** Known colors: Yellow and white. Graphics: Milk Fresh. Maker: **Toyo Plaything**, Japan. Toy marks: A1 (Toyo). Box marks: A1 (Toyo). Box text: *Commercial Van Truck.*
Scarcity: 5. Fine to Excellent (C6-C8): $100-$150, Mint (C10): $250

(Not pictured) **1960s Citroen 2CV 2-door delivery.** 8.25 in (21 cm). **Friction.** Known colors: Assorted. Maker: **Terai**, Japan. Toy marks: Daiya (Terai). Box marks: Daiya (Terai).
Scarcity: 8. Fine to Excellent (C6-C8): $400-$600, Mint (C10): $800

1950s Daihatsu 3 wheel delivery. 6 in (15 cm). **Friction.** Known colors: Assorted two tone. Graphics: (Japanese). Maker: **Nomura**, Japan. Toy marks: TN (Nomura). Box marks: TN (Nomura).
Scarcity: 9. Fine to Excellent (C6-C8): $800-$1,200, Mint (C10): $1,600

(Not pictured) **1950s Daihatsu Midget 3 wheel delivery** with vinyl covered truck bed. **6.5 in** (17 cm). **Friction.** Known colors: Assorted tri tone. Graphics: (Japanese). Maker: **Kokyu**, Japan. Toy marks: K (Kokyu). Box marks: K (Kokyu).
Scarcity: 9. Fine to Excellent (C6-C8): $850-$1,125, Mint (C10): $1,350

1950s Daihatsu Midget 3 wheel delivery with vinyl covered truck bed. **6.5 in** (17 cm). **Friction.** Known colors: Yellow and red. Graphics: Japanese Comedian (Japanese Graphics). Maker: **Kokyu**, Japan. Toy marks: K (Kokyu). Box marks: K (Kokyu). Box text: *Japanese text.*
Scarcity: 10. Fine to Excellent (C6-C8): $1,000-$1,400, Mint (C10): $1,800

1950s Daihatsu Midget 3 wheel delivery. **7 in** (18 cm). **Friction**. Known colors: Yellow and blue. Graphics: Tetsūjin 28. Maker: **Masudaya**, Japan. Toy marks: MT (Masudaya).
Scarcity: 9. Fine to Excellent (C6-C8): $1,200-$1,400, Mint (C10): $1,800

1950s Daihatsu Midget 3 wheel delivery. **8 in** (20 cm). **Friction**. Known colors: Assorted two tone. Maker: **Yonezawa**, Japan. Toy marks: Y (Yonezawa). Box marks: Y (Yonezawa).
Scarcity: 9. Fine to Excellent (C6-C8): $800-$1,100, Mint (C10): $1,300

(Not pictured) **1950s Daihatsu 3 wheel 2-door delivery dump** with dump action. **10.5 in** (27 cm). **Friction**. Known colors: Yellow. Graphics: (Japanese). Maker: **Nomura**, Japan. Toy marks: TN (Nomura). Box marks: TN (Nomura).
Scarcity: 9. Fine to Excellent (C6-C8): $1,200-$1,800, Mint (C10): $2,400

1960s Daihatsu Midget 3 wheel delivery. **8.75 in** (22 cm). **Friction**. Known colors: Assorted. Graphics: Midget. Maker: **Masudaya**, Japan. Toy marks: MT (Masudaya). Box marks: MT (Masudaya).
Scarcity: 9. Fine to Excellent (C6-C8): $800-$1,100, Mint (C10): $1,300

1950s Divco 2-door Ice Cream delivery with opening door and exiting driver with ice cream cone. Activated by bumper. **7.25 in** (18 cm). **Friction**. Known colors: White. Graphics: Carvel's Ice Cream. Maker: **Unknown**, Japan. Toy marks: HTC (Unknown). Box marks: AHI. Box text: *Carvel Ice Cream Truck*. Notes: Promotional toy.
Scarcity: 10. Fine to Excellent (C6-C8): $1,000-$1,200, Mint (C10): $1,500

1950s Divco 2-door bakery delivery. **7.25 in** (18 cm). **Friction**. Known colors: White and green. Graphics: Dugan's Bakers For The Home Since 1878. Maker: **Unknown**, Japan. Toy marks: HTC (Unknown). Box marks: none. Box text: *Dugan's Bakers For The Home Since 1878*. Notes: Promotional toy.
Scarcity: 9. Fine to Excellent (C6-C8): $300-$400, Mint (C10): $600

Commercial Delivery Vehicles 17

1950s Divco 2-door Ice Cream delivery with opening door and exiting driver with ice cream cone. Activated by bumper. **7.25 in** (18 cm). **Friction**. Known colors: White. Graphics: Fresh Delicious Ice Cream. Maker: **Unknown**, Japan. Toy marks: HTC (Unknown).
Scarcity: 10. Fine to Excellent (C6-C8): $800-$1,000, Mint (C10): $1,200

(Not pictured) **1960s Divco 2-door delivery**. **5.25 in** (13 cm). **Friction**. Known colors: White. Graphics: Borden's Milk. Maker: **Linemar**, Japan. Toy marks: Linemar (Marx). Box marks: Linemar (Marx).
Scarcity: 6. Fine to Excellent (C6-C8): $100-$175, Mint (C10): $350

1959 Dodge 100 2-door delivery with pull string, canvas top and rear plastic window. **25 in** (64 cm). **Pull toy**. Known colors: Green. Graphics: Dodge 100 - Dodge hubcaps. License: M-1000/H. Maker: **Mitsuhashi**, Japan. Toy marks: M (Mitsuhashi). Box marks: M (Mitsuhashi).
Scarcity: 10. Fine to Excellent (C6-C8): $1,500-$2,100, Mint (C10): $2,800

(Not pictured) **1959 Dodge 100 2-door dump delivery** with pull string and dump action. **25 in** (64 cm). **Pull toy**. Known colors: Green. Graphics: Dodge 100 - Dodge hubcaps. License: M-1000/H. Maker: **Mitsuhashi**, Japan. Toy marks: M (Mitsuhashi). Box marks: M (Mitsuhashi).
Scarcity: 10. Fine to Excellent (C6-C8): $1,500-$2,100, Mint (C10): $2,800

1958 Dodge 2-door panel van with opening rear tailgate. **6 in** (15 cm). **Friction**. Known colors: Assorted. Maker: **Shioji**, Japan. Toy marks: none. Box marks: SSS (Shioji). Box text: *Dodge Panel Truck*.
Scarcity: 8. Fine to Excellent (C6-C8): $100-$145, Mint (C10): $200

1960s Fiat 1800 4-door sedan with animal graphics. **9.5 in** (24 cm) **Friction**. Known colors: Green. Graphics: Chipi Chip. License: A-8008-A. Maker: **Paya**, Spain. Toy marks: Paya. Box marks: Paya.
Scarcity: 5. Fine to Excellent (C6-C8): $50-$85, Mint (C10): $125

1959 Dodge 100 2-door pick up with pull string. **19 in** (48 cm). **Pull toy**. Known colors: Red and white. Graphics: Dodge 100 - Dodge hubcaps. Maker: **Mitsuhashi**, Japan. Toy marks: M (Mitsuhashi). Box marks: M (Mitsuhashi). Box text: *New Dodge Truck*.
Scarcity: 10. Fine to Excellent (C6-C8): $1,500-$2,100, Mint (C10): $2,800

1932 Ford Model A 2-door Ice Cream delivery with two bells and pink plastic fenders. **8 in** (20 cm). **Friction.** Known colors: White with white fenders (+25%); white with pink fenders. Graphics: Ice Cream. Maker: **Bandai**, Japan. Toy marks: Bandai. Box marks: Bandai.
Notes: Produced 1960s.
Scarcity: 4. Fine to Excellent (C6-C8): $120-$145, Mint (C10): $175

1932 Ford Model A 2-door pick up with top down. **8 in** (20 cm). **Friction.** Known colors: Assorted with black fenders. Maker: **Bandai**, Japan. Toy marks: Bandai. Box marks: Bandai. Box text: *Old Fashioned Ford A Pick up Truck Convertible #936.*
Notes: Produced 1960s.
Scarcity: 3. Fine to Excellent (C6-C8): $60-$80, Mint (C10): $100

1932 Ford Model A 2-door Ice Cream delivery with two bells. **8 in** (20 cm). **Friction.** Known colors: White with white fenders (+25%), white with black fenders. Graphics: Ice Cream. Maker: **Bandai**, Japan. Toy marks: Bandai. Box marks: NGS (Cragstan), Cragstan. Box text: *Antique Car.*
Notes: Produced 1960s.
Scarcity: 4. Fine to Excellent (C6-C8): $100-$125, Mint (C10): $150

1932 Ford Model A 2-door pick up with top up. **8 in** (20 cm). **Friction.** Known colors: Assorted with black fenders. Maker: **Bandai**, Japan. Toy marks: Bandai. Box marks: Bandai. Box text: *Old Fashioned Ford A Pick up Truck Sedan #935.*
Notes: Produced 1960s.
Scarcity: 3. Fine to Excellent (C6-C8): $60-$80, Mint (C10): $100

Commercial Delivery Vehicles 19

1932 Ford Model A 2-door van. **8 in** (20 cm). **Friction**. Known colors: Maroon with black fenders. Graphics: Express Delivery Inc. Maker: **Bandai**, Japan. Toy marks: Bandai. Box marks: Bandai. Box text: *Old Fashioned Van Truck #1010*.
Notes: Produced 1960s.
Scarcity: 3. Fine to Excellent (C6-C8): $60-$80, Mint (C10): $100

1950s Ford 2-door Ice Cream delivery with sliding roof and bell. **7 in** (18 cm). **Friction**. Known colors: White. Graphics: Delicious Ice Cream - Caution Watch Children. Maker: **Unknown**, Japan. Toy marks: none.
Scarcity: 5. Fine to Excellent (C6-C8): $150-$200, Mint (C10): $265

1950s Ford 2-door Ice Cream delivery with tin driver. **4.5 in** (11 cm). **Friction**. Known colors: White. Graphics: Good Humor Ice Cream - Mount Vernon - NY. Maker: **Linemar**, Japan. Toy marks: Linemar (Marx). Box marks: Linemar (Marx). Box text: *Good Humor Truck*.
Scarcity: 9. Fine to Excellent (C6-C8): $300-$500, Mint (C10): $675

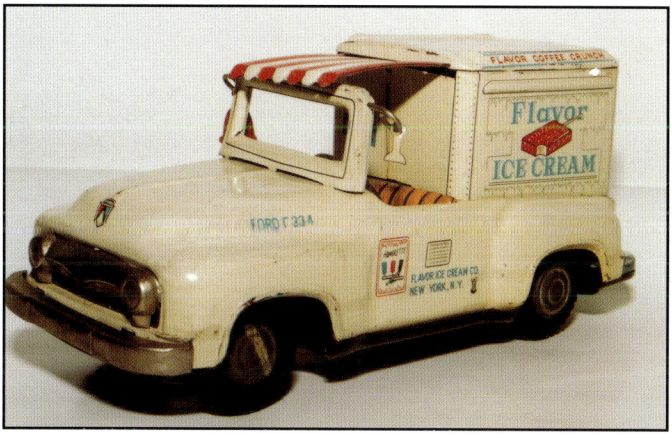

1950s Ford 2-door Ice Cream delivery with sliding canopy, two bells, and opening rear door. **7.25 in** (18 cm). **Friction**. Known colors: White. Graphics: Flavor Ice Cream - Flavor Ice Cream New York, NY - F334. Maker: **Bandai**, Japan. Toy marks: Bandai.
Scarcity: 7. Fine to Excellent (C6-C8): $125-$250, Mint (C10): $375

1950s Ford 2-door delivery. **8.5 in** (22 cm). **Friction**. Known colors: Blue and white. Graphics: Schrafft's Candies. Maker: **Unknown**, Japan. Toy marks: none.
Scarcity: 5. Fine to Excellent (C6-C8): $125-$185, Mint (C10): $265

Commercial Delivery Vehicles

1950s Ford 2-door Ice Cream delivery with sliding roof and bell. **11 in** (28 cm). **Friction**. Known colors: White. Graphics: Good Humor Ice Cream - Caution Watch Children. Maker: **Tatsuya**, Japan. Toy marks: KTS (Tatsuya). Box marks: KTS (Tatsuya), Lang Craft. Box text: *Good Humor Ice Cream Truck*.
Scarcity: 8. Fine to Excellent (C6-C8): $800-$1,000, Mint (C10): $1,400

1956 Ford 2-door pick up with opening tailgate. **12 in** (30 cm). **Friction**. Known colors: Assorted. Graphics: Ford Lasts Longer! (with elephant). Maker: **Bandai**, Japan. Toy marks: Bandai. Box marks: Bandai. Box text: *Ford Pickup*.
Scarcity: 4. Fine to Excellent (C6-C8): $250-$450, Mint (C10): $600

1956 Ford 2-door sedan delivery with opening tailgate and rear window. **12 in** (30 cm). **Friction**. Known colors: Turquoise. Graphics: Flowers for Gracious Living - Ford Lasts Longer. Maker: **Bandai**, Japan. Box marks: Bandai. Box text: *Ford Flower Delivery Wagon*.
Scarcity: 8. Fine to Excellent (C6-C8): $700-$1,300, Mint (C10): $1,800

1956 Ford 2-door pick up with opening tailgate and canvas cover. **12 in** (30 cm). **Friction**. Known colors: Yellow. Graphics: Morinaga (Japanese text). Maker: **Bandai**, Japan. Toy marks: Bandai. Box marks: Bandai. Box text: *Morinaga*. Notes: Private promotional issue for Morinaga Candy Company.
Scarcity: 10. Fine to Excellent (C6-C8): $3,500-$4,500, Mint (C10): $5,500

Box for Morinaga Candy Company Ford pick up.

1956 Ford 2-door sedan delivery with opening tailgate and rear window. **12 in** (30 cm). **Friction**. Known colors: Black and orange. Graphics: Standard Coffee. Maker: **Bandai**, Japan. Toy marks: Bandai. Box marks: Bandai.
Scarcity: 9. Fine to Excellent (C6-C8): $800-$1,400, Mint (C10): $2,000

Commercial Delivery Vehicles 21

1957 Ford 2-door sedan delivery. 11.75 in (30 cm). **Friction**. Known colors: Black and orange. Graphics: Standard Coffee - Rain or Shine I'm on Time. Maker: **Bandai**, Japan. Toy marks: Bandai. Box marks: Bandai. Box text: *Standard Coffee Wagon*.
Scarcity: 9. Fine to Excellent (C6-C8): $1,500-$2,500, Mint (C10): $4,000

1958 Ford Fairlane 2-door pick up. 8 in (20 cm). **Friction**. Known colors: Assorted two tone. Maker: **Bandai**, Japan. Toy marks: Bandai. Box marks: Bandai.
Scarcity: 3. Fine to Excellent (C6-C8): $75-$150, Mint (C10): $225

1957 Ford Ranchero 2-door pick up. 11.75 in (30 cm). **Friction**. Known colors: Assorted two tone. Maker: **Bandai**, Japan. Toy marks: Bandai. Box marks: Bandai. Box text: *New Ford Ranchero*.
Scarcity: 5. Fine to Excellent (C6-C8): $300-$600, Mint (C10): $900

1958 Ford 2-door pick up. 8 in (20 cm). **Friction**. Known colors: Assorted two tone. Maker: **Joustra**, France. Toy marks: Joustra. Box marks: Joustra.
Scarcity: 5. Fine to Excellent (C6-C8): $200-$300, Mint (C10): $400

1957 Ford 2-door pick up. 11.75 in (30 cm). **Friction**. Known colors: Assorted two tone. Maker: **Joustra**, France. Toy marks: Joustra.
Scarcity: 5. Fine to Excellent (C6-C8): $300-$500, Mint (C10): $700

1959 Ford 2-door pick up. 12 in (30 cm). **Friction**. Known colors: Red, white, and blue. Graphics: Daito. Maker: **Daito**, Japan. Toy marks: Daito.
Scarcity: 4. Fine to Excellent (C6-C8): $125-$165, Mint (C10): $225

(Not pictured) **1958 Ford 2-door pick up**. 7 in (18 cm). **Friction**. Known colors: Assorted. Maker: **Asahi**, Japan. Toy marks: Asahitoy (Asahi Toy).
Scarcity: 3. Fine to Excellent (C6-C8): $50-$85, Mint (C10): $110

1960s Ford 2-door pick up with roof marker lights. **8 in** (20 cm). **Friction**. Known colors: Blue and red. Graphics: Ford - Ford (hubcaps). Maker: **Marusan**, Japan. Toy marks: SAN (Marusan).
Notes: Marusan's "Bulldog Series" was deigned for durability and to compete with pressed steel toys.
Scarcity: 3. Fine to Excellent (C6-C8): $60-$90, Mint (C10): $120

1960s Ford Econoline 2-door pick up. **9 in** (23 cm). **Friction**. Known colors: Red and white; Green and white. Graphics: JPF Service Company. License: 5-2500. Maker: **Marx**, Japan. Toy marks: Marx. Box marks: Linemar (Marx). Box text: *New Econoline Truck*.
Scarcity: 3. Fine to Excellent (C6-C8): $135-$210, Mint (C10): $295

1960s Ford 2-door delivery with "Lifesaver roll" truck body. **8.5 in** (22 cm). **Friction**. Known colors: Blue. Graphics: Lifesavers. Maker: **Unknown**, Japan. Toy marks: none.
Scarcity: 5. Fine to Excellent (C6-C8): $75-$165, Mint (C10): $250

1960s Ford 4-door hardtop. **11 in** (28 cm). **Friction**. Known colors: Red and white. Graphics: Coca-Cola - Refresh With Zest. License: Pol 2. Maker: **Taiyo**, Japan. Toy marks: Taiyo World Toy. Box text: *Sturdy Metal Friction Toy - Sedan Series*.
Scarcity: 7. Fine to Excellent (C6-C8): $250-$350, Mint (C10): $450

1960s Ford Falcon 2-door pick up. **9 in** (23 cm). **Friction**. Known colors: Assorted two tone. Maker: **Alps**, Japan. Toy marks: Alps. Box marks: Alps. Box text: *Falcon Pick Up Truck*.
Notes: Also came with wipers.
Scarcity: 3. Fine to Excellent (C6-C8): $75-$100, Mint (C10): $125

1960s Ford Galaxie 2-door sedan delivery. **11.5 in** (29 cm). **Friction**. Known colors: Black and orange. Graphics: Standard Fresh Coffee - Rain or Shine I'm on Time. Maker: **Asakusa Toy and Doll**, Japan. Toy marks: none. Box marks: none. Box text: *Standard Fresh Coffee Ford Station Wagon*.
Scarcity: 8. Fine to Excellent (C6-C8): $800-$1,500, Mint (C10): $2,200

1960s Ford 2-door delivery with operating headlights. **12 in** (30 cm). **Battery operated**. Known colors: White, yellow, and red. Graphics: Drink Coca-Cola. Maker: **Linemar**, Japan. Toy marks: none.
Scarcity: 6. Fine to Excellent (C6-C8): $225-$400, Mint (C10): $600

1960s Ford 2-door pick up with swing out mirrors, opening side panels, and doors. **19 in** (48 cm). **Friction**. Known colors: Red. Maker: **Yonezawa**, Japan. Toy marks: none. Box marks: Y (Yonezawa).
Scarcity: 6. Fine to Excellent (C6-C8): $400-$600, Mint (C10): $800

1960s Ford 2-door pick up. **14.5 in** (37 cm). **Friction**. Known colors: Red and cream. Maker: **Yonezawa**, Japan. Toy marks: Y (Yonezawa).
Scarcity: 6. Fine to Excellent (C6-C8): $300-$400, Mint (C10): $500

1960s Ford-Köln 2-door delivery. **8.5 in** (22 cm). **Friction**. Known colors: Light green and dark green. Maker: **Tatsuya**, Japan. Toy marks: KTS (Tatsuya).
Scarcity: 4. Fine to Excellent (C6-C8): $75-$125, Mint (C10): $165

1960s Ford 2-door pick up with vinyl cargo cover. **14.5 in** (37 cm). **Friction**. Known colors: Red. Graphics: Diamond Delivery Express. Maker: **Yonezawa**, Japan. Toy marks: Y (Yonezawa). Box text: *Diamond Hood Truck*.
Scarcity: 6. Fine to Excellent (C6-C8): $300-$400, Mint (C10): $500

1960s Ford-Köln 2-door delivery. **8.5 in** (22 cm). **Friction**. Known colors: Light blue and dark blue. Maker: **Tatsuya**, Japan. Toy marks: KTS (Tatsuya), Stone.
Scarcity: 4. Fine to Excellent (C6-C8): $75-$125, Mint (C10): $165

Commercial Delivery Vehicles

1960s Ford-Köln 2-door delivery. **8.5 in** (22 cm). **Friction**. Known colors: Red. Graphics: Delivery Van. Maker: **Tatsuya**, Japan. Toy marks: KTS (Tatsuya).
Scarcity: 4. Fine to Excellent (C6-C8) $75-$125, Mint (C10): $165

1931 Franklin 2-door pick up with opening doors, operating headlights, and Goodyear balloon tin tires. **10 in** (25 cm). Known colors: Green, orange, and black. Graphics: Children Commercial Track - Franklin. Maker: **Nomura**, Japan. Toy marks: TN (Nomura), MHT (Unknown). Box marks: TN (Nomura), MHT (Unknown). Box text: *Franklin New Track*.
Scarcity: 10. Fine to Excellent (C6-C8): $10,000-$13,000, Mint (C10): $16,000

1960s Ford-Köln 2-door pick up. **8.5 in** (22 cm). **Friction**. Known colors: Yellow. Graphics: Tires Tubes Batteries. Maker: **Tatsuya**, Japan. Toy marks: KTS (Tatsuya).
Scarcity: 4. Fine to Excellent (C6-C8): $75-$125, Mint (C10): $165

1960s Hino 2-door Ice Cream van with lithographed driver and helper. **8.5 in** (22 cm). **Friction**. Known colors: White. Graphics: Ice Cream. Maker: **Hayashi**, Japan. Toy marks: H (Hayashi).
Scarcity: 9. Fine to Excellent (C6-C8): $100-$200, Mint (C10): $300

1929 Franklin 2-door Ice Cream delivery with hood mounted bell. **7.5 in** (19 cm). **Friction**. Known colors: Yellow and white. Graphics: Ice Cream - Fresh Delicious. Maker: **Shioji**, Japan. Toy marks: none. Box marks: SSS (Shioji). Box text: *Ice Cream Truck - Classic Car Collection*.
Scarcity: 4. Fine to Excellent (C6-C8): $90-$150, Mint (C10): $225

1960s Hino 2-door delivery van. **8.5 in** (22 cm). **Friction**. Known colors: Yellow, white, and blue. Graphics: Borden's Milk. Maker: **Hayashi**, Japan. Toy marks: H (Hayashi).
Scarcity: 6. Fine to Excellent (C6-C8): $150-$200, Mint (C10): $300

1960s Hino 2-door delivery van. 8.5 in (22 cm). **Friction**. Known colors: Light blue, white, and dark blue. Graphics: Snow Crop Frozen Foods. Maker: **Hayashi**, Japan. Toy marks: H (Hayashi).
Scarcity: 5. Fine to Excellent (C6-C8): $125-$175, Mint (C10): $225

1960s Hino 2-door bakery delivery van with roof rack, opening driver (left) door and rear doors. **9.5 in** (24 cm). **Friction**. Known colors: Yellow and white. Graphics: Main Street Bakery. Maker: **Lumar/Hayashi**, Japan. Toy marks: Lumar (Marx).
Scarcity: 5. Fine to Excellent (C6-C8): $250-$350, Mint (C10): $500

1960s Hino Picnic Van 2-door micro-bus with roof rack and passenger seats. **9.5 in** (24 cm). **Friction**. Known colors: Orange and cream. Graphics: Picnic Bus. Maker: **Marusan/Hayashi**, Japan. Toy marks: SAN (Marusan), H (Hayashi). Box marks: SAN (Marusan).
Scarcity: 5. Fine to Excellent (C6-C8): $150-$225, Mint (C10): $300

1960s Hino 2-door flower delivery van with roof rack, opening driver (left) door and rear doors. **9.5 in** (24 cm). **Friction**. Known colors: Green. Graphics: Flowers For Gracious Living. Maker: **Marusan/Hayashi**, Japan. Toy marks: SAN (Marusan), H (Hayashi). Box marks: SAN (Marusan).
Scarcity: 5. Fine to Excellent (C6-C8): $250-$350, Mint (C10): $500

1960s Hino 2-door delivery van with roof rack, lithographed passengers and driver in windows, and rotating scenes in side window. Four different scenes are shown on each side (eight total). **9.5 in** (24 cm). **Friction**. Known colors: Light blue and cream. Graphics: Sightseeing Bus. Maker: **Marusan/Hayashi**, Japan. Toy marks: SAN (Marusan), H (Hayashi).
Scarcity: 9. Fine to Excellent (C6-C8): $350-$450, Mint (C10): $700

26 Commercial Delivery Vehicles

1960s Hino 2-door delivery van with roof rack. **9.5 in** (24 cm). **Friction**. Known colors: Yellow. Graphics: Suburban Cleaners. Maker: **Marusan/Hayashi**, Japan. Toy marks: SAN (Marusan), H (Hayashi). Box marks: SAN (Marusan).
Scarcity: 5. Fine to Excellent (C6-C8): $250-$350, Mint (C10): $500

1960s Hino 2-door bakery delivery van with roof rack, opening driver (left) door and rear doors. **9.5 in** (24 cm). **Friction**. Known colors: Yellow. Graphics: Today Enjoy Baked Goods. Maker: **Marusan/Hayashi**, Japan. Toy marks: SAN (Marusan), H (Hayashi). Box marks: SAN (Marusan).
Scarcity: 5. Fine to Excellent (C6-C8): $250-$350, Mint (C10): $500

1960s International Fuel Tanker 2-door with Budd cab. **9.25 in** (23 cm). **Friction**. Known colors: Red and white. Graphics: Gasoline - Shell - Cicago. License: LP-36-1026. Maker: **Marusan/Hayashi**, Japan. Toy marks: SAN (Marusan), H (Hayashi).
Scarcity: 6. Fine to Excellent (C6-C8): $175-$300, Mint (C10): $450

1950s International 2-door cement delivery with rotating drum and opening doors. **19 in** (48 cm). **Friction**. Known colors: Assorted. License: SSS. Graphics: Cement Mixer. Maker: **Shioji**, Japan. Toy marks: none. Box marks: SSS (Shioji).
Scarcity: 10. Fine to Excellent (C6-C8): $1,200-$1,800, Mint (C10): $2,500

1950s International 2-door dump delivery with dump action and opening doors. **23 in** (58 cm). **Friction**. Known colors: Assorted. License: BC. Maker: **Bandai**, Japan. Toy marks: Bandai.
Scarcity: 10. Fine to Excellent (C6-C8): $1,200-$1,800, Mint (C10): $2,500

1950s International 2-door dump delivery with dump action and opening doors. **23 in** (58 cm). **Friction**. Known colors: Assorted. License: SSS. Maker: **Shioji**, Japan. Toy marks: SSS (Shioji). Box marks: SSS (Shioji).
Scarcity: 10. Fine to Excellent (C6-C8): $1,200-$1,800, Mint (C10): $2,500

(Not pictured) **1960s Isuzu Elf 2-door pick up**. **8 in** (20 cm). **Friction**. Known colors: Assorted. Maker: **Bandai**, Japan. Toy marks: Bandai. Box text: #847.
Scarcity: 6. Fine to Excellent (C6-C8): $300-$400, Mint (C10): $500

1960s Isuzu 2-door dump delivery with lever actuated dumping. **9 in** (23 cm). **Friction**. Known colors: Assorted. Maker: **Asahi**, Japan. Toy marks: ATC (Asahi Toy). Box marks: ATC (Asahi Toy). Box text: *Isuzu Dump Truck*.
Scarcity: 3. Fine to Excellent (C6-C8): $90-$140, Mint (C10): $190

1960s Jeep FC 2-door stake delivery. **7 in** (18 cm). **Windup**. Known colors: Assorted two tone. Graphics: Jeep. Maker: **Bandai**, Japan. Toy marks: Bandai. Box marks: Bandai.
Scarcity: 4. Fine to Excellent (C6-C8): $125-$175, Mint (C10): $250

1950s Jeep CJ 2-door with magnetic crane. **9.5 in** (24 cm). **Battery operated**. Known colors: Green. Graphics: Crane Jeep - CJ - J-002700. Maker: **Bandai**, Japan. Toy marks: Bandai. Box marks: Bandai. Box text: *Magnetic Crane Jeep*.
Scarcity: 5. Fine to Excellent (C6-C8): $100-$160, Mint (C10): $225

1960s Jeep FC 2-door stake delivery. **7 in** (18 cm). **Friction**. Known colors: Assorted two tone. Graphics: Jeep. Maker: **Bandai**, Japan. Toy marks: Bandai. Box marks: Bandai. Box text: *Stake Truck #630*.
Scarcity: 4. Fine to Excellent (C6-C8): $125-$175, Mint (C10): $250

1950s Jeep CJ2, 2-door with attached wagon and moveable bucket. Has interior radio graphics. **13 in** (33 cm). **Friction**. Known colors: Blue and white. Graphics: Jupiter - Reclaim Jupiter Jeep. Maker: **Shioji**, Japan. Toy marks: none. Box marks: SSS (Shioji). Box text: *Jupiter Jeep*.
Scarcity: 5. Fine to Excellent (C6-C8): $125-$175, Mint (C10): $200

28 Commercial Delivery Vehicles

1960s Jeep FC 2-door pick up with opening tailgate. **7 in** (18 cm). **Friction**. Known colors: Assorted two tone. Graphics: Jeep 4 Wheel Drive Forward Control. Maker: **Bandai**, Japan. Toy marks: Bandai. Box marks: Bandai. Box text: *Jeep Truck #629*.
Scarcity: 4. Fine to Excellent (C6-C8): $125-$175, Mint (C10): $250

1960s Jeep FC 2-door stake delivery with opening tailgate. **8 in** (20 cm). **Friction**. Known colors: Assorted two tone. Graphics: Jeep. Maker: **Bandai**, Japan. Toy marks: Bandai. Box marks: Bandai.
Scarcity: 4. Fine to Excellent (C6-C8): $150-$200, Mint (C10): $275

1960s Jeep FC 2-door pick up with opening tailgate and chain. **8 in** (20 cm). **Friction**. Known colors: Assorted two tone. Graphics: Jeep 4 Wheel Drive Forward Control. License: B-605. Maker: **Bandai**, Japan. Toy marks: Bandai. Box marks: Bandai. Box text: *A Great New Jeep Forward Control Truck #605*.
Scarcity: 4. Fine to Excellent (C6-C8): $150-$200, Mint (C10): $275

1960s Jeep FC 2-door delivery. **11 in** (28 cm). **Friction**. Known colors: Red and white. Graphics: Gasoline. Maker: **Nomura**, Japan. Toy marks: TN (Nomura). Box marks: TN (Nomura).
Scarcity: 4. Fine to Excellent (C6-C8): $150-$225, Mint (C10): $300

1960s Jeep stake body 2-door pick up with plastic stakes. **11 in** (28 cm). **Friction**. Known colors: Assorted. Maker: **Nomura**, Japan. Toy marks: none. Box marks: TN (Nomura). Box text: *Jeep Stake Truck*.
Scarcity: 4. Fine to Excellent (C6-C8): $125-$200, Mint (C10): $250

1960s Jeep 2-door stake delivery with modified grille. **12 in** (30 cm). **Friction**. Known colors: Red and yellow. Maker: **Yonezawa**, Japan. Toy marks: Y (Yonezawa). Box marks: Y (Yonezawa).
Scarcity: 3. Fine to Excellent (C6-C8): $150-$250, Mint (C10): $350

Commercial Delivery Vehicles 29

1960s Jeep 2-door dump delivery with modified grille and bumper activated dumping action. **12 in** (30 cm). **Friction**. Known colors: Orange. Graphics: World Transport. Maker: **Yonezawa**, Japan. Toy marks: Y (Yonezawa). Box marks: Y (Yonezawa).
Scarcity: 3. Fine to Excellent (C6-C8): $150-$250, Mint (C10): $350

1950s Mazda 3 wheel delivery. **6.5 in** (17 cm). **Friction**. Known colors: Assorted two tone. Maker: **Bandai**, Japan. Toy marks: Bandai. Box marks: Bandai. Box text: *Three-Wheel Truck*.
Notes: Also came with covered bed (+20%).
Scarcity: 9. Fine to Excellent (C6-C8): $400-$600, Mint (C10): $800

(Not pictured) **1950s Mazda K 360 3 wheel delivery**. **7.5 in** (19 cm). **Friction**. Known colors: Assorted two tone. Graphics: Mazda K 360. Maker: **Bandai**, Japan. Toy marks: Bandai. Box marks: Bandai. Box text: *Three-Wheel Truck*.
Scarcity: 9. Fine to Excellent (C6-C8): $800-$1,000, Mint (C10): $1,200

1950s Mazda 3 Wheel delivery. **8.75 in** (22 cm). **Friction**. Known colors: Assorted. Maker: **Bandai**, Japan. Toy marks: Bandai. Box marks: Bandai. Box text: (Japanese text).
Notes: Also came with covered bed (+20%).
Scarcity: 8. Fine to Excellent (C6-C8): $400-$800, Mint (C10): $1,200

1950s Mazda D-1100 Romper 2-door pick up. **8.75 in** (22 cm). **Friction**. Known colors: Assorted. Maker: **Bandai**, Japan. Toy marks: Bandai. Box marks: Bandai. Box text: *Mazda D-1100 Romper* (in Japanese).
Scarcity: 7. Fine to Excellent (C6-C8): $275-$425, Mint (C10): $600

1960s Mazda Bongo 2-door pick up. **8.75 in** (22 cm). **Friction**. Known colors: Blue/Light Blue two tone. Maker: **Mitsuhashi**, Japan. Toy marks: M (Mitsuhashi). Box marks: M (Mitsuhashi). Box text: *Mazda Bongo* (in Japanese).
Scarcity: 5. Fine to Excellent (C6-C8): $125-$225, Mint (C10): $350

1950s Mitsubishi Leo 2-door delivery. **6 in** (15 cm). **Friction**. Known colors: Assorted two tone. Maker: **Bandai**, Japan. Toy marks: Bandai. Box marks: Bandai.
Scarcity: 9. Fine to Excellent (C6-C8): $600-$800, Mint (C10): $1,000

1950s Nissan/Datsun Junior 2-door pick up with rear window guard. **8 in** (20 cm). **Friction**. Known colors: Assorted. Graphics: Junior. License: 536. Maker: **Bandai**, Japan. Toy marks: Bandai. Box marks: Bandai. Box text: *#536*.
Scarcity: 7. Fine to Excellent (C6-C8): $275-$350, Mint (C10): $475

1950s Mitsubishi 2-door dump delivery with lever action dump. **10 in** (25 cm). **Friction**. Known colors: Assorted tri tone. Maker: **Bandai**, Japan. Toy marks: Bandai. Box marks: Bandai.
Scarcity: 9. Fine to Excellent (C6-C8): $1,000-$1,400, Mint (C10): $1,800

1950s Nissan/Datsun Junior 2-door pick up with rear window guard bars. **9 in** (23 cm). **Friction**. Known colors: Assorted tri tone. Maker: **Unknown**, Japan. Toy marks: none.
Scarcity: 7. Fine to Excellent (C6-C8): $175-$225, Mint (C10): $350

1950s Mitsubishi 3 wheel delivery. **10 in** (25 cm). **Friction**. Known colors: Assorted two tone. Maker: **Bandai**, Japan. Toy marks: Bandai. Box marks: Bandai. Box text: (Japanese text).
Scarcity: 9. Fine to Excellent (C6-C8): $1,000-$1,400, Mint (C10): $1,800

(Not pictured) **1950s Mitsubishi 3 wheel delivery**. **13.75 in** (35 cm). **Friction**. Known colors: Assorted tri tone. Maker: **Yonezawa**, Japan. Toy marks: Y (Yonezawa).
Scarcity: 9. Fine to Excellent (C6-C8): $1,000-$1,400, Mint (C10): $1,800

1950s Nissan/Datsun Junior 2-door pick up with rear window guard bars. **11.5 in** (29 cm). **Friction**. Known colors: Assorted tri tone. Maker: **Yonezawa**, Japan. Toy marks: Y (Yonezawa). Box marks: Y (Yonezawa). Box text: *Junior Truck*.
Scarcity: 8. Fine to Excellent (C6-C8): $250-$300, Mint (C10): $450

1960s Nissan/Datsun Prince Hormer 2-door pick up. 15.75 in (40 cm).
Friction. Known colors: Assorted. Maker: **Yonezawa**, Japan. Toy marks: Y (Yonezawa).
Scarcity: 7. Fine to Excellent (C6-C8): $250-$400, Mint (C10): $575

1950s Orient 3 wheel delivery. 9 in (23 cm). **Friction.** Known colors: Assorted two tone. Graphics: Orient (badge). Maker: **Yonezawa**, Japan. Toy marks: Y (Yonezawa). Box marks: Y (Yonezawa). Box text: *Orient Three-Wheel Truck*.
Scarcity: 9. Fine to Excellent (C6-C8): $800-$1,200, Mint (C10): $1,400

1970s Nissan/Datsun 4-door station wagon with panel delivery body. 18.5 in (47 cm). **Battery operated.** Known colors: Assorted. Maker: **Ichiko**, Japan. Toy marks: Ichiko.
Scarcity: 4. Fine to Excellent (C6-C8): $150-$250, Mint (C10): $350

1958 Pontiac 2-door pick up. 6 in (15 cm). **Friction.** Known colors: Assorted two tone. Maker: **Bandai**, Japan. Toy marks: Bandai. Box marks: Bandai.
Scarcity: 3. Fine to Excellent (C6-C8): $125-$175, Mint (C10): $225

1960 Opel Rekord P2, 2-door pick up. 11 in (28 cm). **Friction.** Known colors: Assorted two tone. License: BC-481. Maker: **Bandai**, Japan. Toy marks: Bandai. Box marks: Bandai. Box text: *Commercial Half Truck # 481*.
Scarcity: 9. Fine to Excellent (C6-C8): $500-$800, Mint (C10): $1,000

1950s Studebaker 2-door pick up. 10 in (25 cm). **Friction.** Known colors: Assorted tri tone. Maker: **Kaname**, Japan. Toy marks: KS (Kaname). Notes: Also sold as battery operated version with operating headlights.
Scarcity: 4. Fine to Excellent (C6-C8): $150-$250, Mint (C10): $350

Commercial Delivery Vehicles

1950s Studebaker 2-door with tin bottle cases. **11 in** (28 cm). **Friction**. Known colors: Red, white, and blue. Graphics: Pepsi-Cola - Pepsi Cola Light Refreshment. Maker: **Unknown**, Japan. Toy marks: Cragstan.
Scarcity: 9. Fine to Excellent (C6-C8): $400-$600, Mint (C10): $800

1950s Studebaker Fuel Tanker 2-door with grounding chain. **13.5 in** (34 cm). **Friction**. Known colors: Red and white. Graphics: Gasoline - Shell. Maker: **Marusan/Hayashi**, Japan. Toy marks: SAN (Marusan), H (Hayashi). Box marks: SAN (Marusan), H (Hayashi). Box text: *Gasoline Tanker*.
Scarcity: 6. Fine to Excellent (C6-C8): $200-$350, Mint (C10): $500

1960s Subaru Sanber 2-door pick up. **9 in** (23 cm). **Friction**. Known colors: White with flowers. Graphics: Flowers (and floral graphics). Maker: **Nomura**, Japan. Toy marks: TN (Nomura). Box marks: TN (Nomura). Box text: *Subaru Sanber* (in Japanese) - *Fancy Color*.
Scarcity: 7. Fine to Excellent (C6-C8): $400-$500, Mint (C10): $700

1950s Toyota Toyoace 2-door pick up. **7.5 in** (19 cm). **Friction**. Known colors: Assorted. License: (Japanese). Maker: **Asahi**, Japan. Toy marks: Asahitoy (Asahi Toy).
Scarcity: 8. Fine to Excellent (C6-C8): $400-$525, Mint (C10): $780

1950s Toyota Toyoace 2-door pick up. **7.5 in** (19 cm). **Friction**. Known colors: Assorted two tone. Maker: **Nomura**, Japan. Toy marks: TN (Nomura).
Scarcity: 8. Fine to Excellent (C6-C8): $400-$525, Mint (C10): $780

(Not pictured) **1950s Toyota Toyopet Crown 2-door pick up** with fender mirrors and chrome gas cap. **9 in** (23 cm). **Friction**. Known colors: Assorted two tone. Graphics: Toyopet. Maker: **Bandai**, Japan. Toy marks: Bandai.
Scarcity: 7. Fine to Excellent (C6-C8): $500-$700, Mint (C10): $900

1960s Toyota Toyoace Delivery 2-door pick up with tilting driver's seatback. **9 in** (23 cm). **Friction**. Known colors: Assorted. Graphics: ToyoAce - Tool Box. Maker: **Asahi**, Japan. Toy marks: ATC (Asahi Toy). Box marks: ATC (Asahi Toy). Box text: *Delivery Truck*.
Notes: Asahi catalog image.
Scarcity: 8. Fine to Excellent (C6-C8): $300-$600, Mint (C10): $900

(Not pictured) **1960s Toyota Toyoace 2-door pick up**. **10 in** (25 cm). **Friction**. Known colors: Assorted. Maker: **Bandai**, Japan. Toy marks: Bandai.
Scarcity: 6. Fine to Excellent (C6-C8): $250-$375, Mint (C10): $500

Commercial Delivery Vehicles 33

1940s Undetermined 2-door delivery. 12 in (30 cm). **Windup.** Known colors: Assorted two tone. Graphics: Rico - IBI. Maker: **Rico**, Spain. Toy marks: Rico.
Scarcity: 10. Fine to Excellent (C6-C8): $200-$350, Mint (C10): $500

1950s Undetermined 2-door Ice Cream delivery. 7.5 in (19 cm). **Friction.** Known colors: White. Graphics: Frosty Bar - Vanilla - Chocolate - Mint - Coconut - Caution. License: 4931. Maker: **Unknown**, Japan. Toy marks: none.
Scarcity: 5. Fine to Excellent (C6-C8): $100-$185, Mint (C10): $290

1950s Undetermined 2-door Ice Cream delivery with driver and mystery action. **7 in** (18 cm). **Friction.** Known colors: White. Graphics: Good Flavor Ice Cream - Ice cream. Maker: **Yoshiya**, Japan. Toy marks: KO (Yoshiya). Box marks: KO (Yoshiya), Frankonia. Box text: Ice Cream Vendor.
Scarcity: 7. Fine to Excellent (C6-C8): $250-$350, Mint (C10): $450

1950s Undetermined 2-door delivery with open sides and cases with bottles. **9 in** (23 cm). **Friction.** Known colors: Yellow and red. Graphics: Coca-Cola. Maker: **Götz & Sohn**, Germany. Toy marks: GÖSO (Götz & Sohn).
Scarcity: 7. Fine to Excellent (C6-C8): $500-$700, Mint (C10): $900

1950s Undetermined 2-door delivery with opening tool box. **7.5 in** (19 cm). **Friction.** Known colors: Blue and yellow. Graphics: Irco Engineering Co. Maker: **IRCO**, Japan. Toy marks: Irco.
Scarcity: 5. Fine to Excellent (C6-C8): $75-$125, Mint (C10): $185

1950s Undetermined 2-door delivery with open sides and cases with bottles. **9 in** (23 cm). **Friction.** Known colors: Yellow and red. Graphics: Enjoy Coca-Cola - Drink Coca-Cola. Maker: **Tipp & Co.**, Germany. Toy marks: TCO (Tipp).
Scarcity: 7. Fine to Excellent (C6-C8): $500-$700, Mint (C10): $900

Commercial Delivery Vehicles

1950s Undetermined 2-door fuel delivery. 11.5 in (29 cm). **Windup**. Known colors: Red and yellow. Graphics: SHELL INFIAMMABILI. Maker: **Marchesini**, Italy. Toy marks: MLB (Marchesini). Box marks: MLB (Marchesini).
Scarcity: 7. Fine to Excellent (C6-C8): $400-$600, Mint (C10): $800

1950s Undetermined Moving Van 2-door delivery with opening rear van doors. **13 in** (33 cm). **Friction**. Known colors: Orange. Graphics: Allied Van Lines - Inc. Nation-Wide Moving. Maker: **Linemar**, Japan. Toy marks: Linemar (Marx). Box marks: Linemar (Marx).
Scarcity: 4. Fine to Excellent (C6-C8): $150-$250, Mint (C10): $350

1950s Undetermined 2-door delivery. 13 in (33 cm). **Friction**. Known colors: Orange. License: I-1956. Maker: **Marusan**, Japan. Toy marks: SAN (Marusan), H (Hayashi).
Scarcity: 8. Fine to Excellent (C6-C8): $250-$350, Mint (C10): $450

1960s Undetermined 2-door van. 9 in (23 cm). **Friction**. Known colors: Blue and white. Graphics: Milk Fresh. Maker: **Kyoei**, Japan. Toy marks: none. Box marks: Kyoei.
Notes: Also came as Fire Rescue and U.S. Mail.
Scarcity: 3. Fine to Excellent (C6-C8): $60-$90, Mint (C10): $125

1960s Undetermined 2-door milk van with tin driver. **9 in** (23 cm). **Friction**. Known colors: Cream. Graphics: Milk - YU-9-0050. Maker: **Unknown**, Japan. Toy marks: none. Box marks: Frankonia.
Scarcity: 3. Fine to Excellent (C6-C8): $75-$125, Mint (C10): $175

1960s Undetermined 2-door van with coin slot, opening rear door, and bell sound. **10 in** (25 cm). **Friction**. Known colors: Silver. Graphics: First National Bank. Maker: **Hayashi**, Japan. Toy marks: H (Hayashi).
Scarcity: 3. Fine to Excellent (C6-C8): $75-$125, Mint (C10): $175

Commercial Delivery Vehicles

1960s Undetermined 2-door Food Service van with opening side panel that reveals food service counter. Bell rings when panel opens. **10 in** (25 cm). **Friction**. Known colors: Blue and white. Graphics: Joe's Kitchen Wagon. Maker: **Hayashi**, Japan. Toy marks: H (Hayashi). Box marks: H (Hayashi). Box text: *Joe's Kitchen Wagon -Lift Up Side Roof & Ring-Ring*.
Scarcity: 5. Fine to Excellent (C6-C8): $250-$325, Mint (C10): $400

1960s Undetermined 2-door dump delivery with bumper activated dumping action. **13 in** (33 cm). **Friction**. Known colors: Blue and orange. Graphics: Mighty Dump. Maker: **Yonezawa**, Japan. Toy marks: Y (Yonezawa). Box marks: Y (Yonezawa). Box text: *Mighty Dump Truck*.
Scarcity: 3. Fine to Excellent (C6-C8): $150-$250, Mint (C10): $350

1960s Undetermined 2-door van with coin slot, opening rear door, and bell sound. **10 in** (25 cm). **Friction**. Known colors: Silver and red; Cream and red. Graphics: Savings Bank - Armored Car. Maker: **Hayashi**, Japan. Toy marks: H (Hayashi), Rosko.
Scarcity: 3. Fine to Excellent (C6-C8): $75-$125, Mint (C10): $175

1960s Volkswagen Beetle 2-door sedan. **8 in** (20 cm). **Friction**. Known colors: Yellow. Graphics: Kreuzer Ball Pen Stylo. Maker: **Bandai**, Japan. Toy marks: Bandai.
Scarcity: 9. Fine to Excellent (C6-C8): $400-$500, Mint (C10): $600

1960s Undetermined 2-door van with celluloid driver, rear opening door, and skylight roof. **12.5 in** (32 cm). **Friction**. Known colors: Red and yellow. Graphics: Home Town Laundry - Y3018. Maker: **IY Metal**, Japan. Toy marks: IY Metal Toy.
Scarcity: 7. Fine to Excellent (C6-C8): $300-$400, Mint (C10): $500

1950/60s Volkswagen Transporter Ice Cream van. **6 in** (15 cm). **Friction**. Known colors: Red, white, and blue. Graphics: Helados Ice Cream No 524. License: P-524-D. Maker: **Payva**, Spain. Toy marks: Payva. Box marks: Payva. Box text: *Furgoneta Volkswagen*.
Notes: Produced 1980s.
Scarcity: 5. Fine to Excellent (C6-C8): $85-$135, Mint (C10): $195

36 Commercial Delivery Vehicles

1950/60s Volkswagen Transporter pick up. **6.25 in** (16 cm). **Friction**. Known colors: Assorted two tone. Maker: **Bandai**, Japan. Toy marks: Bandai. Box marks: Bandai. Box text: *Volkswagen Pick Up #746*.
Scarcity: 4. Fine to Excellent (C6-C8): $125-$175, Mint (C10): $250

1950/60s Volkswagen Transporter pick up. **7.75 in** (20 cm). **Friction**. Known colors: Assorted. Maker: **Bandai**, Japan. Toy marks: Bandai. Box marks: Bandai, Cragstan. Box text: *Volkswagen Pick-Up Truck*.
Scarcity: 5. Fine to Excellent (C6-C8): $175-$225, Mint (C10): $300

1950/60s Volkswagen Transporter pick up with forward/reverse action, operating headlights, and BC Toys cargo box. **7.75 in** (20 cm). **Battery operated**. Known colors: Assorted. Maker: **Bandai**, Japan. Toy marks: Bandai. Box marks: Bandai.
Scarcity: 6. Fine to Excellent (C6-C8): $200-$300, Mint (C10): $425

1950/60s Volkswagen Transporter pick up with livestock truck top and pull down rear ramp. **7.75 in** (20 cm). **Friction**. Known colors: Assorted. License: Volkswagen. Maker: **Bandai**, Japan. Toy marks: Bandai.
Scarcity: 6. Fine to Excellent (C6-C8): $125-$250, Mint (C10): $385

1950/60s Volkswagen Transporter pick up with forward/reverse action and steering. **7.75 in** (20 cm). **R/C battery operated**. Known colors: Assorted. Maker: **Bandai**, Japan. Toy marks: Bandai. Box marks: Bandai. Box text: *Volkswagen Pick Up Truck #4120*.
Scarcity: 5. Fine to Excellent (C6-C8): $125-$185, Mint (C10): $250

1950/60s Volkswagen Transporter van with modern graphics. **7.75 in** (20 cm). **Friction**. Known colors: Assorted two tone. Maker: **Bandai**, Japan. Toy marks: Bandai. Box text: *#533*.
Scarcity: 10. Fine to Excellent (C6-C8): $600-$800, Mint (C10): $1,000

Commercial Delivery Vehicles 37

1950/60s Volkswagen Transporter van. 7.75 in (20 cm). **Friction.** Known colors: Assorted. Maker: **Bandai**, Japan. Toy marks: Bandai. Box marks: Bandai.
Scarcity: 6. Fine to Excellent (C6-C8): $125-$250, Mint (C10): $375

(Not pictured) **1950/60s Volkswagen Transporter van** promotional model. **7.75 in** (20 cm). **Friction.** Known colors: Yellow with red and white stripes and blue roof. Graphics: Parkway Distributors. Maker: **Bandai**, Japan. Toy marks: Bandai.
Scarcity: 9. Fine to Excellent (C6-C8): $600-$900, Mint (C10): $1,200

1950/60s Volkswagen Transporter micro-bus. 9 in (23 cm). **Friction.** Known colors: Red and white. Graphics: Coca-Cola - Drink Coke. Maker: **Taiyo**, Japan. Toy marks: Taiyo World Toy.
Scarcity: 5. Fine to Excellent (C6-C8): $100-$200, Mint (C10): $300

1950/60s Volkswagen Transporter micro-bus with animal graphics and lithographed skylight roof. **9 in** (23 cm). **Friction.** Known colors: Red and white. Graphics: Kindergarten. Maker: **Takatoku**, Japan. Toy marks: TT (Takatoku).
Scarcity: 4. Fine to Excellent (C6-C8): $100-$150, Mint (C10): $200

1950/60s Volkswagen Transporter micro-bus with lithographed children and driver on windows. **9 in** (23 cm). **Friction.** Known colors: Blue, white, and cream. Graphics: Kindergarten Bus (Japanese). License: 35-71. Maker: **Terai**, Japan. Toy marks: Daiya (Terai).
Scarcity: 5. Fine to Excellent (C6-C8): $125-$175, Mint (C10): $250

(Not pictured) **1950/60s Volkswagen Transporter Ice Cream micro-bus** with opening side panel revealing milk and ice cream. **9 in** (23 cm). **Friction.** Known colors: Blue and white. Graphics: Fresh Bakery - Milk - Ice cream. Maker: **Yonezawa**, Japan. Toy marks: Y (Yonezawa).
Scarcity: 8. Fine to Excellent (C6-C8): $300-$400, Mint (C10): $500

1950/60s Volkswagen Transporter micro-bus with lithographed passengers in windows and button-activated camping song, forward/reverse action. **9 in** (23 cm). **Battery operated.** Known colors: Red, yellow, white, and blue. Graphics: Camping Bus. Maker: **Yonezawa/Ichiko**, Japan. Toy marks: Ichiko. Box marks: Y (Yonezawa). Box text: *Camping Bus With Sound Effects.*
Scarcity: 6. Fine to Excellent (C6-C8): $200-$300, Mint (C10): $400

1950/60s Volkswagen Transporter pick up with visible motor and spinning fan. **9.5 in** (24 cm). **Friction.** Known colors: Assorted. Maker: **Bandai**, Japan. Toy marks: Bandai. Box marks: Bandai. Box text: *#809.*
Scarcity: 6. Fine to Excellent (C6-C8): $200-$400, Mint (C10): $600

38 Commercial Delivery Vehicles

1950/60s Volkswagen Transporter delivery with open sides and plastic cases with bottles. **9.5 in** (24 cm). **Friction.** Known colors: Red and white. Graphics: Coca-Cola -504 - Comparte Coca-Cola y una sonrisa. License: Pol-888. Maker: **Poliumex**, Mexico. Toy marks: Poliumex.
Scarcity: 7. Fine to Excellent (C6-C8): $300-$450, Mint (C10): $600

1950/60s Volkswagen Transporter delivery with open sides and plastic cases with bottles. **9.5 in** (24 cm). **Friction.** Known colors: White and blue. Graphics: Pepsi-Cola. License: Pol-888. Maker: **Poliumex**, Mexico. Toy marks: Poliumex.
Scarcity: 7. Fine to Excellent (C6-C8): $300-$450, Mint (C10): $600

1950/60s Volkswagen Transporter pick up with drop down canvas side. **9.5 in** (24 cm). **Friction.** Known colors: Red & blue. Graphics: VW - Express. Maker: **Tipp & Co.**, Germany. Toy marks: TCO (Tipp). Box marks: TCO (Tipp).
Scarcity: 6. Fine to Excellent (C6-C8): $400-$600, Mint (C10): $800

(Not pictured) **1950/60s Volkswagen Transporter van. 9.5 in** (24 cm). **Friction.** Known colors: Light blue and white. Maker: **Tipp & Co.**, Germany. Toy marks: TCO (Tipp). Box marks: TCO (Tipp).
Scarcity: 7. Fine to Excellent (C6-C8): $400-$600, Mint (C10): $800

1950/60s Volkswagen Transporter delivery with open sides and plastic cases with bottles. **9.5 in** (24 cm). **Friction.** Known colors: Yellow and red. Graphics: Coca-Cola -504 - Köstlich Erfrischend. License: TCO-020. Maker: **Tipp & Co.**, Germany. Toy marks: TCO (Tipp).
Notes: US market version does not have German advertising.
Scarcity: 7. Fine to Excellent (C6-C8): $700-$900, Mint (C10): $1,200

(Not pictured) **1950/60s Volkswagen Transporter delivery** with open sides and plastic cases with bottles. **9.5 in** (24 cm). **Friction.** Known colors: White and black. Graphics: Sie güte milch. Maker: **Tipp & Co.**, Germany. Toy marks: TCO (Tipp).
Scarcity: 7. Fine to Excellent (C6-C8): $500-$700, Mint (C10): $1,000

(Not pictured) **1950/60s Volkswagen Transporter micro-bus. 9.5 in** (24 cm). **Friction.** Known colors: Light blue and white. Graphics: Köln Rom. Maker: **Tipp & Co.**, Germany. Toy marks: TCO (Tipp). Box marks: TCO (Tipp).
Scarcity: 7. Fine to Excellent (C6-C8): $700-$900, Mint (C10): $1,200

1950/60s Volkswagen Transporter micro-bus with tin animal passengers and bump and go action. **9.75 in** (25 cm). **Battery operated.** Known colors: Yellow. Graphics: Animal School Bus. Maker: **Takatoku**, Japan. Toy marks: TT (Takatoku). Box marks: TT (Takatoku).
Scarcity: 4. Fine to Excellent (C6-C8): $100-$150, Mint (C10): $200

Commercial Delivery Vehicles 39

1950/60s Volkswagen Transporter micro-bus with siren sound and lithographed people. **10.25 in** (26 cm). **Friction.** Known colors: Yellow and red. Graphics: School Bus (Japanese). Maker: **Ichiko**, Japan. Toy marks: none. Box marks: Ichiko. Box text: *12" VW School Bus with Siren Sound* (Japanese text).
Notes: Produced 1980s.
Scarcity: 2. Fine to Excellent (C6-C8): $35-$45, Mint (C10): $60

1960s White 2-door delivery with lithographed bottles and cases. **8.5 in** (22 cm). **Friction.** Known colors: Light green. Graphics: Canada Dry. License: NH-8437. Maker: **Hayashi**, Japan. Toy marks: H (Hayashi), Rosko.
Scarcity: 5. Fine to Excellent (C6-C8): $150-$300, Mint (C10): $450

1960s White Freightliner 2-door fuel delivery with ground chain. **16 in** (41 cm). **Friction.** Known colors: Red. Graphics: Mobilgas No.159. Maker: **Hayashi**, Japan. Toy marks: H (Hayashi). Box marks: H (Hayashi). Box text: *Mobilgas Tank Truck*.
Scarcity: 4. Fine to Excellent (C6-C8): $150-$225, Mint (C10): $300

Public Service Vehicles

(By Make, Year, Size, and Toy Maker)

Airline Service

1961 Chevrolet Corvair 95, van. **8 in** (20 cm). **Friction**. Known colors: Light blue and white. Graphics: Pan American - Airport Service - Airport Bus. License: 1069. Maker: **Tatsuya**, Japan. Toy marks: KTS (Tatsuya).
Scarcity: 5. Fine to Excellent (C6-C8): $125-$185, Mint (C10): $275

1961 Chevrolet Corvair 2-door van with opening rear door. **9 in** (23 cm). **Friction**. Known colors: Blue. Graphics: PAA Airlines. Maker: **Toyo Plaything**, Japan. Toy marks: none. Box marks: A1 (Toyo). Box text: *Airlines Service Bus*.
Scarcity: 5. Fine to Excellent (C6-C8): $150-$250, Mint (C10): $375

(Not pictured) **1962 Ford Falcon 4-door station wagon** with opening rear tailgate. **9 in** (23 cm). **Friction**. Known colors:. Graphics: American Airlines Airport Service - AA. Maker: **Alps**, Japan. Toy marks: Mitomo.
Scarcity: 3. Fine to Excellent (C6-C8): $60-$90, Mint (C10): $120

(Not pictured) **1962 Ford Falcon 4-door station wagon** with opening rear tailgate. **9 in** (23 cm). **Friction**. Known colors:. Graphics: Pan Am Airport Service Car. Maker: **Alps**, Japan. Toy marks: Mitomo.
Scarcity: 3. Fine to Excellent (C6-C8): $60-$90, Mint (C10): $120

(Not pictured) **1962 Ford Falcon 4-door station wagon** with opening rear tailgate. **9 in** (23 cm). **Friction**. Known colors:. Graphics: United Airlines Airport Service - United Airlines. Maker: **Alps**, Japan. Toy marks: Mitomo.
Scarcity: 3. Fine to Excellent (C6-C8): $60-$90, Mint (C10): $120

1960s Ford-Köln 2-door delivery. **8.5 in** (22 cm). **Friction**. Known colors: Blue. Graphics: Air Transport. Maker: **Tatsuya**, Japan. Toy marks: KTS (Tatsuya).
Scarcity: 4. Fine to Excellent (C6-C8): $75-$125, Mint (C10): $165

1960s Hino 2-door delivery. **8.5 in** (22 cm). **Friction**. Known colors: Silver, red and blue. Graphics: American Airlines. Maker: **Hayashi**, Japan. Toy marks: H (Hayashi). Box text: *Shuttle Truck*.
Scarcity: 4. Fine to Excellent (C6-C8): $75-$125, Mint (C10): $175

1960s Hino 2-door delivery. **8.5 in** (22 cm). **Friction**. Known colors: Red and blue. Graphics: United Air Lines. Maker: **Hayashi**, Japan. Toy marks: H (Hayashi).
Scarcity: 4. Fine to Excellent (C6-C8): $75-$125, Mint (C10): $175

Public Service Vehicles 41

1950s Jeep CJ3, 2-door with rear seat and canopy. **7 in** (18 cm). **Friction**. Known colors: Blue; Yellow; Red. Graphics: AA - American Airlines - Airport. Maker: **Taiyo**, Japan. Toy marks: none. Box marks: Taiyo World Toy. Box text: *Airport Service Jeep Series*.
Scarcity: 5. Fine to Excellent (C6-C8): $75-$150, Mint (C10): $225

(Not pictured) **1950s Jeep CJ3, 2-door** with rear seat and canopy. **7 in** (18 cm). **Friction**. Known colors:. Graphics: TWA - Trans World Airlines. Maker: **Taiyo**, Japan. Toy marks: none. Box marks: Taiyo World Toy. Box text: *Airport Service Jeep Series*.
Scarcity: 5. Fine to Excellent (C6-C8): $75-$150, Mint (C10): $225

(Not pictured) **1950s Jeep CJ3, 2-door** with rear seat and canopy. **7 in** (18 cm). **Friction**. Known colors:. Graphics: United Airlines. Maker: **Taiyo**, Japan. Toy marks: none. Box marks: Taiyo World Toy. Box text: *Airport Service Jeep Series*.
Scarcity: 5. Fine to Excellent (C6-C8): $75-$150, Mint (C10): $225

1964 Plymouth 4-door hardtop with siren sound and lithographed luggage rack. **10 in** (25 cm). **Friction**. Known colors: Red and white. Graphics: Pan Am. Maker: **Kusama/Yoshi**, Japan. Toy marks: K (Kusama). Box marks: Y (Yoshi). Box text: *Airport Service Car Plymouth*.
Scarcity: 3. Fine to Excellent (C6-C8): $125-$165, Mint (C10): $200

(Not pictured) **1964 Plymouth 4-door station wagon** with siren sound and lithographed luggage rack. **10 in** (25 cm). **Friction**. Known colors: Blue and white. Graphics: BOAC. Maker: **Kusama/Yoshi**, Japan. Toy marks: K (Kusama). Box marks: Y (Yoshi). Box text: *Airport Service Car Plymouth*.
Scarcity: 3. Fine to Excellent (C6-C8): $125-$165, Mint (C10): $200

(Not pictured) **1964 Plymouth 4-door station wagon** with siren sound and lithographed luggage rack. **10 in** (25 cm). **Friction**. Known colors: Blue and white. Graphics: KLM. Maker: **Kusama/Yoshi**, Japan. Toy marks: K (Kusama). Box marks: Y (Yoshi). Box text: *Airport Service Car Plymouth*.
Scarcity: 3. Fine to Excellent (C6-C8): $125-$165, Mint (C10): $200

(Not pictured) **1964 Plymouth 4-door station wagon** with siren sound and lithographed luggage rack. **10 in** (25 cm). **Friction**. Known colors: Red and white. Graphics: Pan Am. Maker: **Kusama/Yoshi**, Japan. Toy marks: K (Kusama). Box marks: Y (Yoshi). Box text: *Airport Service Car Plymouth*.
Scarcity: 3. Fine to Excellent (C6-C8): $125-$165, Mint (C10): $200

1960s Toyota Crown 4-door station wagon with roof sign and luggage rack. **11.5 in** (29 cm). **Friction**. Known colors: Blue. Graphics: JAL Japan Air Lines Limousine. Maker: **Nomura**, Japan. Toy marks: TN (Nomura). Box marks: TN (Nomura). Box text: *Super Five Airport Limousine*.
Scarcity: 4. Fine to Excellent (C6-C8): $200-$300, Mint (C10): $400

(Not pictured) **1960s Undetermined 2-door**. **8.75 in** (22 cm). **Friction**. Known colors: Multi colored. Graphics: Airport Service - (Airline logos). Maker: **Takatoku**, Japan. Toy marks: TT (Takatoku).
Scarcity: 3. Fine to Excellent (C6-C8): $75-$115, Mint (C10): $135

1950/60s Volkswagen Transporter micro-bus with lithographed passengers, flashing light, and bump and go action. **9.75 in** (25 cm). **Battery operated**. Known colors: Blue-gray and white. Graphics: Alitalia VW. Maker: **Takatoku**, Japan. Toy marks: TT (Takatoku). Box marks: TT (Takatoku). Box text: *Airport Service Bus*.
Scarcity: 4. Fine to Excellent (C6-C8): $125-$250, Mint (C10): $375

Ambulances

Ambulance box art. *Photo by Rodney Abensur.*

(Not pictured) **1960s Bentley 4-door sedan** with flashing roof light and two red fender sirens. **9 in** (23 cm). **R/C battery operated**. Known colors: White. Graphics: (Red Cross emblem). License: 5647. Maker: **Yonezawa**, Japan. Toy marks: Y (Yonezawa). Box marks: Y (Yonezawa). Box text: *Ambulance Car with Flashing Light*.
Scarcity: 5. Fine to Excellent (C6-C8): $125-$175, Mint (C10): $235

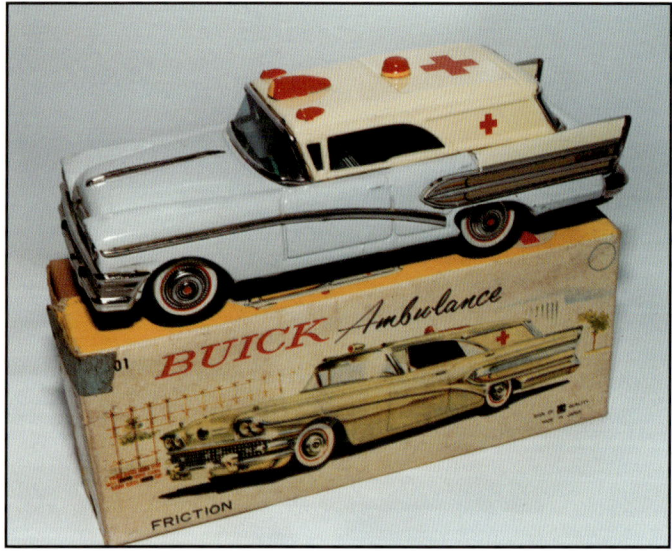

1958 Buick Century Estate Wagon 4-door station wagon with roof light and markers. **8 in** (20 cm). **Friction**. Known colors: White and off white. Graphics: (Red Cross emblem). Maker: **Bandai**, Japan. Toy marks: Bandai. Box marks: Bandai. Box text: *Buick Ambulance #601*.
Scarcity: 5. Fine to Excellent (C6-C8): $125-$175, Mint (C10): $270

(Not pictured) **1959 Buick 2-door hardtop** with fender siren and antenna. **9 in** (23 cm). **Friction**. Known colors: White. Graphics: Ambulance - (Red Cross emblem). Maker: **Masudaya**, Japan. Toy marks: MT (Masudaya). Box marks: MT (Masudaya). Box text: *Buick Ambulance*.
Scarcity: 3. Fine to Excellent (C6-C8): $100-$150, Mint (C10): $200

1961 Buick Le Sabre 4-door hardtop with rotating siren, antenna, and working wipers. **16 in** (41 cm). **Friction**. Known colors: White. Graphics: Ambulance - NO. 105 - Rescue Squad - Buick. Maker: **Nomura**, Japan. Toy marks: TN (Nomura).
Scarcity: 5. Fine to Excellent (C6-C8): $375-$525, Mint (C10): $650

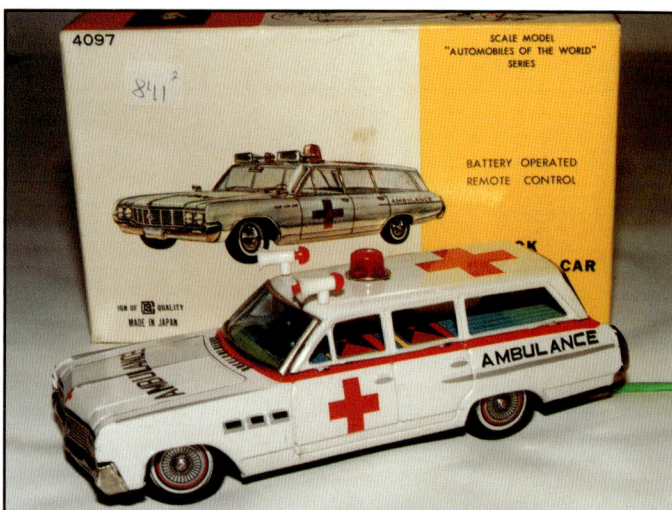

1963 Buick Estate Wagon 4-door station wagon with flashing light, rotating speakers, forward/reverse action, and steering. **8 in** (20 cm). **R/C battery operated**. Known colors: White. Graphics: Ambulance - (Red Cross emblem). Maker: **Bandai**, Japan. Toy marks: Bandai. Box marks: Bandai. Box text: *Buick Ambulance Car #4097*.
Notes: Also produced as friction model.
Scarcity: 3. Fine to Excellent (C6-C8): $60-$90, Mint (C10): $125

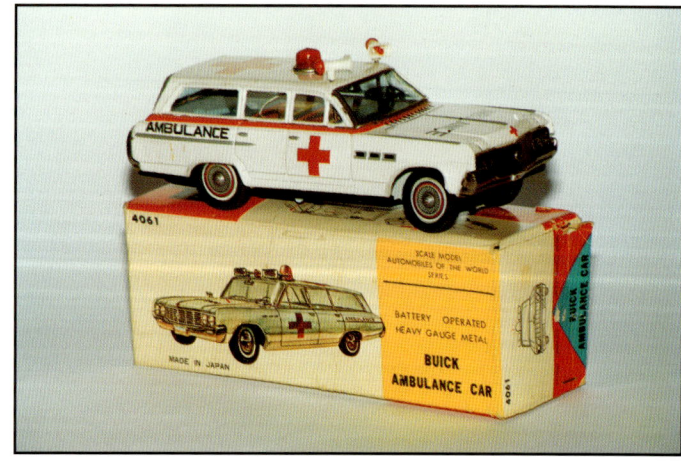

1963 Buick Estate Wagon 4-door station wagon with flashing light, rotating speakers, and forward/reverse action. **8 in** (20 cm). **Battery operated**. Known colors: White. Graphics: Ambulance - (Red Cross emblem). Maker: **Bandai**, Japan. Toy marks: Bandai. Box marks: Bandai. Box text: *Buick Ambulance Car #4061*.
Scarcity: 3. Fine to Excellent (C6-C8): $60-$90, Mint (C10): $125

Public Service Vehicles 43

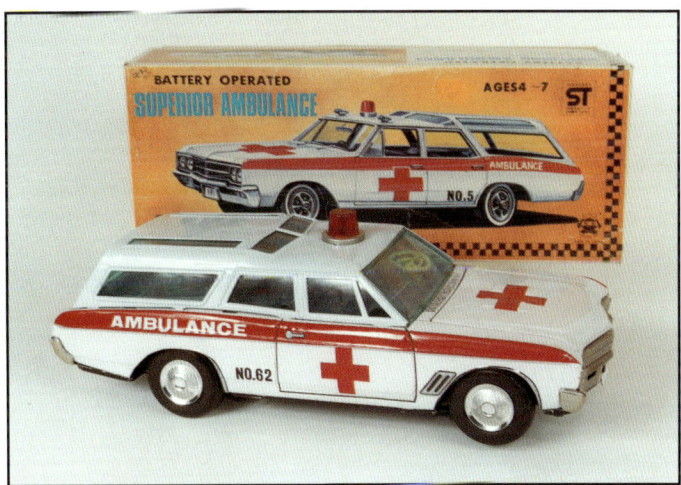

1966 Buick Skylark 4-door station wagon with roof dome light. **11.5 in** (29 cm). **Battery operated**. Known colors: White and red. Graphics: Ambulance No.625. License: 4044. Maker: **Asakusa**, Japan. Toy marks: A1 (Asakusa). Box marks: A1 (Asakusa). Box text: *Superior Ambulance*.
Scarcity: 3. Fine to Excellent (C6-C8): $125-$200, Mint (C10): $325

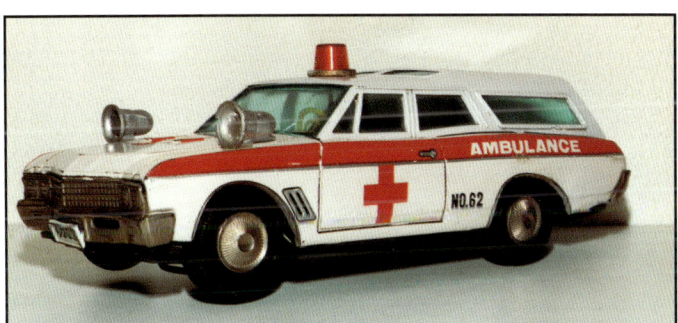

1966 Buick Skylark 4-door station wagon with roof light and two fender mounted sirens. **11.5 in** (29 cm). **Battery operated**. Known colors: White and red. Graphics: Ambulance No.625. License: 6063. Maker: **Asakusa**, Japan. Toy marks: A1 (Asakusa). Box marks: A1 (Asakusa). Box text: *Superior Ambulance*.
Scarcity: 3. Fine to Excellent (C6-C8): $125-$200, Mint (C10): $325

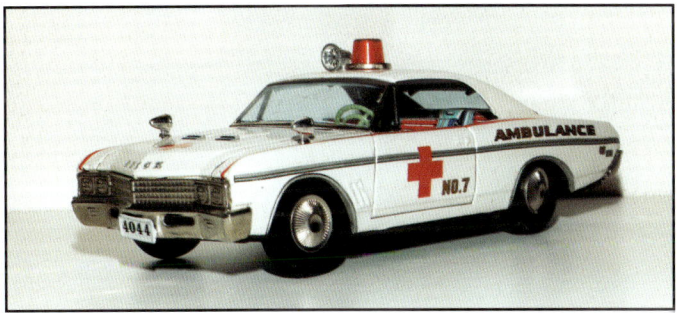

1966 Buick Skylark 2-door hardtop with dome roof light, siren, and fender mirrors. **11.5 in** (29 cm). **Friction**. Known colors: White. Graphics: Ambulance - No.7 - (Red Cross emblem) - Buick. License: 4044. Maker: **Asakusa**, Japan. Toy marks: A1 (Asakusa). Box marks: A1 (Asakusa). Box text: *Ambulance New Buick*.
Scarcity: 3. Fine to Excellent (C6-C8): $125-$200, Mint (C10): $325

1966 Buick Riviera 2-door station wagon with roof light and siren. **15 in** (38 cm). **Friction**. Known colors: White and red. Graphics: Ambulance - 123 - (Red Cross emblem) - Buick. Maker: **Asakusa**, Japan. Toy marks: A1 (Asakusa). Box marks: A1 (Asakusa).
Scarcity: 4. Fine to Excellent (C6-C8): $125-$300, Mint (C10): $500

(Not pictured) **1960 Cadillac 4-door hardtop** with rotating roof light and antenna. **6 in** (15 cm). **Friction**. Known colors: White. Graphics: Ambulance. License: IK-62. Maker: **Ichiko**, Japan. Toy marks: none. Box marks: Ichiko. Box text: *Ambulance With Moving Light*.
Scarcity: 3. Fine to Excellent (C6-C8): $75-$125, Mint (C10): $165

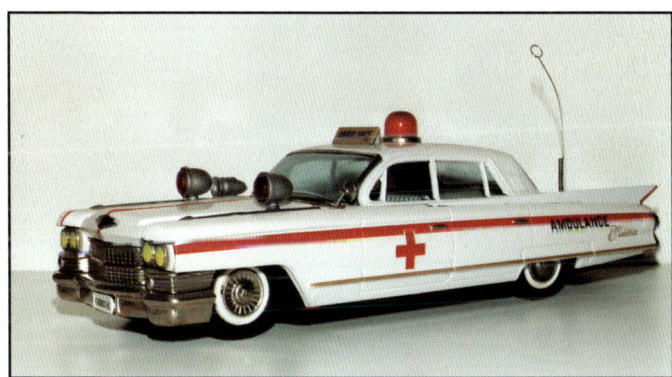

1961 Cadillac 4-door sedan with lights, siren, antenna, and roof sign. **17 in** (43 cm). **Friction**. Known colors: White and red. Graphics: Ambulance - (Red Cross emblem). Maker: **Bandai**, Japan. Toy marks: Bandai. Box text: *Cadillac Ambulance #967*.
Notes: 1963 model front end.
Scarcity: 5. Fine to Excellent (C6-C8): $275-$425, Mint (C10): $500

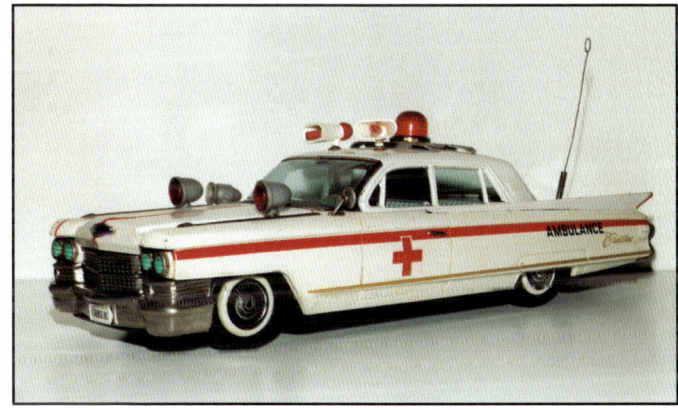

1961 Cadillac 4-door sedan with lights, siren, antenna, and roof speakers. **17 in** (43 cm). **Battery operated**. Known colors: White and red. Graphics: Ambulance - (Red Cross emblem). License: Cadillac. Maker: **Bandai**, Japan. Toy marks: Bandai.
Notes: 1963 model front end.
Scarcity: 5. Fine to Excellent (C6-C8): $275-$425, Mint (C10): $500

44 Ambulances

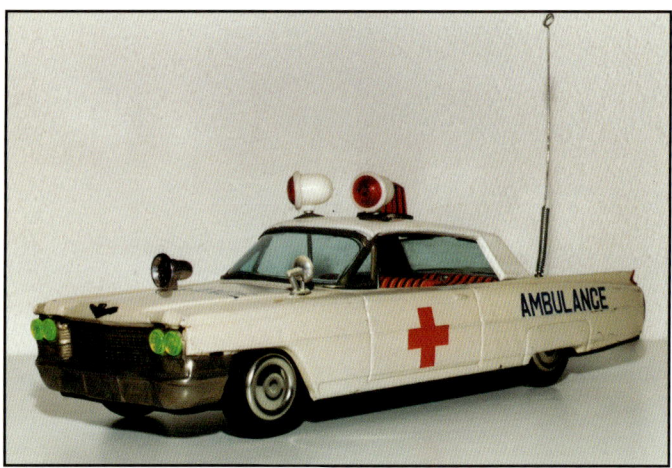

1963 Cadillac 2-door hardtop with dome roof light, rotating lights, fender siren, mirror, and antenna. **11 in** (28 cm). **Friction**. Known colors: White. Graphics: Ambulance - (Red Cross emblem). Maker: **Ichiko**, Japan. Toy marks: Ichiko. Box marks: Ichiko.
Scarcity: 4. Fine to Excellent (C6-C8): $75-$125, Mint (C10): $185

1956 Chevrolet 2-door station wagon. 9.75 in (25 cm). **Friction**. Known colors: White. Graphics: (Red Cross emblem). Maker: **Bandai**, Japan. Toy marks: Bandai. Box marks: Bandai.
Notes: Also came R/C battery operated with 3-button remote.
Scarcity: 4. Fine to Excellent (C6-C8): $100-$175, Mint (C10): $250

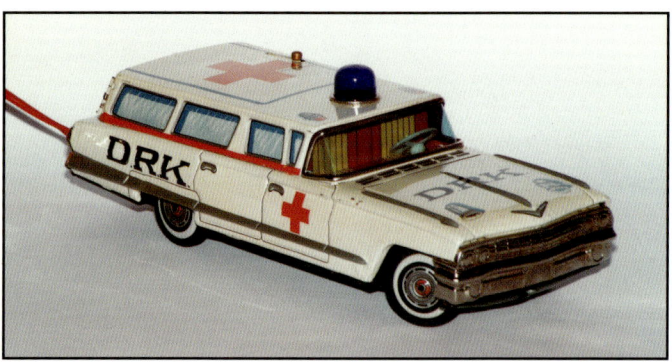

1963 Cadillac 4-door station wagon with blue roof light, opening rear doors, forward/reverse action, and steering. **11.25 in** (29 cm). **R/C battery operated**. Known colors: White. Graphics: DRK - (Red Cross emblem). Maker: **Yonezawa**, Japan. Toy marks: Y (Yonezawa). Box marks: Y (Yonezawa). Box text: *Deutsches Rotes Kreuz*.
Scarcity: 4. Fine to Excellent (C6-C8): $200-$300, Mint (C10): $400

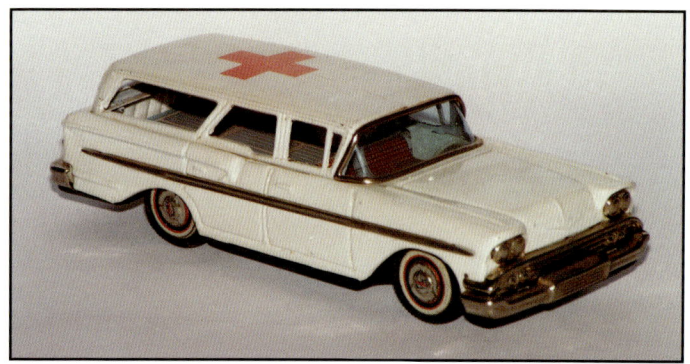

1958 Chevrolet 4-door station wagon. 8 in (20 cm). **Friction**. Known colors: White. Graphics: (Red Cross emblem). Maker: **Bandai**, Japan. Toy marks: Bandai. Box marks: Bandai. Box text: #719.
Scarcity: 4. Fine to Excellent (C6-C8): $75-$150, Mint (C10): $225

1959 Chevrolet 4-door station wagon with roof dome light. **12.5 in** (32 cm). **Friction**. Known colors: Green and white. Graphics: Ambulance - (Red Cross emblem) - Chevrolet. Maker: **Asakusa Toy & Doll,** Japan. Toy marks: ATD (Asakusa Toy & Doll).
Scarcity: 5. Fine to Excellent (C6-C8): $175-$225, Mint (C10): $350

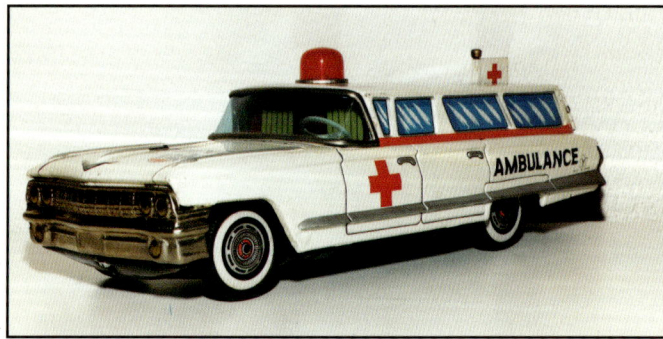

1963 Cadillac 4-door station wagon with extending ladder and roof light. Forward/reverse action with steering. **11.25 in** (29 cm). **R/C battery operated**. Known colors: White. Graphics: Ambulance - (Red Cross emblem). Maker: **Yonezawa**, Japan. Toy marks: Y (Yonezawa).
Scarcity: 4. Fine to Excellent (C6-C8): $250-$325, Mint (C10): $400

(Not pictured) **1960 Chevrolet 4-door hardtop** with rotating roof lights and siren. **7.5 in** (19 cm). **Friction**. Known colors: White. Graphics: (Red Cross emblem). License: Chevrolet - Ichiko. Maker: **Ichiko**, Japan. Toy marks: Ichiko. Box marks: Ichiko.
Scarcity: 4. Fine to Excellent (C6-C8): $85-$125, Mint (C10): $165

Public Service Vehicles 45

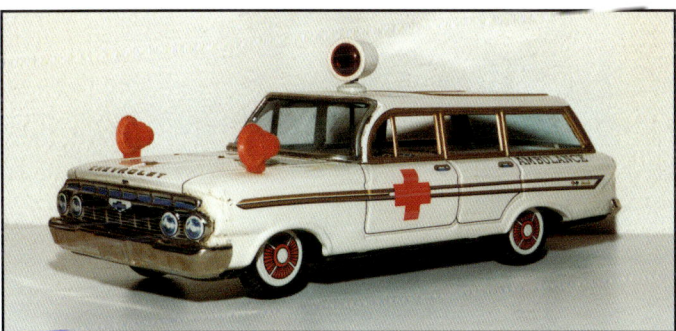

1961 Chevrolet 4-door station wagon with roof light and two fender sirens. **9.75 in** (25 cm). **Friction**. Known colors: White. Graphics: Ambulance - Chevrolet. Maker: **Aoshin**, Japan. Toy marks: ASC (Aoshin). Box marks: ASC (Aoshin).
Scarcity: 3. Fine to Excellent (C6-C8): $150-$200, Mint (C10): $250

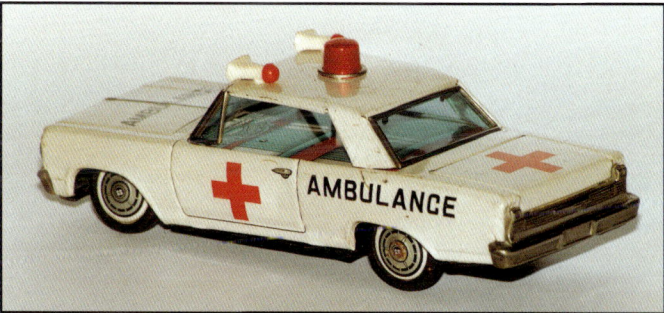

1964 Chevrolet Chevelle Malibu 2-door hardtop with dome roof light and rotating sirens. **8 in** (20 cm). **Friction**. Known colors: White. Graphics: Ambulance (Red Cross emblem). License: Chevrolet. Maker: **Bandai**, Japan. Toy marks: Bandai. Box marks: Bandai. Box text: *Security Car Series Ambulance Car #1098*.
Scarcity: 3. Fine to Excellent (C6-C8): $60-$90, Mint (C10): $125

(Not pictured) **1967 Dodge Dart 4-door hardtop** with red dome roof light, sirens, antenna and, lighted side fender markers. **12.25 in** (31 cm). **Friction**. Known colors: White. Graphics: Ambulance - (Red Cross emblem). Maker: **Nomura**, Japan. Toy marks: TN (Nomura).
Scarcity: 6. Fine to Excellent (C6-C8): $275-$350, Mint (C10): $425

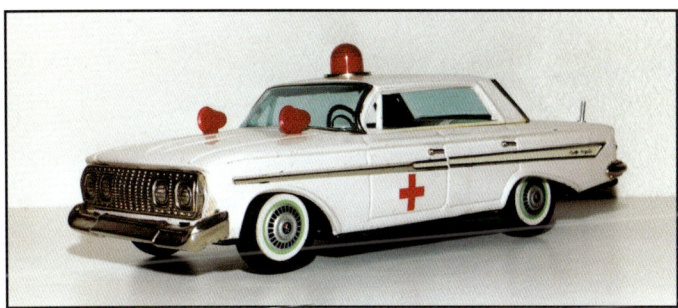

1961 Chevrolet Impala 4-door hardtop with roof dome light, antenna, and fender sirens. **11 in** (28 cm). **Friction**. Known colors: White. Graphics: (Red Cross emblem) - Impala. Maker: **Bandai**, Japan. Toy marks: Bandai. Box marks: Bandai. Box text: *#862*.
Notes: Car sold as 1961, 1962, and 1963 with taillight changes only.
Scarcity: 4. Fine to Excellent (C6-C8): $150-$225, Mint (C10): $300

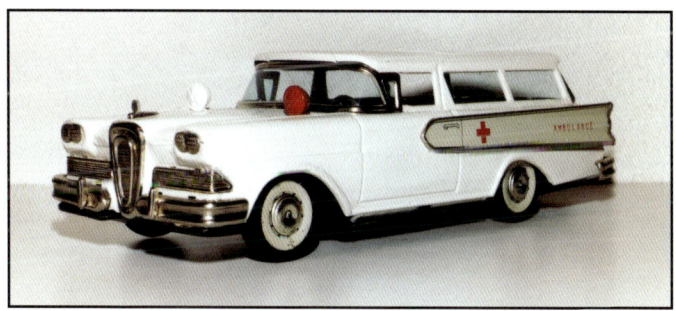

1958 Edsel 2-door station wagon with sirens. **11 in** (28 cm). **Friction**. Known colors: White. Graphics: Ambulance (Red Cross emblem) - Edsel. Maker: **Mansei Toys**, Japan. Toy marks: Haji (Mansei). Box marks: Haji (Mansei).
Scarcity: 6. Fine to Excellent (C6-C8): $300-$385, Mint (C10): $475

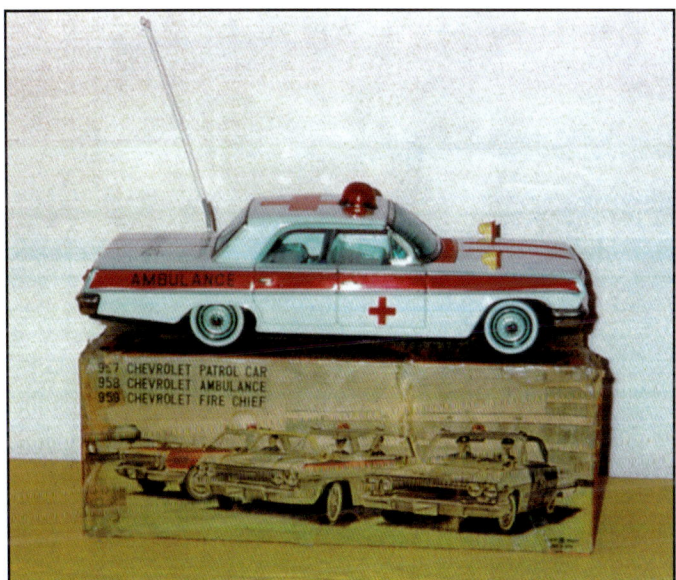

1962 Chevrolet 4-door hardtop with roof light, fender siren, and antenna. **11 in** (28 cm). **Friction**. Known colors: White and red. Graphics: Ambulance (Red Cross emblem). Maker: **Bandai**, Japan. Toy marks: Bandai. Box marks: Bandai. Box text: *Ambulance #958*.
Scarcity: 6. Fine to Excellent (C6-C8): $125-$225, Mint (C10): $350

1932 Ford Model A 2-door sedan. **8 in** (20 cm). **Friction**. Known colors: White with white or black fenders. Graphics: Ambulance - (Red Cross emblem). Maker: **Bandai**, Japan. Toy marks: Bandai. Box marks: Bandai. Box text: *Old fashioned Ambulance truck #1053*.
Notes: Produced 1960s.
Scarcity: 4. Fine to Excellent (C6-C8): $100-$125, Mint (C10): $150

46 Ambulances

1956 Ford 2-door station wagon with two sirens. **12 in** (30 cm). **Friction**. Known colors: White. Graphics: (Red Cross emblem). Maker: **Bandai**, Japan. Toy marks: Bandai. Box marks: Bandai. Box text: *Red Cross Ambulance #355*.
Scarcity: 6. Fine to Excellent (C6-C8): $175-$300, Mint (C10): $525

1957 Ford 2-door station wagon with tin roof light. **11.75 in** (30 cm). **Friction with battery**. Known colors: White. Maker: **Joustra**, France. Toy marks: Joustra.
Scarcity: 4. Fine to Excellent (C6-C8): $200-$250, Mint (C10): $325

1956 Ford 2-door station wagon with two sirens. **12 in** (30 cm). **Friction**. Known colors: White. Graphics: City of Hope - (torch). Maker: **Bandai**, Japan. Toy marks: Bandai. Box marks: Bandai.
Scarcity: 9. Fine to Excellent (C6-C8): $600-$800, Mint (C10): $1,000

1957 Ford 2-door station wagon with two fender sirens. **11.75 in** (30 cm). **Friction**. Known colors: White. Maker: **Joustra**, France. Toy marks: Joustra. Box text: *Serie "Junior" - Voiture Croix Rouge*.
Scarcity: 4. Fine to Excellent (C6-C8): $200-$250, Mint (C10): $325

1958 Ford 4-door station wagon. **8 in** (20 cm). **Friction**. Known colors: White. Graphics: (Red Cross emblem). Maker: **Bandai**, Japan. Toy marks: Bandai. Box marks: Bandai. Box text: *58 Ford Red Cross Ambulance #574*.
Scarcity: 3. Fine to Excellent (C6-C8): $125-$175, Mint (C10): $250

1957 Ford 2-door station wagon with two sirens. **11.75 in** (30 cm). **Friction**. Known colors: White. Graphics: (Red Cross emblem) - Ford. Maker: **Bandai**, Japan. Toy marks: Bandai. Box marks: Bandai. Box text: *Red Cross Ambulance #544*.
Scarcity: 6. Fine to Excellent (C6-C8): $275-$350, Mint (C10): $495

(Not pictured) **1959 Ford Fairlane 500 4-door hardtop**. **8.5 in** (22 cm). **Friction**. Known colors: White. Graphics: Ambulance - (Red Cross emblem). Maker: **Masudaya**, Japan. Toy marks: MT (Masudaya). Box marks: MT (Masudaya).
Scarcity: 5. Fine to Excellent (C6-C8): $100-$150, Mint (C10): $200

Public Service Vehicles 47

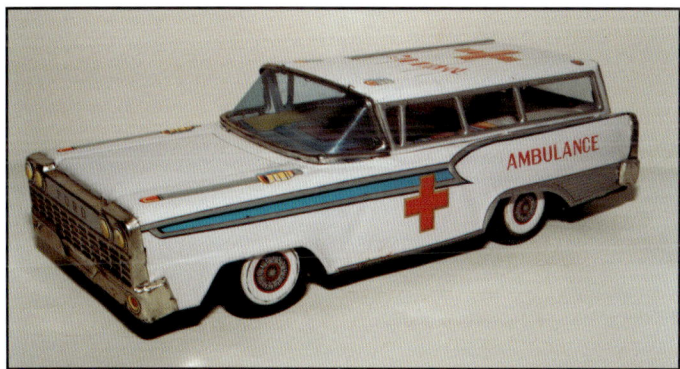

1959 Ford 4-door station wagon. **9 in** (23 cm). **Friction**. Known colors: White. Graphics: Ambulance - (Red Cross emblem). Maker: **Unknown**, Japan. Toy marks: none.
Scarcity: 2. Fine to Excellent (C6-C8): $60-$100, Mint (C10): $150

1961 Ford Galaxie 2-door hardtop with rotating roof lights, siren, and antenna. **9.5 in** (24 cm). **Friction with battery**. Known colors: White. Graphics: Ambulance. License: Ford. Maker: **Ichiko**, Japan. Toy marks: Ichiko. Box marks: Ichiko.
Notes: Ichiko catalog image.
Scarcity: 3. Fine to Excellent (C6-C8): $75-$175, Mint (C10): $275

1963 Ford Thunderbird 2-door hardtop with dome roof light and forward/reverse action. **8 in** (20 cm). **Battery operated**. Known colors: White, green, and red. Graphics: Ambulance (Red Cross). License: Thunderbird. Maker: **Bandai**, Japan. Toy marks: Bandai. Box marks: Bandai. Box text: *Ford Thunderbird Ambulance Car #4019*.
Scarcity: 8. Fine to Excellent (C6-C8): $150-$250, Mint (C10): $350

1964 Ford Galaxie 500 2-door hardtop with roof light, rotating lights, and antenna. **13 in** (33 cm). **Friction**. Known colors: White. Graphics: Ambulance - (Red Cross emblem) - F-1729. License: FG-1729. Maker: **Ichiko**, Japan. Toy marks: Ichiko.
Scarcity: 5. Fine to Excellent (C6-C8): $175-$250, Mint (C10): $325

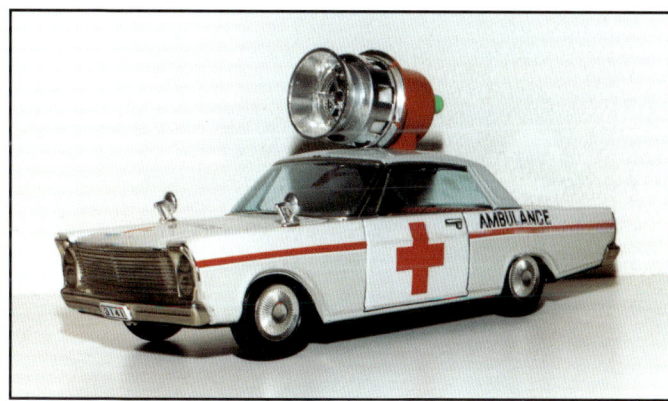

1965 Ford Galaxie 500XL 2-door hardtop with large roof mounted crank siren and fender mirrors. **11.25 in** (29 cm). **Friction**. Known colors: White. Graphics: Ambulance - (Red Cross emblem). License: 3141. Maker: **Masudaya**, Japan. Toy marks: KKY (Yamato). Box marks: MT (Masudaya). Box text: *Ambulance Car With Crank Siren*.
Scarcity: 6. Fine to Excellent (C6-C8): $75-$150, Mint (C10): $225

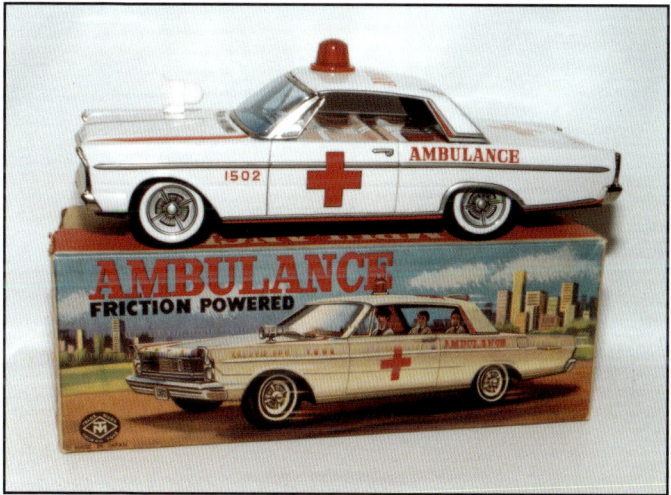

1965 Ford Galaxie 500XL 2-door hardtop with roof light, one siren, and siren sound. **11.25 in** (29 cm). **Friction**. Known colors: White and red. Graphics: Ambulance 1502 - (Red Cross emblem). License: 3141. Maker: **Masudaya**, Japan. Toy marks: KKY (Yamato). Box marks: MT (Masudaya). Box text: *Ambulance*.
Scarcity: 8. Fine to Excellent (C6-C8): $200-$325, Mint (C10): $450

Ambulances

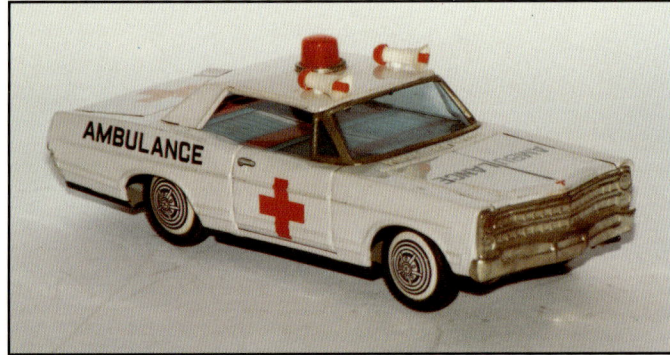

1967 Ford 2-door hardtop with rotating sirens and sound and roof light. **8 in** (20 cm). **Friction**. Known colors: White. Graphics: Ambulance - (Red Cross emblem). Maker: **Bandai**, Japan. Toy marks: Bandai. Box marks: Bandai. Box text: *Security Car Series #1106*.
Scarcity: 3. Fine to Excellent (C6-C8): $75-$110, Mint (C10): $150

(Not pictured) **1969 Ford Capri 2-door sedan** with roof dome light. **11 in** (28 cm). **Friction**. Known colors: White. Graphics: Ambulance (Red Cross emblem). Maker: **Aoshin**, Japan. Toy marks: ASC (Aoshin). Box marks: ASC (Aoshin).
Scarcity: 4. Fine to Excellent (C6-C8): $95-$135, Mint (C10): $175

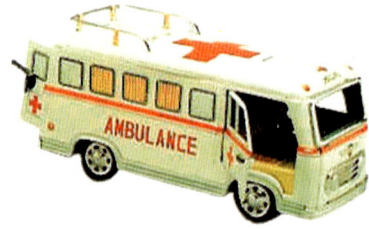

1960s Hino Ambulance Van 2-door with roof rack, opening driver (left) door and rear doors. **9.5 in** (24 cm). **Friction**. Known colors: White. Graphics: Ambulance (Red Cross emblem). Maker: **Marusan/Hayashi**, Japan. Toy marks: SAN (Marusan), H (Hayashi). Box marks: SAN (Marusan).
Scarcity: 4. Fine to Excellent (C6-C8): $75-$150, Mint (C10): $225

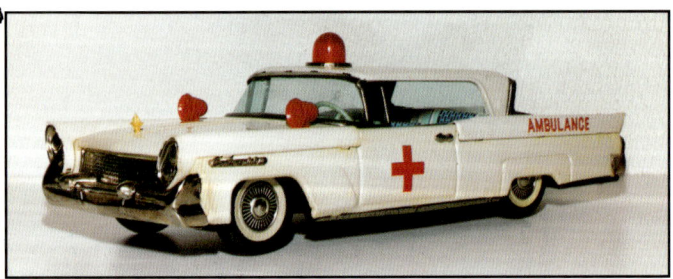

1958 Lincoln Continental Mark III 2-door hardtop with roof dome light and fender sirens. **11.5 in** (29 cm). **Friction**. Known colors: White. Graphics: Ambulance - Continental. Maker: **Bandai**, Japan. Toy marks: Bandai. Box marks: Bandai. Box text: *Lincoln Security Car Series*.
Scarcity: 4. Fine to Excellent (C6-C8): $225-$275, Mint (C10): $350

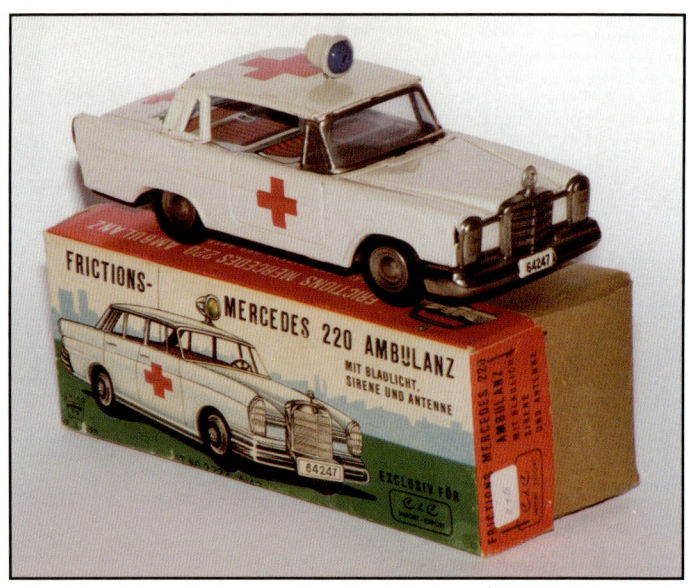

1960s Mercedes Benz 220 2-door hardtop with blue roof light, siren sound, and antenna. **7.5 in** (19 cm). **Friction**. Known colors: White. Graphics: (Red Cross emblem). License: 64247. Maker: **Ichiko**, Japan. Toy marks: Ichiko. Box marks: Ichiko. Box text: *Mercedes 220 Ambulanz Mit Blaulicht, Sirene und Antenne*.
Scarcity: 3. Fine to Excellent (C6-C8): $75-$125, Mint (C10): $175

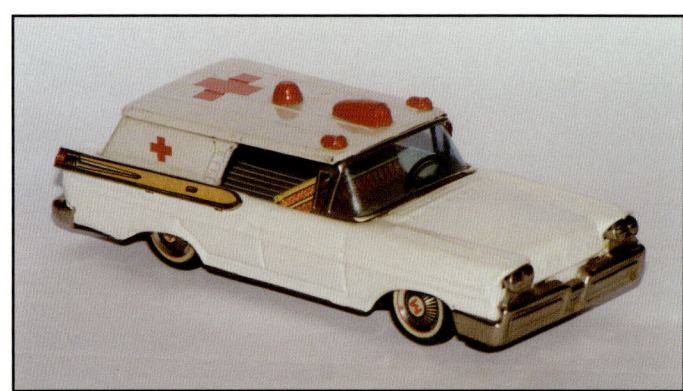

1958 Mercury 4-door station wagon with roof light and markers. **8 in** (20 cm). **Friction**. Known colors: White. Graphics: (Red Cross emblem). Maker: **Bandai**, Japan. Toy marks: Bandai. Box marks: Bandai.
Scarcity: 6. Fine to Excellent (C6-C8): $150-$200, Mint (C10): $250

1967 Mercury Cougar 2-door hardtop with roof light, two sirens, and two mirrors. **15 in** (38 cm). **Friction**. Known colors: White & Red. Graphics: Ambulance No.171 - (Red Cross emblem). License: A-9171. Maker: **Asakusa**, Japan. Toy marks: A1 (Asakusa). Box marks: A1 (Asakusa). Box text: *Ambulance Car Mercury Cougar*.
Scarcity: 7. Fine to Excellent (C6-C8): $250-$350, Mint (C10): $450

Public Service Vehicles 49

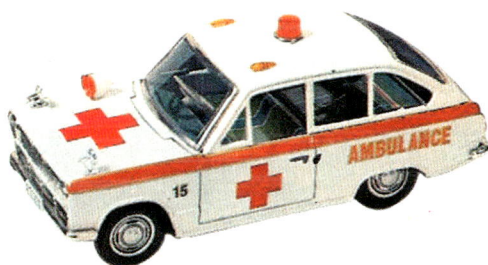

1960s Mitsubishi Colt 1000 2-door sedan with roof dome light, fender mirrors, and siren. **10 in** (25 cm). **Friction**. Known colors: White. Graphics: Ambulance - 15 - (Red Cross emblem). Maker: **Asahi**, Japan. Toy marks: ATC (Asahi Toy). Box marks: ATC (Asahi Toy).
Notes: Asahi catalog image.
Scarcity: 7. Fine to Excellent (C6-C8): $500-$650, Mint (C10): $800

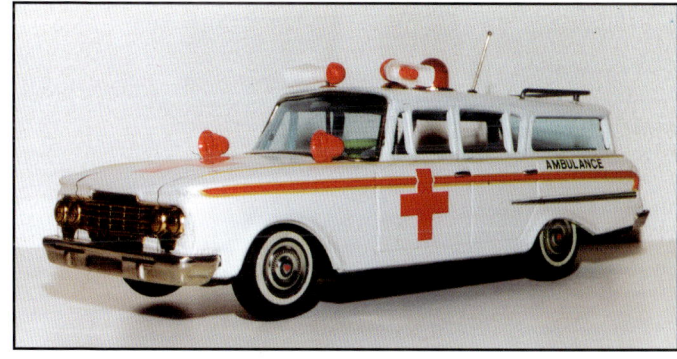

1962 Nash Rambler 4-door station wagon with roof light, two rotating lights, two sirens, and roof antenna. **10.75 in** (27 cm). **Friction**. Known colors: White. Graphics: Ambulance - (Red Cross emblem). Maker: **Bandai**, Japan. Toy marks: Bandai. Box marks: Bandai. Box text: *Rambler Ambulance with Speakers #2006*.
Scarcity: 3. Fine to Excellent (C6-C8): $225-$275, Mint (C10): $325

1959 Nash Rambler 4-door station wagon with two speakers. **10.75 in** (27 cm). **Friction**. Known colors: White. Maker: **Bandai**, Japan. Toy marks: Bandai. Box marks: Bandai.
Scarcity: 3. Fine to Excellent (C6-C8): $125-$175, Mint (C10): $225

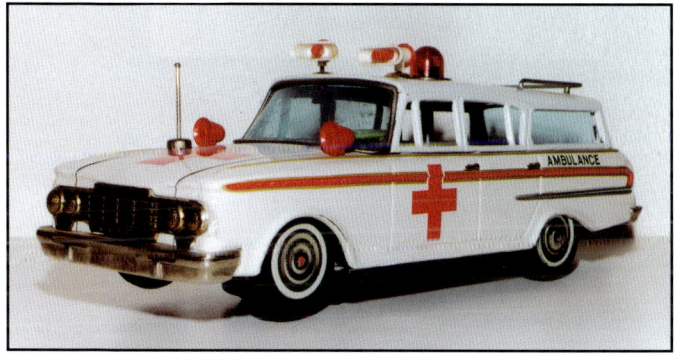

1962 Nash Rambler 4-door station wagon with roof light, two rotating lights, two sirens, and fender antenna. **10.75 in** (27 cm). **Battery operated**. Known colors: White. Graphics: Ambulance - (Red Cross emblem). Maker: **Bandai**, Japan. Toy marks: Bandai. Box marks: Bandai. Box text: *Ambulance Car*.
Scarcity: 3. Fine to Excellent (C6-C8): $225-$275, Mint (C10): $325

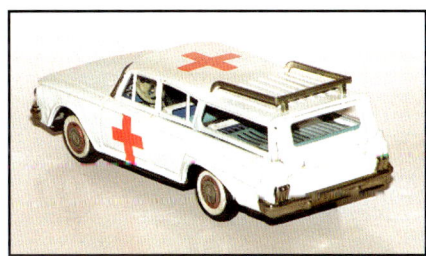

1961 Nash Rambler 4-door station wagon. **8 in** (20 cm). **Friction**. Known colors: White. Graphics: (Red Cross emblem). Maker: **Bandai**, Japan. Toy marks: Bandai. Box marks: Bandai.
Scarcity: 2. Fine to Excellent (C6-C8): $50-$85, Mint (C10): $125

1960s Nissan/Datsun Cedric 4-door station wagon with roof dome light and fender siren. **11 in** (28 cm). **Friction**. Known colors: White and red. Graphics: Ambulance - (Red Cross emblem). Maker: **Asahi**, Japan. Toy marks: ATC (Asahi Toy).
Notes: Asahi catalog image.
Scarcity: 7. Fine to Excellent (C6-C8): $300-$400, Mint (C10): $500

1961 Nash Rambler 4-door station wagon with two fender mounted speakers. **10.75 in** (27 cm). **Friction**. Known colors: White. Graphics: R (hubcaps). Maker: **Bandai**, Japan. Toy marks: Bandai. Box text: #799.
Scarcity: 3. Fine to Excellent (C6-C8): $200-$265, Mint (C10): $325

1970s Nissan/Datsun 4-door micro-bus with lithographed window, two roof dome lights, and siren sound. **7 in** (18 cm). **Friction.** Known colors: White. Graphics: Ambulance (Japanese) - A0978 - (Red Cross). License: A0978. Maker: **Toplay**, Japan. Toy marks: TPS (Toplay), Ueno. Box marks: TPS (Toplay). Box text: *Siren Emergency Series* (Japanese text).
Scarcity: 5. Fine to Excellent (C6-C8): $50-$75, Mint (C10): $100

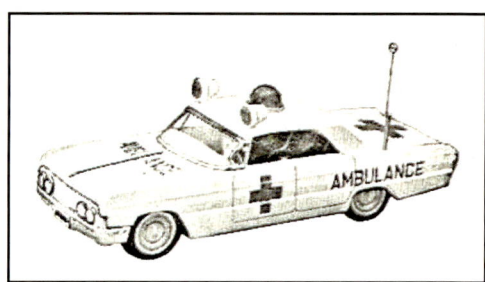

1962 Oldsmobile Starfire 4-door hardtop with dome roof light, rotating lights, and antenna. **11 in** (28 cm). **Friction.** Known colors: White. Graphics: Ambulance - (Red Cross emblem). Maker: **Ichiko**, Japan. Toy marks: Ichiko. Notes: Ichiko catalog image
Scarcity: 6. Fine to Excellent (C6-C8): $225-$275, Mint (C10): $350

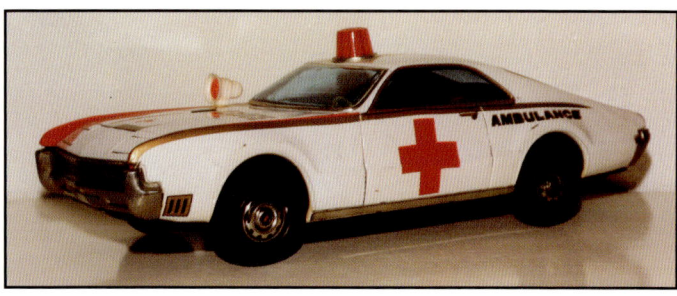

1967 Oldsmobile Toronado 2-door hardtop with roof dome light and fender siren. **15 in** (38 cm). **Friction.** Known colors: White, red, and gold. Graphics: Ambulance - (Red Cross emblem). Maker: **Asahi**, Japan. Toy marks: ATC (Asahi Toy). Box text: *Toronado Ambulance*.
Scarcity: 5. Fine to Excellent (C6-C8): $325-$375, Mint (C10): $450

1959 Oldsmobile 2-door station wagon with roof dome light and two rotating lights. **13 in** (33 cm). **Friction with battery.** Known colors: White. Graphics: Ambulancia - Espanola. Maker: **Rico**, Spain. Toy marks: Rico.
Scarcity: 5. Fine to Excellent (C6-C8): $200-$250, Mint (C10): $325

1960 Opel Rekord P2, 2-door station wagon. 8 in (20 cm). **Friction.** Known colors: White. Graphics: (Red Cross emblem). License: Opel. Maker: **Bandai**, Japan. Toy marks: Bandai. Box marks: Bandai. Box text: #866.
Scarcity: 4. Fine to Excellent (C6-C8): $85-$135, Mint (C10): $185

(Not pictured) **1962 Opel Kadett 2-door sedan. 8.25 in** (21 cm). **Friction.** Known colors: White. Maker: **Ichiko**, Japan. Toy marks: Ichiko. Box marks: Ichiko.
Scarcity: 3. Fine to Excellent (C6-C8): $80-$125, Mint (C10): $175

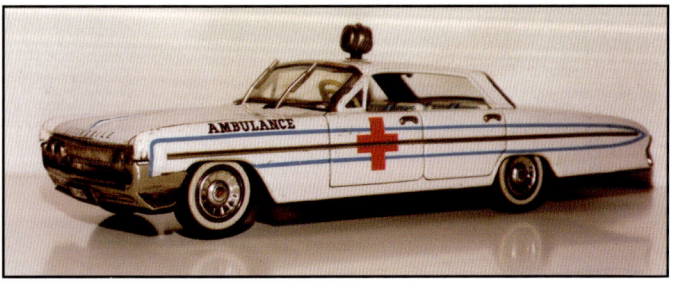

1961 Oldsmobile 4-door hardtop with dome siren and working wipers. **12 in** (30 cm). **Friction.** Known colors: White and blue. Graphics: Ambulance - (Red Cross emblem). Maker: **Yonezawa**, Japan. Toy marks: Y (Yonezawa).
Scarcity: 6. Fine to Excellent (C6-C8): $250-$275, Mint (C10): $350

Public Service Vehicles 51

1963 Opel Rekord 2-door station wagon. 8 in (20 cm). **Friction.** Known colors: White. Graphics: (Red Cross emblem). Maker: **Bandai**, Japan. Toy marks: Bandai. Box marks: Bandai. Box text: *Opel Rekord Ambulance #1016.*
Scarcity: 4. Fine to Excellent (C6-C8): $85-$135, Mint (C10): $185

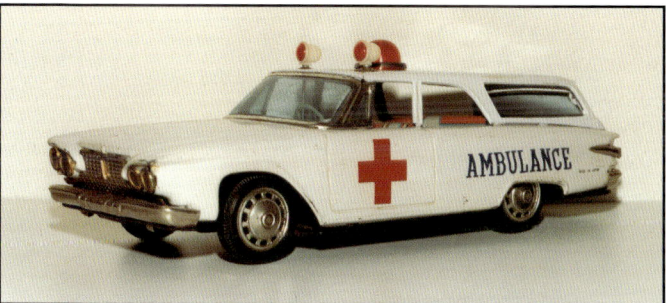

1961 Plymouth 2-door station wagon with red dome roof light, two rotating lights, and no chrome trim. **12 in** (30 cm). **Friction.** Known colors: White. Graphics: Ambulance - (Red Cross emblem). Maker: **Ichiko**, Japan. Toy marks: Ichiko.
Notes: This version was produced without detailed trim, windows, and hubcaps.
Scarcity: 5. Fine to Excellent (C6-C8): $175-$250, Mint (C10): $325

1958 Plymouth Fury 2-door hardtop with roof light, antenna, fender siren, and lithographed side windows. **8 in** (20 cm). **Friction.** Known colors: White. Graphics: Ambulance - (Red Cross emblem). Maker: **Bandai**, Japan. Toy marks: Bandai. Box marks: Bandai.
Notes: Car has 1957 model side trim.
Scarcity: 3. Fine to Excellent (C6-C8): $60-$90, Mint (C10): $150

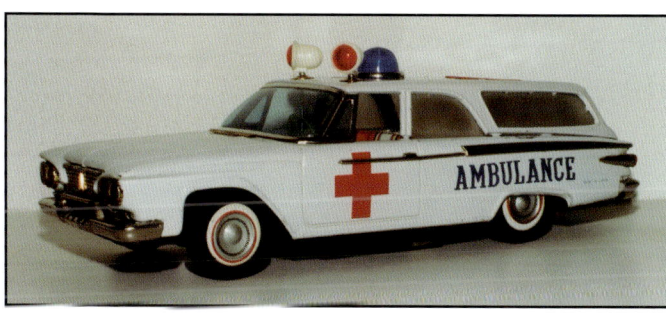

1961 Plymouth 2-door station wagon with blue dome roof light, two rotating lights, and chrome trim. **12 in** (30 cm). **Friction.** Known colors: White. Graphics: Ambulance - (Red Cross emblem). Maker: **Ichiko**, Japan. Toy marks: Ichiko.
Notes: Also came with red roof light.
Scarcity: 5. Fine to Excellent (C6-C8): $200-$275, Mint (C10): $350

1961 Plymouth 2-door station wagon with roof light, two rotating lights, operating large tail lights, and chrome trim. Made for Sweden. **12 in** (30 cm). **Friction with battery.** Known colors: White. Graphics: Ambulans - (Red Cross emblem). License: Plymouth. Maker: **Ichiko**, Japan. Toy marks: Ichiko.
Scarcity: 5. Fine to Excellent (C6-C8): $200-$275, Mint (C10): $350

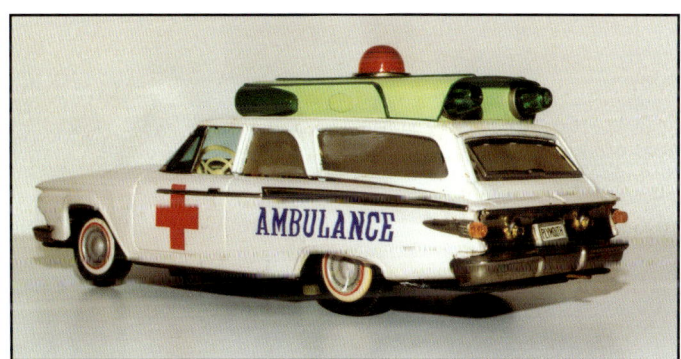

1961 Plymouth 2-door station wagon with raised roof containing flashing red and green lights and red roof light. **12 in** (30 cm). **Friction with battery.** Known colors: White with green roof. Graphics: Ambulance - (Red Cross emblem). License: Plymouth. Maker: **Ichiko**, Japan. Toy marks: Ichiko. Box marks: Ichiko.
Notes: Believed to be a sample, not commercially produced.
Scarcity: 10. Fine to Excellent (C6-C8): $600-$800, Mint (C10): $1,000

(Not pictured) **1958 Pontiac 2-door** with lithographed tin roof light. **6 in** (15 cm). **Friction.** Known colors: White. Maker: **Bandai**, Japan. Toy marks: Bandai. Box marks: Bandai. Box text: *Pontiac Security Car Series #663.*
Scarcity: 9. Fine to Excellent (C6-C8): $150-$300, Mint (C10): $450

52 Ambulances

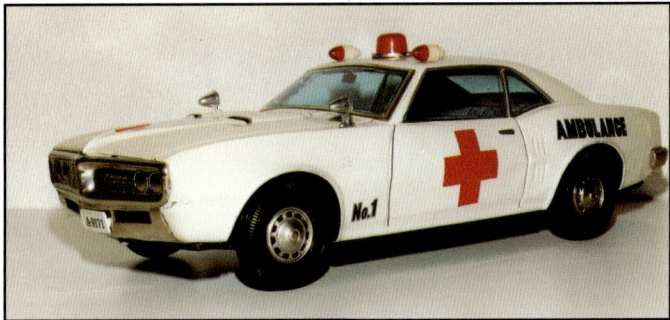

1967 Pontiac Firebird 2-door coupe with dome roof light, markers, and fender mirrors. **16 in** (41 cm). **Friction.** Known colors: White. Graphics: Ambulance - No.1 - (Red Cross emblem) - Firebird. License: A-9171. Maker: **Asakusa**, Japan. Toy marks: A1 (Asakusa). Box marks: A1 (Asakusa). Box text: *Pontiac Ambulance Car*.
Scarcity: 7. Fine to Excellent (C6-C8): $350-$450, Mint (C10): $550

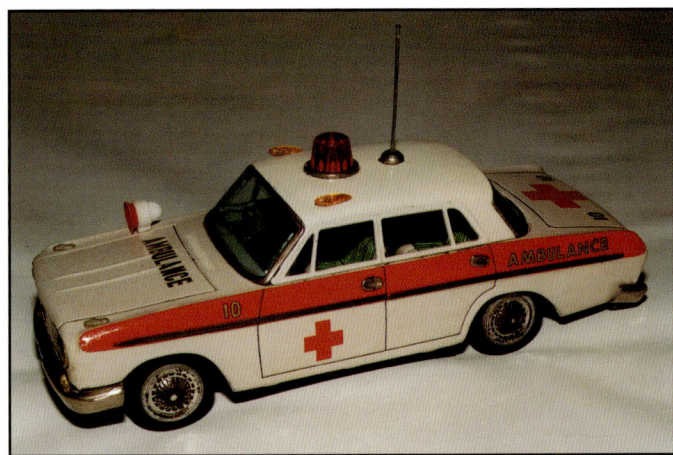

1960s Toyota Crown Deluxe 4-door sedan with roof dome light, antenna, fender mirrors, and siren. **10 in** (25 cm). **Friction.** Known colors: White and red. Graphics: Ambulance 10. Maker: **Asahi**, Japan. Toy marks: ATC (Asahi Toy). Box marks: ATC (Asahi Toy).
Scarcity: 6. Fine to Excellent (C6-C8): $275-$385, Mint (C10): $500

(Not pictured) **1960s Toyota Toyopet Crown 2-door hardtop** with roof dome light and fender siren. **13.75 in** (35 cm). **Friction.** Known colors: White and red. Graphics: Ambulance - (Red Cross emblem). License: Crown. Maker: **Aoshin**, Japan. Toy marks: ASC (Aoshin).
Scarcity: 5. Fine to Excellent (C6-C8): $200-$250, Mint (C10): $300

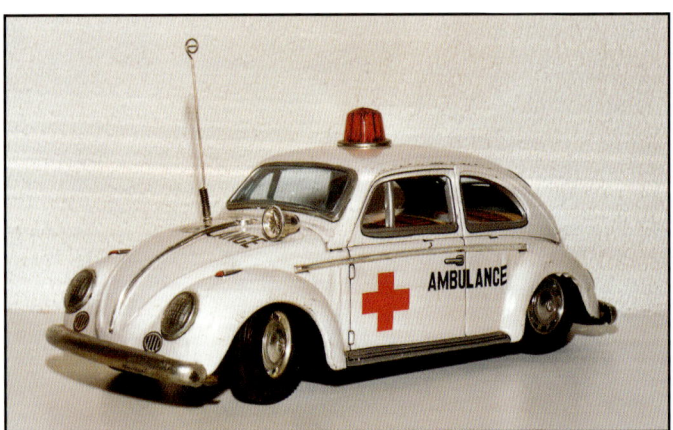

1960s Volkswagen Beetle 2-door sedan with flashing roof light, siren, antenna, and bump and go action. **10.75 in** (27 cm). **Battery operated.** Known colors: White. Graphics: Ambulance - (Red Cross emblem). Maker: **Masudaya**, Japan. Toy marks: MT (Masudaya). Box marks: MT (Masudaya). Notes: Also produced with sirens on roof and as R/C battery operated model.
Scarcity: 5. Fine to Excellent (C6-C8): $75-$150, Mint (C10): $225

(Not pictured) **1950/60s Volkswagen Transporter van. 6 in** (15 cm). **Friction.** Known colors: White. Graphics: Cruz Roja Internacional - No 523. License: P-523-D. Maker: **Payva**, Spain. Toy marks: Payva. Box marks: Payva. Box text: *Furgoneta Volkswagen*.
Notes: Produced 1980s.
Scarcity: 5. Fine to Excellent (C6-C8): $50-$100, Mint (C10): $135

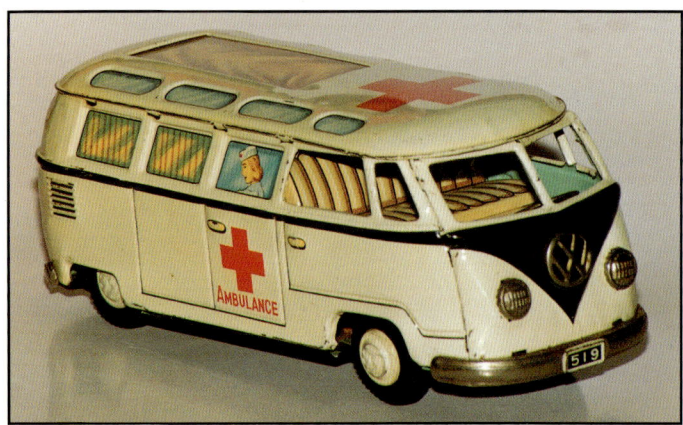

1950/60s Volkswagen Transporter micro-bus with lithographed side windows and roof windows. **7.75 in** (20 cm). **Friction.** Known colors: White and black. Graphics: Ambulance - (Red Cross emblem). License: 519. Maker: **Bandai**, Japan. Toy marks: Bandai. Box marks: Bandai. Box text: *#519*.
Scarcity: 6. Fine to Excellent (C6-C8): $250-$350, Mint (C10): $450

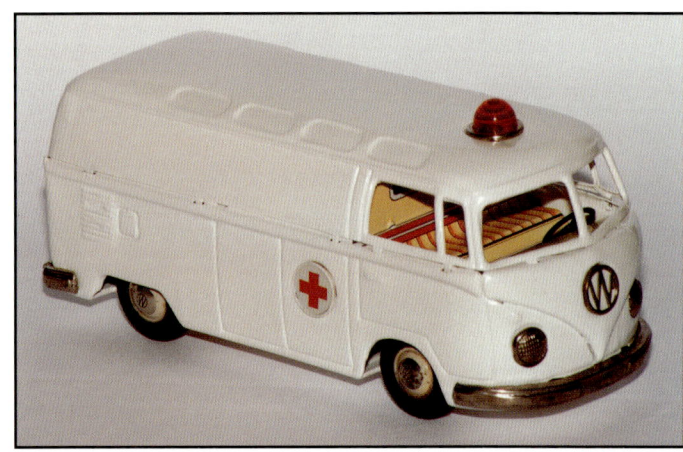

1950/60s Volkswagen Transporter van with red dome roof light. **7.75 in** (20 cm). **Friction.** Known colors: White. Graphics: (Red Cross). Maker: **Bandai**, Japan. Toy marks: Bandai. Box text: *Volkswagen Ambulance #801*. Notes: Found with incorrect "W" logo on front. Also produced battery operated.
Scarcity: 4. Fine to Excellent (C6-C8): $125-$175, Mint (C10): $250

(Not pictured) **1950/60s Volkswagen Transporter micro-bus. 9 in** (23 cm). **Friction.** Known colors: White and blue. Graphics: Ambulance - No.3072 - (Red Cross emblem. Maker: **Taiyo**, Japan. Toy marks: Taiyo World Toy.
Scarcity: 4. Fine to Excellent (C6-C8): $50-$90, Mint (C10): $145

Public Service Vehicles 53

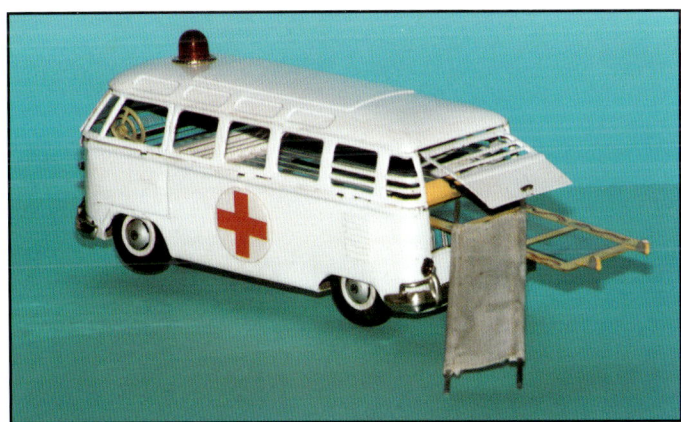

1950/60s Volkswagen Transporter micro-bus with red dome roof light, rear opening door, and pull out stretcher. **9.5 in** (24 cm). **Battery operated.** Known colors: White. Graphics: (Red Cross). Maker: **Bandai**, Japan. Toy marks: Bandai.
Scarcity: 6. Fine to Excellent (C6-C8): $300-$400, Mint (C10): $500

(Not pictured) **1950/60s Volkswagen Transporter micro-bus** with siren sound, dome roof light, and skylights. **10.25 in** (26 cm). **Friction.** Known colors: White. Graphics: 119 (Japanese). Maker: **Ichiko**, Japan. Toy marks: Ichiko. Box marks: Ichiko. Box text: *VW Ambulance*.
Notes: Produced 1980s.
Scarcity: 2. Fine to Excellent (C6-C8): $35-$45, Mint (C10): $60

(Not pictured) **1970s Volvo P 1800 ES 2-door station wagon** with blue roof light. **9 in** (23 cm). **R/C battery operated.** Known colors: White. Graphics: (Red Cross emblem). Maker: **Asahi**, Japan. Box marks: Asahitoy (Asahi Toy). Box text: *Volvo Ambulance Wagon*.
Scarcity: 5. Fine to Excellent (C6-C8): $150-$225, Mint (C10): $320

Fire

Mercury Fire Chief protecting the glaciers. *Photo by Rodney Abensur*

1960s Bedford 2-door. **8.5 in** (22 cm). **Friction.** Known colors: Red. Graphics: Fire Chief. Maker: **Unknown**, Japan. Toy marks: none.
Scarcity: 6. Fine to Excellent (C6-C8): $100-$135, Mint (C10): $185

1959 Buick 2-door hardtop with rotating roof light. **9 in** (23 cm). **Friction.** Known colors: Red. Graphics: F.D. - Fire Chief. Maker: **Aoshin**, Japan. Toy marks: ASC (Aoshin). Box marks: ASC (Aoshin).
Scarcity: 6. Fine to Excellent (C6-C8): $75-$135, Mint (C10): $185

1959 Buick 2-door convertible with fireman driver and windshield siren. **9 in** (23 cm). **Friction.** Known colors: Red. Graphics: F.D. - Fire Chief - Buick. Maker: **Yonezawa**, Japan. Toy marks: Y (Yonezawa). Box text: *Fire Chief With Hand Motion And Siren*.
Scarcity: 4. Fine to Excellent (C6-C8): $125-$175, Mint (C10): $225

(Not pictured) **1959 Buick 2-door hardtop** with roof light. **9 in** (23 cm). **Friction.** Known colors: Red. Graphics: Fire Chief. Maker: **Yonezawa**, Japan. Toy marks: Y (Yonezawa). Box marks: Y (Yonezawa).
Scarcity: 4. Fine to Excellent (C6-C8): $100-$135, Mint (C10): $175

54 Fire Vehicles

1959 Buick 2-door convertible with oversized driver and hood siren. **11 in** (28 cm). **Friction**. Known colors: Red. Graphics: F.D. Feuerwehr. Maker: **Ichiko**, Japan. Toy marks: Ichiko.
Scarcity: 5. Fine to Excellent (C6-C8): $200-$275, Mint (C10): $350

1959 Buick 2-door convertible with oversized fireman driver. **11 in** (28 cm). **Battery operated**. Known colors: Red. Graphics: F.D. Fire Chief. Maker: **Ichiko**, Japan. Toy marks: Ichiko.
Scarcity: 5. Fine to Excellent (C6-C8): $200-$275, Mint (C10): $350

1959 Buick 2-door convertible with oversized fireman driver, antenna, hood siren, and bell. **11 in** (28 cm). **Friction**. Known colors: Red. Graphics: F.D. Fire Chief. Maker: **Ichiko**, Japan. Toy marks: Ichiko.
Scarcity: 5. Fine to Excellent (C6-C8): $200-$275, Mint (C10): $350

1959 Buick 2-door convertible with oversized fireman driver. **11 in** (28 cm). **Friction**. Known colors: Red. Graphics: F.D. Fire Chief. Maker: **Ichiko**, Japan. Toy marks: Ichiko.
Scarcity: 5. Fine to Excellent (C6-C8): $200-$275, Mint (C10): $350

1959 Buick 2-door hardtop with rotating lights and antenna. **11 in** (28 cm). **Friction**. Known colors: Red. Graphics: F.D. Fire Chief. Maker: **Ichiko**, Japan. Toy marks: Ichiko. Box text: *Fire Chief Car*.
Scarcity: 5. Fine to Excellent (C6-C8): $200-$275, Mint (C10): $350

1959 Buick 2-door hardtop with single rotating light. **11 in** (28 cm). **Friction**. Known colors: Red. Graphics: F.D. Fire Chief. Maker: **Ichiko**, Japan. Toy marks: Ichiko.
Scarcity: 5. Fine to Excellent (C6-C8): $200-$275, Mint (C10): $350

1959 Buick 2-door hardtop with siren and dome roof light. **11.5 in** (29 cm). **Friction**. Known colors: Red. Graphics: F.D. Maker: **Nomura**, Japan. Toy marks: TN (Nomura). Box text: *Fire Chief Car*.
Scarcity: 5. Fine to Excellent (C6-C8): $200-$300, Mint (C10): $400

Public Service Vehicles 55

1959 Buick 2-door convertible with two oversized firemen, two fender sirens, hose, flag, radio, and water tank. **11.75 in** (30 cm). **Friction.** Known colors: Red. Graphics: Bomberos Auxilios. License: RA-1962. Maker: **Gorgo**, Argentina. Toy marks: Gorgo. Box marks: Gorgo. Box text: *Bomberos 1 ros Auxilios*.
Scarcity: 8. Fine to Excellent (C6-C8): $150-$250, Mint (C10): $350

(Not pictured) **1961 Buick 4-door hardtop** with rotating roof sirens. **7.5 in** (19 cm). **Friction.** Known colors: Red. Graphics: F.D. - Fire Chief. Maker: **Ichiko**, Japan. Toy marks: Ichiko.
Scarcity: 3. Fine to Excellent (C6-C8): $75-$115, Mint (C10): $150

1961 Buick Le Sabre 4-door hardtop with rotating light and working wipers. **16 in** (41 cm). **Friction.** Known colors: Red. Graphics: Fire Dept. - Fire Chief Car. Maker: **Nomura**, Japan. Toy marks: TN (Nomura). Box text: *Fire Chief Car No. 1 - Siren and Wiper Action*.
Scarcity: 5. Fine to Excellent (C6-C8): $375-$525, Mint (C10): $650

1966 Buick Skylark 2-door station wagon with blue roof light. **11.5 in** (29 cm). **Battery operated.** Known colors: Red. Graphics: FD - Fire Chief - Buick. License: 6063. Maker: **Asakusa**, Japan. Toy marks: A1 (Asakusa). Box marks: A1 (Asakusa).
Scarcity: 3. Fine to Excellent (C6-C8): $125-$200, Mint (C10): $325

(Not pictured) **1960 Cadillac 4-door hardtop** with rotating roof light and antenna. **6 in** (15 cm). **Friction.** Known colors: Red. Graphics: F.D. License: IK-62. Maker: **Ichiko**, Japan. Toy marks: none. Box marks: Ichiko. Box text: *Fire With Moving Light*.
Scarcity: 3. Fine to Excellent (C6-C8): $75-$125, Mint (C10): $165

1960 Cadillac 4-door hardtop with bump and go action. **9.75 in** (25 cm). **Battery operated.** Known colors: Red. Graphics: FD - No.125. Maker: **Plaything**, Japan. Toy marks: Plaything.
Scarcity: 2. Fine to Excellent (C6-C8): $50-$75, Mint (C10): $115

1960 Cadillac 4-door hardtop with antenna, blue roof dome light, and blacked out windows. **18 in** (46 cm). **Radio battery operated.** Known colors: Red. License: Cadillac. Maker: **Yonezawa**, Japan. Toy marks: Y (Yonezawa). Box marks: Y (Yonezawa).
Scarcity: 7. Fine to Excellent (C6-C8): $450-$575, Mint (C10): $680

1961 Cadillac 4-door sedan with Fire Chief roof sign, roof light, fender siren and antenna. **17 in** (43 cm). **Friction.** Known colors: Red and white. Graphics: Chief - F.D. - Fire Chief - Cadillac. License: Cadillac. Maker: **Bandai**, Japan. Toy marks: Bandai. Box marks: Bandai. Box text: *Cadillac Fire #969*. Notes: 1963 model front end.
Scarcity: 5. Fine to Excellent (C6-C8): $275-$475, Mint (C10): $575

Fire Vehicles

1963 Cadillac 2-door hardtop with rotating roof lights, fender siren, dome light, and antenna. **11 in** (28 cm). **Battery operated**. Known colors: Red. Graphics: F.D. - Fire Chief. Maker: **Ichiko**, Japan. Toy marks: Ichiko. Box marks: Ichiko. Box text: *Fire Chief Car Moving Light With Siren and Blinking Light*.
Scarcity: 3. Fine to Excellent (C6-C8): $95-$150, Mint (C10): $225

1965 Cadillac 2-door hardtop with dome roof light, antenna, fender siren, and mirrors. **16.5 in** (42 cm). **Friction**. Known colors: Red. Graphics: Fire Chief. License: Cadillac. Maker: **Asahi**, Japan. Toy marks: ATC (Asahi Toy). Box marks: ATC (Asahi Toy).
Notes. Asahi catalog image.
Scarcity: 5. Fine to Excellent (C6-C8): $350-$450, Mint (C10): $550

1963 Cadillac 4-door station wagon with automatic raising and lowering ladder and extending hose platform. Forward/reverse action and steering. **11.25 in** (29 cm). **Battery operated**. Known colors: Red. Graphics: F.D. Chief with F.D. shield. Maker: **Yonezawa**, Japan. Toy marks: Y (Yonezawa). Box marks: Y (Yonezawa). Box text: *Fire Chief Car With Automatic Ladder Up & Down Action*.
Scarcity: 5. Fine to Excellent (C6-C8): $225-$325, Mint (C10): $425

1956 Chevrolet 4-door sedan with chrome trim, flashing roof light, fender siren, forward/reverse, and steering. **7.75 in** (20 cm). **R/C battery operated**. Known colors: Red. Maker: **Linemar/Iwaya**, Japan. Toy marks: Linemar (Marx). Box marks: Linemar (Marx). Box text: *Fire Chief Car With Siren and Flashing Light*.
Scarcity: 5. Fine to Excellent (C6-C8): $175-$225, Mint (C10): $300

1965 Cadillac 4-door sedan with roof dome light, fender siren, and mirror. **12.25 in** (31 cm). **Friction**. Known colors: Red and white. Graphics: Chief - Fire Chief. License: M888. Maker: **Nomura**, Japan. Toy marks: TN (Nomura).
Notes: Nomura catalog image.
Scarcity: 6. Fine to Excellent (C6-C8): $225-$285, Mint (C10): $365

1959 Chevrolet 2-door hardtop with roof dome light and antenna. **10 in** (25 cm). **Friction**. Known colors: Red and yellow. Graphics: Fire Dept. - Fire Chief. Maker: **Aoshin**, Japan. Toy marks: ASC (Aoshin). Box marks: ASC (Aoshin).
Scarcity: 5. Fine to Excellent (C6-C8): $175-$225, Mint (C10): $350

Public Service Vehicles 57

1959 Chevrolet 4-door hardtop with roof dome light and antenna. **12.5 in** (32 cm). **Friction**. Known colors: Red. Graphics: F.D. Maker: **Daito**, Japan. Toy marks: none.
Scarcity: 3. Fine to Excellent (C6-C8): $125-$165, Mint (C10): $195

1959 Chevrolet 4-door hardtop with roof dome light. **12.5 in** (32 cm). **Friction**. Known colors: Red. Graphics: F.D. Maker: **Daito**, Japan. Toy marks: none.
Scarcity: 3. Fine to Excellent (C6-C8): $125-$165, Mint (C10): $195

(Not pictured) **1960 Chevrolet 4-door hardtop** with rotating roof lights and siren. **7.5 in** (19 cm). **Friction**. Known colors: Red. Graphics: F.D. - Fire Chief. License: Chevrolet - Ichiko. Maker: **Ichiko**, Japan. Toy marks: Ichiko. Box marks: Ichiko.
Scarcity: 3. Fine to Excellent (C6-C8): $65-$95, Mint (C10): $125

1960 Chevrolet Corvair 4-door sedan with rotating light and with or without working wipers. **9 in** (23 cm). **Friction**. Known colors: Red. Graphics: F.D. - Fire Dept. - Chief - 101 - Corvair. Maker: **Yonezawa**, Japan. Toy marks: Y (Yonezawa). Box marks: Y (Yonezawa). Box text: *Turnpike Fire Chief With Turning Light and Windshield Wiper Action*.
Scarcity: 4. Fine to Excellent (C6-C8): $125-$165, Mint (C10): $225

1960 Chevrolet Corvair 4-door sedan with rotating lights. **9.25 in** (23 cm). **Friction**. Known colors: Red. Graphics: F.D. - Fire Chief. License: IK-0973. Maker: **Ichiko**, Japan. Toy marks: Ichiko. Box text: *Fire Chief*.
Scarcity: 3. Fine to Excellent (C6-C8): $100-$175, Mint (C10): $250

1960 Chevrolet Corvair 4-door hardtop. **9.25 in** (23 cm). **Friction**. Known colors: Red. Graphics: F.D. No.5. Maker: **Mitsuhashi**, Japan. Toy marks: M (Mitsuhashi).
Scarcity: 3. Fine to Excellent (C6-C8): $45-$85, Mint (C10): $115

1960 Chevrolet 2-door hardtop. **11.5 in** (29 cm). **Friction**. Known colors: Red. Graphics: Chief - Fire Dept. License: 8100. Maker: **Yoneya**, Japan. Toy marks: ST (Unknown), SY (Yoneya). Box marks: SY (Yoneya), ST (Unknown).
Scarcity: 8. Fine to Excellent (C6-C8): $250-$400, Mint (C10): $600

1961 Chevrolet Corvair 4-door convertible with fireman driver, siren, light, radio box, and antenna. **9 in** (23 cm). **Battery operated**. Known colors: Red. Graphics: Fire Dept. No.7 - Chief - F.D.(shield). Maker: **Unknown**, Japan. Toy marks: HTC (Unknown). Box marks: HTC (Unknown). Box text: *Fire Chief Non Stop Action, Siren and Light*.
Scarcity: 5. Fine to Excellent (C6-C8): $125-$175, Mint (C10): $235

58 Fire Vehicles

1961 Chevrolet Impala 4-door hardtop with roof dome light, antenna, and fender siren. **11 in** (28 cm). **Friction**. Known colors: Red. Graphics: F.D. - Fire Dept. - Chief. License: Chevrolet. Maker: **Bandai**, Japan. Toy marks: Bandai. Box marks: Bandai. Box text: *#863*.
Notes: Car sold as 1961, 1962, and 1963 with taillight changes only.
Scarcity: 5. Fine to Excellent (C6-C8): $175-$225, Mint (C10): $300

(Not pictured) **1962 Chevrolet 4-door hardtop** with roof light, fender siren, and antenna. **11 in** (28 cm). **Friction**. Known colors: Red. Maker: **Bandai**, Japan. Toy marks: Bandai. Box marks: Bandai. Box text: *Chevrolet Fire Chief #959*.
Scarcity: 6. Fine to Excellent (C6-C8): $125-$225, Mint (C10): $350

1963 Chevrolet 2-door hardtop with red roof light, two moving lights, and siren sound. **8 in** (20 cm). **Friction**. Known colors: Red and white. Graphics: Fire Chief 283. Maker: **Ichiko**, Korea. Toy marks: none. Box marks: Ichiko-S. Box text: *Fire Car Two Moving Lights*.
Scarcity: 4. Fine to Excellent (C6-C8): $75-$135, Mint (C10): $185

1963 Chevrolet 4-door hardtop with roof dome light. **12.5 in** (32 cm). **Friction**. Known colors: Red and white. Graphics: Fire Chief - F.D. (shield). Maker: **Daito**, Japan. Toy marks: none.
Scarcity: 3. Fine to Excellent (C6-C8): $125-$165, Mint (C10): $195

1963 Chevrolet 4-door hardtop with dome roof light, antenna, and bump and go action. **13.75 in** (35 cm). **Battery operated**. Known colors: Red and white. Graphics: F.D. - Chief - Chevrolet. Maker: **Okuma**, Japan. Toy marks: Okuma. Box marks: Okuma.
Scarcity: 4. Fine to Excellent (C6-C8): $150-$185, Mint (C10): $265

1963 Chevrolet 4-door sedan with roof speaker, fender sirens, and lithographed firemen windows. Talking car for USA market. **13.75 in** (35 cm). **Battery operated**. Known colors: Red. Graphics: Fire Chief. License: No.1115. Maker: **Yonezawa**, Japan. Toy marks: Y (Yonezawa). Box marks: Y (Yonezawa), Cragstan/NGS. Box text: *Cragstan's Talking Fire Chief Car*.
Scarcity: 3. Fine to Excellent (C6-C8): $125-$175, Mint (C10): $250

1963 Chevrolet 4-door hardtop with dome roof light, siren sound, and antenna. **17.25 in** (44 cm). **Friction**. Known colors: Red. Graphics: F.D. - Fire Chief. License: E-147. Maker: **Nomura**, Japan. Toy marks: TN (Nomura). Box marks: TN (Nomura). Box text: *Fire Chief Car No.2*.
Scarcity: 6. Fine to Excellent (C6-C8): $325-$375, Mint (C10): $450

Public Service Vehicles 59

1964 Chevrolet Chevelle Malibu 2-door hardtop with flashing dome roof light, rotating speakers, and forward/reverse action. **8 in** (20 cm). **Battery operated**. Known colors: Red and white. Graphics: Chief - F.D. License: Chevrolet. Maker: **Bandai**, Japan. Toy marks: Bandai. Box marks: Bandai. Box text: *Chevrolet Fire Chief Car #4062*.
Notes: Box illustrates Chevrolet Impala.
Scarcity: 3. Fine to Excellent (C6-C8): $60-$90, Mint (C10): $125

1964 Chevrolet Chevelle Malibu 2-door hardtop with dome roof light, rotating speakers, and siren sound. **8 in** (20 cm). **Friction**. Known colors: Red and white. Graphics: Fire Chief - F.D. License: Chevrolet. Maker: **Bandai**, Japan. Toy marks: Bandai. Box marks: Bandai. Box text: *Security Car Series Chevrolet Fire Chief Car #1099*.
Scarcity: 3. Fine to Excellent (C6-C8): $60-$90, Mint (C10): $125

1965 Chevrolet 4-door station wagon with siren sound, rotating lights, and lithographed fire passengers. **7 in** (18 cm). **Friction**. Known colors: Red. Graphics: Fire Chief - F.D. Maker: **Ichiko**, Japan. Toy marks: Ichiko. Box marks: Ichiko. Box text: *Fire Chief With Siren And Moving Lights*.
Scarcity: 3. Fine to Excellent (C6-C8): $45-$85, Mint (C10): $125

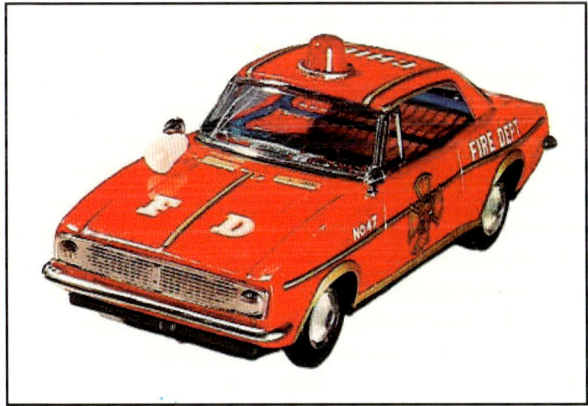

1967 Chevrolet Camaro 2-door hardtop with flashing dome roof light and fender siren. **11 in** (28 cm). **Battery operated**. Known colors: Red. Graphics: Fire Dept. - Chief - No.47. Maker: **Masudaya**, Japan. Toy marks: MT (Masudaya). Box marks: MT (Masudaya).
Notes: Masudaya catalog image.
Scarcity: 4. Fine to Excellent (C6-C8): $100-$160, Mint (C10): $225

(Not pictured) **1968 Chevrolet 4-door sedan** with roof lights and siren sound. **11 in** (28 cm). **Battery operated**. Known colors: Red. Maker: **Alps**, Japan. Toy marks: Alps. Box marks: Alps. Box text: *Real Sound Car*.
Scarcity: 2. Fine to Excellent (C6-C8): $50-$75, Mint (C10): $115

(Not pictured) **1971 Chevrolet Camaro 2-door hardtop** with non-fall action and dome roof light. **10.25 in** (26 cm). **Battery operated**. Known colors: Red and white. Graphics: Fire Chief - 703. Maker: **Taiyo**, Japan. Toy marks: Taiyo. Box marks: Taiyo.
Scarcity: 2. Fine to Excellent (C6-C8): $50-$95, Mint (C10): $135

1976 Chevrolet Monza 2-door coupe with operating siren, lights, and non stop action. **9 in** (23 cm). **Battery operated**. Known colors: Red and white. Graphics: Fire Chief F.D.6033 Fire Dept No.2. License: 6017. Maker: **Alps**, Japan. Toy marks: none. Box marks: Alps, ST (Safe Toy). Box text: *Chevrolet Monza Fire Chief Car*.
Scarcity: 2. Fine to Excellent (C6-C8): $45-$75, Mint (C10): $110

Fire Vehicles

1967 Dodge Dart 4-door hardtop with red dome roof light, sirens, antenna, and lighted side fender markers. **12.25 in** (31 cm). **Battery operated**. Known colors: Red. Graphics: F.D. - Fire Chief. Maker: **Nomura**, Japan. Toy marks: TN (Nomura).
Scarcity: 4. Fine to Excellent (C6-C8): $175-$250, Mint (C10): $325

1952 Ford 2-door sedan with driver and passenger firemen and light. **10.25 in** (26 cm). **Battery operated**. Known colors: Red. Graphics: F.D. - Fire Dept. Maker: **Marusan**, Japan. Toy marks: SAN (Marusan), Kosuge. Box marks: SAN (Marusan), Cragstan. Box text: *Stop-Go Fire Dept*.
Scarcity: 5. Fine to Excellent (C6-C8): $225-$285, Mint (C10): $375

(Not pictured) **1958 Ford 4-door station wagon**. **9.5 in** (24 cm). **Friction**. Known colors: Red and white. Graphics: Fire Chief. Maker: **Mitsuhashi**, Japan. Toy marks: M (Mitsuhashi). Box marks: M (Mitsuhashi). Box text: *Ford Wagon*. Notes: Also came in Police and Ambulance versions.
Scarcity: 3. Fine to Excellent (C6-C8): $60-$90, Mint (C10): $115

1958 Edsel 4-door hardtop. **7.5 in** (19 cm). **Friction**. Known colors: Assorted two tone. Maker: **Sato**, Japan. Toy marks: TOY (Sato). Box marks: Haji (Mansei), AHI. Box text: *Fire Chief Car*.
Notes: Also sold as Olympia Fire Chief and Police Car Set.
Scarcity: 7. Fine to Excellent (C6-C8): $150-$200, Mint (C10): $300

(Not pictured) **1959 Ford Fairlane 500 4-door hardtop**. **8.5 in** (22 cm). **Friction**. Known colors: Red and white. Graphics: Fire Chief. Maker: **Masudaya**, Japan. Toy marks: MT (Masudaya). Box marks: MT (Masudaya).
Scarcity: 5. Fine to Excellent (C6-C8): $100-$150, Mint (C10): $200

1958 Edsel 2-door hardtop with roof light and fender siren. **13.25 in** (34 cm). **Friction**. Known colors: Red, white, and black. Graphics: Fire Chief Car - City Fire Dept. License: Y-3018. Maker: **Daito**, Japan. Toy marks: Daito.
Scarcity: 6. Fine to Excellent (C6-C8): $125-$300, Mint (C10): $450

1960 Ford Falcon 4-door hardtop with rotating roof light, steering, and forward/reverse action. **7.25 in** (18 cm). **R/C battery operated**. Known colors: Red and white. Graphics: Fire Dept F.D. Chief (shield). License: 5-9332. Maker: **Swallow**, Japan. Toy marks: Swallow, SKK (Shinsei).
Scarcity: 3. Fine to Excellent (C6-C8): $75-$125, Mint (C10): $175

1932 Ford Model A 2-door with bell, pump, and lithographed hoses. **8 in** (20 cm). **Friction**. Known colors: Red with black fenders. Graphics: F.D. Maker: **Bandai**, Japan. Toy marks: Bandai. Box marks: Bandai. Box text: *Old Fashioned Fire Engine #1009*.
Notes: Produced 1960s. Also produced as battery operated model.
Scarcity: 3. Fine to Excellent (C6-C8): $60-$80, Mint (C10): $100

Public Service Vehicles 61

1960 Ford Gyron 2-door hardtop with forward/reverse, steering, and opening top. **12 in** (30 cm). **R/C battery operated**. Known colors: Red and white. Graphics: Chief - Fire Dept. Maker: **Ichida**, Japan. Toy marks: none. Box marks: Ichida.
Scarcity: 6. Fine to Excellent (C6-C8): $250-$350, Mint (C10): $450

(Not pictured) **1961 Ford Galaxie 2-door hardtop** with rotating roof lights, siren, and antenna. **9.5 in** (24 cm). **Friction with battery**. Known colors: Red. Graphics: Chief. License: Ford. Maker: **Ichiko**, Japan. Toy marks: Ichiko. Box marks: Ichiko.
Scarcity: 3. Fine to Excellent (C6-C8): $75-$175, Mint (C10): $275

1961 Ford Thunderbird 2 door hardtop with rotating roof lights. **9.5 in** (24 cm). **Friction**. Known colors: Red. Graphics: Fire Chief. Maker: **Ichiko**, Japan. Toy marks: Ichiko. Box marks: Ichiko.
Notes: Ichiko catalog image.
Scarcity: 3. Fine to Excellent (C6-C8): $75-$125, Mint (C10): $160

1961 Ford Galaxie 2-door hardtop with rotating roof light. **9.5 in** (24 cm). **Friction**. Known colors: Red. Graphics: Fire Chief. License: Ford. Maker: **Ichiko**, Japan. Toy marks: Ichiko. Box marks: Ichiko.
Notes: Ichiko catalog image.
Scarcity: 3. Fine to Excellent (C6-C8): $75-$175, Mint (C10): $275

1961 Ford 4-door hardtop with siren sound. **9.5 in** (24 cm). **Friction**. Known colors: Red. Graphics: Fire Chief - No.102. Maker: **Kyoei**, Japan. Toy marks: none. Box marks: Kyoei. Box text: *Emergency Car With Siren*.
Scarcity: 2. Fine to Excellent (C6-C8): $50-$75, Mint (C10): $125

1961 Ford 4-door hardtop. **9.5 in** (24 cm). **Friction**. Known colors: Red. Graphics: F.D. Maker: **Unknown**, Japan. Toy marks: none.
Scarcity: 2. Fine to Excellent (C6-C8): $50-$75, Mint (C10): $125

1962 Ford Falcon 4-door station wagon with lithographed officers, roof speaker, fender siren, siren sound, and shifting antenna for 2-speed action. **9 in** (23 cm). **Friction**. Known colors: Red. Graphics: Chief - Fire Chief - Double Speed Action. Maker: **Alps**, Japan. Toy marks: Alps. Box marks: Alps. Box text: *Fire Chief Double Speed Action*.
Scarcity: 3. Fine to Excellent (C6-C8): $75-$100, Mint (C10): $125

62 Fire Vehicles

1962 Ford Fairlane 2-door station wagon with antenna and red plastic roof light. **9 in** (23 cm). **Friction**. Known colors: Red. Graphics: Fire Chief. Maker: **Tohko-Toy**, Japan. Toy marks: none. Box marks: Tohko-Toy, Cragstan/NGS. Box text: *Cragstan Fire Chief*.
Scarcity: 3. Fine to Excellent (C6-C8): $65-$95, Mint (C10): $135

1963 Ford Galaxie 500 2-door hardtop with trunk mounted windup siren wheel, roof light, and plastic fender siren. **9 in** (23 cm). **Friction**. Known colors: Red. Graphics: F.D. - Fire Chief. Maker: **Terai**, Japan. Toy marks: Daiya (Terai). Box marks: Daiya (Terai). Box text: *Fire Chief Car With Siren*.
Scarcity: 3. Fine to Excellent (C6-C8): $85-$135, Mint (C10): $185

(Not pictured) **1963 Ford 4-door hardtop**. **11 in** (28 cm). **Friction**. Known colors: Red. Graphics: Fire Chief - No.851 - Command. Maker: **Taiyo**, Japan. Toy marks: Taiyo World Toy.
Scarcity: 4. Fine to Excellent (C6-C8): $100-$155, Mint (C10): $225

1963 Ford 4-door hardtop with rotating roof light. **12.5 in** (32 cm). **Friction**. Known colors: Red. Maker: **Taiyo**, Japan. Toy marks: Taiyo World Toy.
Scarcity: 2. Fine to Excellent (C6-C8): $75-$125, Mint (C10): $175

1963 Ford 4-door hardtop with roof dome light, antenna, and bump and go action. **12.5 in** (32 cm). **Battery operated**. Known colors: Red. Graphics: Chief. Maker: **Taiyo**, Japan. Toy marks: Taiyo World Toy.
Scarcity: 3. Fine to Excellent (C6-C8): $75-$125, Mint (C10): $175

1963 Ford 4-door hardtop with roof dome light, roof sirens, fender speaker, mirror, and antenna. **12.5 in** (32 cm). **Battery operated**. Known colors: Red. Graphics: Fire Chief. Maker: **Taiyo**, Japan. Toy marks: Taiyo World Toy.
Scarcity: 2. Fine to Excellent (C6-C8): $75-$125, Mint (C10): $175

1964 Ford 4-door station wagon with roof dome light. **19 in** (48 cm). **Battery operated**. Known colors: Red. Graphics: JEFE DE BOMBEROS. License: Ford. Maker: **Rico**, Spain. Toy marks: Rico.
Scarcity: 7. Fine to Excellent (C6-C8): $100-$200, Mint (C10): $350

Public Service Vehicles 63

1965 Ford Galaxie 500XL 2-door hardtop with large roof siren and fender mirrors. **11.25 in** (29 cm). **Friction**. Known colors: Red and white. Graphics: F.D. - Chief - 110. Maker: **Masudaya**, Japan. Toy marks: KKY (Yamato). Box marks: MT (Masudaya). Box text: *Fire Chief Car With Crank Siren*.
Scarcity: 6. Fine to Excellent (C6-C8): $175-$235, Mint (C10): $285

1965 Ford Galaxie 500XL 2-door hardtop with roof dome light and fender siren. **11.25 in** (29 cm). **Friction**. Known colors: Red. Graphics: F.D. - Fire Dept. - Chief. License: 3141. Maker: **Masudaya**, Japan. Toy marks: KKY (Yamato). Box marks: MT (Masudaya).
Scarcity: 6. Fine to Excellent (C6-C8): $225-$285, Mint (C10): $335

1965 Ford Galaxie 500 4-door sedan with driver and antenna. **13.5 in** (34 cm). **Friction**. Known colors: Red. Graphics: Corpo De Bombeiros. Maker: **Estrela**, Brazil. Toy marks: Estrela.
Scarcity: 8. Fine to Excellent (C6-C8): $200-$285, Mint (C10): $365

1966 Ford Mustang 2-door hardtop with red dome roof light. **11 in** (28 cm). **Friction**. Known colors: Red and white. Graphics: Fire Chief - F.D. Maker: **Clover Toy**, Korea. Toy marks: Clover.
Scarcity: 6. Fine to Excellent (C6-C8): $75-$135, Mint (C10): $190

1966 Ford Mustang Fastback 2-door coupe with siren, dome light, fender mirrors, and antenna. **16 in** (41 cm). **Friction**. Known colors: Red. Graphics: Fire Chief - F.D. License: E-147. Maker: **Nomura**, Japan. Toy marks: TN (Nomura). Box marks: TN (Nomura). Box text: *Mustang GT Fire Chief*.
Scarcity: 7. Fine to Excellent (C6-C8): $375-$485, Mint (C10): $590

1967 Ford 2-door hardtop with rotating sirens and sound and roof dome light. **8 in** (20 cm). **Friction**. Known colors: Red and white. Graphics: Fire Chief - F.D. Maker: **Bandai**, Japan. Toy marks: Bandai. Box marks: Bandai. Box text: *Security Car Series Fire Chief #1107*.
Scarcity: 3. Fine to Excellent (C6-C8): $75-$110, Mint (C10): $150

1968 Ford Thunderbird 2-door hardtop with roof speakers and red dome roof light. **7 in** (18 cm). **Friction**. Known colors: Red and white. Graphics: Fire Chief - Chief - F.D. Maker: **Bandai**, Japan. Toy marks: Bandai. Box marks: Bandai.
Scarcity: 2. Fine to Excellent (C6-C8): $35-$65, Mint (C10): $95

1960s Jeep FC 2-door pick up with revolving roof beacon and tin driver ringing bell. Lithographed chassis. **7.5 in** (19 cm). **Friction**. Known colors: Red. Graphics: Fire Dept. No.1 Emergency Truck - P.D. AHI. Maker: **Nomura**, Japan. Toy marks: TN (Nomura), AHI. Box marks: TN (Nomura), AHI.
Scarcity: 6. Fine to Excellent (C6-C8): $100-$150, Mint (C10): $225

1968 Ford Thunderbird 2-door hardtop with forward/reverse, roof light, and fender siren. **10.75 in** (27 cm). **Battery operated**. Known colors: Red. Graphics: Fire Chief - F.D. Maker: **Ichiko**, Japan. Toy marks: Ichiko. Box marks: Ichiko.
Scarcity: 5. Fine to Excellent (C6-C8): $100-$150, Mint (C10): $225

1960s Jeep CJ3, 2-door with bump and go action, antenna, and two tin fire figures. **11 in** (28 cm). **Battery operated**. Known colors: Red. Graphics: Fire Dept - No.1 - F.D. Maker: **Nomura**, Japan. Toy marks: TN (Nomura), Shinkosa. Box marks: TN (Nomura), Shinkosa. Box text: *Fire Command Car*.
Scarcity: 6. Fine to Excellent (C6-C8): $250-$400, Mint (C10): $550

1969 Ford Mustang Fastback Mach 1, 2-door coupe. **11 in** (28 cm). **Friction**. Known colors: Red and white. Graphics: Fire Chief - F.D. Maker: **Takatoku**, Japan. Toy marks: TT (Takatoku). Box marks: TT (Takatoku). Box text: *Ford Mustang Mach 1*.
Scarcity: 5. Fine to Excellent (C6-C8): $175-$225, Mint (C10): $300

1954 Lincoln 4-door sedan with roof light, fender siren, and antenna. **8.25 in** (21 cm). **Friction**. Known colors: Red. Graphics: Fire Dept. - F.D. Maker: **Masudaya**, Japan. Toy marks: MT (Masudaya).
Scarcity: 3. Fine to Excellent (C6-C8): $75-$125, Mint (C10): $165

Public Service Vehicles 65

1954 Lincoln 4-door sedan with roof light, working rear turn signals and dual on/off switches. Side mounted push buttons allow figure 8 or circular drive pattern. **8.25 in** (21 cm). **Battery operated.** Known colors: Red. Maker: **Mizuno/Alps**, Japan. Toy marks: M (Mizuno). Box marks: M (Mizuno). Box text: *Electromobile With Directional Light Signals and Figure 'Eight' Movement* Notes: This plain color version may not have been designed as a fire car. It is known to have been produced in assorted colors.
Scarcity: 4. Fine to Excellent (C6-C8): $200-$265, Mint (C10): $315

1954 Lincoln 4-door sedan with roof light, headlights, and dual on/off switches. **8.25 in** (21 cm). **Battery operated.** Known colors: Red. Graphics: F.D. No.110. Maker: **Mizuno/Alps**, Japan. Toy marks: M (Mizuno). Box marks: M (Mizuno).
Scarcity: 4. Fine to Excellent (C6-C8): $200-$265, Mint (C10): $315

1958 Lincoln Continental Mark III 2-door hardtop with roof dome light, fender sirens, and antenna. **11.5 in** (29 cm). **Friction.** Known colors: Red. Graphics: F.D. - Chief - Continental. Maker: **Bandai**, Japan. Toy marks: Bandai. Box marks: Bandai. Box text: *Lincoln Security Car Series*.
Scarcity: 4. Fine to Excellent (C6-C8): $175-$275, Mint (C10): $375

1958 Lincoln Continental Mark III 2-door hardtop with rotating lights, siren, and pull-up antenna. **11.5 in** (29 cm). **Battery operated.** Known colors: Red and white. Graphics: F.D. - Fire Chief - Continental. Maker: **Bandai**, Japan. Toy marks: Bandai. Box marks: Bandai. Box text: *Lincoln Fire Chief Car #4077*.
Scarcity: 4. Fine to Excellent (C6-C8): $175-$275, Mint (C10): $375

(Not pictured) **1950s Mercedes Benz 190 SL 2-door roadster** with composition driver and red dome roof light. **8.75 in** (22 cm). **Battery operated.** Known colors: Red and white. Maker: **Schuco**, Germany. Toy marks: Schuco. Box marks: Schuco.
Scarcity: 5. Fine to Excellent (C6-C8): $250-$450, Mint (C10): $650

1950s Mercedes Benz 190 SL 2-door roadster with driver, antenna, siren, and searchlight. **9 in** (23 cm). **Battery operated.** Known colors: Red. Graphics: F.D. Chief. Maker: **Sanshin**, Japan. Toy marks: Sanshin. Box marks: Sanshin. Box text: *Mystery Fire Chief New Car*.
Scarcity: 5. Fine to Excellent (C6-C8): $300-$400, Mint (C10): $550

66 Fire Vehicles

1960s Mercedes Benz 220 S 4-door sedan with siren sound, rotating lights, and roof light. **7.5 in** (19 cm). **Friction**. Known colors: Red. Graphics: Fire Chief. License: Mercedes. Maker: **Ichiko**, Japan. Toy marks: Ichiko. Box marks: Ichiko.
Notes: Ichiko catalog image.
Scarcity: 3. Fine to Excellent (C6-C8): $50-$100, Mint (C10): $150

(Not pictured) **1960s Mercedes Benz 220 SE 4-door sedan** with red dome roof light and yellow plastic fender sirens. **8.75 in** (22 cm). **Friction**. Known colors: Red and white. Graphics: Chief - 119 - F.D. (shield). Maker: **Daishin**, Japan. Toy marks: DSK (Daishin).
Scarcity: 2. Fine to Excellent (C6-C8): $75-$125, Mint (C10): $175

(Not pictured) **1960s Mercedes Benz 220 SE 4-door sedan** with fender mirrors, siren, roof dome light, and antenna. **14 in** (36 cm). **Friction**. Known colors: Red and white. Graphics: Fire Chief - No.1. License: FD-7186. Maker: **Nomura**, Japan. Toy marks: TN (Nomura). Box marks: TN (Nomura). Box text: *Fire Chief*.
Scarcity: 7. Fine to Excellent (C6-C8): $250-$400, Mint (C10): $550

(Not pictured) **1970s Mercedes Benz C 111 concept 2-door coupe** with dome roof light. **7 in** (18 cm). **Friction**. Known colors: Red. Graphics: (Japanese). Maker: **Yoneya/Ichiko**, Japan. Toy marks: Yone (Yoneya), Ichiko. Box marks: Ichiko, Yone (Yoneya).
Scarcity: 4. Fine to Excellent (C6-C8): $75-$150, Mint (C10): $225

(Not pictured) **1970s Mercedes Benz C 111 concept 2-door coupe**. **7 in** (18 cm). **Friction**. Known colors: Red. Graphics: Fire Chief - F.D. Maker: **Yoneya/Ichiko**, Japan. Toy marks: Yone (Yoneya). Box marks: Ichiko, Yone (Yoneya).
Scarcity: 4. Fine to Excellent (C6-C8): $75-$150, Mint (C10): $225

1958 Mercury Montclair 4-door hardtop with roof dome light and fender siren. **11.5 in** (29 cm). **Friction**. Known colors: Red. Graphics: Fire Chief - No.6 - Fire Dept - Mercury. Maker: **Yonezawa**, Japan. Toy marks: Y (Yonezawa).
Scarcity: 6. Fine to Excellent (C6-C8): $225-$295, Mint (C10): $375

1967 Mercury Cougar 2-door hardtop with roof dome light, two sirens, and two mirrors. **15 in** (38 cm). **Friction**. Known colors: Red. Graphics: Fire Chief. License: A-9171. Maker: **Asakusa**, Japan. Toy marks: A1 (Asakusa). Box marks: A1 (Asakusa). Box text: *Fire Chief Car*.
Scarcity: 6. Fine to Excellent (C6-C8): $275-$375, Mint (C10): $475

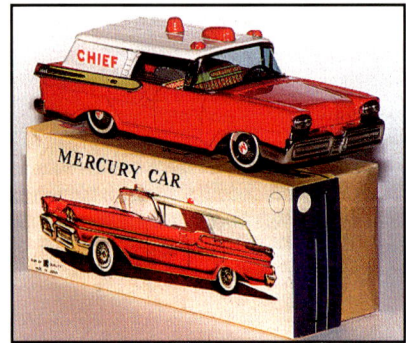

1958 Mercury 4-door station wagon with roof light and markers. **8 in** (20 cm). **Friction**. Known colors: Red and white. Graphics: Chief. Maker: **Bandai**, Japan. Toy marks: Bandai. Box marks: Bandai. Box text: *Mercury Car*.
Scarcity: 6. Fine to Excellent (C6-C8): $150-$200, Mint (C10): $250

1968 Mercury Cougar 2-door hardtop with dome roof light and non-fall action. **10 in** (25 cm). **Battery operated**. Known colors: Red. Graphics: Chief - F.D. - Mercury Cougar. License: Cougar. Maker: **Taiyo**, Japan. Toy marks: Taiyo. Box marks: Taiyo. Box text: *Mercury Cougar Fire Chief*.
Scarcity: 3. Fine to Excellent (C6-C8): $85-$115, Mint (C10): $150

Public Service Vehicles 67

1970s Nissan 4-door micro-bus with lithographed fire personnel on windows, two roof dome lights, and siren sound. **7 in** (18 cm). **Friction**. Known colors: Red. Graphics: Fire (Japanese) - N6250. License: 6250. Maker: **Toplay**, Japan. Toy marks: TPS (Toplay). Box marks: TPS (Toplay). Box text: *Siren Emergency Series* (Japanese text).
Scarcity: 5. Fine to Excellent (C6-C8): $50-$75, Mint (C10): $100

(Not pictured) **1958 Oldsmobile 4-door station wagon** with lithographed tin roof light. **7.25 in** (18 cm). **Friction**. Known colors: Red and white. Graphics: Eighty Eight - Chief - FD. Maker: **Nakamura**, Japan. Toy marks: none. Box marks: NT (Nakamura). Box text: *Fire Dept Chief Patrol Oldsmobile*.
Scarcity: 3. Fine to Excellent (C6-C8): $40-$60, Mint (C10): $85

1959 Oldsmobile 2-door hardtop with rotating lights, roof dome light, siren sound, and antenna. **13 in** (33 cm). **Friction with battery**. Known colors: Red and pink. Graphics: Fire Dept - F.D. License: I.K.0973. Maker: **Ichiko**, Japan. Toy marks: none. Box marks: Ichiko. Box text: *Fire Dept With Authentic Emergency Siren and Blinking Moving Warning Light*.
Scarcity: 4. Fine to Excellent (C6-C8): $200-$275, Mint (C10): $325

1959 Oldsmobile 2-door station wagon with rotating lights and roof dome light. **13 in** (33 cm). **Friction with battery**. Known colors: Red. Graphics: (crest on door). Maker: **Rico**, Spain. Toy marks: Rico.
Scarcity: 5. Fine to Excellent (C6-C8): $200-$250, Mint (C10): $325

1958 Oldsmobile 2-door hardtop with rotating roof light and siren sound. **8.5 in** (22 cm). **Friction**. Known colors: Red. Graphics: Fire Chief - F.D.176 - Oldsmobile. Maker: **Ichiko**, Japan. Toy marks: none. Box text: *Fire Chief Car With Siren and Moving Warning Light*.
Scarcity: 3. Fine to Excellent (C6-C8): $115-$175, Mint (C10): $220

1960 Oldsmobile 2-door hardtop with roof light. **9 in** (23 cm). **Friction**. Known colors: Red. Graphics: Fire Dept - F.D. Maker: **Nomura**, Japan. Toy marks: TN (Nomura), IY Metal Toy. Box marks: TN (Nomura).
Scarcity: 6. Fine to Excellent (C6-C8): $150-$250, Mint (C10): $350

68 Fire Vehicles

1961 Oldsmobile 4-door station wagon with roof light and wipers. **12 in** (30 cm). **Friction**. Known colors: Red. Graphics: Fire Dept. - F.D. License: E-147. Maker: **Yonezawa**, Japan. Toy marks: Y (Yonezawa).
Scarcity: 7. Fine to Excellent (C6-C8): $250-$325, Mint (C10): $400

1962 Oldsmobile Starfire 4-door hardtop with three roof lights and antenna. **11 in** (28 cm). **Friction**. Known colors: Red. Graphics: Fire Chief. License: Oldsmobile. Maker: **Ichiko**, Japan. Toy marks: Ichiko. Box marks: Ichiko.
Scarcity: 6. Fine to Excellent (C6-C8): $225-$275, Mint (C10): $350

1967 Oldsmobile Toronado 2-door hardtop with roof dome light and fender siren. **15 in** (38 cm). **Friction**. Known colors: Red with white and gold trim. Graphics: F.D. - Chief. Maker: **Asahi**, Japan. Toy marks: ATC (Asahi Toy). Box text: *Toronado Fire Chief*.
Scarcity: 5. Fine to Excellent (C6-C8): $325-$375, Mint (C10): $450

(Not pictured) **1968 Oldsmobile Toronado 2-door hardtop** with roof light and non-fall action. **10.25 in** (26 cm). **Battery operated**. Known colors: Red and white. Graphics: Chief - F.D. (shield). Maker: **Taiyo**, Japan. Toy marks: Taiyo. Box marks: Taiyo.
Scarcity: 3. Fine to Excellent (C6-C8): $75-$125, Mint (C10): $175

1960 Opel Rekord P2, 2-door sedan with forward/reverse, steering, roof dome light, antenna, and fender siren. **11 in** (28 cm). **R/C battery operated**. Known colors: Red and white. Graphics: Fire Chief - F.D. License: Opel Rekord. Maker: **Bandai**, Japan. Toy marks: Bandai. Box marks: Bandai. Box text: *Opel Rekord Fire* (in Japanese) #7276.
Scarcity: 7. Fine to Excellent (C6-C8): $200-$350, Mint (C10): $500

1958 Plymouth Fury 2-door hardtop with roof light, fender siren, antenna, and lithographed firemen side windows. **8 in** (20 cm). **Friction**. Known colors: Red and white. Graphics: Fire Dept. - Chief - F.D. Maker: **Bandai**, Japan. Toy marks: Bandai. Box marks: Bandai.
Notes: Car has 1957 model side trim.
Scarcity: 3. Fine to Excellent (C6-C8): $60-$90, Mint (C10): $150

1961 Plymouth 4-door hardtop with dome roof light, rotating roof lights, and antenna. **12 in** (30 cm). **Friction**. Known colors: Red. Graphics: Fire Chief - F.D. Maker: **Ichiko**, Japan. Toy marks: Ichiko.
Notes: Ichiko catalog image. No price established.
Scarcity: 10.

Public Service Vehicles 69

1961 Plymouth 2-door hardtop with roof dome light and siren sound. **12 in** (30 cm). **Friction**. Known colors: Red and yellow. Graphics: Fire Chief - F.D. License: RTC73. Maker: **Raja**, India. Toy marks: Raja. Box marks: Raja. Box text: *Sashank-Car With Siren, Solid Beauty*.
Scarcity: 8. Fine to Excellent (C6-C8): $150-$250, Mint (C10): $350

Box for 1961 Plymouth Fire Chief by Raja.

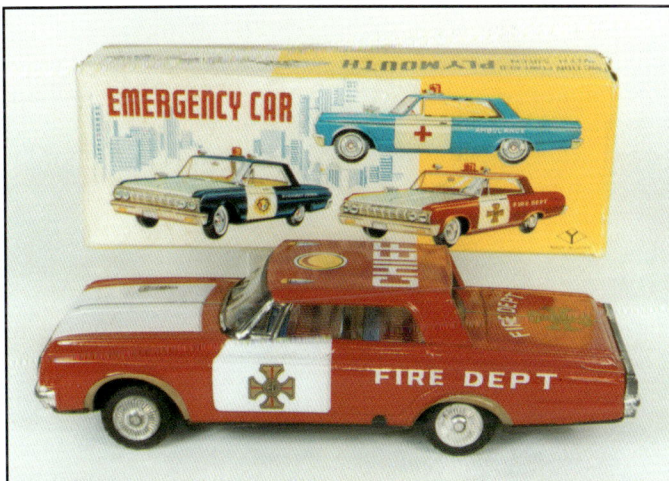

1964 Plymouth Fury 4-door hardtop with siren sound. **10 in** (25 cm). **Friction**. Known colors: Red. Graphics: Fire Dept - Chief. Maker: **Kusama/ Yoshi**, Japan. Toy marks: Y (Yoshi). Box marks: Y (Yoshi). Box text: *Emergency Car*.
Scarcity: 3. Fine to Excellent (C6-C8): $75-$115, Mint (C10): $150

1938 Pontiac 4-door with ladder on roof. **11.5 in** (29 cm). **Windup**. Known colors: Red. Maker: **Kuramochi**, Japan. Toy marks: CK (Kuramochi).
Scarcity: 9. Fine to Excellent (C6-C8): $800-$1,600, Mint (C10): $2,400

1954 Pontiac 2-door sedan with blue roof light. **10 in** (25 cm). **Battery operated**. Known colors: Red. Maker: **Amartoy**, India. Toy marks: Amartoy. Box marks: Amartoy. Box text: *Minister Deluxe - Mechanical & Automatic*.
Scarcity: 8. Fine to Excellent (C6-C8): $25-$60, Mint (C10): $90

(Not pictured) **1958 Pontiac 2-door** with lithographed tin roof light. **6 in** (15 cm). **Friction**. Known colors: Red. Maker: **Bandai**, Japan. Toy marks: Bandai. Box marks: Bandai. Box text: *Pontiac Security Car Series #661*.
Scarcity: 9. Fine to Excellent (C6-C8): $150-$300, Mint (C10): $450

1967 Pontiac Firebird 2-door coupe with siren, sound, and roof light. **8 in** (20 cm). **Friction**. Known colors: Red and white. Graphics: Fire Chief - F.D. - Pontiac (on grille). Maker: **Clover Toy**, Korea. Box marks: Clover. Box text: *2 Asst. Security Cars Fire Department*.
Scarcity: 3. Fine to Excellent (C6-C8): $55-$100, Mint (C10): $150

70 Fire Vehicles

1967 Pontiac Firebird 2-door coupe with tinted windows, roof light, and fender mirrors. **16 in** (41 cm). **Friction**. Known colors: Red. Graphics: F.D.- Fire Chief 10. Maker: **Asakusa**, Japan. Toy marks: A1 (Asakusa). Box marks: A1 (Asakusa).
Notes: Asakusa catalog image.
Scarcity: 7. Fine to Excellent (C6-C8): $350-$450, **Mint (C10):** $550

1960s Toyota Crown Deluxe 4-door sedan with fender mirrors and lights, roof dome light, siren and antenna. **15.5 in** (39 cm). **Battery operated**. Known colors: Red and white. Graphics: (Japanese). Maker: **Yonezawa**, Japan. Toy marks: Y (Yonezawa).
Scarcity: 6. Fine to Excellent (C6-C8): $400-$525, **Mint (C10):** $650

(Not pictured) **1950/60s Volkswagen Transporter van**. **6 in** (15 cm). **Friction**. Known colors: Red and white. Graphics: Bomberos - No. 520. License: P-520-D. Maker: **Payva**, Spain. Toy marks: Payva. Box marks: Payva. Box text: *Furgoneta Volkswagen*.
Notes: Produced 1980s.
Scarcity: 5. Fine to Excellent (C6-C8): $50-$100, **Mint (C10):** $135

(Not pictured) **1950/60s Volkswagen Transporter micro-bus** with flashing dome light and forward/reverse action. **7.5 in** (19 cm). **R/C battery operated**. Known colors: Red. Graphics: F.D. Maker: **Suzuki**, Japan. Box marks: SK (Suzuki). Box text: *Emergency Series*.
Scarcity: 3. Fine to Excellent (C6-C8): $75-$125, **Mint (C10):** $175

1960s Porsche 911 S 2-door coupe with roof dome light, siren, and stand up roll-over action. **10 in** (25 cm). **Battery operated**. Known colors: Red and white. Graphics: Chief - F.D. - Acrobat - Fire Dept. Maker: **Toplay**, Japan. Toy marks: TPS (Toplay). Box marks: TPS (Toplay). Box text: *Acrobat Team Porsche*.
Scarcity: 4. Fine to Excellent (C6-C8): $75-$100, **Mint (C10):** $125

1960s Toyota Crown Deluxe 4-door sedan with roof light, antenna, fender mirrors, and siren. **10 in** (25 cm). **Friction**. Known colors: Red. Graphics: Fire Chief - Fire Dept. Maker: **Asahi**, Japan. Toy marks: ATC (Asahi Toy). Box marks: ATC (Asahi Toy).
Notes: Asahi catalog image.
Scarcity: 6. Fine to Excellent (C6-C8): $275-$385, **Mint (C10):** $500

1950/60s Volkswagen Transporter pick up with extendable ladder and crank actuated rotating ladder assembly. **7.75 in** (20 cm). **Friction**. Known colors: Red. License: Volks Wagen. Maker: **Bandai**, Japan. Toy marks: Bandai. Box marks: Bandai.
Scarcity: 10. Fine to Excellent (C6-C8): $300-$450, **Mint (C10):** $600

Public Service Vehicles 71

1950/60s **Volkswagen Transporter van** with roof dome light. **7.75 in** (20 cm). **Friction**. Known colors: Red. Graphics: F.D. (side plate). Maker: **Bandai**, Japan. Toy marks: Bandai.
Notes: Found with incorrect "W" logo on front.
Scarcity: 6. Fine to Excellent (C6-C8): $125-$250, Mint (C10): $375

1950/60s **Volkswagen Transporter pick up** with extending and rotating ladder. **9.5 in** (24 cm). **Friction**. Known colors: Red. Graphics: VW. Maker: **Tipp & Co.**, Germany. Toy marks: TCO (Tipp). Box marks: TCO (Tipp).
Scarcity: 8. Fine to Excellent (C6-C8): $800-$1,000, Mint (C10): $1,300

(Not pictured) 1960s **Volkswagen 1500, 2-door sedan** with roof lights. **7.5 in** (19 cm). **Windup**. Known colors: Red. Graphics: F.D. - Chief. License: Volkswagen. Maker: **Ichiko**, Japan. Toy marks: none. Box marks: Ichiko.
Scarcity: 5. Fine to Excellent (C6-C8): $90-$140, Mint (C10): $185

1950/60s **Volkswagen Transporter van** with radio control and revolving speaker. Vehicle follows speaker direction. **8 in** (20 cm). **Radio Control Battery**. Known colors: Red and white. Graphics: Fire Dept - F.D. Maker: **Gaaken**, Japan. Toy marks: Gaaken Toy. Box marks: Gaaken Toy.
Scarcity: 0. Fine to Excellent (C6-C8): $175-$300, Mint (C10): $425

1960s **Volkswagen Beetle 2-door sedan** with flashing roof light, siren, antenna, and bump and go action. **10.75 in** (27 cm). **Battery operated**. Known colors: Red. Graphics: F.D. Fire Chief. Maker: **Masudaya**, Japan. Toy marks: MT (Masudaya). Box marks: MT (Masudaya).
Notes: Masudaya catalog image. Also produced as R/C battery operated model.
Scarcity: 4. Fine to Excellent (C6-C8): $90-$150, Mint (C10): $225

1960s **Volvo Amazon 4-door sedan** with roof dome light, forward/reverse, and steering. **9.25 in** (23 cm). **R/C battery operated**. Known colors: Red. Graphics: Chief (side plate). Maker: **Unknown**, Japan. Toy marks: none.
Scarcity: 3. Fine to Excellent (C6-C8): $60-$90, Mint (C10): $145

Military Service

Military Jeeps in action. *Photo by Tosh Wakabayashi*

1950 Cadillac 2-door convertible with tin M.P. driver and two tin M.P.s with guns. **9.5 in** (24 cm). **R/C battery operated**. Known colors: Military green. Graphics: Military Police. Maker: **Linemar**, Japan. Toy marks: Linemar (Marx). Box marks: Linemar (Marx). Box text: *Military Police Car*.
Notes: Box illustrates 1956 Oldsmobile.
Scarcity: 4. Fine to Excellent (C6-C8): $125-$175, Mint (C10): $250

Public Service Vehicles 73

1962 Chevrolet 4-door hardtop with roof light and fender siren. **11.5 in** (29 cm). **Friction**. Known colors: Military green. Graphics: U.S. Army. Maker: **Asahi**, Japan. Toy marks: ATC (Asahi Toy). Box marks: ATC (Asahi Toy). Box text: *Staff Car For 5 Star General*.
Scarcity: 10. Fine to Excellent (C6-C8): $1,400-$1,800, Mint (C10): $2,500

(Not pictured) **1963 Ford 4-door hardtop**. **11 in** (28 cm). **Friction**. Known colors: Olive and white. Graphics: Military Police - 71523 - M.P. Maker: **Taiyo**, Japan. Toy marks: Taiyo World Toy.
Scarcity: 4. Fine to Excellent (C6-C8): $100-$155, Mint (C10): $195

1940s Jeep MB 2-door with siren sound, military driver, and covered rear compartment. **8 in** (20 cm). **Friction**. Known colors: Green and gray. Maker: **Nomura**, Japan. Toy marks: none. Box marks: TN (Nomura). Box text: *Covered Jeep*.
Notes: Produced 1950s.
Scarcity: 6. Fine to Excellent (C6-C8): $95-$140, Mint (C10): $195

1960s Hino 2-door delivery. **8.5 in** (22 cm). **Friction**. Known colors: Military Green. Graphics: Army - (Red Cross emblem). Maker: **Hayashi**, Japan. Toy marks: H (Hayashi).
Scarcity: 5. Fine to Excellent (C6-C8): $85-$135, Mint (C10): $190

1940s Jeep MB 2-door with battery operated rotating searchlight. **9.5 in** (24 cm). **Friction**. Known colors: Maroon. Graphics: Airplane Spotter. Maker: **Bandai**, Japan. Toy marks: Bandai. Box marks: Bandai. Box text: *Airplane Spotter*.
Notes: Produced 1960s.
Scarcity: 5. Fine to Excellent (C6-C8): $100-$140, Mint (C10): $175

1940s Jeep MB 2-door with fold down windshield and tin driver. **7.5 in** (19 cm). **R/C battery operated**. Known colors: Military green. Graphics: (Star). Maker: **Unknown**, Japan. Toy marks: none.
Notes: Produced 1950s.
Scarcity: 3. Fine to Excellent (C6-C8): $50-$75, Mint (C10): $100

Military Service Vehicles

1940s Jeep MB with operating headlights, siren, and three tin soldiers. Rear seat has radio console and map console. Spare tire and gas can. **10.25 in** (26 cm). **Friction with battery**. Known colors: Olive and white. Graphics: Sunbeam - US 54329 - Jeep No.1. Maker: **Unknown**, Japan. Toy marks: none. Box marks: none. Box text: *Sunbeam Jeep*.
Scarcity: 7. Fine to Excellent (C6-C8): $200-$300, Mint (C10): $425

1940s Jeep MB 2-door with fold down windshield, full-figure tin soldier driver and two tin soldiers manning rotating anti-aircraft guns. Tin shovels. **12 in** (30 cm). **Friction**. Known colors: Military green. Maker: **Shioji**, Japan. Toy marks: none. Box marks: SSS (Shioji). Box text: *Anti-Aircraft Jeep*
Notes: Produced 1950s.
Scarcity: 4. Fine to Excellent (C6-C8): $100-$150, Mint (C10): $200

1940s Jeep MB 2-door with fold down windshield, full-figure tin soldier driver and passengers, fold down seats, and opening hood to reveal siren. **12 in** (30 cm). **Friction**. Known colors: Military green. Graphics: Jeep - U.S.2400. License: J-2400. Maker: **Unknown**, Japan. Toy marks: TKK (Unknown). Notes: Produced 1950s.
Scarcity: 5. Fine to Excellent (C6-C8): $150-$200, Mint (C10): $250

1950s Jeep M38A 2-door with fold down windshield, antenna, light, and driver that signals when turning. **7.5 in** (19 cm). **R/C battery operated**. Known colors: White. Graphics: M.P. Maker: **Linemar**, Japan. Toy marks: Linemar (Marx). Box marks: Linemar (Marx). Box text: *Army Radio Jeep U-Turn Jeep*.
Scarcity: 4. Fine to Excellent (C6-C8): $75-$125, Mint (C10): $175

Public Service Vehicles 75

1950s Jeep M38, 2-door with fold down windshield, tin soldiers, and rotating anti-aircraft guns. **7.5 in** (19 cm). **Friction**. Known colors: Military green. Graphics: (Star) - Anti-Aircraft Patrol. License: AHI-5533. Maker: **Yoshiya**, Japan. Toy marks: AHI. Box marks: KO (Yoshiya), AHI. Box text: *Friction Jeep With Swivel Action*.
Scarcity: 4. Fine to Excellent (C6-C8): $100-$150, Mint (C10): $200

1950s Jeep M38A 2-door with fold down windshield and flip over rear seat to reveal machine gun. **8 in** (20 cm). **Friction**. Known colors: Military green. Graphics: 02051 (star) - J35 - Patrol Jeep - J-A NO.7. Maker: **Nomura/Showa**, Japan. Toy marks: TN (Nomura), Showa. Box marks: TN (Nomura), Showa. Box text: *Patrol Jeep*.
Scarcity: 4. Fine to Excellent (C6-C8): $75-$120, Mint (C10): $185

1950s Jeep M38, 2-door with fold down windshield and opening hood with siren motor. **7.75 in** (20 cm). **Friction**. Known colors: Olive and military green. Graphics: King - King Jeep - (star). Maker: **Tanaguchi**, Japan. Toy marks: TS (Tanaguchi). Box marks: TS (Tanaguchi). Box text: *King Jeep*.
Scarcity: 5. Fine to Excellent (C6-C8): $75-$150, Mint (C10): $225

1950s Jeep M38, 2-door with tin soldier driver and passenger. **8.5 in** (22 cm). **Friction**. Known colors: Blue. Graphics: 0257103 (star). Maker: **Nomura**, Japan. Toy marks: TN (Nomura). Box marks: TN (Nomura). Box text: *Army Jeep*.
Scarcity: 5. Fine to Excellent (C6-C8): $100-$150, Mint (C10): $225

76 Military Service Vehicles

1950s Jeep M38, 2-door with adjustable front wheels, stop and go action, and rotating guns with firing sound. Includes tin driver and gunners. **9.25 in** (23 cm). **Battery operated**. Known colors: Military green. Graphics: Anti-Aircraft - 638698 U.S.A. - U.S.A. 35MM. Maker: **Sankei**, Japan. Toy marks: K (Sankei), GW (George Wagner). Box marks: K (Sankei), GW (George Wagner). Box text: *Anti-Aircraft Jeep With Automatic Stop' n Go & Gun Firing Action*. Notes: Produced 1960s.
Scarcity: 6. Fine to Excellent (C6-C8): $100-$150, Mint (C10): $200

1960s Jeep CJ3B 2-door with antenna and fold down windshield. **10 in** (25 cm). **Friction**. Known colors: Camouflage. Graphics: Army. Maker: **Taiyo**, Japan. Toy marks: none. Box marks: Taiyo World Toy. Box text: *Army Jeep*.
Scarcity: 3. Fine to Excellent (C6-C8): $75-$100, Mint (C10): $125

1950s Jeep M38A 2-door with tin MP, firing gun, lights, and bump and go action. **10 in** (25 cm). **Battery operated**. Known colors: White. Graphics: MP. Maker: **Terai**, Japan. Toy marks: none. Box marks: Daiya (Terai). Box text: *M.P. Jeep*.
Scarcity: 3. Fine to Excellent (C6-C8): $75-$125, Mint (C10): $175

1960s Jeep M38, 2-door with fold down windshield. **11 in** (28 cm). **Friction**. Known colors: Military green. Graphics: (star). Maker: **Nomura**, Japan. Toy marks: TN (Nomura). Box marks: TN (Nomura). Box text: *US Army Jeep*.
Scarcity: 3. Fine to Excellent (C6-C8): $75-$125, Mint (C10): $175

1960s Jeep CJ3B 2-door with rotating anti-aircraft guns, tin soldier, folding windshield and figure eight or circle driving patterns. **9.5 in** (24 cm). **Battery operated**. Known colors: Military green. Graphics: Super Control - 502388 U.S.A. Maker: **Bandai/Suzuki & Edward**, Japan. Toy marks: Bandai. Box marks: S&E (Suzuki & Edward). Box text: *Super Control Anti Craft Jeep*.
Scarcity: 5. Fine to Excellent (C6-C8): $95-$155, Mint (C10): $225

1960s Jeep M38, 2-door with lights, bump and go action, articulated driver, telephone answering passenger, machine gun, and radio with pull up antenna. **11 in** (28 cm). **Battery operated**. Known colors: Military green. Graphics: (Tin star). Maker: **Nomura**, Japan. Toy marks: TN (Nomura), Shinkosa. Box marks: TN (Nomura). Box text: *Radio Jeep*.
Scarcity: 5. Fine to Excellent (C6-C8): $175-$275, Mint (C10): $375

Public Service Vehicles 77

1960s Jeep M38A 2-door with bump and go action, tin driver, antenna, flashing hood dome light, and flashing gun which rotates from under hood with sound. **11 in** (28 cm). **Battery operated**. Known colors: Military green. Graphics: 1st. Div. - U.S.A. License: U.S. Army 6607. Maker: **Nomura**, Japan. Toy marks: TN (Nomura). Box marks: TN (Nomura). Box text: *Turn-O-Matic Gun Jeep*.
Scarcity: 4. Fine to Excellent (C6-C8): $175-$275, Mint (C10): $350

(Not pictured) **1950s Mercedes Benz 190 SL 2-door roadster** with tin driver and gunner, anti-aircraft guns, and airplane attached to antenna rod. **9 in** (23 cm). **Battery operated**. Known colors: Light blue and white. Graphics: Air Force - Atom. Maker: **Sanshin**, Japan. Toy marks: Sanshin. Box marks: Sanshin. Box text: *Ack-Ack Squad*.
Scarcity: 6. Fine to Excellent (C6-C8): $350-$450, Mint (C10): $550

(Not pictured) **1950s Mercedes Benz 190 SL 2-door roadster** with tin driver and soldier, radar panel, and gun. **9 in** (23 cm). **Battery operated**. Known colors: Military green. Graphics: Army - Radar. Maker: **Sanshin**, Japan. Toy marks: Sanshin. Box marks: Sanshin.
Scarcity: 6. Fine to Excellent (C6-C8): $350-$450, Mint (C10): $550

1930s Undetermined Armored Motorcar 2-door armored vehicle with four machine guns. **8 in** (20 cm). **Windup**. Known colors: Military brown. Maker: **Masudaya**, Japan. Toy marks: MT (Masudaya). Notes: Celluloid body.
Scarcity: 10. Fine to Excellent (C6-C8): $800-$1,000, Mint (C10): $1,200

1960s Jeep CJ5, 2-door with tin Military Police driver, siren sound, radio, and antenna. **11.25 in** (29 cm). **Friction**. Known colors: White and black. Graphics: Military Police - Jeep. Maker: **Shioji**, Japan. Toy marks: none. Box marks: SSS (Shioji). Box text: *M.P. 'Jeep.'*
Scarcity: 4. Fine to Excellent (C6-C8): $125-$200, Mint (C10): $300

1930s Mercedes Benz 770K 4-door convertible with military driver and two passengers including der Fuehrer. **9 in** (23 cm). **Windup**. Known colors: Black. License: 11A-19357. Maker: **Tipp & Co.**, Germany. Toy marks: TCO (Tipp). Box marks: TCO (Tipp).
Scarcity: 10. Fine to Excellent (C6-C8): $1,200-$1,800, Mint (C10): $2,400

1960s Undetermined 2-door delivery. 9.5 in (24 cm). **Friction**. Known colors: Military green. Graphics: Army. Maker: **Hayashi**, Japan. Toy marks: H (Hayashi). Box marks: H (Hayashi). Box text: *Army Transport Truck*.
Scarcity: 3. Fine to Excellent (C6-C8): $60-$90, Mint (C10): $120

Police

Oldsmobile Highway Patrol, Berkley, California. *Photo by Tosh Wakabayashi*

1960s Aston Martin DB-5 2-door coupe with red dome roof light, two figures, opening door, machine gun and sound, steerable wheels. **11 in** (28 cm). **Battery operated**. Known colors: Black and white. Graphics: Highway Patrol. Maker: **Aoshin**, Japan. Toy marks: ASC (Aoshin). Box marks: ASC (Aoshin). Box text: *Highway Patrol Car*.
Scarcity: 9. Fine to Excellent (C6-C8): $300-$400, Mint (C10): $500

1960s Bentley 4-door sedan with flashing roof light, siren, and antenna. **9 in** (23 cm). **R/C battery operated**. Known colors: Black and white. Graphics: Police - Highway Patrol (and shield). License: 5647. Maker: **Yonezawa**, Japan. Toy marks: Y (Yonezawa). Box marks: Y (Yonezawa). Box text: *Police Car with Flashing Light*.
Scarcity: 5. Fine to Excellent (C6-C8): $125-$175, Mint (C10): $235

1960s BMW 2000 CS 2-door coupe with forward/reverse action and steering. **8.5 in** (22 cm). **R/C battery operated**. Known colors: Assorted. Graphics: Polizei. License: BMW. Maker: **Bandai**, Japan. Toy marks: Bandai. Box marks: Bandai.
Scarcity: 3. Fine to Excellent (C6-C8): $60-$90, Mint (C10): $120

1950 Buick 4-door sedan with headlights, roof light, forward/reverse, and hood mounted machine gun. **8.25 in** (21 cm). **Battery operated**. Known colors: Blue and white. Graphics: Police. Maker: **Mizuno/Alps**, Japan. Toy marks: M (Mizuno). Box marks: M (Mizuno).
Scarcity: 3. Fine to Excellent (C6-C8): $75-$125, Mint (C10): $150

(Not pictured) **1959 Buick 2-door hardtop** with fender siren and antenna. **9 in** (23 cm). **Friction**. Known colors: Black and white. Graphics: Patrol. Maker: **Masudaya**, Japan. Box marks: MT (Masudaya). Box text: *Highway Patrol*.
Scarcity: 3. Fine to Excellent (C6-C8): $100-$150, Mint (C10): $200

(Not pictured) **1959 Buick 2-door hardtop** with rotating roof light and fender siren. **9 in** (23 cm). **Friction**. Known colors: Black and white. Graphics: Police - Police Dept. Maker: **Yonezawa**, Japan. Toy marks: Y (Yonezawa). Box marks: Y (Yonezawa), AHI. Box text: *Turnpike Highway Patrol*.
Scarcity: 4. Fine to Excellent (C6-C8): $100-$135, Mint (C10): $175

1950 Buick 4-door sedan with headlights, roof light, forward/reverse, and hood mounted machine gun. **8.25 in** (21 cm). **Battery operated**. Known colors: Olive, green and white. Graphics: G-Men. Maker: **Mizuno/Alps**, Japan. Toy marks: M (Mizuno). Box marks: M (Mizuno).
Scarcity: 3. Fine to Excellent (C6-C8): $75-$125, Mint (C10): $150

1959 Buick 2-door convertible with oversized police driver, light, and antenna. **11 in** (28 cm). **Friction**. Known colors: Blue and white. Graphics: Patrol - Police Patrol. Maker: **Ichiko**, Japan. Toy marks: Ichiko. Box text: *Gang Buster*.
Scarcity: 5. Fine to Excellent (C6-C8): $225-$275, Mint (C10): $325

1950 Buick 4-door sedan with headlights, roof light, forward/reverse, and hood mounted machine gun. **8.25 in** (21 cm). **Battery operated**. Known colors: Green, red, and cream. Graphics: Police. Maker: **Mizuno/Alps**, Japan. Toy marks: M (Mizuno). Box marks: M (Mizuno).
Scarcity: 3. Fine to Excellent (C6-C8): $75-$125, Mint (C10): $150

1959 Buick 2-door convertible with oversized police driver, twin lights, and antenna. **11 in** (28 cm). **Friction**. Known colors: Blue and white. Graphics: Patrol - RUKS POLITE. Maker: **Ichiko**, Japan. Toy marks: Ichiko.
Scarcity: 5. Fine to Excellent (C6-C8): $225-$275, Mint (C10): $325

1959 Buick 2-door hardtop with two rotating lights. **11 in** (28 cm). **Friction**. Known colors: Blue, white and red. Graphics: Patrol - Highway Patrol (shield). Maker: **Ichiko**, Japan. Toy marks: Ichiko. Box text: *Police Dept Highway Patrol Sedan*.
Scarcity: 5. Fine to Excellent (C6-C8): $225-$275, Mint (C10): $325

1959 Buick 2-door convertible with oversized police driver, machine gun, working lights, and antenna. **11 in** (28 cm). **Friction with battery**. Known colors: Black and white. Graphics: Police - Highway Patrol (shield). Maker: **Ichiko**, Japan. Toy marks: Ichiko.
Scarcity: 5. Fine to Excellent (C6-C8): $225-$275, Mint (C10): $325

1959 Buick 2-door hardtop with one rotating light. **11 in** (28 cm). **Friction**. Known colors: Blue and white. Graphics: Patrol - Highway Patrol (shield). Maker: **Ichiko**, Japan. Toy marks: Ichiko. Box marks: Ichiko. Box text: *Highway Patrol*.
Scarcity: 5. Fine to Excellent (C6-C8): $225-$275, Mint (C10): $325

1959 Buick 2-door convertible with oversized police driver, light, and antenna. **11 in** (28 cm). **Friction**. Known colors: Blue and white. Graphics: Polizei. Maker: **Ichiko**, Japan. Toy marks: Ichiko.
Scarcity: 5. Fine to Excellent (C6-C8): $225-$275, Mint (C10): $325

1959 Buick 2-door hardtop with two rotating lights, antenna, and pop-up roof mounted radar. **11 in** (28 cm). **Friction**. Known colors: Black, white, and red. Graphics: Police - NJ State Police. Maker: **Ichiko**, Japan. Toy marks: Ichiko.
Scarcity: 5. Fine to Excellent (C6-C8): $225-$275, Mint (C10): $325

Public Service Vehicles 81

1959 Buick 2-door hardtop with two rotating lights, operating dome light, and antenna. **11 in** (28 cm). **Friction with battery**. Known colors: Blue, white, and red. Graphics: Polis. Maker: **Ichiko**, Japan. Toy marks: Ichiko.
Scarcity: 5. Fine to Excellent (C6-C8): $225-$275, Mint (C10): $325

1959 Buick 2-door hardtop with two rotating lights, antenna, and pop-up roof mounted radar. **11 in** (28 cm). **Friction**. Known colors: Black, white, and red. Graphics: Polite. Maker: **Ichiko**, Japan. Toy marks: Ichiko.
Scarcity: 5. Fine to Excellent (C6-C8): $225-$275, Mint (C10): $325

1959 Buick 2-door hardtop with two rotating lights, operating dome light, and antenna. **11 in** (28 cm). **Friction with battery**. Known colors: Blue, white, and red. Graphics: Politie. Maker: **Ichiko**, Japan. Toy marks: Ichiko.
Scarcity: 5. Fine to Excellent (C6-C8): $225-$275, Mint (C10): $325

1959 Buick 2-door hardtop with roof dome light, pop-up radar box, antenna, fender light, and siren. On/off switch. **11 in** (28 cm). **Friction with battery**. Known colors: Black and white. Graphics: Rukspolitie - Politie. Maker: **Ichiko**, Japan. Toy marks: Ichiko.
Scarcity: 5. Fine to Excellent (C6-C8): $225-$275, Mint (C10): $325

1959 Buick 2-door hardtop with roof dome light and siren. **11.5 in** (29 cm). **Friction**. Known colors: Black and white. Graphics: Highway Patrol. Maker: **Nomura**, Japan. Toy marks: TN (Nomura). Box marks: TN (Nomura). Box text: *Highway Patrol*.
Scarcity: 5. Fine to Excellent (C6-C8): $300-$350, Mint (C10): $400

1960 Buick Invicta 4-door hardtop with two rotating lights, antenna, and roof dome light. **17.5 in** (44 cm). **Friction**. Known colors: Black, white, and red. Graphics: Buick - Highway Patrol (shield). Maker: **Ichiko**, Japan. Toy marks: Ichiko. Box marks: Ichiko. Box text: *Highway Patrol Car*.
Scarcity: 7. Fine to Excellent (C6-C8): $400-$500, Mint (C10): $650

1960 Buick Invicta 4-door hardtop with two rotating lights, antenna, and pop-up radar box. **17.5 in** (44 cm). **Friction**. Known colors: Black, white, and red. Graphics: Buick - Highway Patrol (shield). Maker: **Ichiko**, Japan. Toy marks: Ichiko.
Scarcity: 7. Fine to Excellent (C6-C8): $400-$500, Mint (C10): $650

Police Vehicles

1961 Buick Le Sabre 4-door hardtop with rotating light, siren, working wipers, and antenna. **16 in** (41 cm). **Friction**. Known colors: Black and white. Graphics: Buick - Patrol No.1125 -Police Patrol (shield). License: E-147. Maker: **Nomura**, Japan. Toy marks: TN (Nomura). Box text: *Police Patrol Car*.
Scarcity: 5. Fine to Excellent (C6-C8): $375-$525, Mint (C10): $650

1964 Buick Wildcat 2-door hardtop with two rotating lights, dome roof light, fender siren, and mirror. **15.5 in** (39 cm). **Friction**. Known colors: Blue and white. Graphics: Highway Patrol - Buick. Maker: **Ichiko**, Japan. Toy marks: Ichiko.
Scarcity: 5. Fine to Excellent (C6-C8): $300-$450, Mint (C10): $600

1962 Buick 2-door hardtop with dome roof light, fender siren, antenna, and trunk mounted speed meter. **12 in** (30 cm). **Friction**. Known colors: Black and white. Graphics: Highway Patrol - Police. Maker: **Nomura/IY Metal**, Japan. Toy marks: Cragstan. Box marks: Cragstan, NGS (Cragstan). Box text: *Cragstan Police Car With Speedmeter*.
Scarcity: 7. Fine to Excellent (C6-C8): $300-$400, Mint (C10): $600

1964 Buick Wildcat 2-door hardtop with two rotating lights and radar speed meter. **15.5 in** (39 cm). **Battery operated**. Known colors: Black and white. Graphics: Highway Patrol (and shield). Maker: **Ichiko**, Japan. Toy marks: Ichiko.
Scarcity: 4. Fine to Excellent (C6-C8): $200-$300, Mint (C10): $425

1964 Buick Wildcat 2-door hardtop with two rotating lights, antenna, and radar speed meter. **15.5 in** (39 cm). **Battery operated**. Known colors: Green. Graphics: (Italy shield) - Buick. Maker: **Ichiko**, Japan. Toy marks: Ichiko.
Scarcity: 4. Fine to Excellent (C6-C8): $200-$300, Mint (C10): $425

1964 Buick Wildcat 2-door hardtop with two rotating lights, dome roof light, antenna, fender siren, and mirror (flat interior). **15.5 in** (39 cm). **Battery operated**. Known colors: Black and white. Graphics: Highway Patrol (and shield). License: Buick. Maker: **Ichiko**, Japan. Toy marks: Ichiko.
Scarcity: 4. Fine to Excellent (C6-C8): $200-$300, Mint (C10): $425

1964 Buick Wildcat 2-door hardtop with two rotating lights, dome roof light, antenna, fender siren, and mirror (**15.5 in** (39 cm). **Friction**. Known colors: Black and white. Graphics: Highway Patrol (and shield). License: Buick. Maker: **Ichiko**, Japan. Toy marks: Ichiko. Box marks: Ichiko. Box text: *Highway Patrol Buick*.
Scarcity: 4. Fine to Excellent (C6-C8): $200-$300, Mint (C10): $425

1964 Buick Wildcat 2-door hardtop with two roof lights, dome roof light, and siren sound. **15.5 in** (39 cm). **Friction**. Known colors: Black and white. Graphics: Highway Patrol (and shield) - Buick. Maker: **Ichiko**, Japan. Toy marks: Ichiko. Box marks: Ichiko. Box text: *Highway Patrol Buick Wildcat*.
Scarcity: 4. Fine to Excellent (C6-C8): $200-$300, Mint (C10): $425

1964 Buick Wildcat 2-door hardtop with two rotating lights, fender mirror, antenna, and radar speed meter. **15.5 in** (39 cm). **Battery operated**. Known colors: Green and white. Graphics: Polizei. License: Buick. Maker: **Ichiko**, Japan. Toy marks: Ichiko.
Scarcity: 4. Fine to Excellent (C6-C8): $200-$300, Mint (C10): $425

1965 Buick Riviera 2-door hardtop with dome roof light, two rotating sirens, pull up antenna, and bump and go action. **10.75 in** (27 cm). **Battery operated**. Known colors: Black and white. Graphics: Highway Patrol - P.D. - Police. License: Buick Riviera. Maker: **Bandai**, Japan. Toy marks: Bandai. Box marks: Bandai. Box text: *High Way Patrol Car #4204*.
Scarcity: 3. Fine to Excellent (C6-C8): $100-$125, Mint (C10): $165

1966 Buick Skylark 2-door hardtop with dome roof light, roof siren, and fender mirrors. **11.5 in** (29 cm). **Friction**. Known colors: Black and white. Graphics: Police Patrol No. 5. License: 4044. Maker: **Asakusa**, Japan. Toy marks: A1 (Asakusa). Box marks: A1 (Asakusa).
Scarcity: 3. Fine to Excellent (C6-C8): $125-$200, Mint (C10): $325

1966 Buick Skylark 2-door hardtop with dome roof light, and roof lights. **11.5 in** (29 cm). **Battery operated**. Known colors: Black and white. Graphics: Police Patrol No. 5. License: 6063. Maker: **Asakusa**, Japan. Toy marks: A1 (Asakusa). Box marks: A1 (Asakusa).
Scarcity: 3. Fine to Excellent (C6-C8): $125-$200, Mint (C10): $325

84　Police Vehicles

1966 Buick Skylark 4-door station wagon with blue dome roof light. **11.5 in** (29 cm). **Battery operated**. Known colors: Black and white. Graphics: Police Patrol No. 5 - Buick. License: 4044. Maker: **Asakusa**, Japan. Toy marks: A1 (Asakusa). Box marks: A1 (Asakusa). Box text: *New Buick Police Car*.
Scarcity: 3. Fine to Excellent (C6-C8): $125-$200, Mint (C10): $325

1966 Buick LeSabre 4-door hardtop with roof dome light, siren, and antenna. **19 in** (48 cm). **Friction**. Known colors: Black and white. Graphics: Highway Patrol - Buick. License: Buick. Maker: **Asahi**, Japan. Toy marks: ATC (Asahi Toy). Box marks: ATC (Asahi Toy). Box text: *Buick Police Car*.
Scarcity: 7. Fine to Excellent (C6-C8): $425-$525, Mint (C10): $625

1966 Buick Riviera 4-door hardtop with roof dome light, sirens, antenna, fender mirror, and speaker. **13.5 in** (34 cm). **Battery operated**. Known colors: Black and white. Graphics: Police Dept. - Police (shield) - Highway Patrol. Maker: **Yonezawa**, Japan. Toy marks: Y (Yonezawa).
Scarcity: 5. Fine to Excellent (C6-C8): $125-$200, Mint (C10): $275

1960 Cadillac 4-door hardtop with rotating roof light and antenna. **6 in** (15 cm). **Friction**. Known colors: Black and white. Graphics: Police - (shield) - Cadillac. License: IK-62. Maker: **Ichiko**, Japan. Toy marks: none. Box marks: Ichiko. Box text: *Police With Moving Light*.
Notes: Also came in "Polizei" version.
Scarcity: 3. Fine to Excellent (C6-C8): $75-$125, Mint (C10): $165

1966 Buick Riviera 2-door hardtop with roof dome light, siren, mirror, and antenna. **15 in** (38 cm). **Battery operated**. Known colors: Blue and White. Graphics: P.D. - Police - Highway Patrol. License: A-1000. Maker: **Asakusa**, Japan. Toy marks: A1 (Asakusa).
Scarcity: 5. Fine to Excellent (C6-C8): $300-$450, Mint (C10): $600

1960 Cadillac 4-door hardtop with dome roof light, rotating speakers, and fender sirens. **11.5 in** (29 cm). **Friction**. Known colors: Black, white, and red. Graphics: Highway Patrol - P.D. (shield). Maker: **Bandai**, Japan. Toy marks: Bandai. Box marks: Bandai.
Scarcity: 3. Fine to Excellent (C6-C8): $80-$120, Mint (C10): $200

Public Service Vehicles 85

1960 Cadillac 4-door hardtop with dome light, two roof lights, two sirens, and antenna. Trunk mounted key on/off switch. **18 in** (46 cm). **Battery operated**. Known colors: Black and white (white rear fender panel). Graphics: Police - Patrol - Highway (shield). License: Cadillac. Maker: **Yonezawa**, Japan. Toy marks: Y (Yonezawa).
Scarcity: 6. Fine to Excellent (C6-C8): $600-$750, Mint (C10): $825

1960 Cadillac 4-door hardtop with three roof lights, two sirens, and antenna. Underbody on/off switch. **18 in** (46 cm). **Battery operated**. Known colors: Black and white (black rear fender panel). Graphics: Police - Patrol - Highway (shield). License: Cadillac. Maker: **Yonezawa**, Japan. Toy marks: Y (Yonezawa).
Scarcity: 6. Fine to Excellent (C6-C8): $600-$750, Mint (C10): $825

1961 Cadillac 4-door hardtop with large roof dome light, two double roof lights, plastic siren, and antenna. **13.75 in** (35 cm). **Friction**. Known colors: Black and white (black rear doors). Graphics: Highway Patrol (and shield). License: A-4684. Maker: **Yonezawa**, Japan. Toy marks: Y (Yonezawa). Box marks: Y (Yonezawa).
Scarcity: 5. Fine to Excellent (C6-C8): $300-$350, Mint (C10): $400

1961 Cadillac 4-door hardtop with roof dome light, plastic siren, and antenna. **13.75 in** (35 cm). **Friction**. Known colors: Black and white (white doors). Graphics: Highway Patrol (and shield). License: A-4684. Maker: **Yonezawa**, Japan. Toy marks: Y (Yonezawa). Box marks: Y (Yonezawa).
Scarcity: 5. Fine to Excellent (C6-C8): $300-$350, Mint (C10): $400

1961 Cadillac 4-door hardtop with roof dome light, siren, and antenna. **13.75 in** (35 cm). **Friction**. Known colors: Black and white. Graphics: Highway Patrol (and shield). License: A-4684. Maker: **Yonezawa**, Japan. Toy marks: Y (Yonezawa). Box marks: Y (Yonezawa). Box text: *Highway Patrol car*.
Scarcity: 5. Fine to Excellent (C6-C8): $300-$350, Mint (C10): $400

1961 Cadillac 4-door sedan with roof dome light, two rotating sirens, two fenders and antenna. **17 in** (43 cm). **Friction**. Known colors: Black and white and gold and red. Graphics: Highway Patrol - P.D. (shield). License: Cadillac. Maker: **Bandai**, Japan. Toy marks: Bandai. Box marks: Bandai.
Notes: 1963 model front end.
Scarcity: 5. Fine to Excellent (C6-C8): $275-$425, Mint (C10): $500

86 Police Vehicles

1961 Cadillac 4-door sedan with dome roof light, rotating speakers, siren, and antenna. Talking speaker. Trunk mounted switch with Japanese markings. **17 in** (43 cm). **Battery operated**. Known colors: Black and white and gold. Graphics: Highway Patrol - Police - P.D. (shield). License: Cadillac. Maker: **Bandai**, Japan. Toy marks: Bandai. Box marks: Bandai. Box text: *Cadillac Highway Patrol, #966*.
Notes: 1963 model front end.
Scarcity: 6. Fine to Excellent (C6-C8): $400-$500, Mint (C10): $600

1961 Cadillac 4-door sedan with Police roof sign, roof dome light, three sirens, and antenna. **17 in** (43 cm). **Friction**. Known colors: Black and white. Graphics: Highway Patrol (and shield) - Police. License: Cadillac. Maker: **Bandai**, Japan. Toy marks: Bandai. Box marks: Bandai.
Notes: 1963 model front end.
Scarcity: 5. Fine to Excellent (C6-C8): $375-$425, Mint (C10): $500

1961 Cadillac Fleetwood 4-door sedan with dome and two roof lights, fender siren, and antenna. **17 in** (43 cm). **Friction**. Known colors: Black and white. Graphics: Highway Patrol. License: Cadillac. Maker: **Shioji**, Japan. Toy marks: SSS (Shioji). Box marks: SSS (Shioji).
Scarcity: 7. Fine to Excellent (C6-C8): $450-$550, Mint (C10): $700

1961 Cadillac Fleetwood 4-door sedan with dome roof light, fender siren, two fender lights, and antenna. **17 in** (43 cm). **Friction**. Known colors: Black and white. Graphics: Highway Patrol - Police (roof sign). License: Cadillac. Maker: **Shioji**, Japan. Toy marks: SSS (Shioji).
Scarcity: 7. Fine to Excellent (C6-C8): $450-$550, Mint (C10): $700

1962 Cadillac 2-door hardtop with dome roof light, two roof lights, sirens, mirror, and pull up antenna. **20 in** (51 cm). **Friction**. Known colors: Black, white, and red. Graphics: Highway Patrol (shield) - Cadillac. Maker: **Ichiko**, Japan. Toy marks: Ichiko. Box marks: Ichiko. Box text: *High Way Patrol Car - Up And Down Antenna*.
Scarcity: 6. Fine to Excellent (C6-C8): $600-$700, Mint (C10): $800

1962 Cadillac 4-door hardtop with roof dome light, two rotating lights, mirror, and antenna. **20 in** (51 cm). **Friction**. Known colors: Black, white, and red. Graphics: Highway Patrol (shield) - Cadillac. Maker: **Ichiko**, Japan. Toy marks: Ichiko. Box marks: Ichiko.
Scarcity: 6. Fine to Excellent (C6-C8): $600-$700, Mint (C10): $800

1962 Cadillac 4-door hardtop with three roof lights, fender siren, and antenna. **22 in** (56 cm). **Friction**. Known colors: Black and white. Graphics: Police Dept. - Patrol -Police - P.D. (shield). Maker: **Yonezawa**, Japan. Toy marks: Y (Yonezawa). Box text: *Police Patrol Car "22"*.
Scarcity: 8. Fine to Excellent (C6-C8): $600-$700, Mint (C10): $850

Public Service Vehicles 87

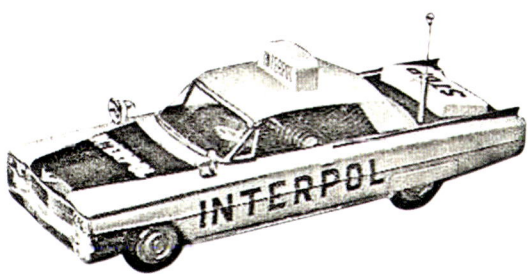

1963 Cadillac 2-door hardtop with flashing roof sign, rear stop sign, fender mirror and siren, and antenna. **11 in** (28 cm). **Battery operated**. Known colors: White and black. Graphics: Interpol. Maker: **Ichiko**, Japan. Toy marks: Ichiko. Box marks: Ichiko.
Notes: Ichiko catalog image.
Scarcity: 5. **Fine to Excellent (C6-C8): $150-$250, Mint (C10): $350**

1963 Cadillac 2-door hardtop with three blue roof lights, fender mirror and siren, and antenna. **11 in** (28 cm). **Battery operated**. Known colors: Green. Graphics: (Italy). Maker: **Ichiko**, Japan. Toy marks: Ichiko. Box marks: Ichiko.
Scarcity: 3. **Fine to Excellent (C6-C8): $75-$125, Mint (C10): $185**

1963 Cadillac 2-door hardtop with three roof lights, fender mirrors, and antenna. **11 in** (28 cm). **Friction**. Known colors: Black and white. Graphics: Police - P.D. (shield). Maker: **Ichiko**, Japan. Toy marks: Ichiko. Box marks: Ichiko.
Scarcity: 3. **Fine to Excellent (C6-C8): $75-$125, Mint (C10): $185**

1963 Cadillac 2-door hardtop with dome roof light, two roof lights, fender siren and mirror, and antenna. **11 in** (28 cm). **R/C battery operated**. Known colors: Black, white, and red. Graphics: Highway Patrol. Maker: **Ichiko**, Japan. Toy marks: Ichiko. Box marks: Ichiko.
Scarcity: 3. **Fine to Excellent (C6-C8): $75-$125, Mint (C10): $185**

1963 Cadillac 2-door hardtop with dome roof light, rotating lights, fender mirror and siren, and antenna. **11 in** (28 cm). **Friction**. Known colors: Black and white. Graphics: Highway Patrol - P.D. (shield). Maker: **Ichiko**, Japan. Toy marks: Ichiko. Box marks: Ichiko.
Notes: Ichiko catalog image.
Scarcity: 3. **Fine to Excellent (C6-C8): $75-$125, Mint (C10): $185**

1963 Cadillac 2-door hardtop with three blue roof lights, fender mirrors, and antenna. **11 in** (28 cm). **R/C battery operated**. Known colors: Green and white. Graphics: Polizei. Maker: **Ichiko**, Japan. Toy marks: Ichiko. Box marks: Ichiko.
Scarcity: 3. **Fine to Excellent (C6-C8): $75-$125, Mint (C10): $185**

88 Police Vehicles

1965 Cadillac 4-door sedan with roof dome light, fender siren, and mirror. **12.25 in (31 cm). Friction**. Known colors: Black and white. Graphics: Police - P.D. (shield). License: M888. Maker: **Nomura**, Japan. Toy marks: TN (Nomura).
Scarcity: 6. Fine to Excellent (C6-C8): $225-$285, Mint (C10): $365

1965 Cadillac 2-door hardtop with dome roof light, antenna, fender siren and mirrors. **16.5 in (42 cm). Friction**. Known colors: Black and white. Graphics: Highway Patrol - 12 (shield). License: Cadillac. Maker: **Asahi**, Japan. Toy marks: ATC (Asahi Toy). Box marks: ATC (Asahi Toy). Box text: *Cadillac Highway Patrol*.
Scarcity: 5. Fine to Excellent (C6-C8): $350-$450, Mint (C10): $550

1965 Cadillac 4-door sedan with dome roof light, markers, plastic siren, and antenna. **25.5 in (65 cm). Friction**. Known colors: Black and white. Graphics: Highway Patrol - 123 - Police - Patrol (shield). License: Cadillac. Maker: **Nomura**, Japan. Toy marks: TN (Nomura).
Scarcity: 6. Fine to Excellent (C6-C8): $400-$600, Mint (C10): $800

1967 Cadillac Eldorado 2-door hardtop. **28 in (71 cm). Friction**. Known colors: Black and white. Graphics: Highway Patrol - Police (shield) - 17. License: Cadillac. Maker: **Ichiko**, Japan. Toy marks: Ichiko.
Scarcity: 6. Fine to Excellent (C6-C8): $475-$575, Mint (C10): $700

1935 Chevrolet 2-door sedan with roof dome light, bump and go, and non-fall action. **10.25 in (26 cm). Battery operated**. Known colors: Red and black; Yellow and black. Graphics: F.B.I. Godfather. Maker: **Taiyo**, Japan. Toy marks: Taiyo. Box marks: Taiyo. Box text: *F.B.I. Godfather*.
Notes: Produced 1960s.
Scarcity: 3. Fine to Excellent (C6-C8): $60-$90, Mint (C10): $125

1954 Chevrolet 2-door sedan with police driver and passenger and roof light. **11 in (28 cm). Battery operated**. Known colors: Black and white. Graphics: Police Car. Maker: **Marusan**, Japan. Toy marks: SAN (Marusan), Kosuge. Box text: *Stop-Go Police Car with Siren and Light*.
Scarcity: 9. Fine to Excellent (C6-C8): $600-$900, Mint (C10): $1,200

Public Service Vehicles 89

1958 Chevrolet 4-door hardtop with roof sign and blue light and antenna. **8 in** (20 cm). **Friction**. Known colors: Black and white. Graphics: Rukspolite (car & roof sign). License: AG-9738. Maker: **Bandai**, Japan. Toy marks: Bandai. Box marks: Bandai.
Scarcity: 8. Fine to Excellent (C6-C8): $200-$300, Mint (C10): $450

1959 Chevrolet 2-door hardtop with roof dome light and antenna. **10 in** (25 cm). **Friction**. Known colors: Black and white. Graphics: Highway Patrol. Maker: **Aoshin**, Japan. Toy marks: ASC (Aoshin). Box marks: ASC (Aoshin).
Scarcity: 5. Fine to Excellent (C6-C8): $175-$225, Mint (C10): $350

(Not pictured) **1959 Chevrolet 4-door station wagon** with roof light. **12.5 in** (32 cm). **Friction**. Known colors: Black and white. Graphics: Highway Patrol. Maker: **Asakusa Toy & Doll**, Japan. Toy marks: ATD (Asakusa Toy & Doll).
Scarcity: 5. Fine to Excellent (C6-C8): $175-$225, Mint (C10): $350

1959 Chevrolet 4-door station wagon with flat dome roof light. **12.5 in** (32 cm). **Friction**. Known colors: Black and white. Graphics: Morgan - Patrol - Chevrolet. License: 9893. Maker: **Asakusa Toy & Doll**, Japan. Toy marks: none.
Scarcity: 6. Fine to Excellent (C6-C8): $175-$225, Mint (C10): $350

1959 Chevrolet 4-door hardtop with flat roof dome light and lithographed trim. Lithographed figures on rear window. **12.5 in** (32 cm). **Friction**. Known colors: Black, white, and red (white roof and white front doors). Graphics: Chevrolet - P.D. - Highway Patrol - Police. License: 9893. Maker: **Daito**, Japan. Toy marks: none.
Notes: 4-door with 2-door handles.
Scarcity: 3. Fine to Excellent (C6-C8): $125-$175, Mint (C10): $250

1959 Chevrolet 4-door hardtop with flat roof dome light and lithographed trim. **12.5 in** (32 cm). **Friction**. Known colors: Black, white, and red (black roof and white front doors). Graphics: Chevrolet - P.D. - Highway Patrol - Police. License: 9893. Maker: **Daito**, Japan. Toy marks: none.
Notes: 4-door with 2-door handles.
Scarcity: 3. Fine to Excellent (C6-C8): $125-$175, Mint (C10): $250

1959 Chevrolet 4-door hardtop with flat roof dome light and lithographed trim. **12.5 in** (32 cm). **Friction**. Known colors: Black and white. Graphics: Chevrolet - Police Patrol. License: 9893. Maker: **Daito**, Japan. Toy marks: none.
Notes: 4-door with 2-door handles.
Scarcity: 3. Fine to Excellent (C6-C8): $125-$175, Mint (C10): $250

1959 Chevrolet 4-door hardtop with flat dome roof light. **12.5 in** (32 cm). **Friction**. Known colors: Black and white. Graphics: Police Patrol - Chevrolet. License: 1961. Maker: **Daito**, Japan. Toy marks: none.
Scarcity: 3. Fine to Excellent (C6-C8): $125-$175, Mint (C10): $250

1959 Chevrolet 4-door sedan with roof dome light and two fender sirens. **12.5 in** (32 cm). **Friction**. Known colors: Black and white. Graphics: Chevrolet - Police. Maker: **Daito**, Japan. Toy marks: none.
Notes: 4-door with 2-door handles.
Scarcity: 3. Fine to Excellent (C6-C8): $125-$175, Mint (C10): $250

1960 Chevrolet 4-door convertible with police driver, machine gun, radar, siren, and light fixture. **7.5 in** (19 cm). **Friction**. Known colors: Black and white. Graphics: Patrol - P.D. - Impala. License: Chevrolet -Ichiko. Maker: **Ichiko**, Japan. Toy marks: Ichiko. Box marks: Ichiko. Box text: *Police Dept. Convertible with Gun - Siren - Light*.
Scarcity: 3. Fine to Excellent (C6-C8): $85-$115, Mint (C10): $145

1960 Chevrolet 4-door hardtop with rotating roof lights and siren. **7.5 in** (19 cm). **Friction**. Known colors: Black and white. Graphics: Police. License: Chevrolet - Ichiko. Maker: **Ichiko**, Japan. Toy marks: Ichiko. Box marks: Ichiko. Box text: *Police Car with Siren and Moving Warning Light*.
Scarcity: 3. Fine to Excellent (C6-C8): $65-$95, Mint (C10): $125

1960 Chevrolet Corvair 4-door sedan with turning roof light and working wipers. **9 in** (23 cm). **Friction**. Known colors: Black and white. Graphics: Police No.112 & P.D. (shield) - Corvair. Maker: **Yonezawa**, Japan. Toy marks: Y (Yonezawa). Box marks: Y (Yonezawa). Box text: *Turnpike Highway Police Patrol Car*.
Scarcity: 5. Fine to Excellent (C6-C8): $125-$165, Mint (C10): $225

1960 Chevrolet Corvair 4-door hardtop with rotating roof lights. **9.25 in** (23 cm). **Friction**. Known colors: Black and white. Graphics: Patrol - P.D. (shield). License: IK-0973 - Ichiko. Maker: **Ichiko**, Japan. Toy marks: Ichiko. Box text: *Police Car*.
Scarcity: 3. Fine to Excellent (C6-C8): $100-$175, Mint (C10): $250

1960 Chevrolet Corvair 4-door hardtop with rotating roof lights. **9.25 in** (23 cm). **Friction**. Known colors: Black and white. Graphics: Polis. License: Ichiko. Maker: **Ichiko**, Japan. Toy marks: Ichiko.
Scarcity: 3. Fine to Excellent (C6-C8): $100-$175, Mint (C10): $250

Public Service Vehicles 91

1960 Chevrolet Corvair 4-door sedan with rotating roof light and tin police figure firing gun. **9.25 in** (23 cm). **Friction**. Known colors: Turquoise and white. License: IK-0973. Maker: **Ichiko**, Japan. Toy marks: Ichiko.
Scarcity: 5. Fine to Excellent (C6-C8): $135-$200, Mint (C10): $275

1960 Chevrolet Corvair 4-door sedan with rotating roof light and tin police figure firing gun. **9.25 in** (23 cm). **Friction**. Known colors: Green and white. License: IK-0973. Maker: **Ichiko**, Japan. Toy marks: Ichiko.
Scarcity: 5. Fine to Excellent (C6-C8): $135-$200, Mint (C10): $275

1960 Chevrolet Corvair 4-door hardtop. **9.25 in** (23 cm). **Friction**. Known colors: Black and white. Graphics: No.7 (and shield). Maker: **Mitsuhashi**, Japan. Toy marks: M (Mitsuhashi).
Scarcity: 3. Fine to Excellent (C6-C8): $45-$85, Mint (C10): $115

1961 Chevrolet 4-door station wagon with rotating roof light and fender sirens. **9.75 in** (25 cm). **Friction**. Known colors: Black and white. Graphics: Highway Patrol - Chevrolet - Patrol (shield). Maker: **Aoshin**, Japan. Toy marks: ASC (Aoshin). Box marks: ASC (Aoshin).
Notes: Also produced with tin fender mirrors instead of sirens.
Scarcity: 3. Fine to Excellent (C6-C8): $150-$200, Mint (C10): $250

1961 Chevrolet Impala 4-door hardtop with dome roof light, antenna, and fender sirens. **11 in** (28 cm). **Friction**. Known colors: Black and white. Graphics: Patrol - P.D. - Impala. License: Chevrolet. Maker: **Bandai**, Japan. Toy marks: Bandai. Box marks: Bandai. Box text: *Chevrolet Police Car #861*.
Notes: Car sold as 1961, 1962, and 1963 with taillight changes only.
Scarcity: 5. Fine to Excellent (C6-C8): $175-$265, Mint (C10): $395

(Not pictured) **1962 Chevrolet 4-door hardtop** with roof light, fender siren, and antenna. **11 in** (28 cm). **Friction**. Known colors: Black and white. Maker: **Bandai**, Japan. Toy marks: Bandai. Box marks: Bandai. Box text: *Patrol Car #957*.
Scarcity: 6. Fine to Excellent (C6-C8): $125-$225, Mint (C10): $350

1962 Chevrolet 4-door hardtop with roof dome light, two sirens, and antenna. **14.75 in** (37 cm). **Battery operated**. Known colors: Black, white, and red. Graphics: Highway Patrol - P.D. (shield). License: Chevrolet. Maker: **Ichiko**, Japan. Toy marks: none.
Scarcity: 5. Fine to Excellent (C6-C8): $300-$375, Mint (C10): $450

1962 Chevrolet 4-door hardtop with roof dome light. **14.75 in** (37 cm). **R/C battery operated**. Known colors: Black and white. Graphics: Police (and shield). License: Chevrolet. Maker: **Ichiko**, Japan. Toy marks: none.
Scarcity: 5. Fine to Excellent (C6-C8): $300-$375, Mint (C10): $450

92 Police Vehicles

1962 Chevrolet 4-door hardtop with roof dome light, two sirens, antenna, and two vinyl police occupants. **14.75 in** (37 cm). **Battery operated**. Known colors: Black and white. Graphics: Police (shield). License: Chevrolet. Maker: **Ichiko**, Japan. Toy marks: none.
Scarcity: 5. Fine to Excellent (C6-C8): $350-$425, Mint (C10): $500

1963 Chevrolet 2-door hardtop with blue roof light, fender siren and mirror, forward/ reverse action, and steering. **8 in** (20 cm). **R/C battery operated**. Known colors: Green and white. Graphics: Polizei. Maker: **Ichiko**, Japan. Toy marks: Ichiko. Box marks: Ichiko. Box text: *Polizei*.
Scarcity: 4. Fine to Excellent (C6-C8): $75-$135, Mint (C10): $185

1962 Chevrolet 4-door convertible Command car with sparking gun, vinyl police driver, bump and go action, siren, and antenna. **14.75 in** (37 cm). **Battery operated**. Known colors: Black, white, red, and gold. Graphics: Star (shield). License: Chevrolet. Maker: **Ichiko/Yanoman**, Japan. Toy marks: none. Box marks: YM (Yanoman). Box text: *Police Command Car*.
Scarcity: 5. Fine to Excellent (C6-C8): $350-$425, Mint (C10): $500

1963 Chevrolet Impala 4-door hardtop with roof dome light, antenna, fender sirens, and plastic hubcaps. **11 in** (28 cm). **Friction**. Known colors: Black and white. Graphics: Patrol - P.D. License: Chevrolet. Maker: **NK Toys**, Korea. Toy marks: NK (NK Toys). Box marks: NK (NK Toys).
Scarcity: 2. Fine to Excellent (C6-C8): $60-$90, Mint (C10): $125

1963 Chevrolet Corvette Sting Ray 2-door coupe with dome roof light. **12 in** (30 cm). **R/C battery operated**. Known colors: Black and white. Graphics: Police - P.D. (shield). License: M-101. Maker: **Bandai/Ichida**, Japan. Toy marks: Bandai, SKK (Shinsei). Box marks: Bandai, Ichida/TET. Box text: *Chevrolet Corvette* (Japanese text).
Scarcity: 6. Fine to Excellent (C6-C8): $300-$375, Mint (C10): $450

1962 Chevrolet 4-door hardtop Secret agent car with pop-up roof dome light, automatic antenna, and two sirens. **14.75 in** (37 cm). **Battery operated**. Known colors: Blue or black. License: Chevrolet. Maker: **Ichiko/Yonezawa**, Japan. Toy marks: none. Box marks: Y (Yonezawa), Spesco. Box text: *Unmarked Secret Agents Car 007* or *Unmarked Police Car*.
Scarcity: 4. Fine to Excellent (C6-C8): $275-$350, Mint (C10): $425

1963 Chevrolet 4-door hardtop with dome roof light. **12.5 in** (32 cm). **Friction**. Known colors: Black, white, and gold. Graphics: Highway Patrol - P.D. (shield). Maker: **Daito**, Japan. Toy marks: none.
Scarcity: 3. Fine to Excellent (C6-C8): $125-$165, Mint (C10): $195

Public Service Vehicles 93

1963 Chevrolet 4-door hardtop with dome roof light, fender siren, mirrors, and antenna. **13.25 in** (34 cm). **Battery operated**. Known colors: Black, white, red, and gold. Graphics: Highway Patrol - P.D. (shield). Maker: **IY Metal**, Japan. Toy marks: KA (Unknown).
Scarcity: 5. Fine to Excellent (C6-C8): $200-$300, Mint (C10): $400

1963 Chevrolet 4-door convertible with two vinyl police figures, hood light, siren, and speed radar box. **13.75 in** (35 cm). **Battery operated**. Known colors: Black and white. Graphics: Highway Patrol - Police - 1978 (shield). Maker: **Terai**, Japan. Toy marks: Daiya (Terai). Box marks: Daiya (Terai). Box text: *Police Convertible with Siren and Flashing Light*.
Scarcity: 3. Fine to Excellent (C6-C8): $250-$325, Mint (C10): $400

1963 Chevrolet 4-door hardtop with dome roof light, fender mirrors and siren, and antenna. **13.25 in** (34 cm). **Battery operated**. Known colors: Black and white. Graphics: R.P.-35, R.P. (shield) - Policia -Radio Policia. License: 33-21-33. Maker: **Metalma**, Brazil. Toy marks: MM (Metalma). Box marks: MM (Metalma). Box text: *Chevrolet - Policia*.
Scarcity: 6. Fine to Excellent (C6-C8): $100-$200, Mint (C10): $300

1963 Chevrolet 4-door convertible with two vinyl police figures, hood light and siren, and speed radar box. **13.75 in** (35 cm). **Battery operated**. Known colors: Green and white. Graphics: Polizei. Maker: **Terai**, Japan. Toy marks: Daiya (Terai).
Scarcity: 3. Fine to Excellent (C6-C8): $250-$325, Mint (C10): $400

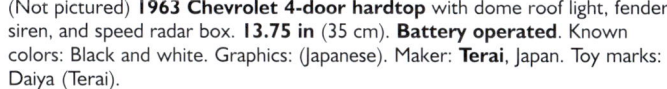

(Not pictured) **1963 Chevrolet 4-door hardtop** with dome roof light, fender siren, and speed radar box. **13.75 in** (35 cm). **Battery operated**. Known colors: Black and white. Graphics: (Japanese). Maker: **Terai**, Japan. Toy marks: Daiya (Terai).
Scarcity: 5. Fine to Excellent (C6-C8): $175-$275, Mint (C10): $375

1963 Chevrolet 4-door hardtop with dome roof light, antenna, and bump and go action. **13.75 in** (35 cm). **Battery operated**. Known colors: Black and white. Graphics: Highway Patrol P.D. (and shield) - P.D.- Impala -. Maker: **Okuma**, Japan. Toy marks: none. Box marks: Okuma. Box text: *Highway Patrol Car*.
Scarcity: 4. Fine to Excellent (C6-C8): $150-$185, Mint (C10): $265

1963 Chevrolet 4-door hardtop with dome roof light, fender siren, and speed radar box. **13.75 in** (35 cm). **Battery operated**. Known colors: Black and white. Graphics: Highway Patrol - 1978 (shield). Maker: **Terai**, Japan. Toy marks: Daiya (Terai). Box text: *Police Car*.
Scarcity: 4. Fine to Excellent (C6-C8): $300-$350, Mint (C10): $450

1963 Chevrolet 4-door sedan with roof speaker, fender sirens, and lithographed windows. Talking car in Japanese. Wakarimasu ka? **13.75 in** (35 cm). **Battery operated**. Known colors: Black and white. Graphics: (Japanese). License: 5-3217. Maker: **Yonezawa**, Japan. Toy marks: Y (Yonezawa). Box marks: Y (Yonezawa).
Scarcity: 3. Fine to Excellent (C6-C8): $150-$200, Mint (C10): $250

1963 Chevrolet 4-door sedan with roof speaker, fender sirens, and lithographed windows. Talking car in German language. Verstehen sie? **13.75 in** (35 cm). **Battery operated**. Known colors: Green and white. Graphics: Polizei (star emblem). License: No.649. Maker: **Yonezawa**, Japan. Toy marks: Y (Yonezawa). Box marks: Y (Yonezawa). Box text: *Das Sprechende Polizei-Auto*.
Scarcity: 3. Fine to Excellent (C6-C8): $150-$200, Mint (C10): $250

1963 Chevrolet 4-door sedan with roof speaker, fender sirens, and lithographed windows. Talking car in German language. Verstehen sie? **13.75 in** (35 cm). **Battery operated**. Known colors: Green and white. Graphics: (shield). License: No.649. Maker: **Yonezawa**, Japan. Toy marks: Y (Yonezawa). Box marks: Y (Yonezawa).
Scarcity: 3. Fine to Excellent (C6-C8): $150-$200, Mint (C10): $250

1963 Chevrolet 4-door sedan with roof speaker, fender sirens, and lithographed windows. Talking car for Italian market. Capisch? **13.75 in** (35 cm). **Battery operated**. Known colors: Black and white. Graphics: Squadra-Mobile. License: No.649. Maker: **Yonezawa**, Japan. Toy marks: Y (Yonezawa). Box marks: Y (Yonezawa). Box text: *Auto Polizia Parlante*.
Scarcity: 3. Fine to Excellent (C6-C8): $150-$200, Mint (C10): $250

1963 Chevrolet 4-door sedan with roof speaker, fender sirens, and lithographed windows. Talking car in English for USA market. Understand? **13.75 in** (35 cm). **Battery operated**. Known colors: Black and white. Graphics: Highway Patrol No.649. License: No.649. Maker: **Yonezawa**, Japan. Toy marks: Y (Yonezawa).
Scarcity: 3. Fine to Excellent (C6-C8): $150-$200, Mint (C10): $250

1963 Chevrolet Impala 4-door hardtop with three roof lights, fender siren, dual mirrors, siren sound, and antenna. **17.25 in** (44 cm). **Friction**. Known colors: Black and white. Graphics: Police - Highway Patrol (and shield). License: E-147. Maker: **Nomura**, Japan. Toy marks: TN (Nomura). Box marks: TN (Nomura). Box text: *Police Patrol Car No. 2 With Siren Sound*.
Scarcity: 6. Fine to Excellent (C6-C8): $325-$375, Mint (C10): $450

1964 Chevrolet Chevelle Malibu 2-door hardtop with dome roof light and rotating sirens. **8 in** (20 cm). **Friction**. Known colors: Black and white. Graphics: Highway Patrol - P.D. License: Chevrolet. Maker: **Bandai**, Japan. Toy marks: Bandai. Box marks: Bandai. Box text: *Security Car Series #1097*. Notes: Also produced as R/C battery operated model.
Scarcity: 3. Fine to Excellent (C6-C8): $60-$90, Mint (C10): $125

1967 Chevrolet Camaro 2-door hardtop with flashing roof light and fender siren. **11 in** (28 cm). **Battery operated**. Known colors: Black and white. Graphics: Police. Maker: **Masudaya**, Japan. Toy marks: MT (Masudaya). Box marks: MT (Masudaya).
Notes: Masudaya catalog image.
Scarcity: 4. Fine to Excellent (C6-C8): $100-$160, Mint (C10): $225

(Not pictured) **1968 Chevrolet Corvette 2-door coupe** with dome roof light and non-fall action. **10.75 in** (27 cm). **Friction or Battery Operated**. Known colors: Blue and white. Graphics: Highway Patrol - P.D. License: Corvette. Maker: **Taiyo**, Japan. Toy marks: Taiyo. Box marks: Taiyo.
Scarcity: 3. Fine to Excellent (C6-C8): $75-$125, Mint (C10): $150

(Not pictured) **1968 Chevrolet 4-door sedan** with roof lights and siren sound. **11 in** (28 cm). **Battery operated**. Known colors: Black and white. Graphics: Highway Patrol - Patrol - P.D.5847 - No.5 - Police. Maker: **Alps**, Japan. Toy marks: Alps. Box marks: Alps. Box text: *Real Sound Car*.
Scarcity: 2. Fine to Excellent (C6-C8): $50-$75, Mint (C10): $115

1967 Chevrolet Camaro 2-door hardtop with flashing roof light and fender siren. **11 in** (28 cm). **Battery operated**. Known colors: Black and white. Graphics: 56 - Police - P.D. - Highway Patrol. Maker: **Masudaya**, Japan. Toy marks: MT (Masudaya). Box marks: MT (Masudaya). Box text: *Police Patrol Car*. Notes: Masudaya catalog image.
Scarcity: 4. Fine to Excellent (C6-C8): $100-$160, Mint (C10): $225

1970 Chevrolet Camaro 2-door hardtop with multi-color roof light bar and siren sound. **11.75 in** (30 cm). **Battery operated**. Known colors: White. Graphics: Police (paper label). Maker: **Gorgo**, Argentina. Toy marks: Gorgo. Box marks: Gorgo.
Scarcity: 3. Fine to Excellent (C6-C8): $75-$110, Mint (C10): $150

1967 Chevrolet Camaro 2-door hardtop with flashing roof dome light, fender mirrors, antenna, and fender siren. **11 in** (28 cm). **Battery operated**. Known colors: Black and white. Graphics: Patrol - 110 - (Japanese). Maker: **Masudaya**, Japan. Toy marks: MT (Masudaya). Box marks: MT (Masudaya).
Scarcity: 6. Fine to Excellent (C6-C8): $250-$350, Mint (C10): $450

1970 Chevrolet Camaro 2-door hardtop with operating dome roof light and siren sound. **11.75 in** (30 cm). **Friction with battery**. Known colors: White and red. Graphics: Police (paper label). Maker: **Gorgo**, Argentina. Toy marks: Gorgo. Box marks: Gorgo.
Scarcity: 3. Fine to Excellent (C6-C8): $75-$110, Mint (C10): $150

96 Police Vehicles

1970 Chevrolet Camaro 2-door hardtop with dome roof light. **11.75 in** (30 cm). **Friction**. Known colors: Blue and white. Graphics: Police (paper label). Maker: **Gorgo**, Argentina. Toy marks: Gorgo. Box marks: Gorgo.
Scarcity: 3. Fine to Excellent (C6-C8): $75-$110, Mint (C10): $150

1979 Chevrolet Camaro 2-door hardtop with dome roof light. **9.5 in** (24 cm). **Windup**. Known colors: Black and white. Graphics: (Japanese). Maker: **Asahi**, Japan. Toy marks: Asahitoy (Asahi Toy).
Scarcity: 2. Fine to Excellent (C6-C8): $35-$65, Mint (C10): $95

1970 Chevrolet Camaro 2-door hardtop with dome roof light and siren sound. **11.75 in** (30 cm). **Friction**. Known colors: Blue and white. Graphics: Police (paper shield). Maker: **Gorgo**, Argentina. Toy marks: Gorgo. Box marks: Gorgo.
Scarcity: 3. Fine to Excellent (C6-C8): $75-$110, Mint (C10): $150

(Not pictured) **1971 Chevrolet Camaro 2-door hardtop** with non-fall action and dome roof light. **10.25 in** (26 cm). **Battery operated**. Known colors: Black and white. Graphics: 701 - Patrol - (Japanese). Maker: **Taiyo**, Japan. Toy marks: Taiyo. Box marks: Taiyo.
Scarcity: 2. Fine to Excellent (C6-C8): $50-$95, Mint (C10): $135

1958 Chrysler New Yorker 4-door convertible with plastic driver, antenna, fender siren, and operating hood light. **13.5 in** (34 cm). **Friction with battery**. Known colors: White. Graphics: Police. Maker: **Joustra**, France. Toy marks: none.
Scarcity: 8. Fine to Excellent (C6-C8): $250-$350, Mint (C10): $500

1971 Chevrolet Camaro 2-door hardtop with dome roof light and fender siren. **14.5 in** (37 cm). **Friction**. Known colors: Black and white. Graphics: Highway Patrol (and shield) - Camaro. Maker: **Nomura**, Japan. Toy marks: TN (Nomura).
Scarcity: 4. Fine to Excellent (C6-C8): $125-$175, Mint (C10): $235

1957 Dodge 2-door coupe with roof light. **9.5 in** (24 cm). **Battery operated**. Known colors: Black and white. Graphics: Police Car. Maker: **Unknown**, China. Toy marks: none.
Scarcity: 6. Fine to Excellent (C6-C8): $75-$150, Mint (C10): $250

Public Service Vehicles 97

1967 Dodge Dart 4-door hardtop with red dome roof light, sirens, and antenna. **12.25 in** (31 cm). **Friction**. Known colors: Black and white. Graphics: Highway Patrol - P.D. (shield) - Dodge. Maker: **Nomura**, Japan. Toy marks: TN (Nomura).
Scarcity: 4. Fine to Excellent (C6-C8): $175-$250, Mint (C10): $325

1967 Dodge Dart 4-door hardtop with red dome roof light, siren, and fender mirror. **12.25 in** (31 cm). **Friction**. Known colors: White. Graphics: State Police - Dodge. Maker: **Nomura**, Japan. Toy marks: TN (Nomura).
Scarcity: 5. Fine to Excellent (C6-C8): $200-$300, Mint (C10): $400

1967 Dodge Dart 4-door hardtop with red dome roof light, sirens, antenna, and lighted side fender markers. **12.25 in** (31 cm). **Battery operated**. Known colors: Black and white. Graphics: Police & P.D. (shield). Maker: **Nomura**, Japan. Toy marks: TN (Nomura).
Scarcity: 4. Fine to Excellent (C6-C8): $175-$250, Mint (C10): $325

1958 Edsel 4-door hardtop. **7.5 in** (19 cm). **Friction**. Known colors: Assorted two tone. Maker: **Sato**, Japan. Toy marks: TOY (Sato). Box marks: TOY (Sato). Box text: *Police Car*.
Notes: Also sold as Olympia Fire Chief and Police Car Set.
Scarcity: 7. Fine to Excellent (C6-C8): $150-$200, Mint (C10): $300

1958 Edsel 2-door hardtop with roof light. **10.5 in** (27 cm). **R/C battery operated**. Known colors: Green and white. Graphics: Police. Maker: **Yonezawa**, Japan. Toy marks: none. Box marks: Y (Yonezawa), SKK (Shinsei).
Scarcity: 6. Fine to Excellent (C6-C8): $200-$300, Mint (C10): $400

1967 Dodge Dart 4-door hardtop with blue dome roof light, sirens, antenna, and lighted side fender markers. **12.25 in** (31 cm). **Battery operated**. Known colors: Green and white. Graphics: Polizei. Maker: **Nomura**, Japan. Toy marks: TN (Nomura).
Scarcity: 4. Fine to Excellent (C6-C8): $175-$250, Mint (C10): $325

98 Police Vehicles

1958 Edsel 2-door hardtop with roof light. **10.5 in** (27 cm). **R/C battery operated**. Known colors: Red and white. Graphics: Police. Maker: **Yonezawa**, Japan. Toy marks: none. Box marks: Y (Yonezawa), SKK (Shinsei).
Scarcity: 6. Fine to Excellent (C6-C8): $200-$300, Mint (C10): $400

1958 Edsel 2-door hardtop with roof light. **10.5 in** (27 cm). **R/C battery operated**. Known colors: Black and white. Graphics: Police. Maker: **Yonezawa**, Japan. Toy marks: none. Box marks: Y (Yonezawa), SKK (Shinsei).
Scarcity: 6. Fine to Excellent (C6-C8): $200-$300, Mint (C10): $400

1958 Edsel 2-door hardtop with roof light, antenna, fender siren, siren sound, and non-stop action. **13.25 in** (34 cm). **Battery operated**. Known colors: Black and white. Graphics: Police. License: Y-3018. Maker: **IY Metal**, Japan. Toy marks: none. Box marks: IY Metal Toy. Box text: *Highway Patrol Car*.
Scarcity: 6. Fine to Excellent (C6-C8): $150-$250, Mint (C10): $400

1958 Edsel 2-door hardtop with roof light, antenna, fender siren, siren sound, and non-stop action. **13.25 in** (34 cm). **Battery operated**. Known colors: Black and white. Graphics: Police - Police Dept. License: FX-1001E. Maker: **Suzuki & Edward**, Japan. Toy marks: S&E (Suzuki & Edward). Box marks: S&E (Suzuki & Edward). Box text: *Highway Patrol Car*.
Scarcity: 6. Fine to Excellent (C6-C8): $125-$300, Mint (C10): $450

1932 Ford Model A Phaeton 4-door sedan. **8 in** (20 cm). **Friction**. Known colors: Blue with black fenders. Graphics: City Police - P.D. Maker: **Bandai**, Japan. Toy marks: Bandai. Box marks: Bandai. Box text: *Old Fashioned City Police #1054*.
Notes: Produced 1960s.
Scarcity: 4. Fine to Excellent (C6-C8): $125-$175, Mint (C10): $250

1952 Ford 2-door sedan with roof light, fender siren, antenna, and two police figures. **10.25 in** (26 cm). **Windup**. Known colors: Black and white. Graphics: Police Car. Maker: **Marusan**, Japan. Toy marks: SAN (Marusan). Box marks: SAN (Marusan). Box text: *Police Car*.
Scarcity: 6. Fine to Excellent (C6-C8): $200-$300, Mint (C10): $375

1952 Ford 2-door sedan with roof light, fender siren, antenna, and two police figures. **10.25 in** (26 cm). **Friction**. Known colors: Black and white. Graphics: Police Car. Maker: **Marusan**, Japan. Toy marks: SAN (Marusan). Box marks: SAN (Marusan). Box text: *Police Car*.
Scarcity: 5. Fine to Excellent (C6-C8): $150-$250, Mint (C10): $350

Public Service Vehicles 99

1955 Ford 4-door sedan with lithographed police in windows. **10 in** (25 cm). **Friction**. Known colors: Blue and cream. Graphics: Police - PD -(shield). Maker: **Asahi**, Japan. Toy marks: ATC (Asahi Toy).
Scarcity: 5. Fine to Excellent (C6-C8): $200-$250, Mint (C10): $300

1952 Ford 2-door sedan with rotating roof light, siren sound, and two police figures. **10.25 in** (26 cm). **Battery operated**. Known colors: Black and white. Graphics: Police Patrol Car. Maker: **Marusan**, Japan. Toy marks: SAN (Marusan). Box marks: SAN (Marusan), Cragston. Box text: *Stop-Go Patrol Car*.
Scarcity: 5. Fine to Excellent (C6-C8): $150-$250, Mint (C10): $350

1956 Ford 2-door hardtop with two police figures lithographed on front and rear window. **12 in** (30 cm). **Friction**. Known colors: Blue and white. Graphics: Patrol - Victoria - Police. Maker: **Marusan**, Japan. Toy marks: SAN (Marusan). Box marks: SAN (Marusan). Box text: *Police Car*.
Scarcity: 10. Fine to Excellent (C6-C8): $400-$600, Mint (C10): $800

1952 Ford 2-door sedan with turning roof light, antenna, and police driver for Scandinavian market. **10.25 in** (26 cm). **Battery operated**. Known colors: Black. Graphics: Polis (roof sign). Maker: **Marusan**, Japan. Toy marks: SAN (Marusan). Box text: *Stop-Go Patrol Car*.
Scarcity: 5. Fine to Excellent (C6-C8): $150-$250, Mint (C10): $325

1957 Ford 2-door hardtop with roof light, siren, and antenna. **16 in** (41 cm). **Friction**. Known colors: Black and white. Graphics: Police - No.6 - Highway Patrol - Ford (hubcaps). Maker: **Yonezawa**, Japan. Toy marks: Y (Yonezawa). Notes: Grille on car is 1956 model.
Scarcity: 6. Fine to Excellent (C6-C8): $450-$550, Mint (C10): $700

1952 Ford 2-door sedan with lithographed figures on windows and hood mounted machine guns, light, and antenna. **10.5 in** (27 cm). **Friction**. Known colors: Red and white. Graphics: Police. Maker: **Niedermeier**, Germany. Toy marks: PN (Niedermeier).
Scarcity: 3. Fine to Excellent (C6-C8): $150-$200, Mint (C10): $250

1958 Ford 2-door hardtop with roof dome light and fender siren. **12.25 in** (31 cm). **Friction**. Known colors: Black, white, and red (black ribbed roof). Graphics: Highway Patrol (shield). License: PD 110. Maker: **Yonezawa**, Japan. Toy marks: Y (Yonezawa). Box marks: Y (Yonezawa).
Scarcity: 7. Fine to Excellent (C6-C8): $350-$450, Mint (C10): $600

1959 Ford 2-door station wagon with lithographed trim. **10.25 in** (26 cm). **Friction**. Known colors: Black and white. Graphics: Police - Highway Patrol. Maker: **Sato Toy**, Japan. Box marks: Sato Toy. Box text: *Highway Patrol*.
Scarcity: 3. Fine to Excellent (C6-C8): $125-$185, Mint (C10): $235

1958 Ford 2-door hardtop with dome roof light, siren, and antenna. **12.25 in** (31 cm). **Battery operated**. Known colors: Black, white, and red (white smooth roof). Graphics: Police - Highway Patrol (shield). License: PD 110. Maker: **Yonezawa**, Japan. Toy marks: Y (Yonezawa). Box marks: Y (Yonezawa). Box text: *Police Car With Mystery Action*.
Scarcity: 7. Fine to Excellent (C6-C8): $350-$450, Mint (C10): $600

(Not pictured) **1959 Ford Fairlane 500 4-door hardtop**. 8.5 in (22 cm). **Friction**. Known colors: Black and white. Graphics: Police. Maker: **Masudaya**, Japan. Toy marks: MT (Masudaya). Box marks: MT (Masudaya).
Scarcity: 5. Fine to Excellent (C6-C8): $100-$150, Mint (C10): $200

(Not pictured) **1959 Ford Fairlane 500 2-door hardtop**. 9 in (23 cm). **Friction**. Known colors: Black and white. Graphics: Police - Highway Patrol. Maker: **Asahi**, Japan. Toy marks: Toymaster (Asahi Toy). Box text: *Sturdy Friction Metal Toy Sedan Series*.
Scarcity: 3. Fine to Excellent (C6-C8): $40-$65, Mint (C10): $95

1960 Ford Galaxie 2-door hardtop with lithographed chassis. **11.5 in** (29 cm). **Friction**. Known colors: Black and white. Graphics: Highway Patrol - Ford - Police (shield). Maker: **Asakusa Toy & Doll**, Japan. Toy marks: ATD (Asakusa Toy & Doll).
Scarcity: 3. Fine to Excellent (C6-C8): $75-$125, Mint (C10): $150

1960 Ford Starliner 2-door hardtop. **11.5 in** (29 cm). **Friction**. Known colors: Black and white. Graphics: Highway Patrol - P.D. - Police (shield). Maker: **Asakusa Toy & Doll**, Japan. Toy marks: none.
Scarcity: 3. Fine to Excellent (C6-C8): $75-$125, Mint (C10): $150

(Not pictured) **1961 Ford Galaxie 2-door hardtop** with rotating roof lights, siren, and antenna. **9.5 in** (24 cm). **Friction with battery**. Known colors: Black, white, and red. Graphics: (Japanese). License: Ford. Maker: **Ichiko**, Japan. Toy marks: Ichiko. Box marks: Ichiko.
Scarcity: 3. Fine to Excellent (C6-C8): $75-$175, Mint (C10): $275

Public Service Vehicles 101

1961 Ford Galaxie 2-door hardtop with rotating roof light. **9.5 in** (24 cm). **Friction**. Known colors: Black, white, and red. Graphics: Highway Patrol. License: Ford. Maker: **Ichiko**, Japan. Toy marks: Ichiko. Box marks: Ichiko. Notes: Ichiko catalog image.
Scarcity: 3. Fine to Excellent (C6-C8): $75-$175, Mint (C10): $275

1961 Ford Thunderbird 2-door hardtop with rotating roof lights. **9.5 in** (24 cm). **Friction**. Known colors: Black and white. Graphics: Highway Patrol - P.D. Maker: **Ichiko**, Japan. Toy marks: Ichiko. Box marks: Ichiko. Notes: Ichiko catalog image.
Scarcity: 3. Fine to Excellent (C6-C8): $75-$125, Mint (C10): $160

1962 Ford Falcon 4-door station wagon with lithographed officers, roof speaker, fender siren, siren sound, and shifting antenna for 2-speed action. **9 in** (23 cm). **Friction**. Known colors: Black and white. Graphics: Highway Police - Patrol - Double Speed Action. Maker: **Alps**, Japan. Toy marks: Alps. Box marks: Alps. Box text: *Highway Patrol Double Speed Action*.
Scarcity: 3. Fine to Excellent (C6-C8): $75-$100, Mint (C10): $125

1961 Ford Galaxie 2-door hardtop with rotating roof lights, trunk mounted sign, mirror, siren, and pull up antenna. **9.5 in** (24 cm). **Friction with battery**. Known colors: White and blue. Graphics: Interpol. License: IK-39-80. Maker: **Ichiko**, Japan. Toy marks: Ichiko. Box marks: Ichiko. Box text: *Ford Interpol*.
Scarcity: 3. Fine to Excellent (C6-C8): $75-$175, Mint (C10): $275

1962 Ford Galaxie 4-door hardtop. **9 in** (23 cm). **Windup**. Known colors: Black and white. Graphics: Patrol - Police Dept (shield). Maker: **Takatoku**, Japan. Toy marks: TT (Takatoku). Box marks: TT (Takatoku). Box text: *Highway Patrol*.
Scarcity: 2. Fine to Excellent (C6-C8): $40-$65, Mint (C10): $90

102 Police Vehicles

1963 Ford Thunderbird 2-door hardtop with roof dome light, sirens and antenna. **8 in** (20 cm). **Friction.** Known colors: Black and white. Graphics: Police - P.D. License: Thunderbird. Maker: **Bandai**, Japan. Toy marks: Bandai. Box marks: Bandai.
Scarcity: 4. Fine to Excellent (C6-C8): $85-$150, Mint (C10): $225

1963 Ford 2-door hardtop with dome roof light, fender sirens, siren sound, and forward/reverse action. **10 in** (25 cm). **R/C battery operated.** Known colors: Black and white. Graphics: Highway Patrol - Galaxie - Ford - Patrol (shield). License: 4341. Maker: **Aoshin**, Japan. Toy marks: ASC (Aoshin). Box marks: ASC (Aoshin). Box text: *New Sound Siren Patrol Car*.
Scarcity: 2. Fine to Excellent (C6-C8): $50-$75, Mint (C10): $100

(Not pictured) **1963 Ford 2-door hardtop** with dome roof light and trunk mounted siren crank. **10 in** (25 cm). **Friction.** Known colors: Black and white. Graphics: Highway Patrol - Galaxie - Ford - Patrol (shield). License: 9511. Maker: **Aoshin**, Japan. Toy marks: ASC (Aoshin).
Scarcity: 2. Fine to Excellent (C6-C8): $50-$75, Mint (C10): $100

(Not pictured) **1963 Ford 2-door hardtop** with dome roof light, siren sound, and forward/reverse action. **10 in** (25 cm). **Battery operated.** Known colors: Black and white. Graphics: Highway Patrol - Galaxie - Ford - Patrol (shield). License: 9511. Maker: **Aoshin**, Japan. Toy marks: ASC (Aoshin).
Scarcity: 2. Fine to Excellent (C6-C8): $50-$75, Mint (C10): $100

1963 Ford Thunderbird 2-door hardtop with dome roof light and forward/reverse action. **8 in** (20 cm). **Battery operated.** Known colors: Black and white. Graphics: Police - P.D. License: Thunderbird. Maker: **Bandai**, Japan. Toy marks: Bandai. Box marks: Bandai.
Scarcity: 3. Fine to Excellent (C6-C8): $100-$150, Mint (C10): $200

1963 Ford 2-door hardtop with blue dome roof light, fender sirens, siren sound, and forward/reverse action. **10 in** (25 cm). **R/C battery operated.** Known colors: Tan. Graphics: Police. License: 4341. Maker: **Aoshin**, Japan. Toy marks: ASC (Aoshin). Box marks: ASC (Aoshin), Telsalda. Box text: *Motorway Patrol Car*.
Scarcity: 2. Fine to Excellent (C6-C8): $50-$75, Mint (C10): $100

(Not pictured) **1963 Ford Galaxie 500 2-door hardtop** with trunk mounted windup siren wheel, dome roof light, and plastic fender siren. **9 in** (23 cm). **Friction.** Known colors: Black and white. Graphics: P-110 (Japanese). Maker: **Terai**, Japan. Toy marks: Daiya (Terai). Box marks: Daiya (Terai).
Scarcity: 3. Fine to Excellent (C6-C8): $85-$135, Mint (C10): $185

(Not pictured) **1963 Ford Galaxie 500 2-door hardtop** with trunk mounted windup siren wheel, dome roof light, and plastic fender siren. **9 in** (23 cm). **Friction.** Known colors: Black and white. Graphics: Police - Patrol - P.D.110. Maker: **Terai**, Japan. Toy marks: Daiya (Terai). Box marks: Daiya (Terai).
Scarcity: 3. Fine to Excellent (C6-C8): $85-$135, Mint (C10): $185

Public Service Vehicles 103

1963 Ford 4-door hardtop with dome roof light, roof sirens, speaker, mirror, antenna, and bump and go action. **12.5 in** (32 cm). **Battery operated**. Known colors: Blue and white. Graphics: Highway Patrol - Police. Maker: **Taiyo**, Japan. Toy marks: Taiyo World Toy.
Scarcity: 5. Fine to Excellent (C6-C8): $125-$175, Mint (C10): $225

1963 Ford 4-door hardtop with dome roof light, roof sirens, speaker, mirror, and antenna. **12.5 in** (32 cm). **Battery operated**. Known colors: Blue and white. Graphics: Police - Emergency. Maker: **Taiyo**, Japan. Toy marks: Taiyo World Toy.
Scarcity: 5. Fine to Excellent (C6-C8): $125-$175, Mint (C10): $225

1963 Ford 4-door hardtop with dome roof light, roof sirens, speaker, mirror, and antenna. **12.5 in** (32 cm). **Battery operated**. Known colors: Black and white. Graphics: P.D. (shield) - Ford. Maker: **Taiyo**, Japan. Toy marks: Taiyo World Toy.
Scarcity: 3. Fine to Excellent (C6-C8): $60-$90, Mint (C10): $130

1963 Ford 4-door hardtop with blue roof light, speakers, siren, mirror, antenna, and trunk mounted speed meter. **12.5 in** (32 cm). **Battery operated**. Known colors: Green. Graphics: Poliziastradale (Map of Italy). Maker: **Taiyo**, Japan. Toy marks: Taiyo World Toy. Box text: *Polizia Stradale*.
Scarcity: 5. Fine to Excellent (C6-C8): $125-$175, Mint (C10): $225

1963 Ford 4-door hardtop with dome roof light, fender siren, mirror, and speed meter. **12.5 in** (32 cm). **Battery operated**. Known colors: Black and white. Graphics: Police - Emergency. Maker: **Taiyo**, Japan. Toy marks: Taiyo World Toy.
Scarcity: 3. Fine to Excellent (C6-C8): $60-$90, Mint (C10): $130

1963 Ford 4-door hardtop with dome roof light, roof sirens, speaker, mirror, antenna, speed meter, and video camera on hood. **12.5 in** (32 cm). **Battery operated**. Known colors: Black and white. Graphics: Squadra Mobile. Maker: **Taiyo**, Japan. Toy marks: Taiyo World Toy.
Scarcity: 5. Fine to Excellent (C6-C8): $125-$175, Mint (C10): $225

104 Police Vehicles

1964 Ford Fairlane 2-door hardtop with flashing light, rotating speakers, and forward/reverse action. **8 in** (20 cm). **Battery operated**. Known colors: Black and white. Graphics: Police - P.D. License: Ford. Maker: **Bandai**, Japan. Toy marks: Bandai. Box marks: Bandai. Box text: *Security car Series #4060*.
Scarcity: 3. Fine to Excellent (C6-C8): $60-$90, Mint (C10): $125

1964 Ford Fairlane 2-door hardtop with flashing light, rotating speakers, forward/reverse action, and steering. **8 in** (20 cm). **R/C battery operated**. Known colors: Black and white. Graphics: Police - P.D. License: Ford. Maker: **Bandai**, Japan. Toy marks: Bandai. Box marks: Bandai. Box text: *Ford Police Car #4096*.
Scarcity: 3. Fine to Excellent (C6-C8): $60-$90, Mint (C10): $125

1964 Ford Taunus 20M 2-door hardtop with blue roof lights, mirror, siren, and forward/reverse action. **9.25 in** (23 cm). **R/C battery operated**. Known colors: Green and white. Graphics: Polizei. License: 64247. Maker: **Ichiko**, Japan. Toy marks: Ichiko. Box marks: Ichiko. Box text: *Elektr. Fernlenk-Polizei Auto Taunus 20M*.
Scarcity: 4. Fine to Excellent (C6-C8): $75-$125, Mint (C10): $175

1964 Ford Thunderbird 2-door hardtop with roof dome light, fender siren, and mirror. **12.25 in** (31 cm). **Friction**. Known colors: Black and white. Graphics: Police - Thunderbird. License: Ford. Maker: **Asahi**, Japan. Toy marks: ATC (Asahi Toy). Box marks: ATC (Asahi Toy). Box text: *Thunderbird Police Car*.
Scarcity: 6. Fine to Excellent (C6-C8): $250-$300, Mint (C10): $375

1964 Ford Galaxie 500, 2-door hardtop with lighted roof sign, siren, blue light, antenna, and speed radar box. **13 in** (33 cm). **Friction with battery**. Known colors: White and blue. Graphics: Interpol. License: FG-1729. Maker: **Ichiko**, Japan. Toy marks: Ichiko.
Scarcity: 4. Fine to Excellent (C6-C8): $175-$250, Mint (C10): $325

1964 Ford Galaxie 500, 2-door hardtop with dome roof light, rotating lights, and antenna. **13 in** (33 cm). **Friction**. Known colors: Black and white. Graphics: Patrol - P.D. (shield). License: FG-1729. Maker: **Ichiko**, Japan. Toy marks: Ichiko.
Scarcity: 4. Fine to Excellent (C6-C8): $150-$225, Mint (C10): $300

Public Service Vehicles 105

1964 Ford Galaxie 500, 2-door hardtop with three roof lights, siren, antenna, driver, and speed radar box. **13 in** (33 cm). **Friction**. Known colors: Black and white. Graphics: Patrol - P.D. (shield). License: FG-1729. Maker: **Ichiko**, Japan. Toy marks: Ichiko.
Scarcity: 4. Fine to Excellent (C6-C8): $150-$225, Mint (C10): $300

1964 Ford Galaxie 500, 2-door hardtop with lighted roof stop sign, siren, red light, antenna, and speed radar box. **13 in** (33 cm). **Friction with battery**. Known colors: Black and white. Graphics: Polis - Ford. License: FG-1729. Maker: **Ichiko**, Japan. Toy marks: Ichiko.
Scarcity: 4. Fine to Excellent (C6-C8): $150-$225, Mint (C10): $300

1964 Ford Galaxie 500, 2-door hardtop with fender siren and light, antenna, and red speed radar box. **13 in** (33 cm). **Friction**. Known colors: Black and white. Graphics: Patrol - P.D. (shield). License: FG-1729. Maker: **Ichiko**, Japan. Toy marks: Ichiko.
Scarcity: 4. Fine to Excellent (C6-C8): $150-$225, Mint (C10): $300

1964 Ford Galaxie 500, 2-door hardtop with lighted roof sign, siren, red light, antenna, and white speed radar box. **13 in** (33 cm). **Friction with battery**. Known colors: White and black. Graphics: Polizei. License: FG-1729. Maker: **Ichiko**, Japan. Toy marks: Ichiko.
Scarcity: 4. Fine to Excellent (C6-C8): $150-$225, Mint (C10): $300

1964 Ford Galaxie 500, 2-door hardtop with lighted roof sign, siren, red light, antenna, and white speed radar box. **13 in** (33 cm). **Friction with battery**. Known colors: Black and white. Graphics: Polis. License: FG-1729. Maker: **Ichiko**, Japan. Toy marks: Ichiko.
Scarcity: 4. Fine to Excellent (C6-C8): $150-$225, Mint (C10): $300

1964 Ford Galaxie 500, 2-door hardtop with lighted roof stop sign, siren, blue light, antenna, and speed radar box. **13 in** (33 cm). **Friction with battery**. Known colors: Blue and white. Graphics: Polizei. License: FG-1729. Maker: **Ichiko**, Japan. Toy marks: Ichiko.
Scarcity: 4. Fine to Excellent (C6-C8): $150-$225, Mint (C10): $300

106 Police Vehicles

1964 Ford Galaxie 500, 2-door hardtop with lighted roof stop sign, siren, blue light, antenna, and speed radar box. **13 in** (33 cm). **Friction with battery**. Known colors: Black and white. Graphics: Polizei. License: FG-1729. Maker: **Ichiko**, Japan. Toy marks: Ichiko.
Scarcity: 4. Fine to Excellent (C6-C8): $150-$225, Mint (C10): $300

1964 Ford Galaxie 500, 2-door hardtop with plastic driver, lighted roof sign, siren, red light, antenna, and white speed radar box. **13 in** (33 cm). **Friction with battery**. Known colors: Black and white. Graphics: Rukspolite - Max Snelheid 50 KM In Bebouwde KOM. License: FG-1729. Maker: **Ichiko**, Japan. Toy marks: Ichiko. Box text: *Rukspolitie*.
Scarcity: 4. Fine to Excellent (C6-C8): $150-$225, Mint (C10): $300

1964 Ford Galaxie 500, 2-door hardtop with lighted roof stop sign, siren, red light, antenna, and speed radar box. **13 in** (33 cm). **Friction with battery**. Known colors: Black and white. Graphics: Polizei (German flag). License: FG-1729. Maker: **Ichiko**, Japan. Toy marks: Ichiko.
Scarcity: 4. Fine to Excellent (C6-C8): $150-$225, Mint (C10): $300

1964 Ford Galaxie 500XL 2-door hardtop with dome roof light, siren, and antenna. **15.25 in** (39 cm). **Friction**. Known colors: Black and white. Graphics: Highway Patrol - Police (shield) Galaxie 500XL. License: XL-500. Maker: **Yonezawa**, Japan. Toy marks: Y (Yonezawa).
Scarcity: 8. Fine to Excellent (C6-C8): $475-$550, Mint (C10): $625

1964 Ford Galaxie 500, 2-door hardtop with lighted roof stop sign, siren, blue light, antenna, and speed radar box. **13 in** (33 cm). **Friction with battery**. Known colors: Black and white. Graphics: Rukspolite - Max Snelheid 50 KM In Bebouwde KOM. License: FG-1729. Maker: **Ichiko**, Japan. Toy marks: Ichiko.
Scarcity: 4. Fine to Excellent (C6-C8): $150-$225, Mint (C10): $300

1964 Ford 4-door hardtop with figure, roof speaker, fender lights, and roof push button. **19 in** (48 cm). **R/C battery operated**. Known colors: Black and white. Graphics: Agente Interpol. License: Ford. Maker: **Rico**, Spain. Toy marks: Rico.
Scarcity: 7. Fine to Excellent (C6-C8): $100-$200, Mint (C10): $350

1964 Ford 4-door hardtop with figure, roof speaker, and roof push button. **19 in** (48 cm). **R/C battery operated**. Known colors: Green and white. Graphics: Policia Trafico. License: Ford. Maker: **Rico**, Spain. Toy marks: Rico.
Scarcity: 7. Fine to Excellent (C6-C8): $100-$200, Mint (C10): $350

1965 Ford Galaxie 500XL 4-door sedan with fender mirrors, flashing bumper machine guns and sound, driver and passenger. **11.25 in** (29 cm). **Battery operated**. Known colors: Black. Graphics: Secret Service - Green Hornet. Maker: **Aoshin**, Japan. Toy marks: ASC (Aoshin). Box marks: ASC (Aoshin). Box text: *Secret Service Action Car - Flashing & Bursting Machine Guns - Throws Lazer Beam - Makes Realistic Sound*
Scarcity: 9. Fine to Excellent (C6-C8): $800-$1,000, Mint (C10): $1,200

1965 Ford Mustang 2-door coupe with dome roof light, siren, mirror, and antenna. **11 in** (28 cm). **Friction**. Known colors: Black and white. Graphics: F.B.I. International - Federal Bureau of Investigation - / -American Automobile Association. License: Mustang. Maker: **Bandai**, Japan. Toy marks: Bandai. Box marks: Bandai. Box text: *Mustang F.B.I. Commander*.
Scarcity: 8. Fine to Excellent (C6-C8): $275-$375, Mint (C10): $480

1965 Ford Galaxie 500XL 2-door convertible. **11.25 in** (29 cm). **Friction**. Known colors: Blue and white. Graphics: Police - 77- P.D. Maker: **Masudaya**, Japan. Toy marks: KKY (Yamato). Box marks: MT (Masudaya).
Scarcity: 6. Fine to Excellent (C6-C8): $75-$150, Mint (C10): $225

1965 Ford Mustang 2-door coupe with dome roof light and forward/reverse action. **11 in** (28 cm). **Battery operated**. Known colors: Green and white. Graphics: Polizei. Maker: **Bandai**, Korea. Toy marks: Bandai.
Scarcity: 4. Fine to Excellent (C6-C8): $75-$125, Mint (C10): $175

1965 Ford Galaxie 500XL 2-door hardtop with large roof mounted crank siren. **11.25 in** (29 cm). **Friction**. Known colors: Black and white. Graphics: (Japanese) Patrol - No.3 - 110. Maker: **Masudaya**, Japan. Toy marks: KKY (Yamato). Box marks: MT (Masudaya).
Notes: Masudaya catalog image.
Scarcity: 4. Fine to Excellent (C6-C8): $75-$125, Mint (C10): $185

1965 Ford Galaxie 500XL 2-door hardtop with antenna, fender mirror, and large roof siren. **11.25 in** (29 cm). **Friction**. Known colors: Black and white. Graphics: P.D. - Highway Patrol - Ford. License: 3141. Maker: **Masudaya**, Japan. Toy marks: KKY (Yamato). Box marks: MT (Masudaya).
Scarcity: 4. Fine to Excellent (C6-C8): $75-$110, Mint (C10): $150

1965 Ford Mustang 2-door convertible with driver, siren, blinking light, push buttons, and antenna. **13.5 in** (34 cm). **Battery operated**. Known colors: Green and white. Graphics: Polizei. License: Polizei. Maker: **Alps**, Japan. Toy marks: none. Box marks: none. Box text: *Polizei-Streifenwagen*.
Scarcity: 4. Fine to Excellent (C6-C8): $150-$300, Mint (C10): $425

1965 Ford Galaxie 500XL 2-door hardtop with dome roof light, fender mirror and siren. **11.25 in** (29 cm). **Friction**. Known colors: Black and white. Graphics: P.D. - Highway Patrol - Police - Ford. License: 3141. Maker: **Masudaya**, Japan. Toy marks: KKY (Yamato). Box marks: MT (Masudaya).
Scarcity: 4. Fine to Excellent (C6-C8): $75-$110, Mint (C10): $150

1966 Ford Mustang Fastback 2-door hardtop with dome roof light and markers, siren, fender mirrors, and antenna. **16 in** (41 cm). **Friction**. Known colors: Black and white. Graphics: Police (and shield). License: Ford and E-147. Maker: **Nomura**, Japan. Toy marks: TN (Nomura). Box marks: TN (Nomura). Box text: *Mustang GT Highway Patrol*.
Scarcity: 7. Fine to Excellent (C6-C8): $350-$450, Mint (C10): $550

1965 Ford Galaxie 500XL 2-door hardtop with large roof mounted crank siren. **11.25 in** (29 cm). **Friction**. Known colors: Blue and white. Graphics: Police - 77- P.D. Maker: **Masudaya**, Japan. Toy marks: KKY (Yamato). Box marks: MT (Masudaya).
Scarcity: 4. Fine to Excellent (C6-C8): $75-$110, Mint (C10): $150

1967 Ford 2-door hardtop with rotating sirens and sound and roof dome light. **8 in** (20 cm). **Friction**. Known colors: Black and white. Graphics: Highway Patrol - P.D. Maker: **Bandai**, Japan. Toy marks: Bandai. Box marks: Bandai. Box text: *Security Car Series #1105*.
Scarcity: 3. Fine to Excellent (C6-C8): $75-$110, Mint (C10): $150

Public Service Vehicles 109

1967 Ford 2-door hardtop with rotating sirens and sound and roof dome light. **8 in** (20 cm). **Battery operated**. Known colors: Blue and white. Graphics: Police - P.D. - 110. Maker: **Bandai**, Japan. Toy marks: Bandai. Box marks: Bandai. Box text: *Ford Police Car #4340*.
Scarcity: 3. Fine to Excellent (C6-C8): $75-$110, Mint (C10): $150

1968 Ford Mustang Fastback 2-door hardtop with dome roof light, rotating speakers, and antenna. **13 in** (33 cm). **Battery operated**. Known colors: Black and white. Graphics: Highway Patrol - P.D. License: 110. Maker: **Bandai**, Japan. Toy marks: Bandai. Box marks: Bandai. Box text: *Highway Patrol Car #4407*.
Scarcity: 5. Fine to Excellent (C6-C8): $200-$275, Mint (C10): $350

1968 Ford Torino GT Fastback 2-door hardtop with dome roof light and markers, fender mirror, and siren. **16 in** (41 cm). **Friction**. Known colors: Black and white. Graphics: Highway Patrol (and shield) - P.D. License: Ford Torino. Maker: **Nomura**, Japan. Toy marks: TN (Nomura). Box marks: TN (Nomura). Box text: *Ford Torino Highway Patrol*.
Scarcity: 7. Fine to Excellent (C6-C8): $350-$450, Mint (C10): $550

(Not pictured) **1969 Ford Capri 2-door sedan** with roof dome light. **11 in** (28 cm). **Friction**. Known colors: Black and white. Graphics: Highway Patrol - P.D. - P.D.9511. Maker: **Aoshin**, Japan. Toy marks: ASC (Aoshin). Box marks: ASC (Aoshin).
Scarcity: 4. Fine to Excellent (C6-C8): $95-$135, Mint (C10): $175

(Not pictured) **1969 Ford Capri 2-door sedan** with roof dome light and twin roof lights. **15 in** (38 cm). **Friction**. Known colors: Black and white. Graphics: Police - 15. Maker: **Ichiko**, Japan. Toy marks: Ichiko. Box marks: Ichiko. Box text: *Ford Capri*.
Scarcity: 4. Fine to Excellent (C6-C8): $150-$225, Mint (C10): $300

1960s Hino Police Van 2-door with opening driver door and roof rack. **9.5 in** (24 cm). **Friction**. Known colors: Black and white. Graphics: Police Dept. - Police. Maker: **Marusan/Hayashi**, Japan. Toy marks: SAN (Marusan), H (Hayashi). Box marks: SAN (Marusan).
Scarcity: 4. Fine to Excellent (C6-C8): $75-$150, Mint (C10): $225

1960s Jeep CJ3, 2 door with vinyl driver, hood light, radar antenna, traffic monitoring console, and forward/reverse action. **7.5 in** (19 cm). **R/C battery operated**. Known colors: White. Graphics: Patrol. Maker: **Bandai**, Japan. Toy marks: Bandai. Box marks: Bandai.
Scarcity: 6. Fine to Excellent (C6-C8): $125-$175, Mint (C10): $225

110 Police Vehicles

1960s Jeep FC 2-door pick up with revolving roof beacon and tin driver ringing bell. Lithographed chassis. **7.5 in** (19 cm). **Friction.** Known colors: Black and white. Graphics: Police Dept. No.2 Emergency Truck - P.D. AHI. Maker: **Nomura**, Japan. Toy marks: TN (Nomura), AHI. Box marks: TN (Nomura), AHI.
Scarcity: 6. Fine to Excellent (C6-C8): $100-$150, Mint (C10): $225

(Not pictured) **1960s Jeep CJ5, 2-door** with bump and go action, tin driver, antenna, flashing hood dome light, and flashing gun which rotates from under hood with sound. **11 in** (28 cm). **Battery operated.** Known colors: Black and white. Graphics: Police. Maker: **Nomura**, Japan. Toy marks: TN (Nomura). Box marks: TN (Nomura). Box text: *Turn-O-Matic Gun Jeep.*
Scarcity: 4. Fine to Excellent (C6-C8): $175-$275, Mint (C10): $375

1960s Jeep CJ3, 2-door with operating lights and siren, engine detail under opening hood, bump-n-go action, antenna, and two tin police figures. **14 in** (36 cm). **Battery operated.** Known colors: White. Graphics: Police Dept - No.3 - Patrol. Maker: **Nomura**, Japan. Toy marks: TN (Nomura). Box marks: TN (Nomura), Rosko. Box text: *Police 'Jeep' with Lights and Siren.*
Scarcity: 6. Fine to Excellent (C6-C8): $250-$400, Mint (C10): $550

(Not pictured) **1960s Jeep CJ3, 2-door. 17.5 in** (44 cm). **Friction.** Known colors: White and black. Graphics: Police - Police Patrol. Maker: **Yonezawa**, Japan. Toy marks: Y (Yonezawa). Box marks: Y (Yonezawa). Box text: *Police Patrol Jeep.*
Notes: Produced 1970s.
Scarcity: 6. Fine to Excellent (C6-C8): $150-$250, Mint (C10): $350

1954 Lincoln 4-door sedan with roof light, headlights, and on/off switch. **8.25 in** (21 cm). **Battery operated.** Known colors: White. Graphics: Police. Maker: **Mizuno/Alps**, Japan. Toy marks: none. Box marks: M (Mizuno). Box text: *Electromobile.*
Scarcity: 4. Fine to Excellent (C6-C8): $200-$275, Mint (C10): $325

1954 Lincoln 4-door sedan with roof light, headlights, and on/off switch. **8.25 in** (21 cm). **Battery operated.** Known colors: Black and white. Graphics: Police. Maker: **Mizuno/Alps**, Japan. Toy marks: none. Box marks: M (Mizuno).
Scarcity: 4. Fine to Excellent (C6-C8): $200-$275, Mint (C10): $325

1956 Lincoln Continental Mark II 2-door sedan with siren, flashing dome light, forward/reverse action. **9.25 in** (23 cm). **R/C battery operated.** Known colors: Black and white. Maker: **Kaname**, Japan. Toy marks: KS (Kaname). Box text: *Police Patrol Car With Siren & Flashing Dome Light.*
Scarcity: 6. Fine to Excellent (C6-C8): $250-$450, Mint (C10): $750

1958 Lincoln Continental Mark III 2-door hardtop with roof dome light, rotating speakers, pull-up antenna, and fender siren. **11.5 in** (29 cm). **Battery operated**. Known colors: Black and white. Graphics: Highway Patrol - P.D. (shield) - Police. Maker: **Bandai**, Japan. Toy marks: Bandai. Box marks: Bandai. Box text: *Lincoln Patrol Car #4075*.
Scarcity: 4. Fine to Excellent (C6-C8): $250-$325, Mint (C10): $400

1960 Lincoln 2-door convertible with fender light and siren, antenna, and radio box. **11.5 in** (29 cm). **Battery operated**. Known colors: Green and white. Graphics: Polizei. License: Lincoln. Maker: **Alps**, Japan. Toy marks: none. Box marks: Alps.
Scarcity: 4. Fine to Excellent (C6-C8): $150-$200, Mint (C10): $250

1958 Lincoln Continental Mark III 2-door hardtop with roof dome light, antenna, and fender sirens. **11.5 in** (29 cm). **Friction**. Known colors: Black and white. Graphics: Highway Patrol - Patrol (shield). Maker: **Bandai**, Japan. Toy marks: Bandai.
Scarcity: 4. Fine to Excellent (C6-C8): $250-$325, Mint (C10): $400

1960 Lincoln 2-door hardtop with blue dome roof light. **11.5 in** (29 cm). **Friction**. Known colors: Green and white. Graphics: Polizei. License: Lincoln. Maker: **Alps**, Japan. Toy marks: none. Box marks: Alps.
Scarcity: 4. Fine to Excellent (C6-C8): $150-$200, Mint (C10): $250

1960 Lincoln 2-door convertible with oversize vinyl police driver, fender light, siren, antenna, and radio box. **11.5 in** (29 cm). **Battery operated**. Known colors: Black, white, and red. Graphics: Police - Patrol (shield). License: Lincoln. Maker: **Alps/Swallow**, Japan. Toy marks: none. Box marks: Alps, Swallow Toys. Box text: *Highway Patrol*.
Scarcity: 3. Fine to Excellent (C6-C8): $150-$200, Mint (C10): $250

1960 Lincoln 2-door hardtop with vinyl driver, roof dome light, antenna, and fender siren. **11.5 in** (29 cm). **Battery operated**. Known colors: Red and white. Graphics: Riot Squad. License: Lincoln. Maker: **Alps**, Japan. Toy marks: Alps. Box marks: Alps. Box text: *Riot Squad Multi Action Patrol Car*.
Scarcity: 4. Fine to Excellent (C6-C8): $150-$200, Mint (C10): $250

112 Police Vehicles

1960 Lincoln 2-door hardtop with vinyl driver, roof dome light, antenna, and fender siren. **11.5 in** (29 cm). **Battery operated**. Known colors: Red and white. Graphics: Riot Squad - (star). License: Lincoln. Maker: **Alps**, Japan. Toy marks: Alps.
Scarcity: 4. Fine to Excellent (C6-C8): $150-$200, Mint (C10): $250

(Not pictured) **1960 Lincoln 2-door hardtop** with vinyl driver, roof dome light, antenna, and fender sirens. **11.5 in** (29 cm). **Battery operated**. Known colors: Black, white, and red. Graphics: (Japanese). License: Lincoln. Maker: **Yonezawa**, Japan. Toy marks: Y (Yonezawa).
Scarcity: 4. Fine to Excellent (C6-C8): $150-$200, Mint (C10): $250

1960 Lincoln 2-door hardtop with roof dome light. **11.5 in** (29 cm). **Friction**. Known colors: Black and white. Graphics: Patrol (shield). License: Lincoln. Maker: **Yonezawa**, Japan. Toy marks: Y (Yonezawa).
Scarcity: 4. Fine to Excellent (C6-C8): $150-$200, Mint (C10): $250

1960 Lincoln 2-door hardtop with roof light. **11.5 in** (29 cm). **Friction**. Known colors: Red and white. Graphics: Police. License: Lincoln. Maker: **Yonezawa**, Japan. Toy marks: none.
Scarcity: 4. Fine to Excellent (C6-C8): $150-$200, Mint (C10): $250

1960 Lincoln 2-door hardtop with blue roof light. **11.5 in** (29 cm). **Friction**. Known colors: Green and white. Graphics: Police. License: Lincoln. Maker: **Yonezawa**, Japan. Toy marks: none.
Scarcity: 4. Fine to Excellent (C6-C8): $150-$200, Mint (C10): $250

1960 Lincoln 2-door hardtop with roof light. **11.5 in** (29 cm). **Friction**. Known colors: Blue and white. Graphics: Police. License: Lincoln. Maker: **Yonezawa/Swallow**, Japan. Toy marks: none. Box marks: Swallow Toys. Box text: *Police Car*.
Scarcity: 4. Fine to Excellent (C6-C8): $150-$200, Mint (C10): $250

1960 Lincoln 2-door hardtop with red roof light. **11.5 in** (29 cm). **Friction**. Known colors: Green and white. Graphics: Police. License: Police. Maker: **Yonezawa**, Japan. Toy marks: none.
Scarcity: 4. Fine to Excellent (C6-C8): $150-$200, Mint (C10): $250

1960 Lincoln 2-door hardtop with vinyl driver with gun, roof dome light, antenna, and fender sirens. **11.5 in** (29 cm). **Battery operated**. Known colors: Black, white, and red. Graphics: Police - Patrol (shield). License: Lincoln. Maker: **Yonezawa**, Japan. Toy marks: Y (Yonezawa).
Scarcity: 4. Fine to Excellent (C6-C8): $175-$225, Mint (C10): $275

Public Service Vehicles 113

1960 Lincoln 2-door hardtop with roof dome light, antenna, and siren. **11.5 in** (29 cm). **Battery operated**. Known colors: Black, white, and red. Graphics: Police - Patrol (shield). License: Lincoln. Maker: **Yonezawa**, Japan. Toy marks: Y (Yonezawa). Box marks: Y (Yonezawa). Box text: *Police Car*. Scarcity: 4. Fine to Excellent (C6-C8): $150-$200, Mint (C10): $250

1950s Mercedes Benz 190 SL 2-door roadster with driver, antenna, siren, and radio light. **9 in** (23 cm). **Battery operated**. Known colors: Black and silver. Graphics: Patrol. Maker: **Sanshin**, Japan. Toy marks: Sanshin. Box marks: Sanshin. Box text: *Mystery Police Car #70*. Scarcity: 5. Fine to Excellent (C6-C8): $300-$400, Mint (C10): $550

1964 Lincoln 4-door hardtop with roof light and forward/reverse action. Large belt mounted remote control. **11 in** (28 cm). **R/C battery operated**. Known colors: Black and white. Graphics: 965 Highway Patrol. Maker: **Nomura**, Japan. Toy marks: TN (Nomura). Box marks: TN (Nomura). Scarcity: 4. Fine to Excellent (C6-C8): $250-$300, Mint (C10): $350

(Not pictured) **1950s Mercedes Benz 190 SL 2-door roadster** with composition driver and blue dome roof light. **8.75 in** (22 cm). **Battery operated**. Known colors: Green and white. Graphics: Polizei. Maker: **Schuco**, Germany. Toy marks: Schuco. Box marks: Schuco. Box text: *Elektro Razzia Car*. Scarcity: 5. Fine to Excellent (C6-C8): $250-$450, Mint (C10): $650

1960s Mercedes Benz 220 S 4-door sedan with siren sound, rotating lights, and roof light. **7.5 in** (19 cm). **Friction**. Known colors: Black and white. Graphics: Police - P.D. (shield). License: Mercedes. Maker: **Ichiko**, Japan. Toy marks: Ichiko. Box marks: Ichiko. Box text: *Highway Patrol With Moving Light*. Scarcity: 3. Fine to Excellent (C6-C8): $50-$100, Mint (C10): $150

(Not pictured) **1960s Mercedes Benz 230 SE 4-door sedan** with blue dome roof light. **8 in** (20 cm). **Windup**. Known colors: Green and white. Graphics: Polizei. Maker: **Aoki**, Japan. Toy marks: Aoki. Scarcity: 4. Fine to Excellent (C6-C8): $150-$200, Mint (C10): $250

1950s Mercedes Benz 300 SL Gullwing 2-door coupe with opening gull wing doors, tin hubcaps, and hood emblem. **9 in** (23 cm). **Friction**. Known colors: Black and white. Graphics: Highway Patrol. Maker: **Bandai**, Japan. Toy marks: Bandai. Scarcity: 7. Fine to Excellent (C6-C8): $225-$275, Mint (C10): $325

114 Police Vehicles

1960s Mercedes Benz 220 4-door hardtop with blue dome roof light, fender siren, forward/reverse action, and steering. **8 in** (20 cm). **R/C battery operated**. Known colors: Green and white. Graphics: Polizei. Maker: **Bandai**, Japan. Toy marks: Bandai. Box marks: Bandai. Box text: *Polizei - Streifenwagen*.
Scarcity: 4. Fine to Excellent (C6-C8): $75-$125, Mint (C10): $160

1960s Mercedes Benz 220 S 4-door sedan with dome roof light and forward/reverse action. **8 in** (20 cm). **R/C battery operated**. Known colors: Green and white. Graphics: Polizei. Maker: **Bandai**, Japan. Toy marks: Bandai. Box marks: Bandai. Box text: *Mercedes Benz Polizei #4041*.
Scarcity: 4. Fine to Excellent (C6-C8): $75-$125, Mint (C10): $160

(Not pictured) **1960s Mercedes Benz 220 SE 4-door sedan** with blue dome roof light and yellow plastic fender sirens. **8.75 in** (22 cm). **Battery operated**. Known colors: Green and white. Graphics: Polizei. Maker: **Daishin**, Japan. Toy marks: DSK (Daishin).
Scarcity: 2. Fine to Excellent (C6-C8): $75-$125, Mint (C10): $175

1960s Mercedes Benz 250 4-door sedan with steering, forward/reverse, blue roof light, and antenna. **9 in** (23 cm). **R/C battery operated**. Known colors: Green and white. Graphics: Polizei. License: Mercedes. Maker: **Shimazaki**, Japan. Toy marks: none. Box marks: SS (Shimazaki). Box text: *Mercedes Benz Polizei*.
Scarcity: 5. Fine to Excellent (C6-C8): $175-$250, Mint (C10): $325

1960s Mercedes Benz 250 SL 2-door convertible with blue roof dome light and fender siren. **10 in** (25 cm). **Friction**. Known colors: Green and white. Graphics: Polizei. License: Benz 250 SL. Maker: **Bandai**, Japan. Toy marks: Bandai. Box marks: Bandai.
Scarcity: 5. Fine to Excellent (C6-C8): $100-$175, Mint (C10): $275

(Not pictured) **1960s Mercedes Benz 280 SE 4-door sedan** with blue roof dome light. **10 in** (25 cm). **Friction**. Known colors: Green and white. Graphics: Polizei. Maker: **Kienberger**, Germany. Toy marks: Huki. Box marks: Huki.
Scarcity: 3. Fine to Excellent (C6-C8): $75-$125, Mint (C10): $175

(Not pictured) **1960s Mercedes Benz 250 4-door sedan** with blue dome roof light, interior and non-fall action. **10.25 in** (26 cm). **Battery operated**. Known colors: Light green and white. Graphics: Polizei. Maker: **Taiyo**, Japan. Toy marks: Taiyo.
Scarcity: 3. Fine to Excellent (C6-C8): $100-$175, Mint (C10): $250

(Not pictured) **1960s Mercedes Benz 250 4-door sedan** with blue dome roof light, blacked out windows, and non-fall action. **10.25 in** (26 cm). **Battery operated**. Known colors: Dark green and white. Graphics: Polizei - C704. Maker: **Taiyo**, Japan. Toy marks: Taiyo.
Scarcity: 3. Fine to Excellent (C6-C8): $100-$150, Mint (C10): $200

(Not pictured) **1960s Mercedes Benz 230 4-door sedan** with red dome roof light, twin roof lights, antenna, and fender sirens. **10.75 in** (27 cm). **Battery operated**. Known colors: Black and white. Graphics: Police - P.D. License: Mercedes Benz 230. Maker: **Ichiko**, Japan. Toy marks: Ichiko. Box marks: Ichiko.
Scarcity: 6. Fine to Excellent (C6-C8): $225-$325, Mint (C10): $500

1960s Mercedes Benz 230 4-door sedan with blue dome roof light, pop up speed meter, antenna, and fender siren and mirror. **10.75 in** (27 cm). **Battery operated**. Known colors: Green and white. Graphics: Polizei. License: Mercedes Benz 230. Maker: **Ichiko**, Japan. Toy marks: Ichiko. Box marks: Ichiko.
Notes: Ichiko catalog image.
Scarcity: 6. Fine to Excellent (C6-C8): $225-$325, Mint (C10): $500

Public Service Vehicles 115

1960s Mercedes Benz 300 SEL 4-door sedan with siren sound, spring antenna, and roof mounted sirens and light. **11 in** (28 cm). **Friction**. Known colors: Black and white. Graphics: Police 12 (Police Dept. Badge). License: A1 4044. Maker: **Asakusa**, Japan. Toy marks: A1 (Asakusa).
Scarcity: 5. Fine to Excellent (C6-C8): $175-$250, Mint (C10): $350

(Not pictured) **1960s Mercedes Benz 230 4-door sedan** with red roof light bar. **11 in** (28 cm). **Battery operated**. Known colors: Black. Graphics: Police. License: Benz 230. Maker: **Bandai**, Japan. Toy marks: Bandai. Box marks: Bandai.
Scarcity: 5. Fine to Excellent (C6-C8): $150-$225, Mint (C10): $300

1960s Mercedes Benz 230 4-door sedan with blue dome roof light. **11 in** (28 cm). **Battery operated**. Known colors: Green and white. Graphics: Polizei. License: Benz 230. Maker: **Bandai**, Japan. Toy marks: Bandai. Box marks: Bandai. Box text: *Tati Tati Benz Police #4073*.
Scarcity: 5. Fine to Excellent (C6-C8): $150-$225, Mint (C10): $300

(Not pictured) **1960s Mercedes Benz 250 SL 2-door coupe** with red dome roof light and fender siren. **11 in** (28 cm). **Battery operated**. Known colors: Black and white. Graphics: Police. Maker: **Terai**, Japan. Toy marks: Daiya (Terai).
Scarcity: 3. Fine to Excellent (C6-C8): $125-$200, Mint (C10): $250

(Not pictured) **1960s Mercedes Benz 250 SL 4-door coupe** with red dome roof light and fender siren. **11 in** (28 cm). **Friction**. Known colors: Black and white. Graphics: (Japanese). Maker: **Terai**, Japan. Toy marks: Daiya (Terai).
Scarcity: 3. Fine to Excellent (C6-C8): $125-$200, Mint (C10): $250

1960s Mercedes Benz 250 SE 4-door sedan with roof speaker, fender sirens, and lithographed windows. Talking car in English. **11 in** (28 cm). **Friction with battery**. Known colors: Black and white. Graphics: Highway Patrol No.483 - P.D. License: MB 250SE. Maker: **Yonezawa**, Japan. Toy marks: Y (Yonezawa).
Scarcity: 3. Fine to Excellent (C6-C8): $150-$225, Mint (C10): $300

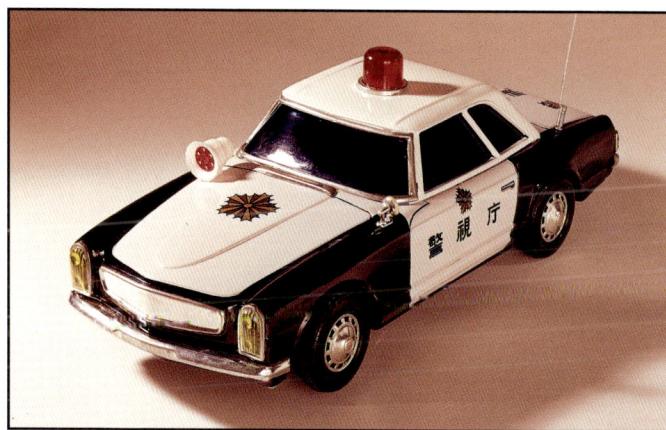

1960s Mercedes Benz 230 SL 2-door coupe with dome roof light, fender siren and mirror, antenna, sound, and no-fall action. **13 in** (33 cm). **Battery operated**. Known colors: Black and white. Graphics: (Japanese). Maker: **Masudaya**, Japan. Toy marks: MT (Masudaya). Box marks: MT (Masudaya). Notes: Masudaya catalog image.
Scarcity: 4. Fine to Excellent (C6-C8): $150-$225, Mint (C10): $300

1960s Mercedes Benz 230 SL 2-door coupe with dome roof light, fender siren and mirror, antenna, sound, and no-fall action. **13 in** (33 cm). **Battery operated**. Known colors: Black and white. Graphics: Highway Patrol - P.D. - 10 - Police. Maker: **Masudaya**, Japan. Toy marks: MT (Masudaya). Box marks: MT (Masudaya). Box text: *New Siren Patrol*.
Notes: Also produced as R/C battery operated model.
Scarcity: 4. Fine to Excellent (C6-C8): $150-$225, Mint (C10): $300

(Not pictured) **1960s Mercedes Benz 280 SE 4-door sedan** with roof dome light, roof sirens, fender siren, and antenna. **13 in** (33 cm). **Battery operated**. Known colors: Black and white. Graphics: Police - P.D. (shield). Maker: **Yonezawa**, Japan. Toy marks: Y (Yonezawa).
Scarcity: 4. Fine to Excellent (C6-C8): $175-$250, Mint (C10): $375

1960s Mercedes Benz 250 S 4-door convertible with fender sirens, hood light, radio box with antenna, and two vinyl police figures. **14 in** (36 cm). **Battery operated**. Known colors: Black and white. Graphics: Police. License: MB 250S. Maker: **Terai**, Japan. Toy marks: Daiya (Terai). Box text: *Police Car*.
Scarcity: 5. Fine to Excellent (C6-C8): $200-$275, Mint (C10): $350

1960s Mercedes Benz 230 SL 2-door coupe with red roof light and Sonicon whistle control. **15.75 in** (40 cm). **Battery operated**. Known colors: Black and white. Graphics: Highway Patrol. Maker: **Masudaya**, Japan. Toy marks: MT (Masudaya). Box marks: MT (Masudaya).
Notes: Masudaya catalog image.
Scarcity: 5. Fine to Excellent (C6-C8): $200-$275, Mint (C10): $325

1960s Mercedes Benz 280 SE 2-door coupe with roof dome light, fender siren, antenna, and fender mirrors. **19.75 in** (50 cm). **Friction**. Known colors: Black and white. Graphics: Patrol - 110 - (Japanese). License: Mercedes Benz. Maker: **Yonezawa**, Japan. Toy marks: Y (Yonezawa).
Scarcity: 7. Fine to Excellent (C6-C8): $250-$350, Mint (C10): $450

(Not pictured) **1970s Mercedes Benz C 111 2-door coupe**. **7 in** (18 cm). **Friction**. Known colors: Black and white. Graphics: Police - P.D. Maker: **Yoneya/Ichiko**, Japan. Toy marks: Yone (Yoneya). Box marks: Ichiko, Yone (Yoneya).
Scarcity: 4. Fine to Excellent (C6-C8): $75-$150, Mint (C10): $225

(Not pictured) **1970s Mercedes Benz C 111 2-door coupe** with blue dome roof light. **8.25 in** (21 cm). **Friction**. Known colors: White. Graphics: Police. Maker: **Nomura**, Japan. Toy marks: TN (Nomura).
Scarcity: 4. Fine to Excellent (C6-C8): $75-$150, Mint (C10): $225

1970s Mercedes Benz 300 SE 2-door coupe with roof dome light and twin roof lights. **24 in** (61 cm). **Friction**. Known colors: Black and white. Graphics: Highway Patrol - Police - 14. License: Mercedes Benz. Maker: **Ichiko**, Japan. Toy marks: Ichiko.
Scarcity: 6. Fine to Excellent (C6-C8): $300-$400, Mint (C10): $500

1958 Mercury 4-door station wagon with roof light and markers. **8 in** (20 cm). **Friction**. Known colors: Black and white. Graphics: Police. Maker: **Bandai**, Japan. Toy marks: Bandai. Box marks: Bandai. Box text: *Mercury Police Car*.
Scarcity: 6. Fine to Excellent (C6-C8): $150-$200, Mint (C10): $250

1958 Mercury Montclair 4-door hardtop with tin fender siren and roof dome light. **11.5 in** (29 cm). **Friction**. Known colors: Black, white, and red. Graphics: Police - Highway Patrol - Mercury. Maker: **Yonezawa**, Japan. Toy marks: Y (Yonezawa).
Scarcity: 5. Fine to Excellent (C6-C8): $275-$350, Mint (C10): $425

Public Service Vehicles

1959 Mercury Montclair 4-door hardtop with working wipers and roof light. **11.5 in** (29 cm). **Friction**. Known colors: Black, white, and red. Graphics: Police - No.110 - P.D. (shield) Mercury. Maker: **Yonezawa**, Japan. Toy marks: Y (Yonezawa).
Scarcity: 5. Fine to Excellent (C6-C8): $250-$325, Mint (C10): $400

1960 Mercury 2-door hardtop with roof dome light. **7 in** (18 cm). **Friction**. Known colors: Black and white. Graphics: Police. Maker: **Shioji**, Japan. Toy marks: none. Box marks: SSS (Shioji). Box text: *Police Car*.
Scarcity: 4. Fine to Excellent (C6-C8): $60-$90, Mint (C10): $150

1967 Mercury Cougar 2-door hardtop with roof dome light, sirens, and fender mirrors. **15 in** (38 cm). **Friction**. Known colors: Black and white. Graphics: Police - Highway Patrol (shield). License: A-9171. Maker: **Asakusa**, Japan. Toy marks: A1 (Asakusa). Box marks: A1 (Asakusa).
Scarcity: 6. Fine to Excellent (C6-C8): $275-$375, Mint (C10): $475

1968 Mercury Cougar 2-door hardtop with roof dome light and non-fall action. **10 in** (25 cm). **Battery operated**. Known colors: Black and white. Graphics: Police - XR-7 - P.D. - Mercury Cougar. License: Cougar. Maker: **Taiyo**, Japan. Toy marks: Taiyo. Box marks: Taiyo. Box text: *Mercury Cougar Police*.
Scarcity: 3. Fine to Excellent (C6-C8): $85-$115, Mint (C10): $150

1960s Nissan/Datsun Bluebird 4-door sedan with fender siren, roof dome light, and antenna. **8.5 in** (22 cm). **Friction**. Known colors: Black and white. Graphics: (Japanese). Maker: **Asahi**, Japan. Toy marks: ATC (Asahi Toy). Box marks: ATC (Asahi Toy).
Notes: Asahi catalog image.
Scarcity: 6. Fine to Excellent (C6-C8): $200-$350, Mint (C10): $500

(Not pictured) **1960s Nissan/Datsun Cedric 2800 4-door sedan** with lithographed trim and siren. **8.75 in** (22 cm). **Friction**. Known colors: Black and white. Graphics: Highway Patrol - NO. 1. Maker: **Takatoku**, Japan. Toy marks: TT (Takatoku).
Scarcity: 5. Fine to Excellent (C6-C8): $175-$250, Mint (C10): $325

1960s Nissan/Datsun Cedric 4-door sedan with roof dome light and fender siren. **11 in** (28 cm). **Friction**. Known colors: Black and white. Graphics: (Japanese). Maker: **Asahi**, Japan. Toy marks: ATC (Asahi Toy). Box marks: ATC (Asahi Toy).
Notes: Asahi catalog image.
Scarcity: 5. Fine to Excellent (C6-C8): $250-$350, Mint (C10): $450

1960s Nissan/Datsun Cedric 4-door convertible with two tin articulated officers, fender siren, antenna, and blue hood light. **15.5 in (39 cm). Battery operated.** Known colors: Dark green and white. Graphics: Highway Patrol - Police - Police Dept. License: P.D.4108. Maker: **Nomura**, Japan. Toy marks: TN (Nomura), Shinkosa.
Scarcity: 6. Fine to Excellent (C6-C8): $350-$600, Mint (C10): $900

1960s Nissan/Datsun Gloria 4-door sedan with roof dome light, fender mirrors, siren, and antenna. **16.5 in (42 cm). Friction.** Known colors: Black and white. Graphics: Nissan Patrol - 110 - (Japanese). Maker: **Yonezawa**, Japan. Toy marks: Y (Yonezawa).
Scarcity: 6. Fine to Excellent (C6-C8): $350-$500, Mint (C10): $650

1960s Nissan/Datsun President 4-door sedan with three roof lights, fender siren, fender mirror, antenna, and siren sound. **18.75 in (48 cm). Friction.** Known colors: Black, white, and red. Graphics: Nissan President (hubcaps) - President (Japanese). License: Japanese. Maker: **Ichiko**, Japan. Toy marks: Ichiko. Box marks: Ichiko. Box text: (Japanese text).
Scarcity: 7. Fine to Excellent (C6-C8): $350-$550, Mint (C10): $750

1970s Nissan 4-door micro-bus with lithographed window, two roof dome lights, and siren sound. **7 in (18 cm). Friction.** Known colors: Black and white. Graphics: Police (Japanese) - N.110. License: A0978. Maker: **Toplay**, Japan. Toy marks: TPS (Toplay). Box marks: TPS (Toplay). Box text: *Siren Emergency Series* (Japanese).
Scarcity: 5. Fine to Excellent (C6-C8): $50-$75, Mint (C10): $100

1956 Oldsmobile 4-door sedan with roof light, siren, antenna, and lithographed police figures on windows. Sonic Radio Control with whistle to change direction. **13.75 in (35 cm). Battery operated.** Known colors: Black and white. Graphics: Police - P.D. (shield). Maker: **Masudaya**, Japan. Toy marks: MT (Masudaya). Box marks: MT (Masudaya). Box text: *Sonicon Patrol Car*.
Scarcity: 4. Fine to Excellent (C6-C8): $250-$325, Mint (C10): $425

(Not pictured) **1958 Oldsmobile 2-door hardtop** with rotating roof light and siren sound. **8.5 in (22 cm). Friction.** Known colors: Blue and white. Graphics: Patrol - High Way Patrol - Oldsmobile. Maker: **Ichiko**, Japan. Toy marks: none.
Scarcity: 3. Fine to Excellent (C6-C8): $115-$175, Mint (C10): $220

Public Service Vehicles 119

1958 Oldsmobile 2-door hardtop with roof dome light, siren, and removable remote control panel with antenna. **11.75 in** (30 cm). **Battery operated**. Known colors: Black and white. Graphics: Highway Patrol (and shield) - Police - Oldsmobile. License: 1962. Maker: **Okuma**, Japan. Toy marks: Okuma. Box marks: Okuma.
Scarcity: 5. Fine to Excellent (C6-C8): $275-$350, Mint (C10): $425

1958 Oldsmobile 2-door hardtop. **12.75 in** (32 cm). **Friction**. Known colors: Black and white. Graphics: Highway Patrol. Maker: **Asahi**, Japan. Toy marks: ATC (Asahi Toy). Box marks: ATC (Asahi Toy).
Notes: Asahi catalog image.
Scarcity: 6. Fine to Excellent (C6-C8): $225-$375, Mint (C10): $475

1959 Oldsmobile 2-door convertible with oversize vinyl police driver, sparking machine gun, hood light, and antenna. **13 in** (33 cm). **Friction with battery**. Known colors: Black, white, and red. Graphics: P.D. - Patrol (shield). Maker: **Ichiko**, Japan. Toy marks: Ichiko.
Scarcity: 4. Fine to Excellent (C6-C8): $200-$275, Mint (C10): $325

1959 Oldsmobile 2-door hardtop with roof sign box that changes cities when pushed down. **13 in** (33 cm). **Friction**. Known colors: Green. Graphics: Map Italy (shield) -Polizia Stradale - V/V. Maker: **Ichiko**, Japan. Toy marks: Ichiko. Box marks: Ichiko. Box text: *Auto Polizia*.
Scarcity: 5. Fine to Excellent (C6-C8): $250-$325, Mint (C10): $375

1959 Oldsmobile 2-door hardtop with rotating roof light and antenna. **13 in** (33 cm). **Battery operated**. Known colors: Black, white, and red. Graphics: P.D. - Patrol (shield). Maker: **Ichiko**, Japan. Toy marks: Ichiko.
Scarcity: 4. Fine to Excellent (C6-C8): $200-$275, Mint (C10): $325

1959 Oldsmobile 2-door hardtop with hood light, antenna, and trunk Speed Meter box. **13 in** (33 cm). **Friction with battery**. Known colors: Black, white and red. Graphics: P.D. - Patrol (shield). Maker: **Ichiko**, Japan. Toy marks: Ichiko. Box marks: Ichiko, Cragstan. Box text: *Highway - P.D. - Patrol*.
Scarcity: 4. Fine to Excellent (C6-C8): $200-$275, Mint (C10): $325

1959 Oldsmobile 2-door hardtop with dome roof light, two rotating lights, and antenna. **13 in** (33 cm). **Friction with battery**. Known colors: Black, white, and red. Graphics: P.D. - Patrol (shield) - Highway Patrol. Maker: **Ichiko**, Japan. Toy marks: Ichiko. Box marks: Ichiko, Cragstan. Box text: *Highway Patrol With Authentic Emergency Siren and Flashing Light*.
Scarcity: 4. Fine to Excellent (C6-C8): $200-$275, Mint (C10): $325

1959 Oldsmobile 2-door hardtop with dome roof light, fender light, antenna, and trunk speed meter box. **13 in** (33 cm). **Friction with battery**. Known colors: Black, white, and red. Graphics: Polizei. Maker: **Ichiko**, Japan. Toy marks: Ichiko.
Scarcity: 4. Fine to Excellent (C6-C8): $200-$275, Mint (C10): $325

1959 Oldsmobile 2-door hardtop with hood light, antenna, and trunk Speed Meter box. No rear fender fins. **13 in** (33 cm). **Friction**. Known colors: Black, white, and red. Graphics: P.D. - Patrol (shield) - Highway Patrol. License: Ichiko. Maker: **Ichiko**, Japan. Toy marks: Ichiko. Box marks: Ichiko, Cragstan/NGS. Box text: *Cragstan Highway Patrol Car - Speed Metering Control Panel*.
Scarcity: 4. Fine to Excellent (C6-C8): $200-$275, Mint (C10): $325

1959 Oldsmobile 2-door hardtop with dome roof light, antenna, and trunk Speed Meter box. **13 in** (33 cm). **Friction with battery**. Known colors: Black, white, and red. Graphics: Rukspolitie. Maker: **Ichiko**, Japan. Toy marks: Ichiko.
Scarcity: 5. Fine to Excellent (C6-C8): $200-$275, Mint (C10): $325

1959 Oldsmobile 2-door hardtop with two rotating roof lights, antenna, and roof Speed Meter box. **13 in** (33 cm). **Friction**. Known colors: Black, white, and red. Graphics: P.D. - Patrol (shield) State Police NJ. Maker: **Ichiko**, Japan. Toy marks: Ichiko. Box text: *Highway Patrol*.
Scarcity: 4. Fine to Excellent (C6-C8): $200-$275, Mint (C10): $325

1959 Oldsmobile 2-door hardtop with dome roof light and rotating lights. **13 in** (33 cm). **Friction with battery**. Known colors: Green and white. Maker: **Rico**, Spain. Toy marks: Rico.
Scarcity: 4. Fine to Excellent (C6-C8): $200-$250, Mint (C10): $325

1959 Oldsmobile 2-door hardtop with roof dome light. **13 in** (33 cm). **R/C battery operated**. Known colors: Black and white. Graphics: Policia. Maker: **Rico**, Spain. Toy marks: Rico.
Scarcity: 4. Fine to Excellent (C6-C8): $200-$250, Mint (C10): $325

1959 Oldsmobile 2-door hardtop with roof dome light and two rotating lights. **13 in** (33 cm). **Friction with battery**. Known colors: Black and white. Graphics: Policia. Maker: **Rico**, Spain. Toy marks: Rico.
Scarcity: 4. Fine to Excellent (C6-C8): $200-$250, Mint (C10): $325

(Not pictured) **1960 Oldsmobile 2-door hardtop** with roof light. **9 in** (23 cm). **Friction**. Known colors: Black and white. Graphics: Police - Highway Patrol. Maker: **Nomura**, Japan. Toy marks: TN (Nomura). Box marks: TN (Nomura). Box text: *Highway Patrol Car*.
Scarcity: 6. Fine to Excellent (C6-C8): $150-$250, Mint (C10): $350

1961 Oldsmobile 4-door hardtop with roof light and working wipers. **12 in** (30 cm). **Friction**. Known colors: Black and white. Graphics: Police - No 10. Maker: **Yonezawa**, Japan. Toy marks: Y (Yonezawa).
Scarcity: 6. Fine to Excellent (C6-C8): $250-$275, Mint (C10): $350

1961 Oldsmobile 4-door station wagon with roof light, siren sound, and working wipers. **12 in** (30 cm). **Friction**. Known colors: Black and white. Graphics: Police Dept. - P.D. (shield). Maker: **Yonezawa**, Japan. Toy marks: Y (Yonezawa). Box marks: Y (Yonezawa), Rosko. Box text: *Highway Patrol*.
Scarcity: 6. Fine to Excellent (C6-C8): $250-$325, Mint (C10): $400

1962 Oldsmobile Starfire 4-door hardtop with dome roof light, rotating lights, and antenna. **11 in** (28 cm). **Friction**. Known colors: Black, white, and red. Graphics: Police - P.D.(shield). Maker: **Ichiko**, Japan. Toy marks: Ichiko.
Scarcity: 6. Fine to Excellent (C6-C8): $225-$275, Mint (C10): $350

1962 Oldsmobile Starfire 4-door hardtop with rotating lights, antenna, and push down speed meter box marked NJ State Police. **11 in** (28 cm). **Friction**. Known colors: Black, white, and red. Graphics: Polis. License: Oldsmobile. Maker: **Ichiko**, Japan. Toy marks: Ichiko.
Scarcity: 6. Fine to Excellent (C6-C8): $225-$275, Mint (C10): $350

1963 Oldsmobile 2-door hardtop with dome roof light and fender siren. **12.5 in** (32 cm). **Friction**. Known colors: Black and white. Graphics: (Japanese) 21. License: 0123 (Japanese). Maker: **Yonezawa**, Japan. Toy marks: Y (Yonezawa). Box marks: Y (Yonezawa).
Scarcity: 6. Fine to Excellent (C6-C8): $300-$400, Mint (C10): $500

122 Police Vehicles

1967 Oldsmobile Toronado 2-door hardtop with dome roof light, siren, and antenna. **15 in** (38 cm). **Friction**. Known colors: Black and white. Graphics: Police - P.D.(shield). Maker: **Asahi**, Japan. Toy marks: ATC (Asahi Toy). Box text: *Toronado Police Car*.
Scarcity: 5. Fine to Excellent (C6-C8): $325-$375, Mint (C10): $450

(Not pictured) **1968 Oldsmobile Toronado 2-door hardtop** with roof light and non-fall action. **10.25 in** (26 cm). **Battery operated**. Known colors: Black and white. Graphics: Police - P.D.-12 -(shield). Maker: **Taiyo**, Japan. Toy marks: Taiyo. Box marks: Taiyo. Box text: *High Way Patrol*.
Scarcity: 3. Fine to Excellent (C6-C8): $75-$125, Mint (C10): $175

1968 Oldsmobile Toronado 2-door hardtop with roof dome light. **17.5 in** (44 cm). **Friction**. Known colors: Black and white. Graphics: Highway Patrol - P.D.(shield) - 11. Maker: **Ichiko**, Japan. Toy marks: Ichiko.
Scarcity: 6. Fine to Excellent (C6-C8): $300-$350, Mint (C10): $400

(Not pictured) **1962 Opel Kadett 2-door sedan** with roof dome light, rotating lights, and antenna. **8.25 in** (21 cm). **Friction**. Known colors: Green and white. Graphics: Polis. Maker: **Ichiko**, Japan. Toy marks: Ichiko. Box marks: Ichiko.
Scarcity: 3. Fine to Excellent (C6-C8): $80-$125, Mint (C10): $175

1965 Opel Admiral 4-door sedan with red dome roof light and antenna. **8 in** (20 cm). **Friction**. Known colors: Red and white. Graphics: Louisiana State Police. Maker: **Bandai**, Japan. Toy marks: Bandai.
Scarcity: 7. Fine to Excellent (C6-C8): $125-$250, Mint (C10): $375

1951 Packard 2-door sedan with lithographed officers on the windows. **9 in** (23 cm). **Friction**. Known colors: Light green and dark green. Graphics: Police - Police Squad - Police car. License: No. 82. Maker: **Masudaya**, Japan. Toy marks: MT (Masudaya).
Scarcity: 4. Fine to Excellent (C6-C8): $125-$250, Mint (C10): $350

1958 Plymouth Fury 2-door hardtop with roof light, antenna, fender siren, and lithographed side windows. **8 in** (20 cm). **Friction**. Known colors: Black and white. Graphics: Highway Patrol - P.D. - Patrol. Maker: **Bandai**, Japan. Toy marks: Bandai. Box marks: Bandai.
Notes: Car has 1957 model side trim.
Scarcity: 3. Fine to Excellent (C6-C8): $60-$90, Mint (C10): $150

1959 Plymouth 4-door hardtop with roof light. **7 in** (18 cm). **Friction**. Known colors: Black and white. Graphics: Police 12. Maker: **Yoneya**, Japan. Toy marks: SY (Yoneya). Box marks: SY (Yoneya). Box text: *Highway Patrol car*.
Scarcity: 4. Fine to Excellent (C6-C8): $60-$110, Mint (C10): $165

Public Service Vehicles 123

1959 Plymouth 4-door hardtop with flashing roof light, siren, antenna, and trunk mounted spare tire. **11 in** (28 cm). **Battery operated**. Known colors: Black and white. Graphics: Police (shield). Maker: **Alps**, Japan. Toy marks: none. Box marks: Alps. Box text: *Police Car With Flashing Light & Realistic Siren*.
Scarcity: 5. Fine to Excellent (C6-C8): $250-$350, Mint (C10): $450

1961 Plymouth 2-door station wagon with roof dome light and radar control box. **12 in** (30 cm). **Friction**. Known colors: Red and white. Graphics: State Police (radar box). Maker: **Ichiko**, Japan. Toy marks: Ichiko.
Scarcity: 5. Fine to Excellent (C6-C8): $200-$275, Mint (C10): $350

1961 Plymouth 4-door hardtop with rotating roof lights and antenna. **12 in** (30 cm). **Friction**. Known colors: Black and white. Graphics: Highway Patrol - P.D. (shield). Maker: **Ichiko**, Japan. Toy marks: Ichiko.
Scarcity: 5. Fine to Excellent (C6-C8): $250-$350, Mint (C10): $450

1961 Plymouth 4-door hardtop with rotating roof lights, antenna, and Speed Meter box. **12 in** (30 cm). **Battery operated**. Known colors: Black and white. Graphics: Highway Patrol - P.D. (shield). Maker: **Ichiko**, Japan. Toy marks: Ichiko. Box text: *Radar Police Car*.
Scarcity: 5. Fine to Excellent (C6-C8): $250-$350, Mint (C10): $450

1961 Plymouth 4-door hardtop with blue roof dome light, rotating roof lights, and antenna. **12 in** (30 cm). **Friction**. Known colors: Green and white. Graphics: Polizei. Maker: **Ichiko**, Japan. Toy marks: Ichiko.
Scarcity: 5. Fine to Excellent (C6-C8): $250-$350, Mint (C10): $450

(Not pictured) **1961 Plymouth 4-door station wagon** with lithographed details. **14 in** (36 cm). **Friction**. Known colors: Black and white. Graphics: Police - Highway Patrol. Maker: **Unknown**, Japan.
Scarcity: 3. Fine to Excellent (C6-C8): $95-$150, Mint (C10): $200

124 Police Vehicles

1938 Pontiac 4-door sedan. **11 in** (28 cm). **Windup.** Known colors: Assorted. Graphics: Police. Maker: **Kuramochi**, Japan. Toy marks: CK (Kuramochi).
Scarcity: 9. Fine to Excellent (C6-C8): $1,000-$2,200, Mint (C10): $3,10

(Not pictured) **1956 Pontiac 2-door hardtop** with roof light, lithographed windows, forward/reverse action, and steering. **9 in** (23 cm). **R/C battery operated.** Known colors: Black and white. Graphics: Police. Maker: **Mitsuhashi**, Japan. Toy marks: M (Mitsuhashi). Box marks: M (Mitsuhashi). Box text: *Police car*.
Scarcity: 3. Fine to Excellent (C6-C8): $80-$120, Mint (C10): $150

1958 Pontiac 2-door station wagon with lithographed tin roof light. **6 in** (15 cm). **Friction.** Known colors: Black and white. Graphics: High Way Patrol. Maker: **Bandai**, Japan. Toy marks: Bandai. Box marks: Bandai. Box text: *Pontiac Security Car Series #662*.
Scarcity: 9. Fine to Excellent (C6-C8): $150-$300, Mint (C10): $450

1967 Pontiac Firebird 2-door coupe with siren and sound and roof light. **8 in** (20 cm). **Friction.** Known colors: Black and white. Graphics: Police - P.D. - Highway Patrol. Maker: **Clover Toy**, Korea. Box marks: Clover. Box text: *2 Asst. Security Cars*.
Scarcity: 3. Fine to Excellent (C6-C8): $55-$100, Mint (C10): $150

1967 Pontiac Firebird 2-door coupe with tinted windows, roof light, and fender mirrors. **16 in** (41 cm). **Friction.** Known colors: Black and white. Graphics: P.D. Police 10. Maker: **Asakusa**, Japan. Toy marks: A1 (Asakusa). Box marks: A1 (Asakusa). Box text: *Pontiac Firebird Police Car*.
Scarcity: 7. Fine to Excellent (C6-C8): $350-$450, Mint (C10): $550

(Not pictured) **1950s Porsche 356 2-door convertible** with blue light and forward/reverse action. **10.5 in** (27 cm). **Battery operated.** Known colors: White. Graphics: Polizei. Maker: **Distler**, Germany. Toy marks: Distler. Box marks: Distler.
Scarcity: 8. Fine to Excellent (C6-C8): $375-$575, Mint (C10): $750

1960s Porsche 911 2-door coupe with steering and forward/reverse action. **7 in** (18 cm). **R/C battery operated.** Known colors: White. Graphics: Polizei. Maker: **Bandai**, Japan. Toy marks: Bandai. Box marks: Bandai. Box text: *Polizei Porsche 911 Elektrisch Mit Fernsteuerung*.
Scarcity: 4. Fine to Excellent (C6-C8): $85-$150, Mint (C10): $235

1960s Porsche 912 2-door coupe with blue roof dome light, steering, and forward/reverse action. Detachable remote control. **7 in** (18 cm). **R/C battery operated.** Known colors: White. Graphics: Polizei. License: 1966. Maker: **Bandai**, Japan. Toy marks: Bandai. Box marks: Bandai. Box text: *#IIF905 Autobahn Streifenwagen set*.
Notes: Combined with ADAC VW as Autobahn Streifenwagen set.
Scarcity: 4. Fine to Excellent (C6-C8): $125-$175, Mint (C10): $225

Public Service Vehicles 125

1960s Porsche 912 2-door coupe with blue roof dome light, steering, and forward/reverse action. **7 in** (18 cm). **R/C battery operated**. Known colors: White. Graphics: Polizei. License: 2016. Maker: **Bandai**, Japan. Toy marks: Bandai. Box marks: Bandai. Box text: *Polizei Porsche Modell 912 Elektrisch Mit Fernsteurerung*.
Scarcity: 4. Fine to Excellent (C6-C8): $125-$175, Mint (C10): $225

1960s Porsche 911S 2-door coupe with roof dome light, siren, and stand up roll-over action. **10 in** (25 cm). **Battery operated**. Known colors: Black and white. Graphics: Police P.D. Acrobat Highway Patrol. Maker: **Toplay**, Japan. Toy marks: TPS (Toplay). Box marks: TPS (Toplay). Box text: *Acrobat Team Porsche*.
Scarcity: 4. Fine to Excellent (C6-C8): $75-$100, Mint (C10): $125

(Not pictured) **1960s Porsche 911S 2-door coupe** with dome roof light and fender siren. **10.25 in** (26 cm). **Friction**. Known colors: Black and white. Graphics: Police - (Japanese). Maker: **Takatoku**, Japan. Toy marks: TT (Takatoku). Box marks: TT (Takatoku).
Scarcity: 4. Fine to Excellent (C6-C8): $125-$175, Mint (C10): $225

(Not pictured) **1960s Porsche 911S 2-door coupe** with dome roof light and fender siren. **10.25 in** (26 cm). **Battery operated**. Known colors: Black and white. Graphics: Police - Highway Patrol - Police Dept. Maker: **Takatoku**, Japan. Toy marks: TT (Takatoku). Box marks: TT (Takatoku).
Scarcity: 4. Fine to Excellent (C6-C8): $125-$175, Mint (C10): $225

(Not pictured) **1960s Porsche 912S 2-door coupe** with roof dome light and siren sound. **11 in** (28 cm). **Battery operated**. Known colors: Black and white. Graphics: Highway Patrol - PD. Maker: **Aoshin**, Japan. Toy marks: Aoshin. Box marks: Aoshin. Box text: *Porsche 912S Patrol Car*.
Scarcity: 4. Fine to Excellent (C6-C8): $150-$275, Mint (C10): $375

(Not pictured) **1960s Porsche 912S 2-door coupe** with roof dome light and European siren sound. **11 in** (28 cm). **Battery operated**. Known colors: White. Graphics: Police. Maker: **Aoshin**, Japan. Toy marks: Aoshin. Box marks: Aoshin. Box text: *Porsche Police Car with Pee-Po Siren and Revolving*.
Scarcity: 4. Fine to Excellent (C6-C8): $150-$275, Mint (C10): $375

(Not pictured) **1950s Renault Floride 4-door sedan** with blue roof dome light, marker lights, fender siren, fender mirror, and antenna. **10.5 in** (27 cm). **Battery operated**. Known colors: Black and white. Graphics: Police. Maker: **Ichiko**, Japan. Toy marks: Ichiko.
Scarcity: 5. Fine to Excellent (C6-C8): $125-$175, Mint (C10): $225

(Not pictured) **1950s Toyota Toyopet Crown 4-door sedan** with antenna and fender mounted sirens. **8.75 in** (22 cm). **Friction**. Known colors: Black and white. Graphics: (Japanese). Maker: **Bandai**, Japan. Toy marks: Bandai. Box marks: Bandai. Box text: *Toyopet Crown Patrol* (in Japanese).
Scarcity: 7. Fine to Excellent (C6-C8): $600-$800, Mint (C10): $1,000

1950s Toyota Toyopet Crown 4-door sedan with antenna and fender and roof siren. **9.25 in** (23 cm). **Friction**. Known colors: Black and white. Graphics: (Japanese). Maker: **Asahi**, Japan. Toy marks: ATC (Asahi Toy). Box marks: ATC (Asahi Toy).
Notes: Asahi catalog image.
Scarcity: 8. Fine to Excellent (C6-C8): $800-$1,000, Mint (C10): $1,300

1960s Toyota Toyopet Crown 4-door sedan with roof dome light, steering, and forward/reverse action. **7.5 in** (19 cm). **R/C battery operated**. Known colors: Black and white. Graphics: (Japanese) 110. Maker: **Bandai**, Japan. Toy marks: Bandai. Box marks: Bandai.
Scarcity: 4. Fine to Excellent (C6-C8): $100-$165, Mint (C10): $225

126 Police Vehicles

1960s Toyota Publica 2-door sedan with roof dome light, fender sirens, forward/reverse, and steering. **8.25 in** (21 cm). **R/C battery operated**. Known colors: Black and white. Graphics: (Japanese). License: 110. Maker: **Bandai**, Japan. Toy marks: Bandai. Box marks: Bandai.
Scarcity: 5. Fine to Excellent (C6-C8): $200-$300, Mint (C10): $400

1960s Toyota Crown Deluxe 4-door sedan with blue dome roof light, fender siren and mirrors, and pull-up antenna. **10 in** (25 cm). **Friction**. Known colors: Black and white. Graphics: Polizei. Maker: **Asahi**, Japan. Toy marks: ATC (Asahi Toy). Box marks: ATC (Asahi Toy).
Scarcity: 6. Fine to Excellent (C6-C8): $350-$400, Mint (C10): $500

1960s Toyota Crown Deluxe 4-door sedan with dome roof light and fender siren. **10 in** (25 cm). **Friction**. Known colors: Black and white. Graphics: Highway Patrol - Police. Maker: **Asahi**, Japan. Toy marks: ATC (Asahi Toy). Box marks: ATC (Asahi Toy).
Scarcity: 7. Fine to Excellent (C6-C8): $325-$400, Mint (C10): $525

1960s Toyota Toyopet Corona 4-door sedan with fender mirrors, siren, dome roof light, and antenna. **10.5 in** (27 cm). **Friction**. Known colors: Black and white. Maker: **Asahi**, Japan. Toy marks: ATC (Asahi Toy). Box marks: ATC (Asahi Toy).
Scarcity: 6. Fine to Excellent (C6-C8): $350-$500, Mint (C10): $650

(Not pictured) **1960s Toyota Toyopet Crown 4-door sedan** with dome roof light, rotating speakers, fender siren, and mirrors. **10.5 in** (27 cm). **Battery operated**. Known colors: Black and white. Graphics: (Japanese). Maker: **Bandai**, Japan. Toy marks: Bandai.
Scarcity: 6. Fine to Excellent (C6-C8): $550-$800, Mint (C10): $1,100

(Not pictured) **1960s Toyota Toyopet Crown 4-door sedan** with antenna and roof mounted light. **10.5 in** (27 cm). **Radio Control battery operated**. Known colors: Black and white. Graphics: (Japanese). Maker: **Bandai**, Japan. Toy marks: Bandai. Box marks: Bandai. Box text: *Toyopet Crown Patrol* (in Japanese).
Scarcity: 7. Fine to Excellent (C6-C8): $700-$900, Mint (C10): $1,100

1960s Toyota Crown Deluxe 4-door sedan with roof dome light, antenna, and fender mirrors and siren. **10 in** (25 cm). **Friction**. Known colors: Black and white. Graphics: (Japanese). Maker: **Asahi**, Japan. Toy marks: ATC (Asahi Toy). Box marks: ATC (Asahi Toy).
Scarcity: 7. Fine to Excellent (C6-C8): $375-$425, Mint (C10): $575

Public Service Vehicles 127

1960s Toyota Crown Deluxe 4-door sedan with fender siren and dome roof light. **11.25 in** (29 cm). **Friction**. Known colors: Black and white. Maker: **Asahi**, Japan. Toy marks: ATC (Asahi Toy). Box marks: ATC (Asahi Toy). Notes: Asahi catalog image.
Scarcity: 5. Fine to Excellent (C6-C8): $300-$400, Mint (C10): $500

(Not pictured) **1960s Toyota Crown 4-door sedan** with roof dome light, rotating lights, fender mirrors, and antenna. **12.5 in** (32 cm). **Friction**. Known colors: Black and white. Graphics: (Japanese). Maker: **Ichiko**, Japan. Toy marks: Ichiko. Box marks: Ichiko.
Scarcity: 5. Fine to Excellent (C6-C8): $200-$300, Mint (C10): $400

(Not pictured) **1960s Toyota Toyopet Crown 2-door hardtop** with roof dome light and fender siren. **13.75 in** (35 cm). **Friction**. Known colors: Black and white. Graphics: (Japanese). License: Crown (Japanese). Maker: **Aoshin**, Japan. Toy marks: ASC (Aoshin).
Scarcity: 5. Fine to Excellent (C6-C8): $200-$250, Mint (C10): $300

1960s Toyota 2000 GT 2-door coupe with roof dome light and fender siren. **14.5 in** (37 cm). **Friction**. Known colors: Black and white. Graphics: Highway Patrol - P.D. - 7. Maker: **Ichiko**, Japan. Toy marks: Ichiko. Box marks: Ichiko.
Scarcity: 4. Fine to Excellent (C6-C8): $150-$250, Mint (C10): $400

1960s Toyota Sports-800 2-door coupe. **15 in** (38 cm). **Friction**. Known colors: Black and white. Graphics: 21 (Japanese). Maker: **Asahi**, Japan. Toy marks: ATC (Asahi Toy). Box marks: ATC (Asahi Toy). Notes: Asahi catalog image.
Scarcity: 6. Fine to Excellent (C6-C8): $400-$600, Mint (C10): $800

(Not pictured) **1960s Toyota Crown Deluxe 4-door sedan** with fender mirrors and lights, dome roof light and siren, and folding antenna. **15.5 in** (39 cm). **Battery operated**. Known colors: Black and white. Graphics: Highway Patrol - Police. Maker: **Yonezawa**, Japan. Toy marks: Y (Yonezawa).
Scarcity: 6. Fine to Excellent (C6-C8): $400-$525, Mint (C10): $650

(Not pictured) **1960s Toyota Corona 2-door hardtop** with dome roof light and fender siren. **16.5 in** (42 cm). **Friction**. Known colors: Black and white. Graphics: Corona Mark II - NO.261 - (Japanese). License: Mark II. Maker: **Aoshin**, Japan. Toy marks: Aoshin.
Scarcity: 5. Fine to Excellent (C6-C8): $200-$250, Mint (C10): $300

(Not pictured) **1960s Toyota Crown Deluxe 4-door sedan** with fender mirrors, fender siren, chrome roof lights, dome light, and antenna. **18 in** (46 cm). **Friction**. Known colors: Black, white, and red. Graphics: (Japanese). License: (Japanese). Maker: **Nomura**, Japan. Toy marks: TN (Nomura).
Scarcity: 8. Fine to Excellent (C6-C8): $500-$650, Mint (C10): $850

1960s Triumph TR-4, 2-door coupe with, fender siren, dome roof light, and trunk mounted crank siren. **8.25 in** (21 cm). **Friction**. Known colors: Black and white. Graphics: Police. Maker: **Terai**, Japan. Toy marks: Daiya (Terai).
Scarcity: 8. Fine to Excellent (C6-C8): $125-$175, Mint (C10): $225

1960s Undetermined 2-door with four tin police figures, red roof light, and front window shield. **10 in** (25 cm). **Friction**. Known colors: Black and white. Graphics: Police Truck. Maker: **Yonezawa**, Japan. Toy marks: Y (Yonezawa).
Scarcity: 9. Fine to Excellent (C6-C8): $1,200-$1,500, Mint (C10): $1,800

(Not pictured) **1950/60s Volkswagen Transporter van**. **6 in** (15 cm). **Friction**. Known colors: Blue and white. Graphics: Police - No 521. License: P-521-D. Maker: **Payva**, Spain. Toy marks: Payva. Box marks: Payva. Box text: *Furgoneta Volkswagen*.
Notes: Produced 1980s.
Scarcity: 5. Fine to Excellent (C6-C8): $50-$100, Mint (C10): $135

128 Police Vehicles

1950/60s Volkswagen Transporter micro-bus with flashing dome light and forward/reverse action. **7 in** (18 cm). **R/C battery operated**. Known colors: Black and white. Graphics: Police - No.20. Maker: **Okyasu**, Japan. Toy marks: EO (Okyasu). Box marks: EO (Okyasu). Box text: *Police Car*.
Scarcity: 2. Fine to Excellent (C6-C8): $40-$80, Mint (C10): $120

1950/60s Volkswagen Transporter micro-bus with flashing dome light and forward/reverse action. **7.5 in** (19 cm). **R/C battery operated**. Known colors: Black and white. Graphics: Police. Maker: **Suzuki**, Japan. Box marks: SK (Suzuki). Box text: *Emergency Series*.
Scarcity: 3. Fine to Excellent (C6-C8): $75-$125, Mint (C10): $175

1950/60s Volkswagen Transporter van with blue roof dome light, forward/reverse action, and steering. **7.75 in** (20 cm). **R/C battery operated**. Known colors: Black and white. Graphics: Police Dept. Maker: **Bandai**, Japan. Toy marks: Bandai.
Scarcity: 5. Fine to Excellent (C6-C8): $150-$225, Mint (C10): $300

1950/60s Volkswagen Transporter van. 9 in (23 cm). **Friction**. Known colors: Black and white. Graphics: Police Dept - P.D. - 7901. License: P-501. Maker: **Taiyo**, Japan. Toy marks: Taiyo World Toy.
Scarcity: 4. Fine to Excellent (C6-C8): $50-$90, Mint (C10): $145

1950/60s Volkswagen Transporter van with lithographed police occupants, blue roof dome light, forward/reverse action, and steering. **9 in** (23 cm). **R/C battery operated**. Known colors: Black and white. Graphics: Polizei – Verkehrsunfall Bereitschaft. Maker: **Terai**, Japan. Toy marks: Daiya (Terai).
Scarcity: 5. Fine to Excellent (C6-C8): $85-$145, Mint (C10): $195

(Not pictured) **1950/60s Volkswagen Transporter micro-bus** with opening side doors and dome roof light. **9.5 in** (24 cm). **Friction**. Known colors: White and black. Graphics: Police. Maker: **Tipp & Co.**, Germany. Toy marks: TCO (Tipp).
Scarcity: 7. Fine to Excellent (C6-C8): $600-$800, Mint (C10): $1,000

(Not pictured) **1950/60s Volkswagen Transporter van** with opening side doors. **9.5 in** (24 cm). **Friction**. Known colors: Green and white. Graphics: Polizeiwagen. Maker: **Tipp & Co.**, Germany. Toy marks: TCO (Tipp).
Scarcity: 8. Fine to Excellent (C6-C8): $800-$1,000, Mint (C10): $1,200

(Not pictured) **1950/60s Volkswagen Transporter micro-bus** with siren sound, dome roof light, and darkened windows. **10 in** (25 cm). **R/C battery operated**. Known colors: Black and white. Graphics: Police. Maker: **Terai**, Japan. Toy marks: Daiya (Terai). Box marks: Daiya (Terai). Box text: *VW Police Van*.
Scarcity: 4. Fine to Excellent (C6-C8): $100-$150, Mint (C10): $210

(Not pictured) **1950/60s Volkswagen Transporter micro-bus** with siren sound, dome roof light, and skylights. **10.25 in** (26 cm). **Friction**. Known colors: Black and white. Graphics: 110 (Japanese). Maker: **Ichiko**, Japan. Toy marks: Ichiko. Box marks: Ichiko. Box text: *VW Patrol*.
Notes: Produced 1980s.
Scarcity: 2. Fine to Excellent (C6-C8): $35-$45, Mint (C10): $60

Public Service Vehicles 129

(Not pictured) **1950/60s Volkswagen Transporter micro-bus** with flashing dome light, siren sound, and two plastic dogs. **11.25 in** (29 cm). **Battery operated**. Known colors: Blue and white. Graphics: Police Canine Patrol Car. Maker: **Yonezawa**, Japan. Toy marks: Y (Yonezawa). Box marks: Y (Yonezawa). Box text: *Canine Patrol Car With 2 Dogs*.
Scarcity: 7. Fine to Excellent (C6-C8): $200-$325, Mint (C10): $450

(Not pictured) **1950/60s Volkswagen Transporter micro-bus** with flashing dome light, siren sound, and bump and go action. **11.25 in** (29 cm). **Battery operated**. Known colors: Green and white. Graphics: Polizei - 537. Maker: **Yonezawa**, Japan. Toy marks: Y (Yonezawa).
Scarcity: 5. Fine to Excellent (C6-C8): $150-$250, Mint (C10): $325

1960s Volkswagen Beetle 2-door convertible with driver, policeman, light, and forward/reverse action. **7 in** (18 cm). **R/C battery operated**. Known colors: Red. License: 1967. Maker: **Bandai**, Japan. Toy marks: Bandai.
Scarcity: 4. Fine to Excellent (C6-C8): $75-$125, Mint (C10): $185

1960s Volkswagen 1500 2-door sedan. **7.5 in** (19 cm). **Windup**. Known colors: Black and white. Graphics: Police - P.D. License: Volkswagen. Maker: **Ichiko**, Japan. Toy marks: none. Box marks: Ichiko. Box text: *Volkswagen 1500 Police car*.
Scarcity: 5. Fine to Excellent (C6-C8): $90-$140, Mint (C10): $185

1960s Volkswagen Beetle 2-door convertible with police driver and passenger, light, and forward/reverse action. **7 in** (18 cm). **R/C battery operated**. Known colors: Green and white. Graphics: Polizei. License: 2016. Maker: **Bandai**, Japan. Toy marks: Bandai.
Scarcity: 4. Fine to Excellent (C6-C8): $75-$125, Mint (C10): $185

1960s Volkswagen 1500 2-door sedan with blue dome roof light. **8 in** (20 cm). **Friction**. Known colors: Green and white. Graphics: Polizei. License: Volkswagen 1500. Maker: **Bandai**, Japan. Toy marks: Bandai. Box marks: Bandai.
Scarcity: 7. Fine to Excellent (C6-C8): $150-$250, Mint (C10): $350

1960s Volkswagen Beetle 2-door sedan with blue roof light and two sirens. **7 in** (18 cm). **Battery operated**. Known colors: Green. Maker: **Unknown**, Japan. Toy marks: none.
Scarcity: 3. Fine to Excellent (C6-C8): $60-$90, Mint (C10): $125

130 Police Vehicles

1960s Volkswagen Beetle 2-door sedan with blue dome roof light. **8 in** (20 cm). **Friction**. Known colors: Black. Graphics: Politie. Maker: **Bandai**, Japan. Toy marks: Bandai. Box marks: Bandai. Box text: *Volkswagen Police Car*.
Scarcity: 4. Fine to Excellent (C6-C8): $125-$175, Mint (C10): $250

1960s Volkswagen Beetle 2-door sedan with blue dome roof light. **8 in** (20 cm). **Friction**. Known colors: Green and white. Graphics: Politie. Maker: **Bandai**, Japan. Toy marks: Bandai. Box marks: Bandai. Box text: *Volkswagen Police Car #824*.
Scarcity: 4. Fine to Excellent (C6-C8): $90-$140, Mint (C10): $200

1960s Volkswagen Beetle 2-door sedan with blue roof dome light and antenna. **8 in** (20 cm). **Friction**. Known colors: White. Graphics: Politie. License: HP 82-05. Maker: **Bandai**, Japan. Toy marks: Bandai. Box marks: Bandai.
Notes: Note the variations of this model.
Scarcity: 4. Fine to Excellent (C6-C8): $125-$175, Mint (C10): $250

1960s Volkswagen Beetle 2-door sedan with roof sign and speaker and fender siren. **8 in** (20 cm). **Friction**. Known colors: Black. Graphics: Politie (roof sign). License: ZX64-02. Maker: **Bandai**, Japan. Toy marks: Bandai. Box marks: Bandai.
Scarcity: 5. Fine to Excellent (C6-C8): $200-$300, Mint (C10): $400

1960s Volkswagen Beetle 2-door sedan with blue roof dome light, tinted windows, and headlights. **8 in** (20 cm). **Friction**. Known colors: Green and white. Graphics: Polizei. Maker: **Bandai**, Japan. Toy marks: Bandai.
Scarcity: 3. Fine to Excellent (C6-C8): $60-$90, Mint (C10): $125

1960s Volkswagen Beetle 2-door sedan with blue roof dome light. **10 in** (25 cm). **Friction**. Known colors: White. Maker: **Asahi**, Japan. Toy marks: Toymaster (Asahi Toy).
Scarcity: 3. Fine to Excellent (C6-C8): $50-$100, Mint (C10): $150

Public Service Vehicles 131

1960s Volkswagen Beetle 2-door sedan with flashing blue dome roof light, siren sound, and lithographed police in windows. **10 in** (25 cm). **Battery operated**. Known colors: Green and white. Graphics: Polizei. Maker: **Masudaya**, Japan. Toy marks: MT (Masudaya). Box marks: MT (Masudaya). Box text: *Volkswagen Polizei*.
Scarcity: 6. Fine to Excellent (C6-C8): $200-$300, Mint (C10): $400

1960s Volkswagen Beetle 2-door sedan with large roof siren, antenna, and bump and go action. **10.75 in** (27 cm). **Battery operated**. Known colors: Black and white. Graphics: P.D. - Police. Maker: **Masudaya**, Japan. Toy marks: MT (Masudaya). Box marks: MT (Masudaya). Box text: *V.W. Riot Squad Car*.
Scarcity: 4. Fine to Excellent (C6-C8): $90-$150, Mint (C10): $200

1960s Volkswagen Beetle 2-door sedan with blue dome roof light. **10.5 in** (27 cm). **Battery operated**. Known colors: Grün und weiss. Maker: **Bandai**, Japan. Toy marks: Bandai. Box marks: Bandai. Box text: *#4074*.
Scarcity: 6. Fine to Excellent (C6-C8): $250-$350, Mint (C10): $475

1960s Volkswagen Beetle 2-door sedan with flashing blue roof light, two sirens, antenna, and bump and go action. **10.75 in** (27 cm). **Battery operated**. Known colors: Black and white. Graphics: P.D. - Polis. Maker: **Masudaya**, Japan. Toy marks: MT (Masudaya). Box marks: MT (Masudaya).
Scarcity: 4. Fine to Excellent (C6-C8): $90-$150, Mint (C10): $200

(Not pictured) **1960s Volkswagen Beetle 2-door sedan** with flashing roof light, sirens, antenna, and bump and go action. **10.75 in** (27 cm). **Battery operated**. Known colors: Green and white. Graphics: Polizei. Maker: **Masudaya**, Japan. Toy marks: MT (Masudaya). Box marks: MT (Masudaya).
Scarcity: 4. Fine to Excellent (C6-C8): $90-$150, Mint (C10): $200

1960s Volkswagen Beetle 2-door sedan with flashing roof dome light, sirens, antenna, and bump and go action. **10.75 in** (27 cm). **Battery operated**. Known colors: Black and white. Graphics: P.D. - Police. Maker: **Masudaya**, Japan. Toy marks: MT (Masudaya). Box marks: MT (Masudaya). Notes: Also produced as R/C model.
Scarcity: 4. Fine to Excellent (C6-C8): $90-$150, Mint (C10): $200

1960s Volkswagen Beetle 2-door convertible with bump and go action and blue flashing light. **13 in** (33 cm). **Battery operated**. Known colors: Green and white. Maker: **Nomura**, Japan. Toy marks: TN (Nomura). Box marks: TN (Nomura).
Scarcity: 9. Fine to Excellent (C6-C8): $600-$800, Mint (C10): $1,000

132 Police Vehicles

1960s Volkswagen Karmann Ghia 2-door coupe with two rotating roof lights and fender siren. **8.75 in** (22 cm). **Friction**. Known colors: Black and white. Graphics: Polis. Maker: **Ichiko**, Japan. Toy marks: Ichiko. Box marks: Ichiko. Box text: *Polis with 2 Moving Lights*.
Notes: Also produced as Polizei model and R/C battery operated model.
Scarcity: 5. Fine to Excellent (C6-C8): $125-$165, Mint (C10): $225

(Not pictured) **1950s Volvo P 1900 2-door coupe** with siren and flashing dome roof light. **8.25 in** (21 cm). **R/C battery operated**. Known colors: Black and white. Graphics: Police. Maker: **Kaname**, Japan. Toy marks: none. Box marks: Cragstan. Box text: *Police Car*.
Scarcity: 7. Fine to Excellent (C6-C8): $200-$325, Mint (C10): $450

1960s Volvo 144 4-door sedan with yellow dome roof light, forward/reverse action, and steering. **8 in** (20 cm). **R/C battery operated**. Known colors: Black and white. Graphics: Polis. License: 144. Maker: **Bandai**, Japan. Toy marks: Bandai. Box marks: Bandai.
Scarcity: 4. Fine to Excellent (C6-C8): $60-$90, Mint (C10): $120

1960s Volvo 144 4-door sedan with blue dome roof light, forward/reverse action, and steering. **8 in** (20 cm). **R/C battery operated**. Known colors: Black and white. Graphics: Politi. License: 144. Maker: **Bandai**, Japan. Toy marks: Bandai. Box marks: Bandai. Box text: *Volvo Politi*.
Scarcity: 4. Fine to Excellent (C6-C8): $60-$90, Mint (C10): $120

1960s Volvo 164 4-door sedan with red dome roof light, steering, and forward/reverse action. **8 in** (20 cm). **R/C battery operated**. Known colors: Black and white. Graphics: Police - P.D. Maker: **Bandai**, Japan. Toy marks: Bandai. Box marks: Bandai.
Scarcity: 3. Fine to Excellent (C6-C8): $60-$90, Mint (C10): $120

1960s Volvo 164 4-door sedan with blue roof dome light, steering, and forward/reverse action. **8 in** (20 cm). **R/C battery operated**. Known colors: Black and white. Graphics: Polis. Maker: **Bandai**, Japan. Toy marks: Bandai. Box marks: Bandai.
Scarcity: 3. Fine to Excellent (C6-C8): $60-$90, Mint (C10): $120

1960s Volvo 164 4-door sedan with yellow dome roof light. **8 in** (20 cm). **Friction**. Known colors: Black and white. Graphics: Polis. Maker: **Bandai**, Japan. Toy marks: Bandai. Box marks: Bandai.
Scarcity: 3. Fine to Excellent (C6-C8): $60-$90, Mint (C10): $120

1960s Volvo Amazon 2-door sedan with yellow roof dome light, steering and forward/reverse action. **8 in** (20 cm). **R/C battery operated**. Known colors: Black and white. Graphics: Polis. License: Volvo. Maker: **Bandai**, Japan. Toy marks: Bandai.
Scarcity: 4. Fine to Excellent (C6-C8): $150-$225, Mint (C10): $300

Postal Service

1950s Daihatsu Midget 3 wheel delivery. 7 in (18 cm). **Friction.** Known colors: Red. Graphics: (Japanese) Postal. Maker: **Masudaya**, Japan. Box marks: MT (Masudaya). Box text: (Japanese text).
Scarcity: 7. Fine to Excellent (C6-C8): $1,000-$1,200, Mint (C10): $1,600

1950s Dodge 2-door van with opening side door, rear doors and coin slot. Separate safe mounted inside. **7 in** (18 cm). **Friction.** Known colors: Blue and white; Red. Graphics: Post - Postal Saving Truck or Royal Mail Canada - Dodge. License: 3S-6540. Maker: **Shioji**, Japan. Toy marks: SSS (Shioji). Box marks: SSS (Shioji).
Scarcity: 3. Fine to Excellent (C6-C8): $75-$125, Mint (C10): $175

1950s Dodge 2-door van with opening side door, rear doors, and coin slot. **7 in** (18 cm). **Friction.** Known colors: Gray. Graphics: Barnkopings - Sparbank - Dodge. Maker: **Shioji**, Japan. Toy marks: none.
Scarcity: 5. Fine to Excellent (C6-C8): $100-$150, Mint (C10): $200

1950s Dodge 2-door van with opening side door and rear doors. **8.25 in** (18 cm). **Friction.** Known colors: Blue and white. Graphics: U.S. Mail - Dodge. Maker: **Shioji**, Japan. Toy marks: SSS (Shioji). Box marks: SSS (Shioji).
Scarcity: 3. Fine to Excellent (C6-C8): $100-$175, Mint (C10): $250

1950s Dodge 2-door van with opening side door and rear doors. Bank versions have separate coin slot with safe mounted inside. **7 in** (18 cm). **Friction.** Known colors: Assorted. Graphics: UPS; REA; Armored Truck; Armored Bank Truck. Maker: **Shioji**, Japan. Toy marks: SSS (Shioji). Notes: UPS (+100%), REA (+50%).
Scarcity: 4. Fine to Excellent (C6-C8): $75-$125, Mint (C10): $175

1960s Opel Kadett A 2-door station wagon. 9 in (23 cm). **Friction.** Known colors: Yellow. Graphics: Deutsche Bundespost. Maker: **Kienberger**, Germany. Toy marks: Huki.
Scarcity: 4. Fine to Excellent (C6-C8): $100-$150, Mint (C10): $200

134 Postal Service Vehicles/Road Service Vehicles

1961 Plymouth 4-door station wagon with small roof lights and siren sound. **12 in** (30 cm). **Friction**. Known colors: Red. Graphics: (Japanese) Post Office (Japanese). Maker: **Ichiko**, Japan. Toy marks: Ichiko. Box marks: Ichiko. Box text: (Japanese text) *Mail Motor Van*.
Scarcity: 9. Fine to Excellent (C6-C8): $600-$800, Mint (C10): $1,000

1960s Volkswagen Beetle 2-door sedan. **6 in** (15 cm). **Friction**. Known colors: Yellow and black. Graphics: PTT (Swiss cross). Maker: **Yoshiya**, Japan. Toy marks: KO (Yoshiya). Box marks: KO (Yoshiya). Box text: *Volkswagen*. Notes: PTT stands for Postes Telegraphie Television.
Scarcity: 2. Fine to Excellent (C6-C8): $50-$85, Mint (C10): $125

1960s Volkswagen Beetle 2-door sedan. **8 in** (20 cm). **Friction**. Known colors: Yellow and black. Graphics: PTT (Swiss cross). Maker: **Bandai**, Japan. Toy marks: Bandai. Box marks: Bandai.
Scarcity: 4. Fine to Excellent (C6-C8): $150-$225, Mint (C10): $325

1950/60s Volkswagen Transporter van with opening side doors. **9.5 in** (24 cm). **Friction**. Known colors: Yellow and black. Maker: **Tipp & Co.**, Germany. Toy marks: TCO (Tipp).
Scarcity: 7. Fine to Excellent (C6-C8): $600-$800, Mint (C10): $1,000

Road Service

Cadillac station wagon Emergency Service, Toronto, Canada. *Photo by Tosh Wakabayashi*

Public Service Vehicles 135

1960 Buick 2-door pick up with tow truck winch. **12 in** (30 cm). **Friction**. Known colors: Assorted. Maker: **Gorgo**, Argentina. Toy marks: Gorgo. Box marks: Gorgo. Box text: *Auxilio Gorgo*.
Scarcity: 8. Fine to Excellent (C6-C8): $150-$250, Mint (C10): $350

1960s Jeep FC 2-door pick up with revolving roof beacon and tin driver ringing bell. Lithographed chassis. **7.5 in** (19 cm). **Friction**. Known colors: Red and white. Graphics: AAA - AHI - Jeep -Emergency Utility Truck. Maker: **Nomura**, Japan. Toy marks: TN (Nomura), AHI. Box marks: TN (Nomura), AHI. Box text: *Emergency Utility Truck*.
Scarcity: 6. Fine to Excellent (C6-C8): $100-$150, Mint (C10): $225

1960s Jeep 2-door pick up with yellow roof light and crank activated winch. **11 in** (28 cm). **Friction**. Known colors: White. License: Jeep S-5. Maker: **Unknown**, Japan. Toy marks: none.
Scarcity: 3. Fine to Excellent (C6-C8): $125-$175, Mint (C10): $225

1963 Cadillac 4-door station wagon with automatic raising and lowering ladder and extending tool platform. Forward/reverse action and steering. **11.25 in** (29 cm). **R/C battery operated**. Known colors: Yellow. Graphics: EES - Electrical Emergency Service. Maker: **Yonezawa**, Japan. Toy marks: Y (Yonezawa). Box marks: Y (Yonezawa). Box text: *Electrical Emergency Service With Automatic Ladder Up and Down Action*.
Scarcity: 5. Fine to Excellent (C6-C8): $225-$325, Mint (C10): $425

1950/60s Volkswagen Transporter van with blinking light, forward/reverse action, and steering. **7.75 in** (20 cm). **R/C battery operated**. Known colors: Yellow and black. Graphics: ADAC Strassenwacht - Wagen NR 23. Maker: **Bandai**, Japan. Toy marks: Bandai. Box marks: Bandai. Box text: *ADAC-Strassenwacht*.
Notes: ADAC stands for: Allgemeiner Deutscher Automobil Club.
Scarcity: 6. Fine to Excellent (C6-C8): $200-$300, Mint (C10): $400

(Not pictured) **1950/60s Volkswagen Transporter pick up** with drop down sides and truck mounted winch. **9.5 in** (24 cm). **Friction**. Known colors: Red and white; Blue and yellow. Graphics: VW - Service. Maker: **Tipp & Co.**, Germany. Toy marks: TCO (Tipp). Box marks: TCO (Tipp).
Scarcity: 7. Fine to Excellent (C6-C8): $600-$800, Mint (C10): $1,100

1960s Volkswagen Beetle 2-door sedan with blacked out windows, yellow roof light, and forward/reverse action. **7 in** (18 cm). **R/C battery operated**. Known colors: Yellow. Graphics: ADAC Strassenwacht. Maker: **Unknown**, Japan.
Scarcity: 3. Fine to Excellent (C6-C8): $60-$90, Mint (C10): $135

1960s Volkswagen Beetle 2-door convertible with detachable remote control. **7 in** (18 cm). **R/C battery operated**. Known colors: Yellow. Graphics: ADAC Strassenwacht. License: 1966. Maker: **Bandai**, Japan. Toy marks: Bandai. Box text: *Autobahn Streifenwagen #IF790B*.
Notes: Came with Police Porsche as boxed set.
Scarcity: 5. Fine to Excellent (C6-C8): $125-$175, Mint (C10): $225

1960s Volkswagen Beetle 2-door sedan with roof light and visible engine. **10.5 in** (27 cm). **Battery operated**. Known colors: Yellow with gray roof. Graphics: ADAC Strassenwacht. Maker: **Bandai**, Japan. Toy marks: Bandai.
Scarcity: 3. Fine to Excellent (C6-C8): $125-$175, Mint (C10): $225

1960s Volkswagen Beetle 2-door sedan with roof light, steering, and forward/reverse action. **7 in** (18 cm). **R/C battery operated**. Known colors: Yellow with gray roof. Graphics: ADAC Strassenwacht. License: 2016. Maker: **Bandai**, Japan. Toy marks: Bandai. Box text: *ADAC-Strassenwacht IF-922*.
Scarcity: 6. Fine to Excellent (C6-C8): $250-$350, Mint (C10): $450

1960s Volkswagen Beetle 2-door sedan with driver, roof light, visible engine, steering, and forward/reverse action. **10.5 in** (27 cm). **R/C battery operated**. Known colors: Yellow with gray roof. Graphics: ADAC Strassenwacht. Maker: **Bandai**, Japan. Toy marks: Bandai.
Scarcity: 6. Fine to Excellent (C6-C8): $250-$350, Mint (C10): $450

(Not pictured) **1960s Volkswagen Beetle 2-door sedan** with flashing blue roof light, siren, antenna, and bump and go action. **10.75 in** (27 cm). **Battery operated**. Known colors: Red. Maker: **Masudaya**, Japan. Toy marks: MT (Masudaya). Box marks: MT (Masudaya).
Scarcity: 4. Fine to Excellent (C6-C8): $90-$150, Mint (C10): $200

Public Service Vehicles 137

1960s Volkswagen Beetle 2-door sedan with flashing yellow roof light and bump-n-go action. **10.75 in** (27 cm). **Battery operated**. Known colors: Yellow and black. Graphics: ADAC - Strassenwacht. Maker: **Masudaya**, Japan. Toy marks: MT (Masudaya). Box marks: MT (Masudaya).
Scarcity: 4. Fine to Excellent (C6-C8): $90-$150, Mint (C10): $200

Taxis, Limousines, and Transportation

Dodge Taxi, New York. *Photo by Rodney Abensur*

138 Taxis, Limousines, and Transportation

1908 Baker 2-door sedan with tin lanterns and tin door sign. **6 in** (15 cm). **Friction**. Known colors: Yellow. Graphics: Taxi. Maker: **Bandai**, Japan. Toy marks: Bandai. Box marks: Bandai, Frankonia. Box text: *Old Fashion Car Series - Yellow Cab 1908*.
Notes: Produced 1960s.
Scarcity: 2. Fine to Excellent (C6-C8): $30-$60, Mint (C10): $95

1950 Buick 4-door sedan with headlights, roof light, and forward/reverse action. **8.25 in** (21 cm). **Battery operated**. Known colors: Red and cream. Graphics: Taxi. Maker: **Mizuno/Alps**, Japan. Toy marks: M (Mizuno). Box marks: M (Mizuno).
Scarcity: 3. Fine to Excellent (C6-C8): $75-$125, Mint (C10): $150

(Not pictured) **1955 Buick 2-door coupe** with roof sign, steering, and forward/reverse. **7.5 in** (19 cm). **R/C battery operated**. Known colors: Yellow. Graphics: Yellow Cab - Taxi. Maker: **Linemar**, Japan. Toy marks: Linemar (Marx). Box marks: Linemar (Marx). Box text: *Taxi With Light and Siren*.
Scarcity: 4. Fine to Excellent (C6-C8): $150-$175, Mint (C10): $250

1959 Buick 2-door hardtop with roof sign board and fare meter and checkered markings. **9 in** (23 cm). **Friction**. Known colors: Yellow and black. Graphics: Yellow Taxi No.15. Maker: **Yonezawa**, Japan. Toy marks: Y (Yonezawa).
Scarcity: 4. Fine to Excellent (C6-C8): $125-$175, Mint (C10): $225

1960 Buick 2-door hardtop with roof sign and two antennas. **12 in** (30 cm). **Friction**. Known colors: Black and yellow. Graphics: Taxi. Maker: **Gorgo**, Argentina. Toy marks: Gorgo. Box marks: Gorgo.
Scarcity: 8. Fine to Excellent (C6-C8): $60-$90, Mint (C10): $125

1961 Buick 4-door sedan with push-down Taxi roof sign. **7.5 in** (19 cm). **Friction**. Known colors: Yellow. Graphics: Taxi - Cab - 25¢ per/mile. Maker: **Ichiko**, Japan. Toy marks: Ichiko. Box marks: Ichiko.
Scarcity: 3. Fine to Excellent (C6-C8): $75-$115, Mint (C10): $150

1963 Buick Estate Wagon 4-door station wagon with luggage rack and two pieces baggage, wood grained sides, forward/reverse, and steering. **8 in** (20 cm). **R/C battery operated**. Known colors: Assorted. Graphics: Airport Limousine. Maker: **Bandai**, Japan. Toy marks: Bandai. Box marks: Bandai. Box text: *Buick Airport Limousine #4136*.
Scarcity: 5. Fine to Excellent (C6-C8): $150-$225, Mint (C10): $300

Public Service Vehicles 139

1950 Cadillac 4-door sedan with lighted roof sign and trunk safety sign. **8.5 in** (22 cm). **R/C battery operated**. Known colors: Yellow. Graphics: Yellow Cab - Taxi. Maker: **Linemar**, Japan. Toy marks: Linemar (Marx). Box marks: Linemar (Marx).
Scarcity: 3. Fine to Excellent (C6-C8): $65-$95, Mint (C10): $135

1951 Cadillac 2-door coupe with roof sign, trunk sign, and rotating meter in window. **6.25 in** (16 cm). **Friction**. Known colors: Assorted. Graphics: Taxi - Rate - Always Be Careful Crossing Streets. Maker: **Bandai/Tanaguchi**, Japan. Toy marks: Hadson. Box marks: Bandai. Box text: *Yellow Cab*.
Notes: Note color, graphic, and trunk sign variation. Variation marked TS (Tanaguchi) and AHI.
Scarcity: 4. Fine to Excellent (C6-C8): $50-$75, Mint (C10): $115

1959 Cadillac 4-door hardtop. **7 in** (18 cm). **Friction**. Known colors: Yellow. Graphics: Yellow Cab. Maker: **Unknown**, Japan. Toy marks: none.
Scarcity: 3. Fine to Excellent (C6-C8): $60-$90, Mint (C10): $140

1955 Chevrolet 4-door sedan with roof luggage rack, lithographed passengers on windows, and bank coin slot. **9 in** (23 cm). **Battery operated**. Known colors: Yellow and red. Graphics: Yellow Cab and Taxi roof sign board. Maker: **Kanto/Ichiko**, Japan. Toy marks: Kanto, Ichiko. Box marks: Kanto, Ichiko. Box text: *Coin Operated Battery Cab*.
Scarcity: 6. Fine to Excellent (C6-C8): $250-$400, Mint (C10): $550

1959 Chevrolet 4-door hardtop with roof sign and antenna. **8.75 in** (22 cm). **Friction**. Known colors: Yellow and red. Graphics: Chevrolet - Taxi - (rates). Maker: **Asahi**, Japan. Toy marks: ATC (Asahi Toy). Box marks: ATC (Asahi Toy). Box text: *Chevrolet Yellow Cab*.
Scarcity: 6. Fine to Excellent (C6-C8): $250-$325, Mint (C10): $400

1963 Chevrolet 4-door hardtop with roof sign and two fender mounted mirrors. **12.5 in** (32 cm). **Friction**. Known colors: Red, yellow, and blue. Graphics: Deluxe - Taxi (Japanese). Maker: **Daito**, Japan. Toy marks: none. Box marks: Hope. Box text: *Taxi* (Japanese).
Scarcity: 8. Fine to Excellent (C6-C8): $250-$350, Mint (C10): $450

(Not pictured) **1966 Chevrolet 4-door hardtop** with siren sound and pull-up antenna. **11 in** (28 cm). **Friction**. Known colors: Yellow and black. Maker: **Saxo**, Argentina. Toy marks: Saxo. Box text: *Chevrolet Impala Taxi*.
Scarcity: 3. Fine to Excellent (C6-C8): $65-$100, Mint (C10): $150

140   Taxis, Limousines, and Transportation

1970 Chevrolet Camaro 2-door hardtop with siren sound. **11.75 in** (30 cm). **Friction**. Known colors: Black and yellow. Graphics: Taxi L.2263 MCBS (adhesive label) - Taxi roof sign. Maker: **Gorgo**, Argentina. Toy marks: Gorgo. Box marks: Gorgo.
Scarcity: 3. Fine to Excellent (C6-C8): $75-$125, Mint (C10): $175

1970 Chevrolet Camaro 2-door hardtop with roof sign and siren sound. **11.75 in** (30 cm). **Friction**. Known colors: Black and yellow. Graphics: Taxi Radiollamada (adhesive label) - Taxi. Maker: **Gorgo**, Argentina. Toy marks: Gorgo. Box marks: Gorgo.
Scarcity: 3. Fine to Excellent (C6-C8): $75-$125, Mint (C10): $175

1967 Dodge Dart 4-door hardtop with yellow roof sign. **12.25 in** (31 cm). **Friction**. Known colors: Green and yellow. Graphics: Checker Cab - Metro Cab -126 - Air Conditioned. Maker: **Nomura**, Japan. Toy marks: TN (Nomura).
Scarcity: 7. Fine to Excellent (C6-C8): $300-$500, Mint (C10): $700

1967 Dodge 4-door hardtop with yellow roof sign and fender mirror. **12.25 in** (31 cm). **Friction**. Known colors: Yellow. Graphics: Yellow Cab - Yellow Cab Co. Inc -30. Maker: **Nomura**, Japan. Toy marks: TN (Nomura).
Scarcity: 6. Fine to Excellent (C6-C8): $250-$450, Mint (C10): $650

1958 Edsel 4-door hardtop with lithographed chassis. **7.5 in** (19 cm). **Friction**. Known colors: Yellow and orange. Graphics: City Cab - Taxi - NY-2900 - Edsel - 32. License: DN-1256. Maker: **Sato/Mansei**, Japan. Toy marks: TOY (Sato). Box marks: Haji (Mansei).
Scarcity: 7. Fine to Excellent (C6-C8): $175-$250, Mint (C10): $350

1958 Edsel 2-door hardtop with lithographed roof. **13.25 in** (34 cm). **Friction**. Known colors: Yellow and red. Graphics: Taxi - Checker Taxi Co. - Checker Cab. License: Y-3018. Maker: **Daito**, Japan. Toy marks: Daito.
Scarcity: 5. Fine to Excellent (C6-C8): $150-$350, Mint (C10): $500

1958 Edsel 2-door hardtop with rear antenna and roof sign. **13.25 in** (34 cm). **Friction**. Known colors: Yellow and red. Graphics: Taxi Checker Taxi Co. License: D-3972 or Y-3018. Maker: **Daito**, Japan. Toy marks: Daito.
Scarcity: 5. Fine to Excellent (C6-C8): $150-$350, Mint (C10): $500

Public Service Vehicles 141

1960s Fiat 1800 4-door sedan with taxi roof sign and window sticker. **9.5 in** (24 cm). **Friction**. Known colors: Black and yellow. Graphics: Metro Taxi - 24 Hour Package Delivery. License: C752152. Maker: **Gorgo**, Argentina. Toy marks: Gorgo. Box marks: Gorgo.
Scarcity: 2. Fine to Excellent (C6-C8): $75-$115, Mint (C10): $150

1955 Ford 4-door sedan with blue Taxi roof sign and lithographed passengers on windows. **8.25 in** (21 cm). **Battery operated**. Known colors: Yellow. Graphics: Yellow Cab - Call Tel.3078. Maker: **Nomura**, Japan. Toy marks: TN (Nomura).
Scarcity: 4. Fine to Excellent (C6-C8): $75-$150, Mint (C10): $215

1952 Ford 2-door sedan with roof sign board, fare meter, and lithographed chassis. **10.25 in** (26 cm). **Friction**. Known colors: Black. Graphics: SAN - (Japanese). Maker: **Marusan**, Japan. Toy marks: SAN (Marusan). Box marks: SAN (Marusan).
Scarcity: 9. Fine to Excellent (C6-C8): $500-$700, Mint (C10): $900

1955 Ford 4-door sedan with white Taxi roof sign and lithographed passengers on windows. **8.25 in** (21 cm). **Friction with battery**. Known colors: Yellow. Graphics: Yellow Cab - Call Tel.3877. Maker: **Nomura**, Japan. Toy marks: TN (Nomura).
Scarcity: 4. Fine to Excellent (C6-C8): $75-$150, Mint (C10): $215

1952 Ford 2-door sedan with red Taxi roof sign board, fare meter, and lithographed chassis. **10.25 in** (26 cm). **Friction**. Known colors: Yellow. Graphics: Yellow Cab (with rates) - Taxi. Maker: **Marusan**, Japan. Toy marks: SAN (Marusan). Box marks: SAN (Marusan). Box text: Taxi, Real Fare Meter.
Scarcity: 7. Fine to Excellent (C6-C8): $400-$600, Mint (C10): $800

1955 Ford 2-door sedan with lithographed Taxi roof sign and antenna. **9 in** (23 cm). **Friction**. Known colors: Yellow and red. Graphics: Yellow Cab - Taxi - (rocket symbol). Maker: **Asahi**, Japan. Toy marks: ATC (Asahi Toy). Box marks: ATC (Asahi Toy). Box text: Yellow Cab.
Notes: Box illustration shows 1958 Ford.
Scarcity: 6. Fine to Excellent (C6-C8): $300-$400, Mint (C10): $500

142 Taxis, Limousines, and Transportation

1956 Ford 2-door sedan with lighted roof sign, rear advertising board, and 1957 style fins. **7.75 in** (20 cm). **Friction with battery**. Known colors: Yellow. Graphics: Yellow Cab. Maker: **Unknown**, Japan. Toy marks: none.
Scarcity: 3. Fine to Excellent (C6-C8): $50-$75, Mint (C10): $100

(Not pictured) **1958 Ford 2-door sedan**. **7 in** (18 cm). **Friction**. Known colors: Yellow. Graphics: Ford (hubcaps). Maker: **Asahi**, Japan. Toy marks: ATC (Asahi Toy). Box marks: ATC (Asahi Toy). Box text: *Yellow Cab*.
Scarcity: 5. Fine to Excellent (C6-C8): $125-$150, Mint (C10): $200

1959 Ford Fairlane 500 2-door hardtop with Taxi roof sign. **9 in** (23 cm). **Friction**. Known colors: Yellow. Graphics: Yellow Cab - Taxi - 66 - (Horse and Carriage). Maker: **Asahi**, Japan. Toy marks: Toymaster (Asahi Toy). Box text: *Sturdy Friction Metal Toy Sedan Series*.
Scarcity: 3. Fine to Excellent (C6-C8): $60-$85, Mint (C10): $125

(Not pictured) **1959 Ford 4-door station wagon** with roof rack. **9 in** (23 cm). **Friction**. Known colors: Black and white. Graphics: Airport Limousine. Maker: **Unknown**, Japan. Toy marks: none. Box marks: Cragstan. Box text: *Airport Limousine*.
Scarcity: 4. Fine to Excellent (C6-C8): $50-$10, Mint (C10): $150

1961 Ford 2-door convertible with retractable roof. **9 in** (23 cm). **Friction**. Known colors: Yellow and orange. Graphics: Yellow Taxi. Maker: **Daito**, Japan. Toy marks: Daito.
Scarcity: 3. Fine to Excellent (C6-C8): $60-$90, Mint (C10): $125

1963 Ford 4-door hardtop with fender mirrors and roof sign. **12 in** (30 cm). **Friction**. Known colors: Red and yellow with blue/white checker. Graphics: (Japanese). Maker: **Miura**, Japan. Toy marks: M (Miura).
Scarcity: 7. Fine to Excellent (C6-C8): $275-$350, Mint (C10): $425

1964 Ford Fairlane 2-door hardtop with lighted roof sign. **8 in** (20 cm). **Battery operated**. Known colors: Yellow and red. Graphics: Yellow Cab - Taxi roof sign. License: Ford. Maker: **Bandai**, Japan. Toy marks: Bandai. Box marks: Bandai.
Scarcity: 5. Fine to Excellent (C6-C8): $175-$275, Mint (C10): $400

(Not pictured) **1964 Ford Taunus 20M 2-door sedan** with lighted roof sign, fender mirrors, steering, and forward/reverse action. **9.25 in** (23 cm). **R/C battery operated**. Known colors: Blue. Maker: **Ichiko**, Japan. Toy marks: Ichiko. Box marks: Ichiko. Box text: *Korskola*.
Scarcity: 5. Fine to Excellent (C6-C8): $75-$115, Mint (C10): $145

(Not pictured) **1964 Ford Taunus 20M 2-door sedan** with lighted roof sign, fender mirrors, steering, and forward/reverse action. **9.25 in** (23 cm). **R/C battery operated**. Known colors: Black. Graphics: Taxi. Maker: **Ichiko**, Japan. Toy marks: Ichiko. Box marks: Ichiko.
Scarcity: 5. Fine to Excellent (C6-C8): $75-$115, Mint (C10): $145

Public Service Vehicles 143

1964 Ford Galaxie 500 2-door hardtop with push roof sign that changes between Caracas, Maracay, Valencia, and Maracaibo, antenna, and siren. **13 in** (33 cm). **Friction**. Known colors: Turquoise. License: MX-38-90. Maker: **Ichiko**, Japan. Toy marks: Ichiko. Box marks: Ichiko, Harely. Box text: *Carro de Alquiler*.
Scarcity: 8. Fine to Excellent (C6-C8): $350-$450, Mint (C10): $575

1964 Ford Galaxie 500 2-door hardtop with push roof sign that changes between Caracas, Maracay, Valencia, and Maracaibo, antenna, and siren. **13 in** (33 cm). **Friction**. Known colors: Red. License: MX-38-90. Maker: **Ichiko**, Japan. Toy marks: Ichiko. Box marks: Ichiko, Harely. Box text: *Carro de Alquiler*.
Scarcity: 8. Fine to Excellent (C6-C8): $350-$450, Mint (C10): $575

1964 Ford Galaxie 500 2-door hardtop with push roof sign that changes between Caracas, Maracay, Valencia, and Maracaibo, antenna, and siren. **13 in** (33 cm). **Friction**. Known colors: Blue. Graphics: Libre - Aotopista Americana. License: MX-38-90. Maker: **Ichiko**, Japan. Toy marks: Ichiko. Box marks: Ichiko, Harely. Box text: *Carro de Alquiler*.
Scarcity: 8. Fine to Excellent (C6-C8): $350-$450, Mint (C10): $575

Box for 1964 Ford Galaxie taxis.

1965 Ford Galaxie 500XL 2-door hardtop. **11.25 in** (29 cm). **Friction**. Known colors: Yellow. Graphics: Taxi Yellow Cab. Maker: **Masudaya**, Japan. Toy marks: KKY (Yamato). Box marks: MT (Masudaya). Notes: Masudaya catalog image.
Scarcity: 8. Fine to Excellent (C6-C8): $450-$700, Mint (C10): $950

1954 Lincoln 4-door sedan with roof sign, headlights, and on/off switch. **8.25 in** (21 cm). **Battery operated**. Known colors: Green and cream. Graphics: Taxi. Maker: **Mizuno/Alps**, Japan. Toy marks: M (Mizuno). Box marks: M (Mizuno).
Scarcity: 6. Fine to Excellent (C6-C8): $250-$300, Mint (C10): $350

1957 Lincoln 2-door hardtop with Taxi roof sign. **8.25 in** (21 cm). **Friction**. Known colors: Yellow. Graphics: Yellow Taxi. Maker: **Masudaya**, Japan. Toy marks: MT (Masudaya).
Scarcity: 2. Fine to Excellent (C6-C8): $50-$75, Mint (C10): $100

144 Taxis, Limousines, and Transportation

1958 Lincoln Continental Mark III 4-door hardtop. **9 in** (23 cm). **Friction**. Known colors: Yellow. Graphics: Yellow Cab. Maker: **Sanyo**, Japan. Toy marks: none. Box marks: Sanyo.
Scarcity: 5. Fine to Excellent (C6-C8): $120-$180, Mint (C10): $250

1960 Lincoln 4-door station wagon with roof rack. **9 in** (23 cm). **Friction**. Known colors: Black and white; Blue and white. Graphics: Airport Limousine. Maker: **Nihon Boeki**, Japan. Toy marks: KKK (Nihon Boeki). Box marks: Cragstan. Box text: *Airport Limousine*.
Scarcity: 4. Fine to Excellent (C6-C8): $150-$175, Mint (C10): $250

(Not pictured) **1950s Mercedes Benz 250 SE 4-door sedan** with lighted roof sign. **8 in** (20 cm). **R/C battery operated**. Known colors: Yellow. Maker: **Ichiko**, Japan. Toy marks: Ichiko. Box marks: Ichiko. Box text: *Mercedes Benz*.
Scarcity: 3. Fine to Excellent (C6-C8): $75-$125, Mint (C10): $175

1950s Mercedes Benz 250 SE 4-door sedan with lever operated pop-up taxi roof sign and antenna. **8 in** (20 cm). **Friction**. Known colors: Black. Graphics: K-MN-887. Maker: **Ichiko**, Japan. Toy marks: Ichiko. Box marks: Ichiko. Box text: *Taxi Cab*.
Scarcity: 3. Fine to Excellent (C6-C8): $75-$125, Mint (C10): $175

(Not pictured) **1960s Mercedes Benz 220 S 4-door sedan** with roof sign, fender mirror, and antenna. **7.5 in** (19 cm). **Friction**. Known colors: Black. Graphics: Taxi. License: Mercedes. Maker: **Ichiko**, Japan. Toy marks: Ichiko. Box marks: Ichiko.
Scarcity: 4. Fine to Excellent (C6-C8): $75-$125, Mint (C10): $175

1960s Mercedes Benz 220 S 4-door sedan with lighted roof sign and forward/reverse action. **8 in** (20 cm). **Battery operated**. Known colors: Black. Graphics: Taxi (roof sign). Maker: **Bandai**, Japan. Toy marks: Bandai. Box marks: Bandai. Box text: *Mercedes Benz Taxi #4118*.
Scarcity: 3. Fine to Excellent (C6-C8): $85-$135, Mint (C10): $185

1960s Mercedes Benz 230 4-door sedan with flashing lights, opening door, and bump and go action. **10.5 in** (27 cm). **Battery operated**. Known colors: Black. Graphics: Taxi (roof sign). License: Benz 230. Maker: **Bandai**, Japan. Toy marks: Bandai. Box marks: Bandai. Box text: *Mercedes Benz Taxi With Flashing Lamp and Openable Door. #4195 or #1F807*.
Scarcity: 5. Fine to Excellent (C6-C8): $150-$225, Mint (C10): $300

1959 Mercury Montclair 4-door hardtop with roof signboard. **11.5 in** (29 cm). **Friction**. Known colors: Yellow. Graphics: (Japanese). Maker: **Yonezawa**, Japan. Toy marks: Y (Yonezawa).
Scarcity: 9. Fine to Excellent (C6-C8): $350-$500, Mint (C10): $750

1953 Nash 4-door sedan with roof sign, door sign, and trunk sign. **8.25 in** (21 cm). **Friction**. Known colors: Yellow or maroon. Graphics: Taxi (roof sign) and Rate sign. Maker: **Tanaguchi/Miyazawa**, Japan. Toy marks: MSK (Miyazawa), TS (Tanaguchi).
Scarcity: 4. Fine to Excellent (C6-C8): $100-$175, Mint (C10): $250

1959 Oldsmobile 2-door hardtop with push roof sign that changes between Caracas, Maracay, Valencia, and Maracaibo. **13 in** (33 cm). **Friction**. Known colors: Green. Graphics: Libre Autopista Americana. License: Ichiko. Maker: **Ichiko**, Japan. Toy marks: Ichiko.
Scarcity: 5. Fine to Excellent (C6-C8): $375-$450, Mint (C10): $575

1959 Oldsmobile 2-door hardtop with push roof signboard that changes between Milano, Bologna, Roma, and Napoli. **13 in** (33 cm). **Friction**. Known colors: Green and light green. Graphics: Taxi. Maker: **Ichiko**, Japan. Toy marks: Ichiko. Box text: *Autopubblica Frizone Taxi*.
Scarcity: 5. Fine to Excellent (C6-C8): $375-$450, Mint (C10): $575

1959 Oldsmobile 2-door hardtop with push roof signboard that changes cities (New York, Chicago, Cleveland). **13 in** (33 cm). **Friction**. Known colors: Yellow and red. Graphics: Taxi - 35 cent 1/4 mile. Maker: **Ichiko**, Japan. Toy marks: Ichiko.
Scarcity: 5. Fine to Excellent (C6-C8): $375-$450, Mint (C10): $575

1959 Oldsmobile 2-door hardtop. **13 in** (33 cm). **Friction**. Known colors: Yellow and black. Graphics: Taxi stick on label. Maker: **Rico**, Spain. Toy marks: Rico. Box marks: Rico. Box text: *Coche Oldsmobile*.
Notes: Produced 1960s.
Scarcity: 8. Fine to Excellent (C6-C8): $200-$300, Mint (C10): $400

1960 Oldsmobile 2-door hardtop with Taxi roof sign. **9 in** (23 cm). **Friction**. Known colors: Yellow and orange. Graphics: Yellow Cab - Dynamic 88. Maker: **Nomura**, Japan. Toy marks: TN (Nomura), IY Metal Toy. Box marks: TN (Nomura). Box text: *Taxi*.
Scarcity: 8. Fine to Excellent (C6-C8): $300-$400, Mint (C10): $500

1953 Opel Olympia Rekord 4-door sedan with roof luggage rack. **7 in** (18 cm). **Friction.** Known colors: Red and cream. Graphics: Hotel New York - Airport. License: B-296. Maker: **Bandai**, Japan. Toy marks: Bandai. Box marks: Bandai. Box text: *Airport Transportation Limousine*.
Scarcity: 4. Fine to Excellent (C6-C8): $75-$100, Mint (C10): $150

1953 Opel Olympia Rekord 4-door sedan with forward/reverse action and roof luggage rack. **7 in** (18 cm). **Battery operated.** Known colors: Red and cream. Graphics: Opel - Opel Limousine. License: B-383. Maker: **Bandai**, Japan. Toy marks: Bandai. Box marks: Bandai. Box text: *Opel Limousine #383*.
Scarcity: 4. Fine to Excellent (C6-C8): $65-$90, Mint (C10): $135

1953 Opel Olympia Rekord 4-door sedan with lithographed people in windows and roof sign. **7 in** (18 cm). **Friction.** Known colors: Yellow. Graphics: Yellow Cab - Taxi (roof sign) - Tel MA5-3042. Maker: **Bandai**, Japan. Toy marks: Bandai.
Scarcity: 4. Fine to Excellent (C6-C8): $90-$140, Mint (C10): $200

1933 Packard 4-door sedan. **8 in** (20 cm). **Windup.** Known colors: Red, blue, and black. Graphics: Taxi. Maker: **Unknown**, Japan. Toy marks: none.
Scarcity: 6. Fine to Excellent (C6-C8): $200-$400, Mint (C10): $600

1960s Peugeot 404 4-door sedan with roof sign, luggage rack, and fender mounted meter. **11.75 in** (30 cm). **Battery operated.** Known colors: Assorted. Graphics: Taxi roof sign. License: 4876-NM-75. Maker: **Joustra**, France. Toy marks: Joustra. Box marks: Joustra. Box text: *Taxi Peugeot 404 Electrique*.
Scarcity: 8. Fine to Excellent (C6-C8): $500-$650, Mint (C10): $900

1958 Plymouth 2-door hardtop with roof sign. **6 in** (15 cm). **Friction.** Known colors: Yellow. Graphics: Taxi - Taxi (roof sign) - Plymouth. Maker: **Unknown**, Japan. Toy marks: none.
Scarcity: 3. Fine to Excellent (C6-C8): $40-$80, Mint (C10): $120

Public Service Vehicles 147

1960s Toyota Toyopet 1900 4-door sedan with roof sign, fender mirrors, and antenna. **9 in** (23 cm). **Friction**. Known colors: Yellow and blue. Graphics: Toyopet 1900 (Japanese). License: Tokyo. Maker: **Bandai**, Japan. Toy marks: Bandai.
Scarcity: 8. Fine to Excellent (C6-C8): $800-$1,400, Mint (C10): $2,000

1960s Toyota Toyopet 4-door sedan with Taxi roof sign, fender mirrors, and trunk mounted turn lights. **10.5 in** (27 cm). **Battery operated**. Known colors: Yellow and orange. Graphics: Taxi. Maker: **Bandai**, Japan. Toy marks: Bandai.
Scarcity: 7. Fine to Excellent (C6-C8): $800-$1,300, Mint (C10): $1,800

1970s Toyota Toyopet Crown 2-door hardtop with Taxi roof sign. **13.75 in** (35 cm). **Friction**. Known colors: Yellow and red. Graphics: Nippon Taxi (Japanese). Maker: **Aoshin**, Japan. Toy marks: ASC (Aoshin). Box marks: ASC (Aoshin).
Scarcity: 5. Fine to Excellent (C6-C8): $225-$275, Mint (C10): $350

1970s Toyota Mark II 4-door hardtop with Japanese Taxi roof sign. **14 in** (36 cm). **Friction**. Known colors: Red and white with checker stripe. Graphics: (Japanese) 5677. Maker: **Nomura**, Japan. Toy marks: TN (Nomura). Box marks: TN (Nomura). Box text: *Deluxe Taxi* (Japanese and English).
Scarcity: 5. Fine to Excellent (C6-C8): $225-$275, Mint (C10): $350

1920s Undetermined 4-door sedan with tin driver and opening door. **9 in** (23 cm). **Windup**. Known colors: Yellow and black. Graphics: Yellow Taxi - 890. Maker: **Gunthermann**, Germany. Toy marks: SG (Gunthermann).
Scarcity: 9. Fine to Excellent (C6-C8): $1,500-$1,700, Mint (C10): $2,000

1920s Undetermined 4-door sedan with tin driver, opening door, side lamps, meter, and vacant indicator sign. **10.5 in** (27 cm). **Windup**. Known colors: Yellow and black. Maker: **Unknown**, Germany.
Scarcity: 9. Fine to Excellent (C6-C8): $3,000-$4,000, Mint (C10): $5,000

1960s Volkswagen Beetle 2-door sedan with flashing taxi roof sign, siren, antenna, and bump-n-go action. **10.75 in** (27 cm). **Battery operated**. Known colors: Yellow. Graphics: Taxi. Maker: **Masudaya**, Japan. Toy marks: MT (Masudaya). Box marks: MT (Masudaya).
Notes: Also produced as R/C model.
Scarcity: 5. Fine to Excellent (C6-C8): $150-$250, Mint (C10): $375

Television and Broadcasting

Porsche 911 TV World News, Michigan International Speedway. *Photo by Tosh Wakabayashi*

1957 Ford 2-door pick up with tin camera and cameraman. **11.75 in** (30 cm). **Windup**. Known colors: Red and cream. Graphics: Radio Television. Maker: **Joustra**, France. Toy marks: Joustra.
Scarcity: 10. Fine to Excellent (C6-C8): $850-$1,075, Mint (C10): $1,400

1963 Ford 4-door hardtop with rotating TV camera. **11 in** (28 cm). **Friction**. Known colors: Light blue and yellow. Graphics: Fernsehen - Wagen 2 - Sport-Und-Nachrichtendienst. License: Ford. Maker: **Taiyo**, Japan. Toy marks: Taiyo World Toy.
Scarcity: 7. Fine to Excellent (C6-C8): $200-$300, Mint (C10): $400

Public Service Vehicles 149

1963 Ford 4-door hardtop with rotating TV camera and lithographed TV screen. **11 in** (28 cm). **Friction**. Known colors: Light blue and white. Graphics: TV News - Colour TV News. License: Ford. Maker: **Taiyo**, Japan. Toy marks: Taiyo World Toy.
Scarcity: 6. Fine to Excellent (C6-C8): $150-$250, Mint (C10): $350

1961 Plymouth 2-door station wagon with TV cameraman. **12 in** (30 cm). **Battery operated**. Known colors: Silver. Graphics: International T.V. Car. Maker: **Ichiko**, Japan. Toy marks: Ichiko. Box marks: Ichiko. Box text: *International T.V. Car.*
Scarcity: 9. Fine to Excellent (C6-C8): $750-$900, Mint (C10): $1,100

1964 Ford Galaxie 500 2-door hardtop with fender mounted camera, mirror, antenna, and TV control. **13 in** (33 cm). **Friction**. Known colors: Silver. Graphics: TV-Radio - Kamera Gar (roof sign). License: FG-1729. Maker: **Ichiko**, Japan. Toy marks: Ichiko.
Scarcity: 10. Fine to Excellent (C6-C8): $800-$1,000, Mint (C10): $1,250

1961 Plymouth 2-door station wagon with TV cameraman. **12 in** (30 cm). **Battery operated**. Known colors: Blue. Graphics: NTS Nederlandse Televisie Stichting. Maker: **Ichiko**, Japan. Toy marks: Ichiko.
Scarcity: 9. Fine to Excellent (C6-C8): $750-$900, Mint (C10): $1,100

1961 Plymouth 2-door station wagon with TV cameraman. **12 in** (30 cm). **Battery operated**. Known colors: Silver. Graphics: RAI Radiotelevisione Italiana. Maker: **Ichiko**, Japan. Toy marks: Ichiko.
Scarcity: 9. Fine to Excellent (C6-C8): $750-$900, Mint (C10): $1,100

1960s Hino TV Truck 2-door with camera and rotating (battery) antenna. **9.5 in** (24 cm). **Friction with battery**. Known colors: Blue and white. Graphics: C.B.S.-TV - Columbia Broadcasting System - TV Car. Maker: **Marusan/Hayashi**, Japan. Toy marks: SAN (Marusan), H (Hayashi). Box marks: SAN (Marusan). Box text: *Television Car With Camera & Battery Antenna*.
Scarcity: 9. Fine to Excellent (C6-C8): $300-$450, Mint (C10): $600

(Not pictured) **1960s Porsche 911 S 2-door coupe** with U-turn action and TV cameraman and camera on roof. **10 in** (25 cm). **Battery operated**. Known colors: Red and white. Graphics: TV Service Car. Maker: **Toplay**, Japan. Toy marks: TPS (Toplay). Box marks: TPS (Toplay).
Scarcity: 9. Fine to Excellent (C6-C8): $350-$450, Mint (C10): $600

150 Television and Broadcasting

1960s Porsche 911 S 2-door coupe with TV cameraman and camera on roof. **10 in** (25 cm). **Battery operated**. Known colors: White. Graphics: World News (with world logos). Maker: **Toplay**, Japan. Toy marks: TPS (Toplay). Box marks: TPS (Toplay). Box text: *News Service Car*.
Scarcity: 7. Fine to Excellent (C6-C8): $300-$400, Mint (C10): $550

(Not pictured) **1953 Studebaker 2-door coupe** with rotating tin camera and cameraman on roof, roof rails, and NBC fender flag. **7.5 in** (19 cm). **Friction**. Known colors: Assorted. Graphics: NBC - NBC Television Car. Maker: **Unknown**, Japan. Toy marks: none.
Scarcity: 9. Fine to Excellent (C6-C8): $800-$1,000, Mint (C10): $1,200

1950s Undetermined with two roof mounted TV cameras. **7 in** (18 cm). **Friction**. Known colors: Green and white. Graphics: NBC Television - Cragstan Broadcasting Company Inc. Maker: **Asahi**, Japan. Toy marks: ATC (Asahi Toy). Box marks: ATC (Asahi Toy), Cragstan. Box text: *Friction Television Car*.
Scarcity: 6. Fine to Excellent (C6-C8): $200-$300, Mint (C10): $400

1950s Undetermined with two roof mounted TV cameras. **7 in** (18 cm). **Friction**. Known colors: Brown and cream. Graphics: CBC Television - Cragstan Broadcasting Company Inc. Maker: **Asahi**, Japan. Toy marks: ATC (Asahi Toy). Box marks: ATC (Asahi Toy), Cragstan. Box text: *Friction Television Car*.
Scarcity: 6. Fine to Excellent (C6-C8): $200-$300, Mint (C10): $400

1950s Undetermined NBC Television Truck with rotating TV camera, cameraman, and side TV screen with moving space pictures. **8 in** (20 cm). **Battery operated**. Known colors: Blue and white. Graphics: NBC Television - RCA Victor - Color Television. Maker: **Yonezawa**, Japan. Toy marks: Y (Yonezawa). Box marks: Y (Yonezawa), Cragstan. Box text: *RCA-NBC Mobile Color T.V. Truck*.
Scarcity: 7. Fine to Excellent (C6-C8): $650-$775, Mint (C10): $900

(Not pictured) **1960s Undetermined News Service Car (Bus)** with fold down antenna, rotating roof TV camera, and lithographed technician. **8.75 in** (22 cm). **Friction**. Known colors: Blue and silver. Graphics: R.C.A. T.V., RCA Telecast Station News Service Car. Maker: **Aoshin**, Japan. Toy marks: ASC (Aoshin). Box marks: ASC (Aoshin). Box text: *R.C.A. T.V. Television News Service Car*.
Scarcity: 6. Fine to Excellent (C6-C8): $250-$350, Mint (C10): $450

1960s Undetermined 2-door with driver, rotating camera, and cameraman. **9 in** (23 cm). **Friction**. Known colors: Red, orange, blue, and white. Graphics: ABC TV - No.2. License: No. 402. Maker: **Nishimura**, Japan. Toy marks: SN (Nishimura). Box text: *ABC TV Truck*.
Scarcity: 6. Fine to Excellent (C6-C8): $100-$200, Mint (C10): $300

Public Service Vehicles 151

1960s Undetermined Television Remote Car 2-door with lithographed interior on windows. **9 in** (23 cm). **Friction**. Known colors: Green. Graphics: Television Remote Car T.V. Maker: **Unknown**, Japan. Toy marks: none. Box marks: none. Box text: *Television Remote Car*.
Scarcity: 5. Fine to Excellent (C6-C8): $100-$200, Mint (C10): $300

1960s Undetermined with lighted screen, stop and go action, and two moveable cameras. **11.25 in** (29 cm). **Battery operated**. Known colors: Blue. Graphics: NAR Television - WBST - WRCA. Maker: **Linemar**, Japan. Toy marks: Linemar (Marx). Box marks: Linemar (Marx). Box text: *Television Truck*.
Scarcity: 7. Fine to Excellent (C6-C8): $400-$600, Mint (C10): $800

1960s Undetermined with roof mounted TV cameraman and light. Bump and go action. **9.25 in** (23 cm). **Battery operated**. Known colors: Blue and light blue. Graphics: WDR - Deutsches Fernsehen - Aufnahme Wagen No.5. Maker: **Alps**, Japan. Toy marks: none. Box marks: Alps. Box text: *World T.V. Bus*.
Scarcity: 7. Fine to Excellent (C6-C8): $350-$450, Mint (C10): $600

1950/60s Volkswagen Transporter van with rotating roof mounted cameraman and camera. Bump and go action. **7.75 in** (20 cm). **Battery operated**. Known colors: Orange and yellow. Graphics: International T.V. Service. Maker: **Bandai**, Japan. Toy marks: Bandai. Box marks: Bandai. Box text: *Volkswagen TV Bus #4310*.
Scarcity: 8. Fine to Excellent (C6-C8): $400-$600, Mint (C10): $800

1950/60s Volkswagen Transporter van with button control and revolving antenna. Vehicle follows antenna direction. **8 in** (20 cm). **Battery operated**. Known colors: Gray and light blue. Graphics: Central T.V. Channel 7 - C.T.V. Maker: **Gaaken**, Japan. Toy marks: Gaaken Toy. Box marks: Gaaken Toy. Box text: *Volkswagen*.
Scarcity: 8. Fine to Excellent (C6-C8): $250-$450, Mint (C10): $625

1950/60s Volkswagen Transporter van with radio control and revolving antenna. Vehicle follows antenna direction. **8 in** (20 cm). **Radio Control Battery**. Known colors: Blue and light blue. Graphics: International TV Broadcasting Van - I.T.V. Maker: **Gaaken**, Japan. Toy marks: Gaaken Toy. Box marks: Gaaken Toy. Box text: *TV Broadcasting Van*.
Scarcity: 8. Fine to Excellent (C6-C8): $250-$450, Mint (C10): $675

1950/60s Volkswagen Transporter van with roof mounted TV camera. **9 in** (23 cm). **Friction**. Known colors: Light blue and dark blue. Graphics: Nederlandse Televisie Stichting. Maker: **Taiyo**, Japan. Toy marks: Taiyo World Toy.
Scarcity: 5. Fine to Excellent (C6-C8): $100-$185, Mint (C10): $375

Hot Rods and Jalopies
(By Year, Size, and Toy Maker)

Hot Rod, Coronado, California. *Photo by Tosh Wakabayashi*

1920s Hot Rod 2-door with visible engine. **7.75 in** (20 cm). **Friction**. Known colors: Red; Green. Graphics: 23. Maker: **Marx**, Japan. Toy marks: Marx. Box marks: Marx. Box text: *Little Big Red Hot Rod*. Notes: Produced 1960s.
Scarcity: 3. Fine to Excellent (C6-C8): $70-$95, Mint (C10): $145

154 Hot Rods and Jalopies

1930s Ford Jalopy 4-door with eccentric rear wheels. **5 in** (12 cm). **Friction**. Known colors: Blue. Graphics: (graffiti all over car). License: Silver Springs. Maker: **Linemar**, Japan. Toy marks: Marx, Linemar (Marx). Box marks: Linemar (Marx).
Notes: Produced 1950s. This car is a miniature version of the windup 7.25 inch Jalopy produced by Marx in the U.S. as it contains the same graffiti markings.
Scarcity: 5. Fine to Excellent (C6-C8): $50-$75, Mint (C10): $100

1930s Hot Rod 2-door with piston action visible engine. **7 in** (18 cm). **Friction**. Known colors: Red and gold. Graphics: The Bug. License: H12. Maker: **Nomura**, Japan. Toy marks: TN (Nomura). Box marks: TN (Nomura). Box text: *Hot Rod - The Bug With Piston Action*.
Notes: Produced 1960s.
Scarcity: 4. Fine to Excellent (C6-C8): $150-$200, Mint (C10): $265

1930s Jalopy 2-door with celluloid driver and forward/reverse action. **7 in** (18 cm). **R/C battery operated**. Known colors: Red. Graphics: (graffiti all over car). License: I-775. Maker: **Linemar**, Japan. Toy marks: Linemar (Marx). Box marks: Linemar (Marx). Box text: *Jalopy*.
Notes: Produced 1950s.
Scarcity: 6. Fine to Excellent (C6-C8): $175-$275, Mint (C10): $375

1930s Ford Jalopy 4-door with tin driver, eccentric rear wheels, and adjustable front wheels. **7.25 in** (18 cm). **Windup**. Known colors: Black. Graphics: (graffiti all over car). License: Silver Springs. Maker: **Marx**, USA. Toy marks: Marx. Box marks: Marx.
Notes: Produced 1950s. Two earlier versions of this car were produced with variations in the graphics. A miniature version of this Jalopy was produced by Marx (Linemar) in Japan and contains the same graffiti markings.
Scarcity: 6. Fine to Excellent (C6-C8): $100-$175, Mint (C10): $250

Hot Rods and Jalopies 155

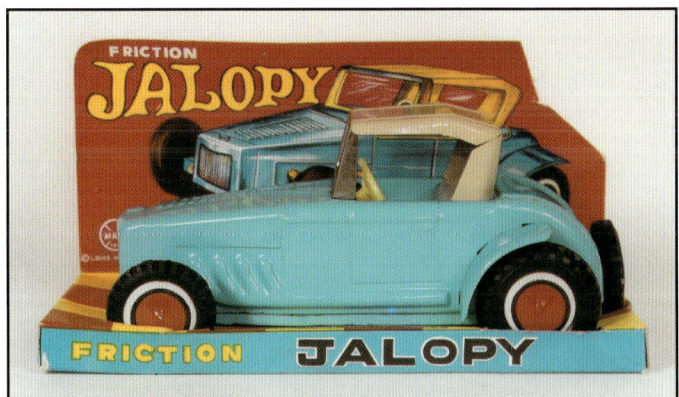

1930s Ford Hot Rod 2-door with no hood or fenders and visible engine. **8 in** (20 cm). **Friction**. Known colors: Assorted. Graphics: 7. License: No. B-306. Maker: **Bandai**, Japan. Toy marks: Bandai. Box marks: Bandai. Box text: *Hot Rod #306*.
Notes: Produced 1960s.
Scarcity: 3. Fine to Excellent (C6-C8): $75-$125, Mint (C10): $175

1930s Jalopy 2-door. 7.25 in (18 cm). **Friction**. Known colors: Assorted. Maker: **Marx**, Japan. Toy marks: Marx. Box marks: Marx. Box text: *Jalopy*.
Notes: Produced 1960s.
Scarcity: 2. Fine to Excellent (C6-C8): $40-$60, Mint (C10): $90

(Not pictured) **1930s Hot Rod 2-door** with rocking engine. **7.25 in** (18 cm). **Friction**. Known colors: Assorted. Graphics: Hot Rod. Maker: **Nomura**, Japan. Toy marks: TN (Nomura). Box text: *Hot Rod Friction Car with Piston Action*.
Notes: Produced 1950s.
Scarcity: 3. Fine to Excellent (C6-C8): $100-$150, Mint (C10): $200

1930s Hot Rod 2-door with bump and go action, lighted engine, and tin driver with head that turns as car turns. **7.25 in** (18 cm). **Battery operated**. Known colors: Blue and yellow; Red and yellow. Graphics: Hot Rod - Dream Boat, Rock n' Roll. License: H12. Maker: **Nomura**, Japan. Toy marks: TN (Nomura). Box marks: TN (Nomura). Box text: *Hot Rod*.
Notes: Produced 1950s.
Scarcity: 5. Fine to Excellent (C6-C8): $125-$175, Mint (C10): $250

(Not pictured) **1930s Ford Hot Rod 2-door** with no fenders, engine noise, and side pipes extending from exposed engine. **8 in** (20 cm). **Friction**. Known colors: Assorted. Maker: **Bandai**, Japan. Toy marks: Bandai. Box marks: Bandai. Box text: *Hot Rod With Clack Clack Noise*.
Notes: Produced 1960s.
Scarcity: 3. Fine to Excellent (C6-C8): $100-$150, Mint (C10): $200

1930s Ford Hot Rod 2-door with civilian driver. **8 in** (20 cm). **Battery operated**. Known colors: White and red with black fenders. Graphics: Hot Rod - (Flame graphics). Maker: **Bandai**, Japan. Toy marks: Bandai. Box marks: Bandai. Box text: *Old Fashioned Hot Rod With Driver #4080*.
Notes: Produced 1960s.
Scarcity: 4. Fine to Excellent (C6-C8): $80-$125, Mint (C10): $150

156 Hot Rods and Jalopies

1930s Ford Hot Rod Jalopy 2-door coupe. 8 in (20 cm). **Friction.** Known colors: Red, black, and white. Graphics: 3 - 30 HP. - Pure - Champion. Maker: **Bandai**, Japan. Toy marks: Bandai. Box marks: Cragstan, NGS (Cragstan). Box text: *Cragstan Jalopy Stock Car*.
Notes: Produced 1960s.
Scarcity: 3. Fine to Excellent (C6-C8): $75-$100, Mint (C10): $125

1930s Ford Hot Rod Jalopy 2-door roadster. 8 in (20 cm). **Friction.** Known colors: White, black, and red. Graphics: 8 - 28 HP. - (flame graphics) - Speed Demon. Maker: **Bandai**, Japan. Toy marks: Bandai. Box marks: Cragstan, NGS (Cragstan). Box text: *Cragstan Jalopy Stock Car*.
Notes: Produced 1960s.
Scarcity: 3. Fine to Excellent (C6-C8): $75-$100, Mint (C10): $125

1930s Ford Hot Rod 4-door convertible. 8 in (20 cm). **Friction.** Known colors: Blue and white. Graphics: 10 - 32 HP. Maker: **Bandai**, Japan. Toy marks: Bandai. Box marks: Cragstan, NGS (Cragstan).
Notes: Produced 1960s.
Scarcity: 3. Fine to Excellent (C6-C8): $75-$100, Mint (C10): $125

1930s Ford Hot Rod 4-door sedan. 8 in (20 cm). **Friction.** Known colors: Black and red. Graphics: 5 - 27 HP. Maker: **Bandai**, Japan. Toy marks: Bandai. Box marks: Cragstan, NGS (Cragstan).
Notes: Produced 1960s.
Scarcity: 3. Fine to Excellent (C6-C8): $75-$100, Mint (C10): $125

1930s Hot Rod 2-door with sparking engine. 8 in (20 cm). **Friction.** Known colors: Red. Graphics: 7 - Hot Rod. Maker: **Nomura**, Japan. Toy marks: TN (Nomura), Mitomo.
Notes: Produced 1960s.
Scarcity: 4. Fine to Excellent (C6-C8): $85-$165, Mint (C10): $225

1930s Hot Rod 2-door with visible engine (tin or plastic). 8 in (20 cm). **Friction.** Known colors: Blue and cream. Graphics: Hot Rod. License: 6483. Maker: **Nomura**, Japan. Toy marks: TN (Nomura).
Notes: Produced 1960s.
Scarcity: 4. Fine to Excellent (C6-C8): $85-$165, Mint (C10): $225

Hot Rods and Jalopies

1930s Hot Rod 2-door with rocking engine. **8 in** (20 cm). **Friction**. Known colors: Blue. Graphics: N62. License: 1350. Maker: **Nomura**, Japan. Toy marks: TN (Nomura). Box marks: TN (Nomura). Box text: *Hot Rod*.
Notes: Produced 1960s.
Scarcity: 4. Fine to Excellent (C6-C8): $85-$165, Mint (C10): $225

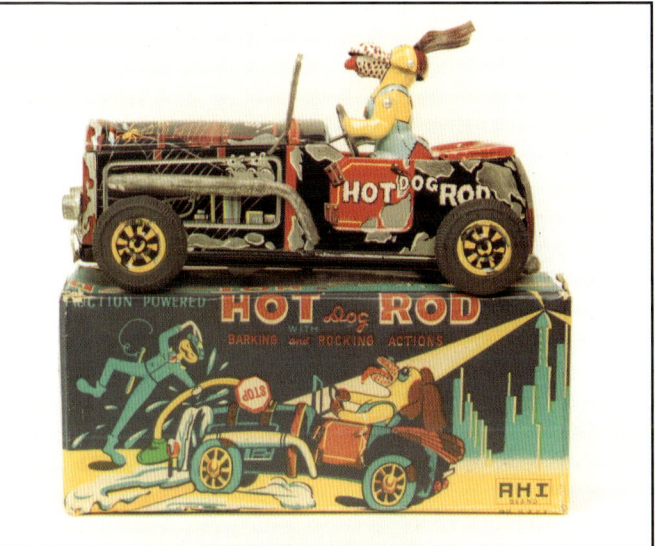

1930s Hot Rod 2-door with barking and bouncing dog driver. **9 in** (23 cm). **Friction**. Known colors: Black and red. Graphics: Hot Dog Rod. Maker: **Masuya**, Japan. Toy marks: Masuya. Box marks: Masuya, AHI. Box text: *Hot Dog Rod With Barking and Rocking Actions*.
Notes: Produced 1960s.
Scarcity: 6. Fine to Excellent (C6-C8): $125-$200, Mint (C10): $325

(Not pictured) **1930s Hot Rod 2-door** with bouncing duck driver. **9 in** (23 cm). **Friction**. Known colors: Red. Graphics: Hot Rod. Maker: **Masuya**, Japan. Toy marks: Masuya. Box marks: Masuya. Box text: *Hot Rod With Driver*.
Notes: Produced 1960s.
Scarcity: 6. Fine to Excellent (C6-C8): $100-$175, Mint (C10): $275

1930s Hot Rod 2-door with tin driver, lithographed chassis, and visible engine with moving piston. **8.5 in** (22 cm). **Friction**. Known colors: Mohave Mauve. Graphics: 3 - (Indian head). License: 1935. Maker: **Terai**, Japan. Toy marks: Daiya (Terai).
Notes: Produced 1960s.
Scarcity: 8. Fine to Excellent (C6-C8): $150-$275, Mint (C10): $425

1930s Hot Rod Jalopy 4-door with four tin figures, lights, steering, and forward/reverse action. Writing all over car. **9.75 in** (25 cm). **R/C battery operated**. Known colors: Red. Graphics: Hot Rod Special - etc. Maker: **Linemar**, Japan. Toy marks: Linemar (Marx). Box marks: Linemar (Marx). Box text: *College Jalopy*.
Notes: Produced 1960s.
Scarcity: 6. Fine to Excellent (C6-C8): $200-$300, Mint (C10): $425

1930s Hot Rod 2-door with moving piston engine. **8.5 in** (22 cm). **Friction**. Known colors: Yellow. Graphics: Hot Rod. License: 1963. Maker: **Unknown**, Japan. Toy marks: none.
Notes: Produced 1960s.
Scarcity: 3. Fine to Excellent (C6-C8): $85-$115, Mint (C10): $135

158 Hot Rods and Jalopies

1930s Ford Hot Rod 2-door with smoking engine with lights, vibration, and stop and go action. **10 in** (25 cm). **Battery operated**. Known colors: Assorted. License: NKW-682. Maker: **Alps**, Japan. Toy marks: Alps. Box marks: Alps. Box text: *Hot Rod Custom "T" Ford with Overheated Boiling Radiator*.
Notes: Produced 1960s.
Scarcity: 3. Fine to Excellent (C6-C8): $95-$140, Mint (C10): $200

1930s Ford Hot Rod 2-door with lighted, smoking engine. **10 in** (25 cm). **Battery operated**. Known colors: Yellow and orange. Graphics: (Psychedelic graphics). Maker: **Alps**, Japan. Toy marks: Alps. Box marks: Alps. Box text: *Big Slicks Hot Rod Limousine*.
Notes: Produced 1960s.
Scarcity: 3. Fine to Excellent (C6-C8): $95-$140, Mint (C10): $200

1930s Ford Hot Rod 2-door with lighted, smoking engine. **10 in** (25 cm). **Battery operated**. Known colors: Yellow. Graphics: (Psychedelic graphics). Maker: **Alps**, Japan. Toy marks: Alps. Box marks: Alps. Box text: *Big Slicks Hot Rod Custom 'T' Ford*.
Notes: Produced 1960s.
Scarcity: 3. Fine to Excellent (C6-C8): $95-$140, Mint (C10): $200

1930s Ford Hot Rod 2-door with lighted interior showing silhouettes, smoking engine, sound, and stop and go action. **10 in** (25 cm). **Battery operated**. Known colors: Red, white, and blue. Graphics: (Stars and stripes). Maker: **Alps**, Japan. Toy marks: Alps. Box marks: Alps. Box text: *Smoking Limousine - The Spirit Of America*.
Notes: Produced 1960s.
Scarcity: 4. Fine to Excellent (C6-C8): $150-$200, Mint (C10): $250

(Not pictured) **1930s Ford Jalopy 2-door** with two figures in front seat and two figures in jump seat. **10 in** (25 cm). **Friction**. Known colors: Yellow. Graphics: Tin Lizzy (graffiti). Maker: **Arnold**, Germany. Toy marks: Arnold. Box marks: Arnold. Box text: *Tin Lizzy*.
Notes: Produced 1950s.
Scarcity: 6. Fine to Excellent (C6-C8): $600-$900, Mint (C10): $1,200

Hot Rods and Jalopies 159

1930s Hot Rod 2-door with driver and bump and go action. **10.25 in** (26 cm). **Battery operated**. Known colors: Red. Graphics: 15B - Super Power. Maker: **Nomura**, Japan. Toy marks: TN (Nomura), Shinkosa. Box marks: TN (Nomura), Shinkosa. Box text: *Hot Rod Mystery Action*.
Notes: Produced 1960s.
Scarcity: 6. Fine to Excellent (C6-C8): $200-$325, Mint (C10): $450

1930s Hot Rod 2-door with tin driver (vinyl head), bump and go action, spinning fan, and lighted vibrating engine. **10.25 in** (26 cm). **Battery operated**. Known colors: Red and yellow. Graphics: 999. Maker: **Nomura**, Japan. Toy marks: TN (Nomura), Shinkosa.
Notes: Produced 1960s.
Scarcity: 6. Fine to Excellent (C6-C8): $200-$325, Mint (C10): $450

(Not pictured) **1930s Hot Rod 2-door** with bump and go action and blinking light. **10.25 in** (26 cm). **Battery operated**. Known colors: Red and white. Graphics: Hot Rod - Mongoose. Maker: **Taiyo**, Japan. Toy marks: Taiyo. Box marks: Taiyo. Box text: *Speed Jack*.
Notes: Produced 1960s.
Scarcity: 4. Fine to Excellent (C6-C8): $120-$175, Mint (C10): $225

1930s Hot Rod 2-door with roll bar, header pipes, plastic engine, lights, sound, and bump and go action. Numbered decals. **10.5 in** (27 cm). **Battery operated**. Known colors: Red; Blue. Graphics: (numbered decals). Maker: **Bandai**, Japan. Toy marks: Bandai. Box marks: Bandai. Box text: *Hot Rod Racer #4383*.
Notes: Produced 1960s.
Scarcity: 3. Fine to Excellent (C6-C8): $75-$120, Mint (C10): $165

1930s Hot Rod 2-door with vinyl head driver, lighted piston engine, bump and go, fan, and engine noise. **11.5 in** (29 cm). **Battery operated**. Known colors: Red. Graphics: 8 - Roadster. Maker: **Terai**, Japan. Toy marks: Daiya (Terai). Box marks: Daiya (Terai), MEGO. Box text: *V8 Roadster*.
Notes: Produced 1960s.
Scarcity: 4. Fine to Excellent (C6-C8): $100-$200, Mint (C10): $300

1930s Ford Hot Rod 2-door with plastic race driver and moving pistons. **12 in** (30 cm). **Battery operated**. Known colors: Red. Maker: **Bandai**, Japan. Toy marks: Bandai. Box marks: Bandai. Box text: *Hot Rod Speed Demon Racer #4148*.
Notes: Produced 1960s.
Scarcity: 5. Fine to Excellent (C6-C8): $200-$325, Mint (C10): $450

1960s Hot Rod 2-door with moving rear engine pistons & propeller. **9 in** (23 cm). **Friction**. Known colors: Black and yellow. Graphics: Prop-Rod 8821. Maker: **Asahi**, Japan. Toy marks: ATC (Asahi Toy). Box marks: ATC (Asahi Toy).
Scarcity: 4. Fine to Excellent (C6-C8): $85-$155, Mint (C10): $225

Race Cars

Dragsters

(By Year, Size, and Toy Maker)

1930s Dragster open-wheel style with tin driver, visible lighted engine, and piston action. **8.5 in** (22 cm). **Battery operated**. Known colors: Red. Graphics: 7 (tin). Maker: **Sankei**, Japan. Toy marks: none. Box marks: K (Sankei), GW (George Wagner). Box text: *Drag Racer With Lighted Piston Action*. Notes: Produced 1960s.
Scarcity: 4. Fine to Excellent (C6-C8): $115-$225, Mint (C10): $325

1960s Dragster open-wheel style with tin driver and hood mounted roulette wheel. **8.5 in** (22 cm). **Friction**. Known colors: Red. Graphics: 7. Maker: **Masuya**, Japan. Toy marks: MS (Masuya).
Scarcity: 5. Fine to Excellent (C6-C8): $150-$225, Mint (C10): $295

1960s Dragster open-wheel style. **8.5 in** (22 cm). **Friction**. Known colors: Yellow. Graphics: World Championship - Big Drag. Maker: **Takatoku**, Japan. Toy marks: TT (Takatoku).
Scarcity: 3. Fine to Excellent (C6-C8): $60-$90, Mint (C10): $135

1960s Dragster open-wheel style with tin driver. **9 in** (23 cm). **Friction**. Known colors: Red. Graphics: 99 - Star. Maker: **Meiko**, Japan. Toy marks: none. Box marks: Meiko. Box text: *Drag Racer*.
Scarcity: 5. Fine to Excellent (C6-C8): $150-$225, Mint (C10): $300

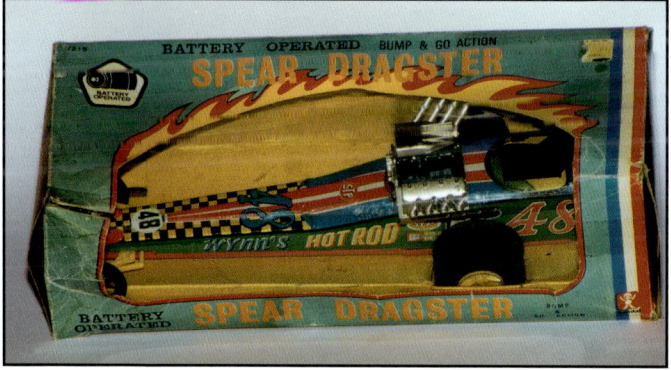

1960s Dragster open-wheel style with bump and go action. **10 in** (25 cm). **Battery operated**. Known colors: Multi. Graphics: 48 – Wynn's Hot Rod. Maker: **Bandai**, Japan. Toy marks: Bandai. Box marks: Bandai. Box text: *Spear Dragster #7215*.
Scarcity: 3. Fine to Excellent (C6-C8): $85-$150, Mint (C10): $235

162 Dragsters

1960s Dragster open-wheel style with vinyl driver head and plastic chassis. **11.5 in** (29 cm). **Friction**. Known colors: Blue and yellow. Graphics: The Winner - Starlucky. Maker: **Unknown**, Japan. Toy marks: none. **Scarcity: 4. Fine to Excellent (C6-C8): $85-$135, Mint (C10): $225**

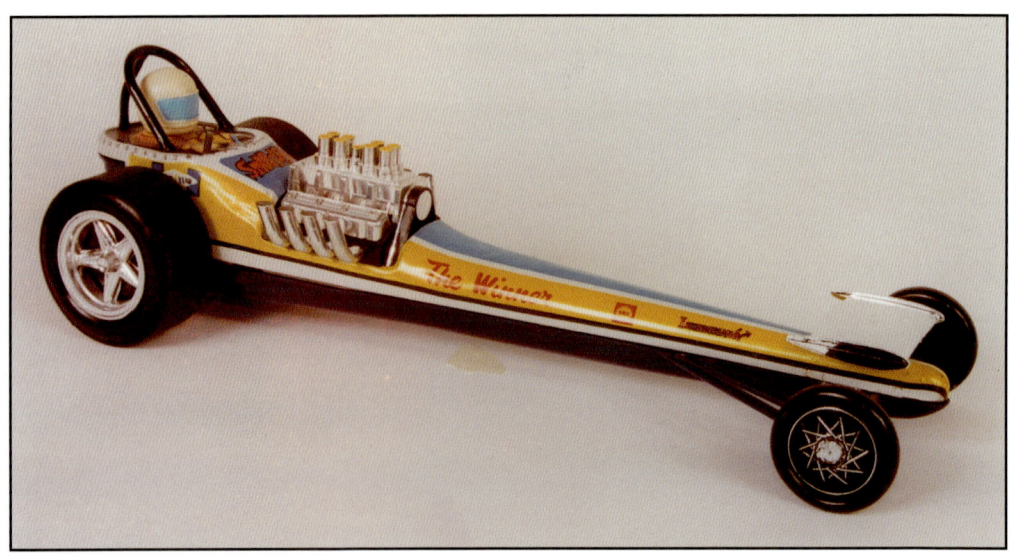

1960s Dragster open-wheel style with engine light, sound, and adjustable front wheels. **12.25 in** (31 cm). **Battery operated**. Known colors: Green and gold. Graphics: Charger. Maker: **Terai**, Japan. Toy marks: Daiya (Terai). Box marks: Daiya (Terai). Box text: *Drag Coupe*. **Scarcity: 4. Fine to Excellent (C6-C8): $250-$325, Mint (C10): $400**

1960s Dragster with vinyl driver head and lithographed chassis. **13.75 in** (35 cm). **Friction**. Known colors: Red. Graphics: 3. Maker: **Unknown**, Japan. Toy marks: none. **Scarcity: 7. Fine to Excellent (C6-C8): $250-$375, Mint (C10): $500**

Speed Record

(By Size and Toy Maker)

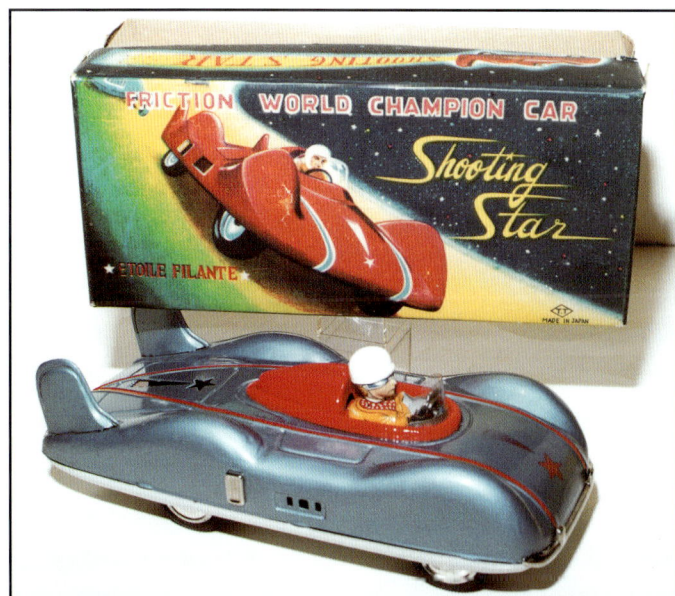

1950/60s Racer with tin driver. **9.5 in** (24 cm). **Friction**. Known colors: Two tone green and red. Graphics: 36. Maker: **Masudaya**, Japan. Toy marks: MT (Masudaya). Box marks: MT (Masudaya). Box text: *Super Sonic Race Car No.36*.
Scarcity: 4. Fine to Excellent (C6-C8): $125-$170, Mint (C10): $225

1950/60s Renault Racer with tin driver and rear fins. **8 in** (20 cm). **Friction**. Known colors: Assorted. Graphics: (Star graphics). Maker: **Takatoku**, Japan. Toy marks: TT (Takatoku). Box marks: TT (Takatoku). Box text: *World Champion Car Shooting Star *Etoile Filante*.
Scarcity: 6. Fine to Excellent (C6-C8): $250-$350, Mint (C10): $500

1950/60s Land Speed Racer with tin driver. **9.5 in** (24 cm). **Friction**. Known colors: Red and yellow. Graphics: 777 – Wynn's Friction Proofing - Streamliner. Maker: **Masudaya**, Japan. Toy marks: MT (Masudaya). Box marks: MT (Masudaya). Box text: *Race Car 777*.
Scarcity: 7. Fine to Excellent (C6-C8): $500-$600, Mint (C10): $700

1950/60s Racer with tin driver head. **8.75 in** (22 cm). **Battery operated**. Known colors: Silver-blue. Graphics: 7 - Meteor. Maker: **Nomura**, Japan. Toy marks: TN (Nomura).
Scarcity: 4. Fine to Excellent (C6-C8): $150-$265, Mint (C10): $350

1950/60s Racer with tin driver, canopy, and sparking action. **9.75 in** (25 cm). **Friction**. Known colors: Red and cream. Graphics: 76. Maker: **Tanaguchi**, Japan. Toy marks: TKK (Unknown), TS (Tanaguchi).
Scarcity: 5. Fine to Excellent (C6-C8): $300-$400, Mint (C10): $525

1950/60s Racer with tin driver, siren sound, and spinning exhaust flames. **9 in** (23 cm). **Friction**. Known colors: White and red. Graphics: 25. Maker: **Nomura**, Japan. Toy marks: TN (Nomura).
Scarcity: 5. Fine to Excellent (C6-C8): $225-$300, Mint (C10): $400

164 Speed Record

1950/60s Renault Racer with plastic driver and fins. **10.5 in** (27 cm). **Friction**. Known colors: Blue. Graphics: Renault - Etoile Filante Renault. Maker: **Mont Blanc**, France. Toy marks: Mont-Blanc. Box marks: Mont-Blanc. Box text: *Record Du Monde 308,9 Km/h - L'etoile Filante - Auto De Course Record De Vitesse*.
Scarcity: 5. Fine to Excellent (C6-C8): $125-$175, Mint (C10): $250

1950/60s Fiat Abarth 750 Racer with tin driver and siren sound. **10 in** (25 cm). **Friction**. Known colors: Red, white, yellow, and blue. Graphics: 45. Maker: **Mansei Toys**, Japan. Toy marks: Haji (Mansei). Box marks: Haji (Mansei). Box text: *Champion Racer*.
Scarcity: 5. Fine to Excellent (C6-C8): $175-$275, Mint (C10): $375

1950/60s Fiat Abarth 750 Racer with tin driver and sparking wheel. **10 in** (25 cm). **Friction**. Known colors: Red and cream. Graphics: Fiat 750 Abarth - Pinin Farina. Maker: **Mansei Toys**, Japan. Toy marks: none. Box marks: HTC (Unknown).
Scarcity: 5. Fine to Excellent (C6-C8): $175-$275, Mint (C10): $375

1950/60s Astro Racer with tin driver head, plastic canopy, blinking engine, and jet exhaust. **12 in** (30 cm). **Battery operated**. Known colors: Red and white. Graphics: Astro. Maker: **Terai**, Japan. Toy marks: Daiya (Terai). Box marks: Daiya (Terai). Box text: *Astro Racer With Multi Action*.
Scarcity: 7. Fine to Excellent (C6-C8): $600-$800, Mint (C10): $1,000

1950/60s Bonneville Racer. **10 in** (25 cm). **Friction**. Known colors: Assorted. Graphics: Mobilgas and various stick on numbers and stripes. Maker: **Mattel**, USA. Toy marks: none. Box marks: Mattel. Box text: *Bonneville Salt-Flats Special*.
Scarcity: 4. Fine to Excellent (C6-C8): $150-$250, Mint (C10): $375

1950/60s Racer with tin driver, canopy, and sparking action. **12.25 in** (31 cm). **Friction**. Known colors: Light green, yellow, and black. Maker: **Tanaguchi**, Japan. Toy marks: TKK (Unknown). Box marks: TKK (Unknown), Cragstan. Box text: *Jet Racer*.
Scarcity: 5. Fine to Excellent (C6-C8): $300-$400, Mint (C10): $525

Race Cars 165

1950/60s Racer with tin driver, canopy, and sparking action. **12.25 in** (31 cm). **Friction**. Known colors: Light blue-green. Graphics: 8 - King Jet. Maker: **Tanaguchi**, Japan. Toy marks: TKK (Unknown), TS (Tanaguchi).
Scarcity: 5. Fine to Excellent (C6-C8): $300-$400, Mint (C10): $525

1950/60s Open-wheel style Racer with tin driver head, chrome nose cone, three wheels, and sparking engine. **12.75 in** (32 cm). **Friction**. Known colors: Blue, red, and yellow. Graphics: 55 - Atom. Maker: **Unknown**, Japan. Toy marks: none.
Scarcity: 8. Fine to Excellent (C6-C8): $475-$725, Mint (C10): $1,000

1950/60s Racer with tin driver head, plastic canopy, and rear gearshift lever. **12.25 in** (31 cm). **Battery operated**. Known colors: Red and white. Maker: **Terai**, Japan. Toy marks: Daiya (Terai). Box marks: Daiya (Terai).
Scarcity: 7. Fine to Excellent (C6-C8): $550-$750, Mint (C10): $950

1950/60s NSU Land Speed Racer. Motorcycle based racer by Neckarsulm Strickmaschinen Union. **13.5 in** (34 cm). **Friction**. Known colors: Red and white. Graphics: 7 - Record Racer - NSU. Maker: **Bandai**, Japan. Toy marks: Bandai. Box text: *NSU Record Racer*.
Notes: (And you thought it was a car!).
Scarcity: 7. Fine to Excellent (C6-C8): $300-$500, Mint (C10): $650

1950/60s Racer with engine noise. **12.75 in** (32 cm). **Friction**. Known colors: Red and white. Graphics: 7 (7 stars). Maker: **Masudaya**, Japan. Toy marks: MT (Masudaya). Box marks: MT (Masudaya). Box text: *Race Car Seven Star*.
Notes: Masudaya catalog image.
Scarcity: 5. Fine to Excellent (C6-C8): $250-$350, Mint (C10): $450

1950/60s Atom Jet Racer with tin driver. **27 in** (69 cm). **Friction**. Known colors: Green. Graphics: 58 - Atom Jet - Atom (hubcaps). Maker: **Yonezawa**, Japan. Toy marks: Y (Yonezawa). Box marks: Y (Yonezawa). Box text: *Atom-54*.
Scarcity: 10. Fine to Excellent (C6-C8): $1,500-$2,200, Mint (C10): $2,900

Rally and Stock Cars
(By Make, Year, Size, and Toy Maker)

Rally Ford Mustang Fastback. *Photo by Rodney Abensur*

1958 Austin Healey 2-door convertible with driver and rally tonneau. **6 in** (15 cm).
Friction. Known colors: Red. **Maker: Unknown**, Japan. Toy marks: none.
Notes: Produced 1980s.
Scarcity: 4. Fine to Excellent (C6-C8): $50-$100, Mint (C10): $150

Race Cars 167

1958 Austin Healey 100 Six 2-door convertible with retainer for race car number. **8 in** (20 cm). **Friction**. Known colors: Red-orange and white. Graphics: (Apply your own number from box cutouts). Maker: **Bandai**, Japan. Toy marks: Bandai. Box marks: Bandai.
Scarcity: 7. Fine to Excellent (C6-C8): $200-$300, Mint (C10): $450

1958 Austin Healey 100 Six 2-door convertible. 8 in (20 cm). **Friction**. Known colors: Red-orange and white. Graphics: 8. Maker: **Bandai**, Japan. Toy marks: Bandai. Box marks: Bandai. Box text: *Austin Healey Sports Car #810*.
Scarcity: 7. Fine to Excellent (C6-C8): $200-$300, Mint (C10): $450

1958 Austin Healey 100 Six 2-door convertible with top up. **8 in** (20 cm). **Friction**. Known colors: Red-orange and white. Graphics: 8 or 5 (on roof and doors), Austin Healey script on hood. Maker: **Bandai**, Japan. Toy marks: Bandai. Box marks: Bandai.
Scarcity: 7. Fine to Excellent (C6-C8): $200-$300, Mint (C10): $450

(Not pictured) **1960s BMW 3.5 CSL** with bump and go action. **8 in** (20 cm). **Battery operated**. Known colors: White. Graphics: 14 - Dunlop. Maker: **Taiyo**, Japan. Toy marks: Taiyo. Box marks: Taiyo. Box text: *BMW 3.5 CSL Turbo*.
Scarcity: 2. Fine to Excellent (C6-C8): $75-$135, Mint (C10): $200

1960s BMW 2000 CS 2-door coupe with blinking directional headlights as it travels in figure eight pattern. **8.5 in** (22 cm). **Battery operated**. Known colors: Blue. Graphics: 6 - Champion. License: BMW. Maker: **Bandai**, Japan. Toy marks: Bandai. Box marks: Bandai.
Scarcity: 4. Fine to Excellent (C6-C8): $110-$160, Mint (C10): $225

1960s BMW 2000 CS 2-door coupe. 8.5 in (22 cm). **Friction**. Known colors: Silver. Graphics: 93 - 2000CS - Champion Spark Plug. License: BMW. Maker: **Bandai**, Japan. Toy marks: Bandai. Box marks: Bandai. Box text: *Grand Prix Race Car Series #2037*.
Scarcity: 4. Fine to Excellent (C6-C8): $110-$160, Mint (C10): $225

1962 Buick 2-door hardtop with smoking exhaust, antenna, siren sound, bump and go action, and checkered flag. **12 in** (30 cm). **Battery operated**. Known colors: Red. Graphics: 8 - Champion - 380HP. Maker: **Nomura/IY Metal**, Japan. Toy marks: none. Box marks: Cragstan, NGS (Cragstan). Box text: *Cragstan Stock Car It's a Winner*.
Scarcity: 9. Fine to Excellent (C6-C8): $300-$600, Mint (C10): $900

168 Rally and Stock Cars

1968 Cadillac 2-door hardtop with rollover action and plastic chassis. **11.25 in** (29 cm). **Battery operated**. Known colors: Red and yellow. Graphics: 17 or 27 - Stunt Car. Maker: **Masudaya**, Japan. Toy marks: MT (Masudaya). Box marks: Sears. Box text: *Stunt Car*.
Scarcity: 3. Fine to Excellent (C6-C8): $75-$125, Mint (C10): $165

(Not pictured) **1960 Chevrolet 4-door hardtop** with racing graphics and space motif. **7.5 in** (19 cm). **Friction**. Known colors: Blue and red. Graphics: 77 - Pure - 375 HP. License: Chevrolet - Ichiko. Maker: **Ichiko**, Japan. Toy marks: Ichiko. Box marks: Ichiko. Box text: *Stock Racing Car Series Chevrolet*.
Scarcity: 5. Fine to Excellent (C6-C8): $95-$125, Mint (C10): $165

1960 Chevrolet Corvair 4-door sedan. **9.25 in** (23 cm). **Friction**. Known colors: Black and red. Graphics: 7 - 375 H.P. License: IK-0973. Maker: **Ichiko**, Japan. Toy marks: Ichiko. Box marks: Cragstan. Box text: *Cragstan Stock Racing Car Corvair*.
Scarcity: 5. Fine to Excellent (C6-C8): $135-$200, Mint (C10): $275

1965 Chevrolet 4-door sedan with trunk on-off switch and bump and go action. **11 in** (28 cm). **Battery operated**. Known colors: Yellow and black. Graphics: 55. License: A-5822. Maker: **Ichiko**, Japan. Toy marks: Ichiko. Box marks: Ichiko. Box text: *Multi-Action Stock Car*.
Scarcity: 7. Fine to Excellent (C6-C8): $150-$225, Mint (C10): $375

(Not pictured) **1971 Chevrolet Camaro 2-door hardtop** with blinking lights, non-fall and bump and go action. **10.25 in** (26 cm). **Battery**. Known colors: Blue and red. Graphics: Chevrolet Camaro, Supercar Engineering, Stripblazer. Maker: **Taiyo**, Japan. Toy marks: Taiyo. Box marks: Taiyo. Box text: *Rusher Z28 Camaro*.
Scarcity: 2. Fine to Excellent (C6-C8): $40-$65, Mint (C10): $100

1962 Chevrolet Corvette 2-door convertible with racing graphics and insertable numbers. **8 in** (20 cm). **Friction**. Known colors: Racing orange. Maker: **Bandai**, Japan. Toy marks: Bandai. Box marks: Bandai. Box text: *Corvette Race Car #1020*.
Scarcity: 4. Fine to Excellent (C6-C8): $150-$200, Mint (C10): $250

1962 Chevrolet Corvette 2-door coupe. **8 in** (20 cm). **Friction**. Known colors: Red and white. Graphics: 12 - Cragstan - Champion - Pure - 365 H.P. License: Corvette. Maker: **Bandai**, Japan. Toy marks: Bandai. Box marks: Cragstan, NGS (Cragstan). Box text: *Cragstan Racing Stock Car Chevrolet Corvette Sedan*.
Notes: Sold as coupe but modeled after up-top convertible.
Scarcity: 4. Fine to Excellent (C6-C8): $150-$200, Mint (C10): $250

Race Cars 169

1962 Chevrolet Corvette 2-door coupe. 8 in (20 cm). **Friction.** Known colors: Racing orange. Graphics: 7 - Chevrolet Corvette - Checkered stripe. Maker: **Bandai**, Japan. Toy marks: Bandai. Box marks: Bandai. Notes: Sold as coupe but modeled after up-top convertible.
Scarcity: 4. Fine to Excellent (C6-C8): $150-$200, Mint (C10): $250

1963 Chevrolet Corvette Sting Ray 2-door with wind screens, side pipes, head rest, driver, and machine guns hidden in hood. 12 in (30 cm). **Battery operated.** Known colors: Red and white. Graphics: Diamond Finger 001. License: DF-001. Maker: **Ichida**, Japan. Toy marks: none. Box marks: Ichida, SKK (Shinsei). Box text: *001 The Diamond Finger*.
Scarcity: 10. Fine to Excellent (C6-C8): $1,500-$2,200, Mint (C10): $3,000

1964 Chevrolet Corvette Sting Ray 2-door coupe. 8.25 in (21 cm). **Friction.** Known colors: Metallic blue. Graphics: 8 - Corvette Sting Ray - GP-II - (racing stripe). License: Corvette. Maker: **Bandai**, Japan. Toy marks: Bandai. Box marks: Bandai.
Scarcity: 4. Fine to Excellent (C6-C8): $150-$200, Mint (C10): $250

1964 Chevrolet Corvette Sting Ray 2-door coupe. 9.75 in (25 cm). **Friction.** Known colors: Yellow. Graphics: Ramchargers. License: A-1191. Maker: **Unknown**, Japan. Toy marks: none.
Scarcity: 2. Fine to Excellent (C6-C8): $40-$60, Mint (C10): $90

1966 Chevrolet Corvette 2-door convertible with driver and side pipes. 9 in (23 cm). **Battery operated.** Known colors: Red. Maker: **Kogure**, Japan. Toy marks: Kogure.
Scarcity: 10. Fine to Excellent (C6-C8): $500-$800, Mint (C10): $1,200

(Not pictured) **1968 Chevrolet Corvette Sting Ray 2-door coupe** with bump and go action. 10.25 in (26 cm). **Battery operated.** Known colors: White. Graphics: 33. Maker: **Taiyo**, Japan. Toy marks: Taiyo. Box marks: Taiyo.
Scarcity: 3. Fine to Excellent (C6-C8): $100-$150, Mint (C10): $195

(Not pictured) **1968 Chevrolet Corvette Sting Ray 2-door coupe** with bump and go action and blinking light. 10.25 in (26 cm). **Battery operated.** Known colors: White, blue, and red or red and yellow. Graphics: 7. Maker: **Taiyo**, Japan. Toy marks: Taiyo. Box marks: Taiyo. Box text: *New Rusher Stingray*.
Scarcity: 3. Fine to Excellent (C6-C8): $100-$150, Mint (C10): $195

1968 Chevrolet Corvette Sting Ray 2-door coupe with bump and go non-fall action and blinking lights. 10.25 in (26 cm). **Battery operated.** Known colors: Red and white. Graphics: Red Cyclone - Stingray - Chevrolet. Maker: **Taiyo**, Japan. Toy marks: Taiyo. Box marks: Taiyo. Box text: *Rusher Stingray Corvette*.
Scarcity: 3. Fine to Excellent (C6-C8): $100-$150, Mint (C10): $195

170 Rally and Stock Cars

1970s Citroen DS 19 GS 4-door sedan. 9.25 in (23 cm). **Friction.** Known colors: Red and gold. Graphics: 34 - Goodyear - Shell - Citroen GS. License: A-8034-F. Maker: **Paya**, Spain. Toy marks: Paya. Box marks: Paya. Box text: *Citroen GS Rallye*.
Scarcity: 3. Fine to Excellent (C6-C8): $80-$115, Mint (C10): $135

1965 Excalibur Phaeton 2-door convertible with bump and go action. **10 in** (25 cm). **Battery operated.** Known colors: White and yellow. Graphics: (bat). License: Excalibur. Maker: **Bandai**, Japan. Toy marks: Bandai. Box marks: Bandai. Box text: *Excalibur #4413*.
Scarcity: 3. Fine to Excellent (C6-C8): $75-$110, Mint (C10): $150

1960s Cunningham 2-door with tin driver head and waving No.1 flag. **8.25 in** (21 cm). **Battery operated.** Known colors: Blue, red, and yellow. Graphics: 7 - Special - Champion. Maker: **Unknown**, Japan. Toy marks: GW (George Wagner).
Scarcity: 6. Fine to Excellent (C6-C8): $150-$275, Mint (C10): $375

1965 Excalibur 2-door convertible with driver, engine sound, bump and go action, and plastic bumpers. **10.75 in** (27 cm). **Battery operated.** Known colors: White. Graphics: 65 - Excalibur. Maker: **Daishin**, Japan. Toy marks: Daishin. Box marks: Daishin. Box text: *Excalibur SSK*.
Scarcity: 3. Fine to Excellent (C6-C8): $75-$125, Mint (C10): $200

1958 Dodge 4-door hardtop. 9.25 in (23 cm). **Friction.** Known colors: Cream. Graphics: 26 - Rocket. License: V-1002. Maker: **Unknown**, Japan. Toy marks: AN (Unknown).
Scarcity: 3. Fine to Excellent (C6-C8): $95-$125, Mint (C10): $185

Race Cars 171

1965 Excalibur 2-door convertible with driver, engine sound, bump and go action, and plastic bumpers. **10.75 in** (27 cm). **Battery operated**. Known colors: White. Graphics: 27 - Excalibur. Maker: **Tada**, Japan. Toy marks: Tada. Box marks: Tada. Box text: *Excalibur Supercharged Custom Speedster*.
Scarcity: 3. Fine to Excellent (C6-C8): $75-$125, Mint (C10): $200

1960s Ferrari 275 GT 2-door coupe with operating headlights, forward/reverse action, and steering. Antenna controls speed. **8.75 in** (22 cm). **Battery operated**. Known colors: Green. Graphics: 3 - Racing stripe and sponsor litho. Maker: **Bandai**, Japan. Toy marks: Bandai. Box marks: Bandai. Box text: *Ferrari 275 GT #4275*.
Scarcity: 6. Fine to Excellent (C6-C8): $175-$250, Mint (C10): $325

1960s Ferrari 275 GT 2-door coupe. **8.75 in** (22 cm). **Friction**. Known colors: Blue. Graphics: 275 - (racing graphics). License: Ferrari. Maker: **Bandai**, Japan. Toy marks: Bandai. Box marks: Bandai. Box text: *Grand Prix Race Car Series #2038*.
Scarcity: 6. Fine to Excellent (C6-C8): $175-$250, Mint (C10): $325

1960s Ferrari 312 2-door with plastic chassis. **11.25 in** (29 cm). **Friction**. Known colors: Orange. Graphics: 24. Maker: **Mont Blanc**, France. Toy marks: Mont-Blanc. Box marks: Mont-Blanc. Box text: *Ferrari 312*.
Scarcity: 3. Fine to Excellent (C6-C8): $60-$90, Mint (C10): $125

(Not pictured) **1960s Ferrari 365 GT BB 2-door coupe** with bump and go action. **10 in** (25 cm). **Battery operated**. Known colors: Yellow. Graphics: 75 - Total. Maker: **Taiyo**, Japan. Toy marks: Taiyo. Box marks: Taiyo.
Scarcity: 2. Fine to Excellent (C6-C8): $65-$85, Mint (C10): $125

172 Rally and Stock Cars

1960s Ferrari 813 . **8 in** (20 cm). **Friction**. Known colors: Assorted. Graphics: 1 (assorted tin numbers and flags). Maker: **Bandai**, Japan. Toy marks: Bandai. Box marks: Bandai.
Scarcity: 4. Fine to Excellent (C6-C8): $125-$175, Mint (C10): $300

1960s Ferrari 813 with vinyl driver head. **9.25 in** (23 cm). **Friction**. Known colors: Red. Graphics: 15 - Ferrari. Maker: **Sanko**, Japan. Toy marks: Y (Sanko).
Scarcity: 2. Fine to Excellent (C6-C8): $20-$40, Mint (C10): $60

1960s Ferrari 813 . **8 in** (20 cm). **Friction**. Known colors: Assorted. Graphics: 2 (assorted tin numbers and flags). Maker: **Bandai**, Japan. Toy marks: Bandai. Box marks: Bandai.
Scarcity: 4. Fine to Excellent (C6-C8): $125-$175, Mint (C10): $300

1960s Ferrari Berlinetta 250 2-door coupe. **11 in** (28 cm). **Friction**. Known colors: Red. Graphics: 1 - 2 - or 3. Maker: **Asahi**, Japan. Toy marks: ATC (Asahi Toy). Box marks: ATC (Asahi Toy). Box text: *Berlinetta 250 Le Mans*.
Notes: Asahi catalog image.
Scarcity: 3. Fine to Excellent (C6-C8): $75-$125, Mint (C10): $175

1960s Ferrari 813 . **8 in** (20 cm). **Friction**. Known colors: Assorted. Graphics: 3 (assorted tin numbers and flags. Maker: **Bandai**, Japan. Toy marks: Bandai. Box marks: Bandai.
Scarcity: 4. Fine to Excellent (C6-C8): $125-$175, Mint (C10): $300

1960s Ferrari Berlinetta 250 2-door coupe with roaring visible engine. **11 in** (28 cm). **Battery operated**. Known colors: Red. Graphics: 1 - 2 - or 3. Maker: **Asahi**, Japan. Toy marks: ATC (Asahi Toy). Box marks: ATC (Asahi Toy). Box text: *Berlinetta 250 Le Mans*.
Scarcity: 3. Fine to Excellent (C6-C8): $75-$125, Mint (C10): $175

(Not pictured) **1960s Ferrari Berlinetta 250 2-door coupe**. **11 in** (28 cm). **Friction**. Known colors: Red. Graphics: 1 - 2 - or 3. Maker: **Siro**, Italy. Toy marks: FSC (Siro Ferrari). Box marks: FSC (Siro Ferrari).
Scarcity: 5. Fine to Excellent (C6-C8): $125-$225, Mint (C10): $375

1960s Ferrari 813 with hood scoop, center seat, driver, and roll bar. **8 in** (20 cm). **Friction**. Known colors: Silver, blue, and white. Graphics: 3 (star). Maker: **Bandai**, Japan. Toy marks: Bandai. Box marks: Bandai.
Scarcity: 6. Fine to Excellent (C6-C8): $225-$300, Mint (C10): $400

Race Cars 173

1960s Ferrari Super America 2-door convertible. 11 in (28 cm). **Friction.** Known colors: Red. Maker: **Siro**, Italy. Toy marks: FSC (Siro Ferrari). Box marks: FSC (Siro Ferrari).
Scarcity: 5. Fine to Excellent (C6-C8): $125-$225, Mint (C10): $375

1960s Ferrari Super America 2-door convertible with tin driver and stunt actions. 11.5 in (29 cm). **Battery operated.** Known colors: Assorted. Maker: **Bandai**, Japan. Toy marks: Bandai. Box marks: Bandai. Box text: *Stunt Car #4151*.
Scarcity: 7. Fine to Excellent (C6-C8): $350-$450, Mint (C10): $550

1960s Ferrari Super America 2-door convertible with tin driver and stunt actions. 11.5 in (29 cm). **Battery operated.** Known colors: Assorted. Graphics: 27 - Speed Demon. Maker: **Bandai**, Japan. Toy marks: Bandai. Box marks: Bandai. Box text: *Stunt Car #4086*.
Scarcity: 7. Fine to Excellent (C6-C8): $350-$450, Mint (C10): $550

1960s Ferrari Super America 2-door coupe. 11.5 in (29 cm). **Friction.** Known colors: Silver. Graphics: 12 - Ferrari. Maker: **Bandai**, Japan. Toy marks: Bandai. Box marks: Bandai, A1 (Asakusa). Box text: *Ferrari Race Car #2033*.
Scarcity: 8. Fine to Excellent (C6-C8): $450-$550, Mint (C10): $650

1960s Fiat 2300 S Rally 2-door coupe with antenna, mirror, steering, and forward/reverse action. 9.5 in (24 cm). **R/C battery operated.** Known colors: Yellow and black. Graphics: 9. Maker: **Ichiko**, Japan. Toy marks: Ichiko.
Scarcity: 4. Fine to Excellent (C6-C8): $200-$300, Mint (C10): $500

1959 Ford Stock car 2-door hardtop. 9 in (23 cm). **Friction.** Known colors: Blue and white. Graphics: 27 - 375 H.P. - Speed King. Maker: **Asahi**, Japan. Toy marks: Toymaster (Asahi Toy).
Scarcity: 3. Fine to Excellent (C6-C8): $60-$85, Mint (C10): $125

(Not pictured) **1961 Ford Galaxie 2-door hardtop.** 9.5 in (24 cm). **Friction.** Known colors: Red, white, and black. Graphics: 12 - Champion - Pure - 365 H.P. Maker: **Takatoku/Ichiko**, Japan. Toy marks: TT (Takatoku). Box marks: TT (Takatoku), Cragstan/NGS. Box text: *Stock Racing Car Ford Galaxy*.
Scarcity: 3. Fine to Excellent (C6-C8): $85-$135, Mint (C10): $175

174 Rally and Stock Cars

1961 Ford Galaxie 4-door hardtop. 9.5 in (24 cm). **Friction.** Known colors: Red and black. Graphics: 5 - Champion - 405 H.P. Maker: **Unknown**, Japan. Toy marks: none. Box marks: Cragstan, NGS (Cragstan). Box text: *Cragstan Stock Racing Car Galaxie*.
Scarcity: 2. Fine to Excellent (C6-C8): $75-$95, Mint (C10): $135

1963 Ford Galaxie 500 4-door hardtop with bump and go action, flashing engine, and engine sound. **12.5 in** (32 cm). **Battery operated.** Known colors: Orange and blue. Graphics: 5 - Track Demon. Maker: **Taiyo**, Japan. Toy marks: none. Box marks: Taiyo World Toy. Box text: *Stock Race Car*.
Scarcity: 4. Fine to Excellent (C6-C8): $100-$175, Mint (C10): $250

(Not pictured) **1963 Ford 4-door hardtop.** 13.5 in (34 cm). **Friction.** Known colors: Blue and white. Graphics: 27 - Speed King - 375 HP. Maker: **Mitake**, Japan. Toy marks: K (Mitake).
Scarcity: 2. Fine to Excellent (C6-C8): $60-$115, Mint (C10): $150

1962 Ford 2-door hardtop. 9.25 in (23 cm). **Friction.** Known colors: Red and white. Graphics: 22 - England - (British Flag). Maker: **Tohko-Toy**, Japan. Toy marks: Tohko-Toy. Box marks: Tohko-Toy. Box text: *International Stock Race Car*.
Notes: Came in assorted colors, numbers, and countries.
Scarcity: 3. Fine to Excellent (C6-C8): $50-$85, Mint (C10): $110

1963 Ford 4-door hardtop with working wipers and antenna. **13.5 in** (34 cm). **Friction.** Known colors: Red and black. Graphics: 5 - Champion - 405 H.P. License: 1831. Maker: **Mitake**, Japan. Toy marks: K (Mitake). Box marks: Cragstan, NGS (Cragstan). Box text: *Cragstan Stock Racing Car*.
Scarcity: 3. Fine to Excellent (C6-C8): $75-$125, Mint (C10): $175

1963 Ford 2-door hardtop. 11 in (28 cm). **Friction.** Known colors: White with psychedelic stripes. License: Ford. Maker: **Taiyo**, Japan. Toy marks: Taiyo World Toy.
Scarcity: 4. Fine to Excellent (C6-C8): $60-$90, Mint (C10): $150

1964 Ford Galaxie 500, 2-door hardtop with trunk mounted speed meter. **13 in** (33 cm). **Friction.** Known colors: Red, white, and black. Graphics: 12 - Champion - Pure - 420 HP. License: FG-1729. Maker: **Ichiko**, Japan. Toy marks: Ichiko. Box marks: Ichiko.
Scarcity: 5. Fine to Excellent (C6-C8): $250-$400, Mint (C10): $625

Race Cars 175

1965 Ford GT40, 2-door coupe. **8 in** (20 cm). **Friction**. Known colors: Assorted. Maker: **Bandai**, Japan. Toy marks: Bandai. Box marks: Bandai. Box text: *GT Car Series Ford GT #1095*.
Scarcity: 3. Fine to Excellent (C6-C8): $40-$80, Mint (C10): $120

1965 Ford GT40, 2-door coupe with lever switch to change from running to spin out action. **10 in** (25 cm). **Battery operated**. Known colors: Assorted. Graphics: 72 - Ford (or apply your own decals). Maker: **Alps/Koa**, Japan. Toy marks: S (Koa). Box marks: Alps. Box text: *The 'Swinger' Ford G.T.40*.
Scarcity: 4. Fine to Excellent (C6-C8): $95-$150, Mint (C10): $200

1965 Ford GT40, 2-door coupe. **10 in** (25 cm). **Battery operated**. Known colors: Assorted. Maker: **Bandai**, Japan. Toy marks: Bandai. Box marks: Bandai. Box text: *Ford GT #4190*.
Scarcity: 3. Fine to Excellent (C6-C8): $40-$80, Mint (C10): $120

1965 Ford Galaxie 500XL 2-door hardtop. **11.25 in** (29 cm). **Friction**. Known colors: White. Graphics: star dust - QX Racing Team. License: 1965 or 3141. Maker: **Masudaya**, Japan. Toy marks: KKY (Yamato), MT (Masudaya). Box marks: MT (Masudaya).
Notes: Masudaya catalog image. No price established.
Scarcity: 10.

1965 Ford Galaxie 500XL 2-door hardtop. **11.25 in** (29 cm). **Friction**. Known colors: Blue. Graphics: Thunder Flame - J-33 Racing Team. License: 1965 or 3141. Maker: **Masudaya**, Japan. Toy marks: KKY (Yamato), MT (Masudaya). Box marks: MT (Masudaya).
Notes: Masudaya catalog image. No price established.
Scarcity: 10.

1965 Ford Galaxie 500XL 2-door hardtop. **11.25 in** (29 cm). **Friction**. Known colors: Yellow. Graphics: Wild Boar - Masu Racing Team. License: 1965 or 3141. Maker: **Masudaya**, Japan. Toy marks: KKY (Yamato), MT (Masudaya). Box marks: MT (Masudaya).
Notes: Masudaya catalog image. No price established.
Scarcity: 10.

1969 Ford Capri 2-door coupe. **8.75 in** (22 cm). **Friction**. Known colors: Yellow; Red. Graphics: 27 - 410 H.P. or 18 - 400 H.P. Maker: **Yoneya**, Japan. Toy marks: Yone (Yoneya).
Scarcity: 3. Fine to Excellent (C6-C8): $125-$165, Mint (C10): $225

176 Rally and Stock Cars

1969 Ford Capri 2-door coupe. 8.75 in (22 cm). **Friction.** Known colors: Blue. Graphics: 35 - 420 HP - Pro Stock. Maker: **Yoneya**, Japan. Toy marks: Yone (Yoneya).
Scarcity: 3. Fine to Excellent (C6-C8): $125-$165, Mint (C10): $225

1969 Ford Capri 2-door coupe with running straight and sharp turning action. 11 in (28 cm). **Battery operated.** Known colors: Red (8); Blue (27). Graphics: 8 or 27. License: Ford Capri. Maker: **Aoshin**, Japan. Toy marks: Aoshin. Box marks: Aoshin. Box text: *Ford Capri, Touring Rally*.
Scarcity: 4. Fine to Excellent (C6-C8): $145-$185, Mint (C10): $250

1965 Ford Mustang 2-door convertible with vinyl driver. 13.5 in (34 cm). **Battery operated.** Known colors: Red. Graphics: 12. Maker: **Yonezawa**, Japan. Toy marks: Y (Yonezawa). Box marks: Y (Yonezawa). Box text: *Ford Mustang*.
Scarcity: 5. Fine to Excellent (C6-C8): $200-$325, Mint (C10): $475

1960s Ford Mustang Fastback 2-door coupe with lithographed driver and passenger on windows, steering, and forward/reverse action. 7 in (18 cm). **R/C battery operated.** Known colors: Red. Graphics: 36. Maker: **Daishin**, Japan. Toy marks: none. Box marks: DSK (Daishin). Box text: *Ford Mustang Rally Car*.
Scarcity: 3. Fine to Excellent (C6-C8): $65-$85, Mint (C10): $110

1960s Ford Mustang Fastback GT 2-door coupe with forward/reverse action and steering. 10 in (25 cm). **R/C battery operated.** Known colors: Orange. Graphics: 23 - Ford GT - STP. License: Ford Mustang. Maker: **Bandai**, Japan. Toy marks: Bandai. Box marks: Bandai. Box text: *Ford Mustang GT Mit Pneumatische Fernsteuerung*.
Scarcity: 4. Fine to Excellent (C6-C8): $125-$175, Mint (C10): $225

1960s Ford Mustang Fastback GT 2-door coupe. 10 in (25 cm). **Friction.** Known colors: Red and yellow. Graphics: 5. Maker: **Bandai**, Japan. Toy marks: Bandai. Box marks: Bandai. Box text: *Rally Car*.
Scarcity: 4. Fine to Excellent (C6-C8): $125-$175, Mint (C10): $225

Race Cars 177

1960s Ford Mustang Fastback GT 2-door hardtop with lithographed windows and bump' n go action. **10.5 in** (27 cm). **Battery operated**. Known colors: Red. Graphics: 27 (with racing stripe). Maker: **Taiyo**, Japan. Toy marks: Taiyo. Box marks: Taiyo. Box text: *Mystery Ford Mustang GT*.
Scarcity: 3. Fine to Excellent (C6-C8): $75-$100, Mint (C10): $125

1960s Ford Mustang Fastback Mach 1, 2-door hardtop with raise up and barrel roll action. **10.75 in** (27 cm). **Battery operated**. Known colors: Silver and red with flames. Graphics: 1 - Stunt Champion Ford Racing Team. Maker: **Toplay**, Japan. Toy marks: TPS (Toplay). Box marks: TPS (Toplay). Box text: *Champion Stunt Car*.
Scarcity: 5. Fine to Excellent (C6-C8): $100-$125, Mint (C10): $150

1960s Ford Mustang Fastback Mach 1, 2-door hardtop with bump and go action and blinking light. **10.5 in** (27 cm). **Battery operated**. Known colors: Red, white, and blue. Graphics: 3 or USA-1. Maker: **Taiyo**, Japan. Toy marks: Taiyo. Box marks: Taiyo. Box text: *New Rusher Mach 1*.
Scarcity: 3. Fine to Excellent (C6-C8): $85-$115, Mint (C10): $150

1960s Ford Mustang Fastback Mach 1, 2-door hardtop with raise up and barrel roll action. **10.75 in** (27 cm). **Battery operated**. Known colors: Black and gold with flames. Graphics: 1 - Stunt Champion Ford Racing Team. Maker: **Toplay**, Japan. Toy marks: TPS (Toplay). Box marks: TPS (Toplay). Box text: *Big Stunt Car*.
Scarcity: 5. Fine to Excellent (C6-C8): $100-$125, Mint (C10): $150

178 Rally and Stock Cars

1960s Ford Mustang Fastback Mach 1, 2-door hardtop with stopping, reversing, and spinning action. **10.75 in** (27 cm). **Battery operated**. Known colors: Lime green and black. Graphics: 5 - The Swinger (with racing logos). Maker: **Toplay**, Japan. Toy marks: TPS (Toplay). Box marks: TPS (Toplay). Box text: *The Swinger*.
Scarcity: 5. Fine to Excellent (C6-C8): $100-$125, Mint (C10): $150

1960s Ford Mustang Fastback Mach 1, 2-door hardtop with stopping, reversing, and spinning action. **10.75 in** (27 cm). **Battery operated**. Known colors: Light blue and red with racing logos. Graphics: 7 - The Hustler. Maker: **Toplay**, Japan. Toy marks: TPS (Toplay). Box marks: TPS (Toplay). Box text: *The Hustler Mustang Handling Test Car*.
Scarcity: 6. Fine to Excellent (C6-C8): $140-$175, Mint (C10): $225

1960s Ford Mustang Fastback Mach 1, 2-door hardtop with stopping and reversing action. **10.75 in** (27 cm). **Battery operated**. Known colors: Red, white, and blue. Graphics: 7 & 377 The Hustler. Maker: **Toplay**, Japan. Toy marks: TPS (Toplay). Box marks: TPS (Toplay). Box text: *The Hustler*.
Scarcity: 5. Fine to Excellent (C6-C8): $100-$125, Mint (C10): $150

1960s Ford Mustang Fastback Mach 1, 2-door hardtop with stopping, reversing, and spinning action. **10.75 in** (27 cm). **Battery operated**. Known colors: Blue, yellow, and red. Graphics: 757 - The Swinger (with racing logos). Maker: **Toplay**, Japan. Toy marks: TPS (Toplay). Box marks: TPS (Toplay).
Scarcity: 5. Fine to Excellent (C6-C8): $100-$135, Mint (C10): $175

1960s Ford Mustang Fastback Mach 1, 2-door hardtop with opening hood, raise up and barrel roll action. **10.75 in** (27 cm). **Battery operated**. Known colors: White, blue, and red. Graphics: Stunt 712 with flames. Maker: **Toplay**, Japan. Toy marks: TPS (Toplay). Box marks: TPS (Toplay). Box text: *Open-Shut Bonnet Stunt Car*.
Scarcity: 4. Fine to Excellent (C6-C8): $100-$125, Mint (C10): $150

1960s Ford Mustang Fastback Mach 1, 2-door hardtop with raise up and barrel roll action. **10.75 in** (27 cm). **Battery operated**. Known colors: Red and black with flames. Graphics: Stunt with flames. Maker: **Toplay**, Japan. Toy marks: TPS (Toplay). Box marks: TPS (Toplay). Box text: *Ford Mustang Stunt Car*.
Scarcity: 5. Fine to Excellent (C6-C8): $100-$135, Mint (C10): $175

Race Cars

1960s Ford Mustang Fastback Mach 1, 2-door coupe. **11 in** (28 cm). **Friction**. Known colors: Yellow and blue. Graphics: 37 - Sports Car World Champion. Maker: **Takatoku**, Japan. Toy marks: none. Box marks: TT (Takatoku). Box text: *Ford Mustang Mach 1*.
Scarcity: 5. Fine to Excellent (C6-C8): $275-$325, Mint (C10): $375

1961 Ford Thunderbird Stock Car 2-door hardtop. **9.5 in** (24 cm). **Friction**. Known colors: Blue and white. Graphics: 27 - 375 H.P. - Speed King. Maker: **Ichiko**, Japan. Toy marks: Ichiko. Box marks: Cragstan, NGS (Cragstan). Box text: *Cragstan Stock Racing Car*.
Scarcity: 3. Fine to Excellent (C6-C8): $75-$125, Mint (C10): $160

1960s Ford Mustang Fastback GT 2-door coupe with fender mirrors. **16 in** (41 cm). **Friction**. Known colors: Red. Graphics: 23 - Ford - Mustang. License: E-147. Maker: **Nomura**, Japan. Toy marks: TN (Nomura). Box marks: TN (Nomura).
Scarcity: 5. Fine to Excellent (C6-C8): $200-$275, Mint (C10): $375

1963 Ford Thunderbird 2-door hardtop. **8.25 in** (21 cm). **Friction**. Known colors: Red and yellow. Graphics: 12 - 370 H.P. Maker: **Bandai**, Japan. Toy marks: Bandai. Box marks: Bandai.
Scarcity: 3. Fine to Excellent (C6-C8): $70-$100, Mint (C10): $150

1961 Ford Thunderbird 2-door convertible with retainer for race car number. **8.25 in** (21 cm). **Friction**. Known colors: Gold and red. Graphics: Thunderbird. Maker: **Bandai**, Japan. Toy marks: Bandai. Box marks: Bandai.
Scarcity: 3. Fine to Excellent (C6-C8): $70-$100, Mint (C10): $150

1963 Ford Thunderbird 2-door hardtop. **8.25 in** (21 cm). **Friction**. Known colors: Blue and white. Graphics: 12 - Thunderbird. Maker: **Bandai**, Japan. Toy marks: Bandai. Box marks: Bandai.
Scarcity: 3. Fine to Excellent (C6-C8): $70-$100, Mint (C10): $150

180 Rally and Stock Cars

1964 Ford Thunderbird 2-door hardtop. 8 in (20 cm). **Friction.** Known colors:. Graphics: 6 - Thunderbird - GP III - Champion. Maker: **Bandai**, Japan. Toy marks: Bandai. Box marks: Bandai.
Notes: Bandai catalog image.
Scarcity: 4. Fine to Excellent (C6-C8): $125-$175, Mint (C10): $225

1950s Jaguar XK 120, 2-door coupe. 7 in (18 cm). **Windup.** Known colors: Blue and white. Graphics: 48 - Grand Prix. Maker: **Unknown**, Japan. Toy marks: none. Box text: *Wind - Up Jaguar*.
Scarcity: 5. Fine to Excellent (C6-C8): $125-$175, Mint (C10): $250

1965 Ford Thunderbird 2-door hardtop. 10.5 in (27 cm). **Friction.** Known colors: Blue. Graphics: 17 - Thunderbird - Ford. Maker: **Bandai**, Japan. Toy marks: Bandai. Box marks: Bandai. Box text: *Grand Prix Race Car Series Thunderbird Race Car #2032*.
Scarcity: 5. Fine to Excellent (C6-C8): $125-$200, Mint (C10): $285

1950s Jaguar XK 120, 2-door convertible with tin driver and push horn. **7.5 in** (19 cm). **Friction.** Known colors: Red. Maker: **Masudaya**, Japan. Toy marks: MT (Masudaya). Box marks: MT (Masudaya).
Scarcity: 4. Fine to Excellent (C6-C8): $150-$175, Mint (C10): $250

1965 Ford Thunderbird 2-door hardtop. 10.5 in (27 cm). **Friction.** Known colors: Red and yellow. Graphics: 21 - Thunderbird - 1968 Rallye Monte-Carlo. Maker: **Bandai**, Japan. Toy marks: Bandai. Box marks: Bandai. Box text: *Grand Prix Race Car Series Thunderbird Race Car #2032*.
Scarcity: 5. Fine to Excellent (C6-C8): $175-$250, Mint (C10): $335

1950s Jaguar XK 140, 2-door coupe. 6 in (15 cm). **Friction.** Known colors: Red, yellow, and blue. Graphics: Official Pace Car Jaguar. Maker: **Bandai**, Japan. Toy marks: Bandai. Box marks: Bandai. Box text: *Jaguar Coupe*.
Scarcity: 5. Fine to Excellent (C6-C8): $125-$195, Mint (C10): $285

Race Cars 181

1950s Jaguar XK 150, 2-door coupe with lever action retractable top. **10 in** (25 cm). **Friction**. Known colors: Red and white. Graphics: 2. Maker: **Bandai**, Japan. Toy marks: Bandai. Box marks: Bandai. Box text: *Jaguar Coupe With Openable Hard Top #677*.
Scarcity: 10. Fine to Excellent (C6-C8): $1,200-$1,600, Mint (C10): $2,200

1960s Jaguar XKE 2-door coupe with rollover action. **10 in** (25 cm). **Battery operated**. Known colors: Assorted. Graphics: 15, 27 or 77. Maker: **Masudaya**, Japan. Toy marks: MT (Masudaya). Box marks: MT (Masudaya). Box text: *Jaguar Stunt Car - Goes Forward - Tumbles Continually*.
Scarcity: 3. Fine to Excellent (C6-C8): $100-$135, Mint (C10): $175

1960s Jaguar XKE 2-door coupe. **8.25 in** (21 cm). **Friction**. Known colors: White and red. Graphics: 11 - Speed Demon - 385 H.P. Maker: **Bandai**, Japan. Toy marks: Cragstan. Box marks: Cragstan.
Scarcity: 5. Fine to Excellent (C6-C8): $125-$175, Mint (C10): $230

1960s Jaguar XKE GTX-753 2-door coupe. **10.5 in** (27 cm). **Friction**. Known colors: Yellow and black. Graphics: GTX-753. Maker: **Takatoku**, Japan. Toy marks: TT (Takatoku). Box marks: TT (Takatoku). Box text: *Jaguar Best GT/Sports*.
Notes: Also produced as R/C model.
Scarcity: 4. Fine to Excellent (C6-C8): $150-$250, Mint (C10): $350

1960s Jaguar XKE 2-door coupe. **8.25 in** (21 cm). **Friction**. Known colors: Yellow leopard. Graphics: 3 - Jaguar XKE - Champion (leopard lithograph). Maker: **Bandai**, Japan. Toy marks: Bandai. Box marks: Bandai. Box text: *#1055*.
Scarcity: 5. Fine to Excellent (C6-C8): $125-$175, Mint (C10): $230

1960s Jaguar XKE 2-door coupe. **12 in** (30 cm). **Friction**. Known colors: Blue and white. Graphics: 7 - Toy - Toys. License: AF211. Maker: **Unknown**, China. Toy marks: none.
Scarcity: 2. Fine to Excellent (C6-C8): $40-$80, Mint (C10): $120

182 Rally and Stock Cars

1960s Lotus Elan 2-door coupe. 7.5 in (19 cm). **Friction.** Known colors: Red. Graphics: 8. License: Lotus. Maker: **Asahi**, Japan. Toy marks: ATC (Asahi Toy). Box marks: ATC (Asahi Toy). Box text: *Lotus Elan*.
Scarcity: 5. Fine to Excellent (C6-C8): $150-$250, Mint (C10): $375

1960s Lotus Elan 2-door coupe. 8 in (20 cm). **Friction.** Known colors: Cream, red, and black. Graphics: 7 - Lotus - GP-II - Champion. License: Lotus. Maker: **Bandai**, Japan. Toy marks: Bandai. Box marks: Bandai. Box text: *Lotus Elan GT Car Series #1096*.
Scarcity: 4. Fine to Excellent (C6-C8): $100-$150, Mint (C10): $250

1950s Mercedes Benz 300 SL Gullwing 2-door coupe with lithographed driver in window. **6 in** (15 cm). **Friction.** Known colors: Yellow and green. Graphics: 7. Maker: **Bandai**, Japan. Toy marks: Bandai. Box marks: Bandai.
Scarcity: 4. Fine to Excellent (C6-C8): $85-$150, Mint (C10): $225

1950s Mercedes Benz 300 SL 2-door roadster with top down and insertable numbers in hood bracket. 8 in (20 cm). **Friction.** Known colors: Blue and yellow. Maker: **Bandai**, Japan. Toy marks: Bandai. Box marks: Bandai. Box text: *Benz Racing Car #1019*.
Scarcity: 7. Fine to Excellent (C6-C8): $200-$300, Mint (C10): $500

1950s Mercedes Benz 300 SL 2-door roadster with top up. **8 in** (20 cm). **Friction.** Known colors: Blue and red. Graphics: 4 - Benz 300 SL. Maker: **Bandai**, Japan. Toy marks: Bandai. Box marks: Bandai.
Scarcity: 6. Fine to Excellent (C6-C8): $175-$250, Mint (C10): $450

1950s Mercedes Benz 300 SL 2-door roadster with top up. **8 in** (20 cm). **Friction.** Known colors: Black and red. Graphics: 7 - Champion - 375 H.P. Maker: **Bandai**, Japan. Toy marks: Bandai. Box marks: Bandai.
Scarcity: 6. Fine to Excellent (C6-C8): $175-$250, Mint (C10): $450

1950s Mercedes Benz 300 SL 2-door roadster with top down. **8 in** (20 cm). **Friction.** Known colors: Black and red. Graphics: 7 - Champion - 375 H.P. Maker: **Bandai**, Japan. Toy marks: Bandai. Box marks: Bandai.
Scarcity: 6. Fine to Excellent (C6-C8): $175-$250, Mint (C10): $450

Race Cars 103

1960s Mercedes Benz 220 S 4-door sedan. **7.5 in** (19 cm). **Windup**. Known colors: Black and red. Graphics: 7 - Champion - 375 H.P. Maker: **Ichiko**, Japan. Toy marks: Ichiko. Box marks: Ichiko.
Scarcity: 3. Fine to Excellent (C6-C8): $50-$75, Mint (C10): $110

1950s MGA 1600 2-door convertible with interchangeable hood numbers. **8 in** (20 cm). **Friction**. Known colors: Red and cream. Graphics: racing stripe. License: MGA 1600. Maker: **Bandai**, Japan. Toy marks: Bandai. Box marks: Bandai.
Scarcity: 4. Fine to Excellent (C6-C8): $125-$200, Mint (C10): $300

1950s MG Midget 2-door convertible with dual windscreens. **8.25 in** (21 cm). **Friction**. Known colors: Cream and red. Graphics: 7 - Winner 1956 or 1955 Overland Race. Maker: **Bandai**, Japan. Toy marks: Bandai. Box marks: Bandai. Box text: *MG Racer #263*.
Scarcity: 7. Fine to Excellent (C6-C8): $400-$525, Mint (C10): $700

1950s MGA 1600 2-door coupe. **8 in** (20 cm). **Friction**. Known colors: Blue, white, red, and yellow. Graphics: 27 - Speed King - 375 HP. License: MGA 1600. Maker: **Bandai**, Japan. Toy marks: Bandai. Box marks: Bandai.
Scarcity: 5. Fine to Excellent (C6-C8): $125-$250, Mint (C10): $335

1950s MGA 2-door coupe with lithographed trim and driver. **7.5 in** (19 cm). **Friction**. Known colors: Black. Graphics: M.G. 11 - MGA Coupe. Maker: **Toplay**, Japan. Toy marks: TPS (Toplay).
Scarcity: 6. Fine to Excellent (C6-C8): $250-$350, Mint (C10): $450

1950s Nissan/Datsun 210 4-door sedan with Rally markings to commemorate Australia Mobil Gas Trial Run. **5 in** (13 cm). **Friction**. Known colors: Cream. Graphics: Datsun Mobilgas Trial 1958 Round Australia Nissan. Maker: **Bandai**, Japan. Toy marks: Bandai.
Scarcity: 10. Fine to Excellent (C6-C8): $800-$1,100, Mint (C10): $1,400

184 Rally and Stock Cars

1967 Oldsmobile Toronado 2-door hardtop. 15 in (38 cm). **Friction.** Known colors: Red and white. Graphics: 18 - GT 500 - Oldsmobile. License: Toronado. Maker: **Asahi**, Japan. Toy marks: ATC (Asahi Toy). Box marks: ATC (Asahi Toy). Box text: *Toronado LeMans*. Notes: Produced 1970s.
Scarcity: 6. Fine to Excellent (C6-C8): $400-$500, Mint (C10): $600

(Not pictured) **1968 Oldsmobile Toronado 2-door hardtop. 10.25 in** (26 cm). **Battery operated.** Known colors: White and black. Graphics: Olds Toronado - Toronado. Maker: **Taiyo**, Japan. Toy marks: Taiyo. Box marks: Taiyo.
Scarcity: 3. Fine to Excellent (C6-C8): $75-$125, Mint (C10): $175

1960 Plymouth Valiant 2-door sedan. 7 in (18 cm). **Friction.** Known colors: Cream. Graphics: 68 - 360 H.P. Maker: **Ichiko**, Japan. Toy marks: Ichiko.
Scarcity: 3. Fine to Excellent (C6-C8): $75-$110, Mint (C10): $165

1964 Plymouth Fury 4-door hardtop with siren sound. **10 in** (25 cm). **Friction.** Known colors: Green; Red, white, and blue; Red and yellow. Graphics: 27 - Pegasus or 45 - Tiger or 63 - Eagle. Maker: **Kusama/Yoshi**, Japan. Toy marks: Y (Yoshi).
Scarcity: 5. Fine to Excellent (C6-C8): $125-$165, Mint (C10): $200

1967 Pontiac Firebird 2-door coupe. 10 in (25 cm). **Friction.** Known colors: Yellow. Graphics: 11. License: Firebird. Maker: **Bandai**, Japan. Toy marks: Bandai. Box marks: Bandai.
Scarcity: 8. Fine to Excellent (C6-C8): $150-$225, Mint (C10): $350

(Not pictured) **1970 Pontiac Firebird 2-door coupe** with bump and go action. **9 in** (23 cm). **Battery operated.** Known colors: Red. Graphics: 45 - Transam - Pontiac. Maker: **Taiyo**, Japan. Toy marks: Taiyo. Box marks: Taiyo. Box text: *Pontiac Firebird*.
Scarcity: 2. Fine to Excellent (C6-C8): $65-$85, Mint (C10): $125

(Not pictured) **1960s Porsche 935** with bump and go action. **8 in** (20 cm). **Battery operated.** Known colors: White. Graphics: 40 - Martini Porsche Racing. Maker: **Taiyo**, Japan. Toy marks: Taiyo. Box marks: Taiyo. Box text: *Porsche 935 Turbo*.
Scarcity: 2. Fine to Excellent (C6-C8): $75-$135, Mint (C10): $200

1960s Porsche 914, 2-door convertible with roll bar. **8.75 in** (22 cm). **Friction.** Known colors: Red. Graphics: 34 - Porsche (rally graphics). Maker: **Terai**, Japan. Toy marks: Daiya (Terai). Box marks: Daiya (Terai).
Scarcity: 4. Fine to Excellent (C6-C8): $225-$300, Mint (C10): $375

1960s Porsche 914, 2-door convertible with roll bar, steering, and forward/reverse action. **8.75 in** (22 cm). **R/C battery operated.** Known colors: Assorted. Graphics: 71 - Porsche (rally graphics). License: VW 914. Maker: **Terai**, Japan. Toy marks: Daiya (Terai). Box marks: Daiya (Terai).
Scarcity: 4. Fine to Excellent (C6-C8): $225-$300, Mint (C10): $375

Race Cars 185

1960s Porsche 911, 2-door coupe. 9 in (23 cm). **Friction.** Known colors: Assorted. Graphics: 11 (rally graphics). Maker: **Joustra**, France. Toy marks: Joustra.
Notes: Produced in a variety of color schemes and numbers.
Scarcity: 4. Fine to Excellent (C6-C8): $150-$225, Mint (C10): $300

1960s Porsche 911, 2-door coupe with bump' n go action. **10 in** (25 cm). **Battery operated.** Known colors: Red. Graphics: 6 - Rallye Monte Carlo - Porsche. Maker: **Bandai**, Japan. Toy marks: Bandai. Box marks: Bandai.
Scarcity: 5. Fine to Excellent (C6-C8): $115-$200, Mint (C10): $265

1960s Porsche 911, 2-door coupe with hood mounted lights and bump' n go action. **10 in** (25 cm). **Battery operated.** Known colors: Yellow and green. Graphics: 38. Maker: **Bandai**, Japan. Toy marks: Bandai. Box marks: Bandai.
Scarcity: 8. Fine to Excellent (C6-C8): $150-$250, Mint (C10): $475

1960s Porsche 911, 2-door coupe. 10 in (25 cm). **Friction.** Known colors: White and green. Graphics: 7. Maker: **Bandai**, Japan. Toy marks: Bandai. Box marks: Bandai. Box text: *Rally Car*.
Scarcity: 5. Fine to Excellent (C6-C8): $115-$275, Mint (C10): $400

1960s Porsche 911, 2-door coupe. 10 in (25 cm). **Friction.** Known colors: Assorted. Graphics: 5 (rally graphics). Maker: **Bandai**, Japan. Toy marks: Bandai. Box marks: Bandai. Box text: *Rally Monte Carlo Porsche 912*.
Scarcity: 4. Fine to Excellent (C6-C8): $150-$225, Mint (C10): $300

1960s Porsche 911S 2-door coupe with raise up and turning action. **10 in** (25 cm). **Battery operated.** Known colors: Red. Graphics: 17 or 6 (rally logos). Maker: **Toplay**, Japan. Toy marks: TPS (Toplay). Box marks: TPS (Toplay). Box text: *High Technical Rally or Rally Car*.
Scarcity: 6. Fine to Excellent (C6-C8): $125-$155, Mint (C10): $200

186 Rally and Stock Cars

1960s Porsche 911S 2-door coupe with roof light and stand up and turn over action. **10 in** (25 cm). **Battery operated**. Known colors: Blue and gray. Graphics: 20 - Martini with racing graphics. Maker: **Toplay**, Japan. Toy marks: TPS (Toplay). Box marks: TPS (Toplay). Box text: *Acrobat Porsche*.
Scarcity: 4. Fine to Excellent (C6-C8): $75-$100, Mint (C10): $125

1960s Porsche 911S 2-door coupe. **10.25 in** (26 cm). **Friction**. Known colors: Red. Graphics: 37 (rally graphics). Maker: **Takatoku**, Japan. Toy marks: none. Box marks: TT (Takatoku). Box text: *Porsche 911S Rallye Champion*.
Scarcity: 5. Fine to Excellent (C6-C8): $300-$400, Mint (C10): $500

1960s Porsche 911S 2-door coupe with U-turn action. **10 in** (25 cm). **Battery operated**. Known colors: Orange and black. Graphics: U-Turn 27. Maker: **Toplay**, Japan. Toy marks: TPS (Toplay). Box marks: TPS (Toplay). Box text: *U-Turn Rally*.
Scarcity: 7. Fine to Excellent (C6-C8): $150-$200, Mint (C10): $250

1960s Porsche 911S 2-door coupe. **10.25 in** (26 cm). **Friction**. Known colors: White. Graphics: 37 (rally stripes). Maker: **Takatoku**, Japan. Toy marks: TT (Takatoku). Box marks: TT (Takatoku). Box text: *Porsche 911S Rallye Champion*.
Scarcity: 5. Fine to Excellent (C6-C8): $300-$400, Mint (C10): $500

1960s Porsche 911S 2-door coupe. **10.25 in** (26 cm). **Friction**. Known colors: Blue. Graphics: 18 (rally graphics). Maker: **Takatoku**, Japan. Toy marks: none. Box marks: TT (Takatoku). Box text: *Porsche 911S Rallye Champion*.
Scarcity: 5. Fine to Excellent (C6-C8): $300-$400, Mint (C10): $500

1960s Porsche 911S 2-door coupe. **10.25 in** (26 cm). **Friction**. Known colors: Red. Graphics: Porsche (rally graphics). Maker: **Takatoku**, Japan. Toy marks: none. Box marks: TT (Takatoku). Box text: *Porsche Sportomatic*.
Scarcity: 5. Fine to Excellent (C6-C8): $300-$400, Mint (C10): $500

(Not pictured) **1960s Porsche 912S 2-door coupe** with fender mirrors. **11 in** (28 cm). **Friction**. Known colors: Red. Graphics: 18. Maker: **Aoshin**, Japan. Toy marks: Aoshin. Box marks: Aoshin.
Scarcity: 4. Fine to Excellent (C6-C8): $100-$185, Mint (C10): $275

Race Cars 187

1970s Porsche 917 2-door with forward/reverse action. **7.25 in** (18 cm). **Battery operated**. Known colors: Silver. Graphics: 8. Maker: **Terai**, Japan. Toy marks: Daiya (Terai).
Scarcity: 4. Fine to Excellent (C6-C8): $95-$150, Mint (C10): $200

1970s Porsche 911S 2-door coupe with bump-n-go action and flashing hood light. **9 in** (23 cm). **Battery operated**. Known colors: Silver-blue with red. Graphics: 12 - Martini Racing - Porsche. License: SAY2611. Maker: **Daishin**, Japan. Toy marks: Daishin.
Scarcity: 2. Fine to Excellent (C6-C8): $50-$70, Mint (C10): $100

1970s Porsche 917, 2-door coupe with steering and forward/reverse action. **10 in** (25 cm). **R/C battery operated**. Known colors: Red. Maker: **Bandai**, Japan. Toy marks: Bandai. Box marks: Bandai.
Scarcity: 4. Fine to Excellent (C6-C8): $100-$175, Mint (C10): $285

(Not pictured) **1970s Porsche 911 Carrera 2-door coupe** with roof rack, spoiler, and headlights. **10.5 in** (27 cm). **Friction with battery**. Known colors: Yellow. Graphics: Carrera. Maker: **Alps**, Japan. Toy marks: none. Box marks: Alps. Box text: *Porsche*.
Scarcity: 3. Fine to Excellent (C6-C8): $125-$175, Mint (C10): $225

(Not pictured) **1970s Porsche 911 Carrera 2-door coupe** with driver and visible engine. **10.5 in** (27 cm). **Battery operated**. Known colors: Red. Graphics: 10 - P. Maker: **Asahi**, Japan. Toy marks: A (Asahi Trading). Box marks: A (Asahi Trading). Box text: *Porsche Carrera 10*.
Scarcity: 4. Fine to Excellent (C6-C8): $175-$250, Mint (C10): $325

(Not pictured) **1970s Porsche 911 Carrera 2-door coupe** with roof rack and bump and go action. **10.5 in** (27 cm). **Battery operated**. Known colors: White. Graphics: 19 - Team Porsche East African Safari. Maker: **Taiyo**, Japan.
Scarcity: 3. Fine to Excellent (C6-C8): $100-$125, Mint (C10): $150

1970s Porsche 911 Carrera 2-door coupe with bump-n-go non fall-action and blinking lights. **10.5 in** (27 cm). **Battery operated**. Known colors: Silver. Graphics: 46 - Martini Racing Team. Maker: **Taiyo**, Japan. Toy marks: Taiyo. Box marks: Taiyo. Box text: *Rusher Porsche Carrera*.
Scarcity: 3. Fine to Excellent (C6-C8): $75-$100, Mint (C10): $125

1960s Renault Floride 2-door coupe. **7.75 in** (20 cm). **Friction**. Known colors: Blue and white. Graphics: 27 - 375 H.P. - Speed King. Maker: **Ichiko**, Japan. Toy marks: Ichiko. Box marks: Ichiko.
Scarcity: 4. Fine to Excellent (C6-C8): $85-$165, Mint (C10): $225

1960s Saab 99, 2-door sedan with steering and forward/reverse action. **8 in** (20 cm). **R/C battery operated**. Known colors: Assorted. Maker: **Bandai**, Japan. Toy marks: Bandai. Box marks: Bandai. Box text: *IF 79 RS Rally Saab*.
Scarcity: 4. Fine to Excellent (C6-C8): $75-$185, Mint (C10): $250

1960s Saab 99, 2-door sedan with steering and forward/reverse action. **8 in** (20 cm). **R/C battery operated**. Known colors: Yellow. Graphics: 99 - S. License: Saab 99. Maker: **Bandai**, Japan. Toy marks: Bandai. Box marks: Bandai.
Scarcity: 4. Fine to Excellent (C6-C8): $75-$185, Mint (C10): $250

1960s Toyota Sports-800, 2-door coupe with roaring engine. **10 in** (25 cm). **Battery operated**. Known colors: Red. Graphics: 5 - GP (racing stripes). License: 5-1380. Maker: **Asahi**, Japan. Toy marks: ATC (Asahi Toy). Box marks: ATC (Asahi Toy).
Notes: Asahi catalog image.
Scarcity: 5. Fine to Excellent (C6-C8): $400-$600, Mint (C10): $800

1950s Triumph TR 3, 2-door convertible with closed top. **8 in** (20 cm). **Friction**. Known colors: Red and white. Graphics: 5 - Triumph TR3. Maker: **Bandai**, Japan. Toy marks: Bandai. Box text: *#1063*.
Scarcity: 4. Fine to Excellent (C6-C8): $150-$250, Mint (C10): $350

1950s Triumph TR 3, 2-door convertible with closed top, door mounted rally lights, luggage rack, and chrome side pipes. **8 in** (20 cm). **Friction**. Known colors: Yellow and black. Graphics: 15. License: Triumph. Maker: **Bandai**, Japan. Toy marks: Bandai.
Scarcity: 9. Fine to Excellent (C6-C8): $700-$1,100, Mint (C10): $1,350

1950s Triumph TR 3, 2-door convertible with top down, door mounted rally lights, luggage rack, and chrome side pipes. **8 in** (20 cm). **Friction**. Known colors: Red. Graphics: 6. License: Triumph. Maker: **Bandai**, Japan. Toy marks: Bandai. Box marks: Bandai.
Scarcity: 9. Fine to Excellent (C6-C8): $700-$1,100, Mint (C10): $1,350

1950s Triumph TR 3, 2-door convertible with top down and fold down windshield. **8 in** (20 cm). **Friction**. Known colors: Red and white. Graphics: 3 - Triumph TR3. Maker: **Bandai**, Japan. Toy marks: Bandai. Box marks: Bandai. Box text: *Triumph Race Car*.
Scarcity: 4. Fine to Excellent (C6-C8): $150-$250, Mint (C10): $350

1950s Triumph TR 3, 2-door convertible with open top, fold down windshield, and interchangeable numbers. **8 in** (20 cm). **Friction**. Known colors: Red and white. Graphics: Triumph TR3. Maker: **Bandai**, Japan. Toy marks: Bandai. Box marks: Bandai.
Scarcity: 4. Fine to Excellent (C6-C8): $150-$250, Mint (C10): $350

Race Cars 189

1960s Volkswagen Karmann Ghia 2-door sedan. 7.75 in (20 cm). **Friction.**
Known colors: Blue, red, yellow, and black. Graphics: 35 - Challenger - 375 H.P.
License: Volkswagen. Maker: **Ichiko**, Japan. Toy marks: Ichiko.
Scarcity: 4. Fine to Excellent (C6-C8): $75-$135, Mint (C10): $195

1960s Volkswagen Beetle 2-door sedan with bump-n-go non-fall action and blinking lights. **9.75 in** (25 cm). **Battery operated.** Known colors: White. Graphics: 53. Maker: **Taiyo**, Japan. Toy marks: Taiyo. Box marks: Taiyo. Box text: *Volkswagen*.
Scarcity: 3. Fine to Excellent (C6-C8): $80-$100, Mint (C10): $125

1960s Volkswagen Beetle 2-door coupe with bump and go non-fall action and blinking lights. **9.75 in** (25 cm). **Battery operated.** Known colors: White. Graphics: Hunter VW1303S Racing Team. Maker: **Taiyo**, Japan. Toy marks: Taiyo. Box marks: Taiyo. Box text: *Racer VW 1303S*.
Notes: Produced 1970s.
Scarcity: 3. Fine to Excellent (C6-C8): $75-$100, Mint (C10): $125

1960s Volkswagen Beetle 2-door sedan with bump-n-go non-fall action and blinking lights. **9.75 in** (25 cm). **Battery operated.** Known colors: Yellow and black. Graphics: Volkswagen. Maker: **Taiyo**, Japan. Toy marks: Taiyo. Box marks: Taiyo.
Scarcity: 3. Fine to Excellent (C6-C8): $80-$100, Mint (C10): $125

1960s Volkswagen Beetle 2-door sedan with bump and go non-fall action and blinking lights. **9.75 in** (25 cm). **Battery operated.** Known colors: Assorted. Graphics: 32. Maker: **Taiyo**, Japan. Toy marks: Taiyo. Box marks: Taiyo. Box text: *Love Bug beetle*.
Scarcity: 3. Fine to Excellent (C6-C8): $80-$100, Mint (C10): $125

1960s Volkswagen Beetle 2-door sedan with steering and forward/reverse action. **10.5 in** (27 cm). **R/C battery operated.** Known colors: White. Graphics: 55. Maker: **Bandai**, Japan. Toy marks: Bandai. Box text: *Volkswagen Rallye*.
Scarcity: 4. Fine to Excellent (C6-C8): $150-$225, Mint (C10): $285

(Not pictured) **1970s Volkswagen Golf 2-door coupe** with bump and go action. **8 in** (20 cm). **Battery operated.** Known colors: Yellow and green. Graphics: 7. Maker: **Unknown**, Japan.
Scarcity: 4. Fine to Excellent (C6-C8): $50-$70, Mint (C10): $90

1960s Volvo 164, 4-door sedan. 8 in (20 cm). **Friction.** Known colors: Green. Graphics: V 18. License: Volvo 164. Maker: **Bandai**, Japan. Toy marks: Bandai. Box text: *V Rally Volvo*.
Scarcity: 4. Fine to Excellent (C6-C8): $125-$175, Mint (C10): $225

1960s Volvo 164, 4-door sedan with steering and forward/reverse action. **8 in** (20 cm). **R/C battery operated.** Known colors: Blue. Graphics: V 26. License: Volvo 164. Maker: **Bandai**, Japan. Toy marks: Bandai. Box text: *V Rally Volvo*.
Scarcity: 4. Fine to Excellent (C6-C8): $125-$175, Mint (C10): $225

Single Seat Racers

(By Car Number, Size, and Toy Maker)

Race car, Michigan International Speedway. *Photo by Tosh Wakabayashi*

(Not pictured) **1950s Open-wheel style Champion Racer** with vinyl head driver. **9.25 in** (23 cm). **Friction.** Known colors: White and red. Graphics: *#1 - Indianapolis Special*. Maker: **Yonezawa**, Japan. Toy marks: Y (Yonezawa). Box marks: Y (Yonezawa). Box text: *Champion Racer*.
Scarcity: 4. Fine to Excellent (C6-C8): $350-$500, Mint: (C10): $750

1960s Open-wheel style Racer with tin driver head. **10 in** (25 cm). **Friction.** Known colors: Red and white. Graphics: **#1** - Belond Special - Star. Maker: **Asahi**, Japan. Toy marks: Toymaster (Asahi Toy).
Scarcity: 4. Fine to Excellent (C6-C8): $150-$250, Mint: (C10): $350

1960s Open-wheel style Racer with two speed operation, vinyl driver head, and smoking exhaust. **12 in** (30 cm). **Battery operated.** Known colors: Red. Graphics: **#1** - Speed Challenger. Maker: **Alps**, Japan. Toy marks: Alps. Box marks: Alps. Box text: *Speed Challenger*.
Scarcity: 6. Fine to Excellent (C6-C8): $400-$600, Mint: (C10): $800

1960s Open-wheel style Racer with built-in jack mechanism to change tires, two extra tires, forward/reverse, cockpit light, and detachable remote control. **14.75 in** (37 cm). **R/C battery operated.** Known colors: Cream and red orange. Graphics: **#1** - Indianapolis 500 Racer. Maker: **Shioji**, Japan. Toy marks: none (Japan). Box marks: Sears. Box text: *Indianapolis 500 Racer*.
Notes: Sold only by Sears.
Scarcity: 8. Fine to Excellent (C6-C8): $800-$1,400, Mint: (C10): $1,800

1960s Open-wheel style Racer with vinyl driver representing A.J. Foyt. **17 in** (43 cm). **Friction.** Known colors: Red and white. Graphics: **#1** - Indianapolis Special - Speed King. Maker: **Yonezawa**, Japan. Toy marks: Y (Yonezawa). Box marks: Y (Yonezawa).
Scarcity: 9. Fine to Excellent (C6-C8): $1,200-$1,800, Mint: (C10): $2,600

(Not pictured) **1930s Bugatti open-wheel style Racer** with tin driver. **19.75 in** (50 cm). **Windup.** Known colors: Blue. Graphics: **#1** 1-970. Maker: **Paya**, Spain. Toy marks: Paya. Box marks: Paya.
Notes: Starting in 1985, reproductions of this toy are being made from the original molds.
Scarcity: 9. Fine to Excellent (C6-C8): $2,500-$3,800, Mint: (C10): $5,000

1930s Bugatti open-wheel style Racer with tin driver. **19.75 in** (50 cm). **Windup.** Known colors: Assorted. Graphics: **#1** 1-970. Maker: **Paya**, Spain. Toy marks: Paya. Box marks: Paya.
Notes: Paya catalog image. Current production. Limited edition reproduction of 5000 pieces.
Scarcity: 2. Mint: (C10): $400

1960s Open-wheel style Racer 8 in (20 cm). **Friction.** Known colors: Assorted. Graphics: **#2** (tin). Maker: **Unknown**, Japan. Toy marks: none (Japan).
Scarcity: 3. Fine to Excellent (C6-C8): $40-$65, Mint: (C10): $90

Single Seat Racers

1960s Ford Lotus open-wheel style Racer with engine sound and steerable front wheels. **9.5 in** (24 cm). **Battery operated**. Known colors: Black. Graphics: **#2** - John Player Special - JPS. Maker: **Bandai**, Japan. Toy marks: Bandai. Box marks: Bandai. Box text: *Lotus Racer With realistic engine sound*.
Scarcity: 3. Fine to Excellent (C6-C8): $150-$200, Mint: (C10): $265

1960s Racer with tin driver head. **12 in** (30 cm). **Friction**. Known colors: White, red, and black. Graphics: **#2** - Thunderbird. Maker: **Kyowa**, Japan. Toy marks: Kyowa. Box marks: Kyowa. Box text: *Jet Racer*.
Scarcity: 3. Fine to Excellent (C6-C8): $130-$180, Mint: (C10): $235

1960s Open-wheel style Racer with vinyl driver head. **12.75 in** (32 cm). **Friction**. Known colors: Red and white. Graphics: **#2**. Maker: **Yonezawa**, Japan. Toy marks: Y (Yonezawa). Box marks: Y (Yonezawa). Box text: *Formula Racer*.
Scarcity: 4. Fine to Excellent (C6-C8): $150-$225, Mint: (C10): $300

1930s Open-wheel style Racer with tin driver. **13.5 in** (34 cm). **Windup**. Known colors: Light blue. Graphics: **#2**. Maker: **Paya**, Spain. Toy marks: Paya. Box marks: Paya.
Notes: Current production. This is a re-issue from original dies.
Scarcity: 2. Mint: (C10): $150

1920s Alfa Romeo open-wheel style Racer. 21 in (53 cm). **Friction**. Known colors: Assorted. Graphics: **#2**. Maker: **CIJ**, France. Toy marks: CIJ.
Scarcity: 10. Fine to Excellent (C6-C8): $1,500-$2,000, Mint: (C10): $2,500

1950s Open-wheel style Racer with tin driver, chrome exhaust, and radius rods. **7 in** (18 cm). **Friction**. Known colors: Assorted. Graphics: **#3** or **#5** or **#6** or **#8** or **#63**, Special, AAA, Sanyo (tires). Maker: **Yonezawa/Tomy**, Japan. Toy marks: Y (Yonezawa), ETC (Tomy). Box marks: Y (Yonezawa), ETC (Tomy). Box text: *Champion Midget Racer*.
Notes: A reproduction of midget racer #5 was produced in 2000. Total production of 1000 pieces.
Scarcity: 8. Fine to Excellent (C6-C8): $500-$900, Mint: (C10): $1,300

Race Cars 193

1950s Open-wheel style Racer with tin driver head. **7.25 in** (18 cm). **Friction**. Known colors: Red and white. Graphics: **#3** - X - X3. Maker: **Bandai**, Japan. Toy marks: Bandai. Box marks: Bandai. Box text: *X-3 Race*.
Scarcity: 4. Fine to Excellent (C6-C8): $100-$175, Mint: (C10): $250

(Not pictured) **1960s Open-wheel style Racer** with plastic driver and tin number badge. **8 in** (20 cm). **Friction**. Known colors: Red. Graphics: **#3**. Maker: **Bandai**, Japan. Toy marks: Bandai. Box marks: Bandai. Box text: *Atom Racer #887*.
Scarcity: 4. Fine to Excellent (C6-C8): $100-$175, Mint: (C10): $250

1960s Open-wheel style Racer with tin driver head. **9.5 in** (24 cm). **Friction**. Known colors: Blue-silver and red. Graphics: **#3** - Hero. Maker: **Takatoku**, Japan. Toy marks: TT (Takatoku).
Scarcity: 2. Fine to Excellent (C6-C8): $35-$65, Mint: (C10): $95

1960s Open-wheel style Racer with tin driver. **11 in** (28 cm). **Friction**. Known colors: Gold, red and white. Graphics: **#3** - Golden Racer. Maker: **Nishimura**, Japan. Toy marks: SN (Nishimura). Box marks: SN (Nishimura). Box text: *Golden Racer*.
Scarcity: 4. Fine to Excellent (C6-C8): $90-$140, Mint: (C10): $185

1960s Open-wheel style Racer with waving driver, lighted engine, smoking exhaust, and forward/reverse action. **14.75 in** (37 cm). **Battery operated**. Known colors: Blue-gray. Graphics: **#3** - Indianapolis 500 - 1107. Maker: **Tomy**, Japan. Toy marks: Tomiyama (Tomy). Box marks: Tomiyama (Tomy). Box text: *Firebird Race Car*.
Scarcity: 7. Fine to Excellent (C6-C8): $600-$800, Mint: (C10): $1,000

1960s Open-wheel style Racer with vinyl driver, removable and inflatable tires, spare, pump, wrench, and engine noise. **14.75 in** (37 cm). **Friction**. Known colors: Red. Graphics: **#3** - Fire Bird - Indianapolis Style. Maker: **Tomy**, Japan. Toy marks: Tomiyama (Tomy). Box marks: Tomiyama (Tomy), Cragstan. Box text: *Firebird Speedway Racer*.
Scarcity: 7. Fine to Excellent (C6-C8): $600-$800, Mint: (C10): $1,000

1960s Open-wheel style Racer with tin driver head. **16 in** (41 cm).
Friction. Known colors: White. Graphics: **#3** - Niki Lauda. Maker: **Rico**, Spain. Toy marks: Rico.
Scarcity: 4. Fine to Excellent (C6-C8): $135-$195, Mint: (C10): $265

1960s Open-wheel style Racer with plastic driver head and chrome side pipes. **6.5 in** (17 cm). **Friction**. Known colors: Red; Blue-gray. Graphics: **#4** - Speedway Racer - Indianapolis Style. Maker: **Linemar**, Japan. Toy marks: Linemar (Marx).
Scarcity: 5. Fine to Excellent (C6-C8): $175-$285, Mint: (C10): $375

(Not pictured) **1950s Mercedes Benz W-196 open-wheel style Racer** with composition driver. **9.5 in** (24 cm). **Battery operated**. Known colors: Assorted. Graphics: **#4** or **#7**. Maker: **Neuhierl**, Germany. Toy marks: JNF (Neuhierl). Box marks: JNF (Neuhierl). Box text: Solo.
Notes: Also produced as windup model.
Scarcity: 6. Fine to Excellent (C6-C8): $300-$500, Mint: (C10): $700

(Not pictured) **1930s Open-wheel style Racer** with tin wheels and tin driver. **12 in** (30 cm). **Windup**. Known colors: Red and yellow. Graphics: **#4** - Dunlop Cord (tires). Maker: **Unknown**, Germany. Toy marks: None.
Scarcity: 8. Fine to Excellent (C6-C8): $750-$1,200, Mint: (C10): $1,700

1950s Mercedes Benz W-196 open-wheel style Racer with composition driver. **13.25 in** (34 cm). **Friction**. Known colors: Assorted. Graphics: **#4** or **#5**. Maker: **Neuhierl**, Germany. Toy marks: JNF (Neuhierl). Box marks: JNF (Neuhierl). Box text: Mercedes Monoposto.
Notes: Also produced as battery operated model.
Scarcity: 7. Fine to Excellent (C6-C8): $400-$600, Mint: (C10): $800

(Not pictured) **1950s Mercedes Benz W-196 open-wheel style Racer** with composition driver. **14 in** (36 cm). **Friction**. Known colors: Assorted. Graphics: **#4**. Maker: **Tipp & Co.**, Germany. Toy marks: TCO (Tipp).
Scarcity: 8. Fine to Excellent (C6-C8): $600-$800, Mint: (C10): $1,000

1960s Open-wheel style Racer with tethered "U-Control," lighted engine, and forward action. **14.75 in** (37 cm). **Battery operated**. Known colors: Bronze. Graphics: **#4** - U-Control Racer - 62 - Indianapolis Special. Maker: **Tomy**, Japan. Toy marks: Cragstan, Tomiyama (Tomy). Box marks: Cragstan. Box text: U-Control Racer With Driver.
Scarcity: 7. Fine to Excellent (C6-C8): $600-$800, Mint: (C10): $1,000

1950s Open-wheel style Racer with tin driver, chrome exhaust, and radius rods. **7 in** (18 cm). **Friction**. Known colors: Red. Graphics: **#5** - Special - AAA - Sanyo (tires). Maker: **Yonezawa/Tomy**, Japan. Toy marks: Y (Yonezawa), ETC (Tomy). Box marks: Y (Yonezawa), ETC (Tomy). Box text: Champion Midget Racer.
Notes: This reproduction of the 1950s Midget Racer #5 was produced in 2000. Total production of 1000 pieces.
Scarcity: 3. Mint: (C10): $300

Race Cars 195

1950s Open-wheel style Racer with tin driver head. **7.25 in** (18 cm). **Friction**. Known colors: Blue and cream. Graphics: **#5** - Champion - 500 Mile Race Between New York and Miami. Maker: **Bandai**, Japan. Toy marks: Bandai.
Scarcity: 5. Fine to Excellent (C6-C8): $100-$160, Mint: (C10): $225

1960s Open-wheel style Racer with spinning prop. **9.25 in** (23 cm). **Friction**. Known colors: Red. Graphics: **(assorted numbers)**. Maker: **Suzuki & Edward**, Japan. Toy marks: S&E (Suzuki & Edward).
Scarcity: 3. Fine to Excellent (C6-C8): $100-$150, Mint: (C10): $185

(Not pictured) **1950s Mercedes Benz W 196 Silver Arrow Racer** with tin driver. **10 in** (25 cm). **Friction**. Known colors: Yellow. Graphics: **#5**. Maker: **Marusan**, Japan. Toy marks: SAN (Marusan). Box marks: SAN (Marusan). Box text: *Benz Racer*.
Scarcity: 6. Fine to Excellent (C6-C8): $200-$300, Mint: (C10): $400

1950s Open-wheel style Racer with tin driver head. **7.25 in** (18 cm). **Friction**. Known colors: Blue and red. Graphics: **#5** - Typhoon. Maker: **Tatsuya**, Japan. Toy marks: KTS (Tatsuya).
Scarcity: 4. Fine to Excellent (C6-C8): $90-$160, Mint: (C10): $235

1960s Lotus Ford open-wheel style Racer with vinyl driver head. **10.5 in** (27 cm). **Friction**. Known colors: Silver. Graphics: **#5** - Grandprix. Maker: **Daito**, Japan. Toy marks: Daito. Box marks: Daito. Box text: *Grand Prix Lotus Ford*.
Scarcity: 3. Fine to Excellent (C6-C8): $75-$135, Mint: (C10): $175

1960s Open-wheel style Racer with moving pistons and spinning prop. **7.5 in** (19 cm). **Friction**. Known colors: Blue; Red. Graphics: **#5** - Super Tiger. Maker: **Nomura**, Japan. Toy marks: TN (Nomura).
Scarcity: 3. Fine to Excellent (C6-C8): $85-$125, Mint: (C10): $165

Single Seat Racers

1950s Mercedes Benz W-196 open-wheel style Racer with tin driver head. **14 in** (36 cm). **Friction**. Known colors: Light blue. Graphics: **#5**. Maker: **Memo**, France. Toy marks: Memo.
Scarcity: 6. Fine to Excellent (C6-C8): $675-$750, Mint: (C10): $825

1950s Open-wheel style Racer with tin driver, chrome exhaust, and radius rods. **7 in** (18 cm). **Friction**. Known colors: Red. Graphics: **#3** or **#5** or **#6** or **#8**, Special, AAA, Sanyo (tires). Maker: **Yonezawa/Tomy**, Japan. Toy marks: Y (Yonezawa), ETC (Tomy). Box marks: Y (Yonezawa), ETC (Tomy). Box text: *Champion Midget Racer*.
Scarcity: 8. Fine to Excellent (C6-C8): $500-$700, Mint: (C10): $1100

1960s Mercedes Benz W-196R Racer with tin driver head and visible spinner in engine compartment. **14 in** (36 cm). **Friction**. Known colors: Cream. Graphics: **#5** - Konryu - Atomic Power Engine. Maker: **Plaything**, Japan. Toy marks: Plaything. Box marks: Plaything. Box text: *Super Speed Racer*.
Scarcity: 4. Fine to Excellent (C6-C8): $200-$300, Mint: (C10): $425

(Not pictured) **1950s Open-wheel style Racer** with driver. **14 in** (36 cm). **Friction**. Known colors: Red. Graphics: **#5**. Maker: **Unknown**, France. Toy marks: none.
Scarcity: 5. Fine to Excellent (C6-C8): $225-$350, Mint: (C10): $475

1960s Open-wheel style Racer with plastic driver and side pipes. **9.5 in** (24 cm). **Friction**. Known colors: Assorted. Graphics: **(assorted numbers)**. Maker: **Linemar**, Japan. Toy marks: Linemar (Marx). Box marks: Linemar (Marx). Box text: *Super Racer With Plastic Figure*.
Scarcity: 4. Fine to Excellent (C6-C8): $150-$210, Mint: (C10): $275

1960s Open-wheel style Racer with detonation sound, sparking, and vinyl head driver. **18 in** (46 cm). **Friction**. Known colors: Red and white. Graphics: **#5** - Panther. Maker: **Masudaya**, Japan. Toy marks: MT (Masudaya). Box marks: MT (Masudaya). Box text: Panther Racer.
Scarcity: 6. Fine to Excellent (C6-C8): $400-$500, Mint: (C10): $600

1930s Open-wheel style Racer with tin driver. **13 in** (33 cm). **Windup**. Known colors: Blue. Graphics: **#6**. Maker: **Mettoy**, Great Britain. Toy marks: Mettoy. Notes: Also came in different colors, numbers, and lithography.
Scarcity: 5. Fine to Excellent (C6-C8): $300-$400, Mint: (C10): $550

Race Cars 197

1950s Open-wheel style Racer with tin driver head and side on/off switch. **6 in** (15 cm). **Battery operated**. Known colors: Red and white. Graphics: **#7** - Champion. Maker: **Nomura**, Japan. Toy marks: TN (Nomura). Box marks: TN (Nomura). Box text: *Champion - Electric Race Car*.
Scarcity: 4. Fine to Excellent (C6-C8): $150-$200, Mint: (C10): $250

1950s Open-wheel style Racer with tin driver head. **6.25 in** (16 cm). **Friction**. Known colors: Yellow and red. Graphics: **#7A**. Maker: **Sato**, Japan. Toy marks: TOY (Sato).
Scarcity: 5. Fine to Excellent (C6-C8): $150-$225, Mint: (C10): $325

1950s Open-wheel style Racer with tin driver and adjustable wheels. **7.25 in** (18 cm). **Friction**. Known colors: Blue. Graphics: **#7** - Comet - 1956 2000 Mile Race. Maker: **Unknown**, Japan. Toy marks: none (Japan). Box text: *Comet Racer*.
Scarcity: 6. Fine to Excellent (C6-C8): $275-$375, Mint: (C10): $485

(Not pictured) **1930s Open-wheel style Racer** 7.5 in (19 cm). **Windup**. Graphics: **#7**. Maker: **Yamada**, Japan. Toy marks: YH (Yamada).
Scarcity: 8. Fine to Excellent (C6-C8): $400-$600, Mint: (C10): $800

1960s Open-wheel style Racer with tin driver head and sparkling. **8 in** (20 cm). **Friction**. Known colors: Yellow, black, and red. Graphics: **#7**. Maker: **Masuya**, Japan. Toy marks: MS (Masuya). Box marks: MS (Masuya). Box text: *Jet Racer With Sparks*.
Scarcity: 4. Fine to Excellent (C6-C8): $135-$195, Mint: (C10): $275

(Not pictured) **1960s Open-wheel style Racer** with composition driver. **8 in** (20 cm). **Friction**. Known colors: Metallic blue. Graphics: **#7**. Maker: **Rico**, Spain. Toy marks: Rico.
Scarcity: 4. Fine to Excellent (C6-C8): $150-$185, Mint: (C10): $250

1950s Open-wheel style Racer with tin driver, popping noise, and sparking. **8.5 in** (22 cm). **Friction**. Known colors: Red, blue, and silver. Graphics: **#7** - Jet. Maker: **Marusan/Kosuge**, Japan. Toy marks: SAN (Marusan), Kosuge. Box marks: SAN (Marusan). Box text: *1955 Jet Racer (Troy Ruttman picture)*.
Scarcity: 5. Fine to Excellent (C6-C8): $225-$325, Mint: (C10): $500

198 Single Seat Racers

1960s Ferrari open-wheel style Racer with siren sound and tin driver head. **9 in** (23 cm). **Friction**. Known colors: Red and cream. Graphics: **#7** - **62** - Indianapolis 500. Maker: **Aoshin**, Japan. Toy marks: ASC (Aoshin). Box marks: ASC (Aoshin). Box text: *Indianapolis Hero Ferrari Racing Car With Siren*.
Scarcity: 5. Fine to Excellent (C6-C8): $150-$250, Mint: (C10): $350

1950s Mercedes Benz W-196 open-wheel style Racer with tin driver. **9.75 in** (25 cm). **Friction**. Known colors: Red and white; Blue-silver and red. Graphics: **#7** - Tornado Special or **25** - Universe. Maker: **Yonezawa**, Japan. Toy marks: Y (Yonezawa). Box marks: Y (Yonezawa). Box text: *Benz Race Car*. Notes: note differences in drivers and lithographed versus tin engine vents.
Scarcity: 6. Fine to Excellent (C6-C8): $450-$650, Mint: (C10): $800

1960s Open-wheel style Racer with tin driver head. **10 in** (25 cm). **Friction**. Known colors: White and red. Graphics: **#7**. Maker: **Kyowa**, Japan. Toy marks: Kyowa.
Scarcity: 3. Fine to Excellent (C6-C8): $85-$135, Mint: (C10): $185

1950s Mercedes Benz W 196 Silver Arrow Racer with tin driver and steerable wheels. **10 in** (25 cm). **Battery operated**. Known colors: Silver. Graphics: **#7**. Maker: **Marusan**, Japan. Toy marks: SAN (Marusan), Kosuge. Box marks: SAN (Marusan). Box text: *Go Stop Benz Racer*.
Scarcity: 6. Fine to Excellent (C6-C8): $200-$300, Mint: (C10): $400

1960s Open-wheel style Racer with tin driver. **10 in** (25 cm). **Friction**. Known colors: Gold and blue. Graphics: **#7**- Golden Wings. Maker: **Nakayama**, Japan. Toy marks: N (Nakayama). Box text: *Race Car Golden Wings*.
Scarcity: 3. Fine to Excellent (C6-C8): $75-$100, Mint: (C10): $125

1960s Open-wheel style Racer with tin driver head and tethered "U-Control." **10 in** (25 cm). **R/C battery operated**. Known colors: Gold and red. Graphics: **#7**- Speed King. Maker: **Suzuki & Edward**, Japan. Toy marks: S&E (Suzuki & Edward). Box marks: S&E (Suzuki & Edward), Rosko. Box text: *U-Control Racing Car "Speed King."*
Scarcity: 5. Fine to Excellent (C6-C8): $250-$300, Mint: (C10): $375

(Not pictured) **1960s Open-wheel style Racer** with tin driver. Car breaks apart on bumping contact. **10.75 in** (27 cm). **Friction**. Known colors: Blue. Graphics: **#7**- (flame graphics). Maker: **Unknown**, Japan. Toy marks: None. Box text: *Break-Apart Racer*.
Scarcity: 6. Fine to Excellent (C6-C8): $250-$450, Mint: (C10): $600

Race Cars 199

1960s Open-wheel style Racer with tin driver head. **11 in** (28 cm).
Friction. Known colors: Red, white, and blue. Graphics: **#7** - Red Arrow.
Maker: **Nishimura**, Japan. Toy marks: SN (Nishimura).
Scarcity: 3. Fine to Excellent (C6-C8): $75-$100, Mint: (C10): $125

1950s Open-wheel style Racer with tin driver, forward/reverse action, steering, and tin hood scoop. **11.25 in** (29 cm). **R/C battery operated**. Known colors: Red and white. Graphics: **#7** - Fire Bird. Maker: **Unknown**, Japan. Toy marks: SSN (Unknown). Box text: *Fire Bird*.
Notes: Photo compares this car with Marusan version which is battery operated.
Scarcity: 5. Fine to Excellent (C6-C8): $250-$350, Mint: (C10): $450

1950s Open-wheel style Racer with tin driver. **11.5 in** (29 cm). **Friction**. Known colors: Blue. Graphics: **#7**. Maker: **Marusan**, Japan. Toy marks: SAN (Marusan).
Scarcity: 6. Fine to Excellent (C6-C8): $200-$300, Mint: (C10): $400

1960s Open-wheel style Racer with tin driver. **11.5 in** (29 cm). **Friction**. Known colors: Gold and white. Graphics: **#7** - Demon. Maker: **Unknown**, Japan. Toy marks: none (Japan). Box marks: HTC (Unknown). Box text: *Demon Racer*.
Scarcity: 3. Fine to Excellent (C6-C8): $85-$135, Mint: (C10): $195

1950s Mercedes Benz W-196 open-wheel style Racer with tin driver. **12 in** (30 cm). **Friction**. Known colors: Red and white. Graphics: **#7** - Tornado Special. Maker: **Linemar**, Japan. Toy marks: Linemar (Marx). Box marks: Linemar (Marx).
Scarcity: 6. Fine to Excellent (C6-C8): $350-$550, Mint: (C10): $750

1960s Open-wheel style Racer with or without tin driver. **12.25 in** (31 cm). **Friction**. Known colors: Blue-green or yellow. Graphics: **#3** - Buffalo or **#7** - Pegasus. Maker: **Marusan**, Japan. Toy marks: SAN (Marusan). Box marks: SAN (Marusan). Box text: *World Speed Racer*.
Scarcity: 5. Fine to Excellent (C6-C8): $165-$285, Mint: (C10): $400

Single Seat Racers

1960s Open-wheel style Racer with lighted engine, steering, speed and noise control, vinyl driver, and white wall tin wheels. **17 in** (43 cm). **Battery operated**. Known colors: Silver. Graphics: **#7** - Jetspeed or **#7** - Marx Jetspeed. Maker: **Yonezawa**, Japan. Toy marks: Y (Yonezawa). Box marks: Y (Yonezawa), Marx. Box text: *Jetspeed Racer* or *Marx Jetspeed Racer*.
Notes: Same racer sold with Yonezawa name or Marx name (Marx Jetspeed).
Scarcity: 6. Fine to Excellent (C6-C8): $400-$600, Mint: (C10): $800

1960s Open-wheel style Racers with connection between the two cars that allows them to alternately pass each other. **7 in** (18 cm). **R/C battery operated**. Known colors: Red; Blue. Graphics: **#5** and **#8**. Maker: **Linemar**, Japan. Toy marks: Linemar (Marx). Box marks: Linemar (Marx). Box text: *Twin Racing Cars*.
Scarcity: 8. Fine to Excellent (C6-C8): $600-$800, Mint: (C10): $1,000

1950s Open-wheel style Racer with tin driver head. **6 in** (15 cm). **Friction**. Known colors: Red, yellow, and white. Graphics: **#8** - Speed King. Maker: **Unknown**, Japan. Toy marks: none.
Scarcity: 3. Fine to Excellent (C6-C8): $75-$110, Mint: (C10): $150

1950s Open-wheel style Racers with two different tin drivers and tie rod between both racers. One racer has friction motor, the other is free wheeling.. **8 in** (20 cm). **Friction**. Known colors: Red and yellow and Blue and cream. Graphics: **#5** and **#8**. Maker: **Alps/Sato**, Japan. Toy marks: Alps, TOY (Sato).
Notes: Individual cars are 6 inches long but the toy is 8 inches.
Scarcity: 6. Fine to Excellent (C6-C8): $175-$250, Mint: (C10): $325

1960s Open-wheel style Racer with tin driver head. **6.5 in** (17 cm). **Friction**. Known colors: Red. Graphics: **#8**. Maker: **Nakayama**, Japan. Toy marks: N (Nakayama).
Scarcity: 3. Fine to Excellent (C6-C8): $85-$135, Mint: (C10): $150

1960s Open-wheel style Racer with tin driver. **8.25 in** (21 cm). **Friction**. Known colors: Red and white. Graphics: **#8** - Champion. Maker: **Asahi**, Japan. Toy marks: ATC (Asahi Toy). Box marks: ATC (Asahi Toy).
Scarcity: 5. Fine to Excellent (C6-C8): $150-$200, Mint: (C10): $275

Race Cars 201

1950s Open-wheel style Racer with tin driver. **8.25 in** (21 cm). **Friction.** Known colors: Light and dark green. Graphics: **#8** - Mars -Sanesu (hubcaps). Maker: **Shioji**, Japan. Toy marks: Sanesu. Box marks: SSS (Shioji). Box text: *Race Car Mars*.
Scarcity: 6. Fine to Excellent (C6-C8): $250-$350, Mint: (C10): $450

1960s Racer with tin driver head. **9 in** (23 cm). **Friction.** Known colors: Silver-blue. Graphics: **#8** - Speed Champion. Maker: **Asahi**, Japan. Toy marks: Toymaster (Asahi Toy).
Scarcity: 3. Fine to Excellent (C6-C8): $40-$60, Mint: (C10): $90

1960s Open-wheel style 3 wheel Racer with tin driver. Racer flips over and goes in reverse direction. **8.5 in** (22 cm). **Friction.** Known colors: Red and silver; Red and gold. Graphics: **#8**. Maker: **Masudaya**, Japan. Toy marks: MT (Masudaya). Box marks: MT (Masudaya). Box text: *Turn Over Race Car*.
Scarcity: 3. Fine to Excellent (C6-C8): $100-$150, Mint: (C10): $225

1960s Open-wheel style Racer with motor sound and vinyl driver head. **9.25 in** (23 cm). **Pullback friction.** Known colors: Red and cream. Graphics: **#8** - Champion Racer - Indianapolis Special. Maker: **Yonezawa**, Japan. Toy marks: Y (Yonezawa). Box marks: Y (Yonezawa). Box text: *Indianapolis Special Champion Racer*.
Scarcity: 8. Fine to Excellent (C6-C8): $300-$425, Mint: (C10): $600

1960s Open-wheel style Racer with tin driver that pops up when bumper hits wall. **8.5 in** (22 cm). **Friction.** Known colors: Yellow and red. Graphics: **#8** - Champion - Stunt Car. Maker: **Yoneya**, Japan. Toy marks: none (Japan). Box marks: SY (Yoneya). Box text: *Stunt Car With Pop-Up Man*.
Scarcity: 5. Fine to Excellent (C6-C8): $175-$225, Mint: (C10): $350

1950s Open-wheel style Racer with tin driver. **9.5 in** (24 cm). **Friction.** Known colors: Red, blue, and yellow. Graphics: **#8** or **#5** - King. Maker: **Momoya**, Japan. Toy marks: ET (Unknown). Box marks: Momoya. Box text: *King Racer*.
Scarcity: 6. Fine to Excellent (C6-C8): $350-$550, Mint: (C10): $750

202 Single Seat Racers

1950s Mercedes Benz W 196 Silver Arrow Racer with tin driver. **10 in** (25 cm). **Friction**. Known colors: Red. Graphics: **(assorted numbers in tin)**. Maker: **Linemar**, Japan. Toy marks: Linemar (Marx). Box marks: Linemar (Marx).
Scarcity: 6. Fine to Excellent (C6-C8): $200-$300, Mint: (C10): $400

1950s Mercedes Benz W 196 Silver Arrow Racer with tin driver and steerable wheels. **10 in** (25 cm). **Friction**. Known colors: White. Graphics: **#8 - Jupiter**. Maker: **Marusan**, Japan. Toy marks: SAN (Marusan), Kosuge. Box marks: SAN (Marusan). Box text: *Jupiter Benz Racer*.
Scarcity: 6. Fine to Excellent (C6-C8): $200-$300, Mint: (C10): $400

1960s Open-wheel style Racer with tin driver. **10 in** (25 cm). **Friction**. Known colors: Assorted. Graphics: **(assorted numbers)**. Maker: **Nakayama**, Japan. Toy marks: N (Nakayama).
Scarcity: 3. Fine to Excellent (C6-C8): $75-$100, Mint: (C10): $125

1960s Open-wheel style Racer with tin driver. **10 in** (25 cm). **Friction**. Known colors: Assorted. Graphics: **(assorted numbers)**. Maker: **Nakayama**, Japan. Toy marks: N (Nakayama).
Scarcity: 3. Fine to Excellent (C6-C8): $75-$100, Mint: (C10): $125

1950s Open-wheel style Racer with tin driver head. **11.5 in** (29 cm). **Friction**. Known colors: Red, yellow, and blue. Graphics: **No.8 - Rocket 8 - Sports** (hubcaps). Maker: **Yonezawa**, Japan. Toy marks: Y (Yonezawa). Box marks: Y (Yonezawa), Alps. Box text: *Sports Motor Car*.
Notes: Also produced with dark helmeted driver.
Scarcity: 10. Fine to Excellent (C6-C8): $1,000-$2,000, Mint: (C10): $3,000

1960s Open-wheel style Racer with tin driver head. **11.75 in** (30 cm). **Friction**. Known colors: Blue, red, and white. Graphics: **#8 - Blue Bird - Champion**. Maker: **Marusan**, Japan. Toy marks: SAN (Marusan). Box marks: SAN (Marusan).
Scarcity: 4. Fine to Excellent (C6-C8): $150-$225, Mint: (C10): $300

1960s Open-wheel style Racer with two speed operation, vinyl driver head, and smoking exhaust. **12 in** (30 cm). **Battery operated**. Known colors: Red and white. Graphics: **#8**. Maker: **Alps**, Japan. Toy marks: Alps. Box marks: Alps. Box text: *Speed Challenger*.
Scarcity: 6. Fine to Excellent (C6-C8): $400-$600, Mint: (C10): $800

(Not pictured) **1960s Open-wheel style Racer** with tin driver head. **12 in** (30 cm). **Friction**. Known colors: Blue and white. Graphics: **#8** - Prince - 200 Mile Racer. Maker: **Marusan**, Japan. Toy marks: SAN (Marusan). **Scarcity: 3. Fine to Excellent (C6-C8): $100-$175, Mint: (C10): $250**

1960s Open-wheel style Racer with vinyl driver head. **12.75 in** (32 cm). **Friction**. Known colors: Silver and red. Graphics: **#8** - Grandprix - Indianapolis. Maker: **Daito**, Japan. Toy marks: Daito. Box marks: Daito. Box text: *Grand Prix Race Car*.
Scarcity: 3. Fine to Excellent (C6-C8): $75-$100, Mint: (C10): $125

1950s Atom Car open-wheel style Racer with tin driver. **16 in** (41 cm). **Friction**. Known colors: Green. Graphics: **#0** - Atom - Sports (hubcaps). Maker: **Yonezawa**, Japan. Toy marks: Y (Yonezawa). Box marks: Y (Yonezawa), KDP (Kyodo). Box text: *Atom Car*.
Notes: Also came marked Atom 27 or 153 and with white or dark helmeted driver.
Scarcity: 7. Fine to Excellent (C6-C8): $1,200-$1,800, Mint: (C10): $2,500

1960s Open-wheel style Racer with built-in jack mechanism to change tires. **14.75 in** (37 cm). **Battery operated**. Known colors: Red orange and white; Red orange and light blue. Graphics: **#8** - Indianapolis 500. Maker: **Shioji**, Japan. Toy marks: none (Japan). Box marks: SSS (Shioji). Box text: *Indianapolis 500 Racer*.
Scarcity: 7. Fine to Excellent (C6-C8): $600-$800, Mint: (C10): $1,200

1960s Open-wheel style Racer with tin driver head and plastic air foil. **10 in** (25 cm). **Friction**. Known colors: Silver. Graphics: **#9**. Maker: **Terai**, Japan. Toy marks: Daiya (Terai). Box marks: Daiya (Terai). Box text: *Formula F-1*.
Scarcity: 2. Fine to Excellent (C6-C8): $60-$90, Mint: (C10): $120

204 Single Seat Racers

1960s Open-wheel style Racer with vinyl head driver and engine sound. **13 in** (33 cm). **Battery operated**. Known colors: Cream and red. Graphics: **#9** - Record Holder. Maker: **Masudaya**, Japan. Toy marks: MT (Masudaya). Box marks: MT (Masudaya). Box text: *Record Holder*.
Scarcity: 5. Fine to Excellent (C6-C8): $300-$425, Mint: (C10): $600

1960s Open-wheel style Racer with tin driver head. **10 in** (25 cm). **Friction**. Known colors: Assorted. Graphics: **#10** - Golden Jet. Maker: **Kyowa**, Japan. Toy marks: none (Japan). Box marks: Kyowa. Box text: *Jet Racer*.
Scarcity: 3. Fine to Excellent (C6-C8): $60-$90, Mint: (C10): $135

1960s Open-wheel style Racer with tin driver head. **10 in** (25 cm). **Friction**. Known colors: Blue. Graphics: **#10**. Maker: **Unknown**, Japan. Toy marks: none (Japan).
Scarcity: 3. Fine to Excellent (C6-C8): $40-$80, Mint: (C10): $120

1960s Racer with composition driver and flap wing. **11 in** (28 cm). **Friction**. Known colors: Red and white. Graphics: **#10**. Maker: **Joustra**, France. Toy marks: Joustra.
Scarcity: 4. Fine to Excellent (C6-C8): $125-$175, Mint: (C10): $250

(Not pictured) **1950s Open-wheel style Racer** with tin driver, steering, and forward/reverse. **11.5 in** (29 cm). **R/C battery operated**. Known colors: Red, white, and blue. Graphics: **#10** - Black Jaguar. Maker: **Marusan**, Japan. Toy marks: SAN (Marusan).
Scarcity: 4. Fine to Excellent (C6-C8): $150-$210, Mint: (C10): $285

1960s Racer with vinyl driver. **13.25 in** (34 cm). **Friction**. Known colors: Cream and red. Graphics: **#10**. Maker: **Unknown**, France. Toy marks: none (France).
Scarcity: 5. Fine to Excellent (C6-C8): $250-$325, Mint: (C10): $400

(Not pictured) **1960s Ford Lotus Formula 1 open-wheel style Racer** with vinyl head driver, flashing engine, exhaust noise, and three position shift. **16 in** (41 cm). **Battery operated**. Known colors: Green and yellow. Graphics: **#10** or **#36** - Team Lotus. Maker: **Asahi/Junior**, Japan. Toy marks: A (Asahi). Box marks: Junior. Box text: *Lotus 49 Ford F-1 Formula Racing Car*.
Scarcity: 5. Fine to Excellent (C6-C8): $150-$200, Mint: (C10): $250

1960s Racer with tin driver. **8.5 in** (22 cm). **Friction**. Known colors: Red. Graphics: **#11** - Red Arrow - Rotor Pfeil. Maker: **Tsujimoto**, Japan. Toy marks: TC (Tsujimoto). Box marks: TC (Tsujimoto). Box text: *Race Car*. Notes: Trademark is similar to Bandai's BC mark but a T rather than B.
Scarcity: 3. Fine to Excellent (C6-C8): $85-$150, Mint: (C10): $225

Race Cars 205

(Not pictured) **1960s Open-wheel style Racer** with tin driver head and lithographed windshield. **10 in** (25 cm). **Friction**. Known colors: Red. Graphics: **#11** - STP - Shell - Esso - Champion. Maker: **Unknown**, Japan. Toy marks: none (Japan). Box marks: none (Japan). Box text: *Jet Racer With Siren*.
Scarcity: 3. Fine to Excellent (C6-C8): $75-$100, Mint: (C10): $125

1960s Racer with siren sound and two speed shifting via antenna. **8.5 in** (22 cm). **Friction**. Known colors: Assorted. Graphics: **#8** or **#12** - GP-II. Maker: **Alps**, Japan. Toy marks: Alps. Box marks: Alps. Box text: *Jet Racer - 2 Speed Shifting With Siren*.
Scarcity: 5. Fine to Excellent (C6-C8): $125-$175, Mint: (C10): $240

1960s Ford Lotus open-wheel style Racer with detonating engine noise, steerable front wheels, and plastic engine and chassis. **11.5 in** (29 cm). **Battery operated**. Known colors: Red and yellow. Graphics: **#12** - Lotus Ford. Maker: **Masudaya**, Japan. Toy marks: MT (Masudaya). Box marks: MT (Masudaya). Notes: Masudaya catalog image.
Scarcity: 4. Fine to Excellent (C6-C8): $125-$250, Mint: (C10): $350

1960s Open-wheel style Racer with composition driver. **11 in** (28 cm). **Friction**. Known colors: Silver and red. Graphics: **#12**, **#13** or **#14**. Maker: **Joustra**, France. Toy marks: Joustra. Box text: *Voiture De Course - Racing Car*.
Scarcity: 5. Fine to Excellent (C6-C8): $200-$300, Mint: (C10): $400

1950s Jet Open-wheel style Racer with tin driver. **12 in** (30 cm). **Friction**. Known colors: Red and silver-blue. Graphics: **T-14** - J.T.T. - JETT-14. Maker: **Nomura**, Japan. Toy marks: TN (Nomura).
Scarcity: 6. Fine to Excellent (C6-C8): $425-$625, Mint: (C10): $800

1960s Mercedes Benz W-196R Racer with composition driver. **16.75 in** (43 cm). **Friction**. Known colors: Silver. Graphics: **#14**. Maker: **Unknown**, Japan. Toy marks: none (Japan).
Scarcity: 4. Fine to Excellent (C6-C8): $150-$225, Mint: (C10): $300

1960s Open-wheel style Racer with vinyl driver head and plastic air foil. **11 in** (28 cm). **Friction**. Known colors: Green and yellow. Graphics: **#15** – Indy' 500. Maker: **Kokyu**, Japan. Toy marks: K (Kokyu).
Scarcity: 5. Fine to Excellent (C6-C8): $125-$240, Mint: (C10): $325

1950s Open-wheel style Racer with composition driver. **11.25 in** (29 cm). **Friction**. Known colors: Blue. Graphics: **#15** or **#18**. Maker: **Tipp & Co.**, Germany. Toy marks: TCO (Tipp). Box marks: TCO (Tipp).
Scarcity: 6. Fine to Excellent (C6-C8): $250-$375, Mint: (C10): $500

Single Seat Racers

1960s Open-wheel style Racer with tin driver head. **11.5 in** (29 cm).
Friction. Known colors: Red and cream. Graphics: **#15** - Mars Jet. Maker: **Marusan**, Japan. Toy marks: SAN (Marusan). Box marks: SAN (Marusan). Box text: *Mars Jet*.
Scarcity: 6. Fine to Excellent (C6-C8): $300-$400, Mint: (C10): $500

1950s Open-wheel style Racer with tin driver head. **8.5 in** (22 cm).
Friction. Known colors: Red and cream. Graphics: **#16** - Speed King. Maker: **Tomy**, Japan. Toy marks: ETC (Tomy).
Scarcity: 5. Fine to Excellent (C6-C8): $175-$275, Mint: (C10): $375

1950s Open-wheel style Racer with tin driver, chrome exhaust pipes, and radius rods. **18 in** (46 cm). **Friction**. Known colors: Orange. Graphics: **#15** - Super Racer. Maker: **Unknown**, Germany. Toy marks: None.
Scarcity: 9. Fine to Excellent (C6-C8): $800-$1,500, Mint: (C10): $2,200

1960s Lotus open-wheel style Racer with plastic driver and gear lever controlled direction and speed. **9.5 in** (24 cm). **Battery operated**. Known colors: Green. Graphics: **#16**. Maker: **Bandai**, Japan. Toy marks: Bandai. Box marks: Bandai. Box text: *Lotus Racer*.
Scarcity: 3. Fine to Excellent (C6-C8): $80-$135, Mint: (C10): $185

1950s Open-wheel style Racer with tin driver head. **8.5 in** (22 cm).
Friction. Known colors: Yellow; Red. Graphics: **#16** - Speed King. Maker: **Alps**, Japan. Toy marks: Alps. Box marks: Alps.
Scarcity: 5. Fine to Excellent (C6-C8): $175-$275, Mint: (C10): $375

1960s Racer with composition driver and sparking. **13.25 in** (34 cm).
Friction. Known colors: Red. Graphics: **#16** - Hurrican - Grand Prix. Maker: **Unknown**, Germany. Toy marks: none (Germany).
Scarcity: 4. Fine to Excellent (C6-C8): $175-$350, Mint: (C10): $500

Race Cars 207

1960s Ferrari open-wheel style Racer with plastic driver and gear lever controlled direction and speed. **9.5 in** (24 cm). **Battery operated**. Known colors: Blue. Graphics: **#17**. Maker: **Bandai**, Japan. Toy marks: Bandai. Box marks: Bandai. Box text: *Ferrari Racer*.
Scarcity: 3. Fine to Excellent (C6-C8): $80-$135, Mint: (C10): $185

1960s Open-wheel style Racer with tin driver head. **10 in** (25 cm). **Friction**. Known colors: Silver and blue. Graphics: **#17** - Silver Jet. Maker: **Kyowa**, Japan. Toy marks: none (Japan).
Scarcity: 3. Fine to Excellent (C6-C8): $85-$100, Mint: (C10): $125

1960s Diamond Open-wheel style Racer with tin driver, lighted rotating color engine, and exhaust. **15.5 in** (39 cm). **Battery operated**. Known colors: Green. Graphics: **#17** - Diamond Racer. Maker: **Yonezawa**, Japan. Toy marks: Y (Yonezawa).
Scarcity: 6. Fine to Excellent (C6-C8): $350-$550, Mint: (C10): $700

1950s Open-wheel style Racer with tin driver, small front wheels, and on/off lever on body. **7.5 in** (19 cm). **Friction**. Known colors: Red and white. Graphics: **#18**. Maker: **Nihon Boeki**, Japan. Toy marks: KKK (Nihon Boeki).
Scarcity: 6. Fine to Excellent (C6-C8): $200-$260, Mint: (C10): $325

1950s Open-wheel style Racer with driver and side exhaust pipes. **8.5 in** (22 cm). **Windup**. Known colors: Silver and red; Silver and blue. Graphics: **#18** - Fairylite. Maker: **Masudaya**, Japan. Toy marks: MT (Masudaya).
Scarcity: 6. Fine to Excellent (C6-C8): $250-$350, Mint: (C10): $475

1960s Formula open-wheel style Racer with steering and forward/reverse action. **9.5 in** (24 cm). **R/C battery operated**. Known colors: Assorted. Graphics: (numbered decals **#12** and **#24**). Maker: **Bandai**, Japan. Toy marks: Bandai. Box marks: Bandai. Box text: *Formula Racing Car*.
Scarcity: 3. Fine to Excellent (C6-C8): $80-$135, Mint: (C10): $185

1960s Mercedes Benz W196R Racer with vinyl driver head and lighted engine. **11 in** (28 cm). **Battery operated**. Known colors: Red. Graphics: **#18**. Maker: **Aoshin**, Japan. Toy marks: ASC (Aoshin).
Scarcity: 4. Fine to Excellent (C6-C8): $150-$225, Mint: (C10): $385

Single Seat Racers

1960s Racer with tin driver head and flap wing. **11 in** (28 cm). **Friction**. Known colors: Silver-blue and red. Graphics: #18. Maker: **Aoshin**, Japan. Toy marks: ASC (Aoshin).
Scarcity: 3. Fine to Excellent (C6-C8): $100-$165, Mint: (C10): $230

(Not pictured) **1960s Strato Racer** with rising airfoil and tin driver. **11 in** (28 cm). **Friction**. Known colors: Blue-gray. Graphics: #18 - Strato. Maker: **Aoshin**, Japan. Toy marks: ASC (Aoshin). Box marks: ASC (Aoshin). Box text: *"Strato" The Flapwing Sports Car A Flare Toy*.
Scarcity: 3. Fine to Excellent (C6-C8): $100-$165, Mint: (C10): $230

1960s Golden Jet Open-wheel style Racer with vinyl driver. **12.5 in** (32 cm). **Friction**. Known colors: Gold and white. Graphics: #18 - Golden Jet. Maker: **Bandai**, Japan. Toy marks: Bandai. Box marks: Bandai. Box text: *Golden Jet Racer #850*.
Scarcity: 3. Fine to Excellent (C6-C8): $90-$130, Mint: (C10): $185

1960s Ford Lotus open-wheel style Racer with 2-speed gear shift, vibrating and lighted engine, and steerable front wheels. **11.5 in** (29 cm). **Battery operated**. Known colors: Red. Graphics: #18 - Team Lotus - Lotus Ford. Maker: **Junior**, Japan. Toy marks: Junior. Box marks: Junior. Box text: *Lotus 49B Formula Racing Car*.
Scarcity: 4. Fine to Excellent (C6-C8): $125-$250, Mint: (C10): $350

1960s Ford Lotus open-wheel style Racer with on-off switch, engine sound, bump and go action, and vinyl driver. **12 in** (30 cm). **Battery operated**. Known colors: Red and white. Graphics: #19 - Lotus - STP. Maker: **Okuma**, Japan. Toy marks: Okuma. Box marks: Okuma. Box text: *Hi-Speed Racer*.
Scarcity: 4. Fine to Excellent (C6-C8): $75-$100, Mint: (C10): $150

1960s Honda Grand Prix Formula 1 open-wheel style Racer with tin driver and engine sound. **12.25 in** (31 cm). **Friction**. Known colors: Red. Graphics: #18 - Honda. Maker: **Asahi**, Japan. Toy marks: ATC (Asahi Toy). Box marks: ATC (Asahi Toy). Box text: *Grand Prix Honda F-1* (Japanese). Notes: Asahi catalog image.
Scarcity: 6. Fine to Excellent (C6-C8): $200-$400, Mint: (C10): $575

1950s Open-wheel style Racer with tin driver head and bumper actuated break-apart action. **6 in** (15 cm). **Friction**. Known colors: Blue and orange. Graphics: #21. Maker: **Unknown**, Japan. Toy marks: none (Japan).
Scarcity: 6. Fine to Excellent (C6-C8): $185-$275, Mint: (C10): $400

Race Cars 209

1960s Racer with tin driver that signals by raising arms as car turns. **7.5 in** (19 cm). **Windup**. Known colors: Orange, yellow, and red. Graphics: **#21** - Mercury - Special. Maker: **Asahi**, Japan. Toy marks: Asahitoy (Asahi Toy), Flare. Box marks: Asahitoy (Asahi Toy). Box text: *Road Wizard*.
Scarcity: 5. Fine to Excellent (C6-C8): $200-$250, Mint: (C10): $350

1950s Open-wheel style Racer with tin driver and lever on/off switch. **10 in** (25 cm). **Battery operated**. Known colors: Red; Blue; Orange. Graphics: **#21** - Electro Special. Maker: **Yonezawa/Tomy**, Japan. Toy marks: Y (Yonezawa), ETC (Tomy). Box marks: Y (Yonezawa), ETC (Tomy). Box text: *Electro Toy Racer*. Notes: One known orange version (add 35 %).
Scarcity: 9. Fine to Excellent (C6-C8): $1,500-$2,200, Mint: (C10): $3,500

(Not pictured) **1960s F1 open-wheel style Racer** with driver, steering, and forward/reverse action. **12 in** (30 cm). **R/C battery operated**. Known colors: Red and yellow. Graphics: **#21**. Maker: **Bandai**, Japan. Toy marks: Bandai. Box marks: Bandai. Box text: *F-1* (Japanese).
Scarcity: 4. Fine to Excellent (C6-C8): $100-$175, Mint: (C10): $250

(Not pictured) **1950s Open-wheel style Racer** with tin driver. **7.75 in** (20 cm). **Friction**. Known colors: Red and cream. Graphics: **#23** - Speed King. Maker: **Unknown**, Japan. Toy marks: none (Japan).
Scarcity: 4. Fine to Excellent (C6-C8): $200-$250, Mint: (C10): $325

(Not pictured) **1960s Mercedes Benz W-196R Racer** with tin driver. **11 in** (28 cm). **Friction**. Known colors: Red. Graphics: **#23** - Speed King. Maker: **Unknown**, Japan. Toy marks: none (Japan).
Scarcity: 3. Fine to Excellent (C6-C8): $75-$100, Mint: (C10): $150

1950s Open-wheel style Racer with tin driver and moving piston engine. **7.75 in** (20 cm). **Friction**. Known colors: Blue and yellow; Red and blue. Graphics: **#21** or **#24**- Special. Maker: **Nomura**, Japan. Toy marks: TN (Nomura). Box marks: TN (Nomura). Box text: *Friction Race Car With Visible Piston Action*.
Scarcity: 6. Fine to Excellent (C6-C8): $200-$300, Mint: (C10): $400

1960s Mercedes Benz W-196R Racer with driver and engine sound. **12 in** (30 cm). **Friction**. Known colors: White, red, and blue. Graphics: **#23**. Maker: **Unknown**, Japan. Toy marks: None. Box marks: Cragstan. Box text: *Cragstan Racer*.
Scarcity: 3. Fine to Excellent (C6-C8): $100-$150, Mint: (C10): $210

(Not pictured) **1950s Open-wheel style Racer** with tin driver head. **8.5 in** (22 cm). **Friction**. Known colors: Red and yellow. Graphics: **#25** - Red Flash. Maker: **Tomy**, Japan. Toy marks: ETC (Tomy).
Scarcity: 5. Fine to Excellent (C6-C8): $250-$300, Mint: (C10): $350

(Not pictured) **1950s Open-wheel style Racer** with tin driver and steerable wheels. **9 in** (23 cm). **Battery operated**. Known colors: Blue and red. Graphics: **#25**. Maker: **Alps**, Japan. Toy marks: Alps.
Scarcity: 6. Fine to Excellent (C6-C8): $400-$650, Mint: (C10): $900

Single Seat Racers

1970s Can-Am Racer with non-fall bump and go action and plastic engine. **10 in** (25 cm). **Battery operated**. Known colors: Red. Graphics: **#25** - Champion. Maker: **Wu Chou**, Taiwan. Toy marks: None. Box marks: Wu Chou. Box text: *New Big Machine*.
Scarcity: 2. Fine to Excellent (C6-C8): $40-$60, Mint: (C10): $90

(Not pictured) **1960s Mercedes open-wheel style Racer** with tin driver. **10 in** (25 cm). **Friction**. Known colors: Silver and red. Graphics: **#25** - Universe. Maker: **Yonezawa**, Japan. Toy marks: Y (Yonezawa).
Scarcity: 7. Fine to Excellent (C6-C8): $400-$550, Mint: (C10): $700

1930s Open-wheel style Racer with rear mounted tin spare tire. **9 in** (23 cm). **Friction**. Known colors: Blue. Graphics: **#27** - Eagle - Grandes Epreuve Racer. Maker: **Takatoku**, Japan. Toy marks: TT (Takatoku).
Notes: Produced 1960s.
Scarcity: 7. Fine to Excellent (C6-C8): $100-$165, Mint: (C10): $265

1960s Open-wheel style Racer with vinyl driver head. **9.5 in** (24 cm). **Windup**. Known colors: Assorted. Graphics: **#27** or **#18** - Lotus. Maker: **Unknown**. Toy marks: none.
Notes: 1980s.
Scarcity: 2. Fine to Excellent (C6-C8): $35-$50, Mint: (C10): $75

1950s Mercedes Benz W-196 Racer with tin driver and sparking engine. **11 in** (28 cm). **Friction**. Known colors: Steel blue. Graphics: **#27** - Racer Special. Maker: **Nomura/Mitomo**, Japan. Toy marks: TN (Nomura), Mitomo. Box marks: TN (Nomura). Box text: *Speed Racer*.
Notes: Also came battery operated with blinking lights as **#25**.
Scarcity: 4. Fine to Excellent (C6-C8): $125-$225, Mint: (C10): $300

1950s Open-wheel style Racer with tin driver. **11.5 in** (29 cm). **Friction**. Known colors: Red and white. Graphics: **#27** - Special. Maker: **Marusan**, Japan. Toy marks: SAN (Marusan). Box marks: SAN (Marusan).
Scarcity: 6. Fine to Excellent (C6-C8): $200-$300, Mint: (C10): $400

1940s Open-wheel style Racer with plastic driver and tin wheels. **11.5 in** (29 cm). **Windup**. Known colors: Red and yellow. Graphics: **#27**. Maker: **Marx**, Japan. Toy marks: Marx. Box text: *Speed Racer*.
Scarcity: 4. Fine to Excellent (C6-C8): $125-$165, Mint: (C10): $225

1950s Atom Car open-wheel style Racer with tin driver. **16 in** (41 cm). **Friction**. Known colors: Green. Graphics: **#27** - Atom - Sports (hubcaps). Maker: **Yonezawa**, Japan. Toy marks: Y (Yonezawa). Box marks: Y (Yonezawa), KDP (Kyodo). Box text: *Atom Car*.
Notes: Also came marked Atom 153.
Scarcity: 7. Fine to Excellent (C6-C8): $1,200-$1,800, Mint: (C10): $2,500

Race Cars 211

1960s Honda open-wheel style Racer with plastic driver and gear lever controlled direction and speed. **9.5 in** (24 cm). **Battery operated.** Known colors: White. Graphics: **#28**. Maker: **Bandai**, Japan. Toy marks: Bandai. Box marks: Bandai. Box text: *Honda Racer*.
Scarcity: 3. Fine to Excellent (C6-C8): $80-$135, Mint: (C10): $185

(Not pictured) **1960s Open-wheel style Racer** with tin driver and siren sound. **10 in** (25 cm). **Friction**. Known colors: Gold and red. Graphics: **#29** - Jet Racer. Maker: **Nakayama**, Japan. Toy marks: N (Nakayama). Box text: *Jet Racer With Siren*.
Scarcity: 3. Fine to Excellent (C6-C8): $75-$100, Mint: (C10): $125

1960s Mercedes Benz W196R Racer with tin driver head. **7 in** (18 cm). **Friction**. Known colors: Blue and yellow. Graphics: **#30**. Maker: **Unknown**, Japan. Toy marks: none (Japan).
Scarcity: 2. Fine to Excellent (C6-C8): $40-$60, Mint: (C10): $80

1960s Mercedes Benz W196R Racer with vinyl driver head and tail fin. **11 in** (28 cm). **Friction**. Known colors: Red and cream. Graphics: **#30** - Thunderbolt. Maker: **Aoshin**, Japan. Toy marks: ASC (Aoshin).
Scarcity: 4. Fine to Excellent (C6-C8): $150-$185, Mint: (C10): $235

(Not pictured) **1950s Fire Jet Open-wheel style Racer** with tin driver. **13 in** (33 cm). **Friction**. Known colors: Green and white. Graphics: **#30** - Fire Jet - Sports (hubcaps). Maker: **Yonezawa**, Japan. Toy marks: Y (Yonezawa).
Scarcity: 8. Fine to Excellent (C6-C8): $1,100-$1,400, Mint: (C10): $1,600

(Not pictured) **1960s Open-wheel style Racer** with tin driver and siren sound. **10 in** (25 cm). **Friction**. Known colors: Blue and silver. Graphics: **#31** - Jet Racer. Maker: **Nakayama**, Japan. Toy marks: N (Nakayama). Box text: *Jet Racer With Siren*.
Scarcity: 3. Fine to Excellent (C6-C8): $75-$100, Mint: (C10): $125

1960s Open-wheel style Racer with tin driver, sparking engine, and hinged chassis engine compartment to change flints. **8.5 in** (22 cm). **Friction**. Known colors: Red and cream. Graphics: **#32**. Maker: **Sanei**, Japan. Toy marks: AAA (Sanei).
Scarcity: 5. Fine to Excellent (C6-C8): $250-$350, Mint: (C10): $450

1960s Ferrari Grand Prix Formula 1 open-wheel style Racer with tin driver and engine sound. **12.25 in** (31 cm). **Friction**. Known colors: Red. Graphics: **#36**. Maker: **Asahi**, Japan. Toy marks: ATC (Asahi Toy). Box marks: ATC (Asahi Toy). Box text: *Grand Prix Ferrari F-1*.
Notes: Asahi catalog image.
Scarcity: 6. Fine to Excellent (C6-C8): $200-$400, Mint: (C10): $575

1950s Open-wheel style Racer with driver (missing in photo). **14.5 in** (37 cm). **Friction**. Known colors: Blue. Graphics: **#36** - Special Bell. Maker: **Bell**, Italy. Toy marks: Bell.
Scarcity: 6. Fine to Excellent (C6-C8): $250-$350, Mint: (C10): $450

212 Single Seat Racers

1960s Jaguar XKE Racer with vinyl driver head. **15 in** (38 cm). **Battery operated**. Known colors: Red. Graphics: **#36** - Thunderchief. Maker: **Aoshin**, Japan. Toy marks: ASC (Aoshin).
Scarcity: 5. Fine to Excellent (C6-C8): $100-$225, Mint: (C10): $350

1950s Open-wheel style Racer with tin driver, chrome exhaust pipes, and radius rods. **18 in** (46 cm). **Friction**. Known colors: White and red; White and blue. Graphics: **#42** - Super Racer - Montlhery. Maker: **GEM**, France. Toy marks: GEM. Box marks: GEM. Box text: *Super Racer*.
Scarcity: 9. Fine to Excellent (C6-C8): $800-$1,500, Mint: (C10): $2,200

1960s Open-wheel style Racer with lighted pistons, sound, and non stop action. **18 in** (46 cm). **Battery operated**. Known colors: Blue, white, and red. Graphics: **#38**. Maker: **Masudaya**, Japan. Toy marks: MT (Masudaya). Box marks: MT (Masudaya). Box text: *Champion Racer 38 Racing Engine Sound*. Notes: Also came in Red #301.
Scarcity: 6. Fine to Excellent (C6-C8): $400-$500, Mint: (C10): $600

1950s Open-wheel style Racer with tin driver, chrome exhaust pipes, and radius rods. **18 in** (46 cm). **R/C battery operated**. Known colors: White and red; White and blue. Graphics: **#42** - Super Racer - Montlhery. Maker: **GEM**, France. Toy marks: GEM. Box marks: GEM.
Scarcity: 9. Fine to Excellent (C6-C8): $800-$1,500, Mint: (C10): $2,200

1960s Open-wheel style Racer with vinyl driver head and clicking sound. **14.75 in** (37 cm). **Friction**. Known colors: Blue and white. Graphics: **#41** - Hurricane Racer. Maker: **Tomy**, Japan. Toy marks: Tomiyama (Tomy). Box marks: Tomiyama (Tomy).
Scarcity: 7. Fine to Excellent (C6-C8): $550-$750, Mint: (C10): $950

1960s Chaparral open-wheel style Racer with forward/reverse and moving wing. **10 in** (25 cm). **Battery operated**. Known colors: Red; White. Graphics: **#43**. Maker: **Bandai**, Japan. Toy marks: Bandai. Box marks: Bandai. Box text: *Chaparral #4277*.
Scarcity: 3. Fine to Excellent (C6-C8): $75-$125, Mint: (C10): $165

1960s Racer with vinyl driver head and lithographed trim. **7.5 in** (19 cm). **Friction**. Known colors: Red and yellow. Graphics: #45 - Red Hawk. Maker: **Yoshi**, Japan. Toy marks: Y (Yoshi).
Scarcity: 3. Fine to Excellent (C6-C8): $40-$65, Mint: (C10): $95

1950s Open-wheel style Racer with lithographed illustrations of 1905 Gordon Bennett Race and 1908 Vanderbilt Cup Race. **11.5 in** (29 cm). **Friction**. Known colors: Red, gold, and white; Red, blue, and white. Graphics: #52 - High Speed - 1908 Vanderbilt Cup Race - 1905 Gordon Bennett Race. Maker: **Marusan**, Japan. Toy marks: SAN (Marusan). Box marks: SAN (Marusan). Box text: *High Speed Racer*.
Scarcity: 7. Fine to Excellent (C6-C8): $250-$500, Mint: (C10): $750

1950s Atom open-wheel style Racer with tin driver. **8.5 in** (22 cm). **Friction**. Known colors: Red, white, and blue. Graphics: #45 - Atom. Maker: **Marusan/Kosuge**, Japan. Toy marks: SAN (Marusan), Kosuge. Box marks: SAN (Marusan). Box text: *Atom Racer*.
Scarcity: 5. Fine to Excellent (C6-C8): $225-$325, Mint: (C10): $500

1950s Open-wheel style Racer with tin driver. **11.5 in** (29 cm). **Friction**. Known colors: Red, yellow, and silver-blue. Graphics: #52 - Star Fire. Maker: **Marusan**, Japan. Toy marks: SAN (Marusan).
Scarcity: 6. Fine to Excellent (C6-C8): $200-$300, Mint: (C10): $400

1960s Ford Lotus open-wheel style Racer with moving lighted visible pistons, engine sound, and bump and go action. **16 in** (41 cm). **Battery operated**. Known colors: Red and yellow. Graphics: #47 - Lotus Ford - Team Lotus. Maker: **Daishin**, Japan. Toy marks: Daishin.
Scarcity: 3. Fine to Excellent (C6-C8): $125-$200, Mint: (C10): $300

1950s Jet Open-wheel style Racer with tin driver and siren sound. **12 in** (30 cm). **Friction**. Known colors: Green and red. Graphics: Y53 - J.T.Y - Jet Y53. Maker: **Yonezawa**, Japan. Toy marks: Y (Yonezawa). Box marks: Y (Yonezawa). Box text: *Jet Race*.
Notes: Also produced marked **Y55**.
Scarcity: 5. Fine to Excellent (C6-C8): $400-$600, Mint: (C10): $800

214 Single Seat Racers

1950s Rocket Car open-wheel style Racer with sparkling rear engine. **7.25 in** (18 cm). **Friction**. Known colors: Red and blue. Graphics: **#54** - Rocket. Maker: **Bandai**, Japan. Toy marks: Bandai. Box marks: Bandai. Box text: *Rocket Car*.
Scarcity: 6. Fine to Excellent (C6-C8): $175-$250, Mint: (C10): $350

(Not pictured) **1950s Jet Open-wheel style Racer** with tin driver. **12 in** (30 cm). **Friction**. Known colors: Red and silver-blue. Graphics: **Y-54** - J.T.Y. - Jet Y54. Maker: **Nomura**, Japan. Toy marks: Hadson, TN (Nomura). Box marks: Hadson.
Notes: Identical to Y53 from Yonezawa.
Scarcity: 6. Fine to Excellent (C6-C8): $400-$600, Mint: (C10): $800

1950s Open-wheel style Racer with side on-off lever and adjustable wheels. **11.5 in** (29 cm). **Battery operated**. Known colors: Red and white. Graphics: **#56** - Fire Bird. Maker: **Marusan**, Japan. Toy marks: SAN (Marusan).
Scarcity: 6. Fine to Excellent (C6-C8): $200-$300, Mint: (C10): $400

1950s Open-wheel style Racer with tin driver head. **10.5 in** (27 cm). **Friction**. Known colors: Light blue and red. Graphics: **#57** - Eagle. Maker: **Mitsuhashi/IY Metal**, Japan. Toy marks: M (Mitsuhashi), IY Metal Toy. Box marks: M (Mitsuhashi), IY Metal Toy.
Scarcity: 6. Fine to Excellent (C6-C8): $225-$375, Mint: (C10): $500

1960s Racer with composition driver. **11 in** (28 cm). **Friction**. Known colors: Red. Graphics: **#57** - Indianapolis Special. Maker: **Unknown**, Germany. Toy marks: none.
Scarcity: 3. Fine to Excellent (C6-C8): $85-$165, Mint: (C10): $225

1960s Ferrari open-wheel style Racer with composition driver, steerable wheels, and gear on-off switch. **12 in** (30 cm). **Windup**. Known colors: Red. Graphics: **#58**. Maker: **Ingap**, Italy. Toy marks: Ingap.
Scarcity: 10. Fine to Excellent (C6-C8): $1,500-$2,250, Mint: (C10): $3,000

1950s Open-wheel style Racer with tin driver head. **6 in** (15 cm). **Friction**. Known colors: Red, yellow, and blue. Graphics: **#60**. Maker: **Epoch**, Japan. Toy marks: none (Japan). Box marks: F (Epoch). Box text: *Champion*.
Scarcity: 4. Fine to Excellent (C6-C8): $125-$175, Mint: (C10): $235

Race Cars 215

1960s Diamond Open-wheel style Racer with tin driver, lighted rotating color engine, and exhaust. **15.5 in** (39 cm). **Battery operated.** Known colors: Yellow. Graphics: **#60** - Diamond Racer. Maker: **Yonezawa**, Japan. Toy marks: Y (Yonezawa).
Scarcity: 7. Fine to Excellent (C6-C8): $500-$750, Mint: (C10): $950

1960s Open-wheel style Racer with tin driver. **11.5 in** (29 cm). **Friction.** Known colors: Blue and yellow. Graphics: **#77** - Grand Prix. Maker: **Maruya**, Japan. Toy marks: YA (Maruya). Box marks: YA (Maruya).
Scarcity: 5. Fine to Excellent (C6-C8): $125-$225, Mint: (C10): $325

1960s Open-wheel style Racer with sparking action and "S.K." hood flag. **11.5 in** (29 cm). **Friction.** Known colors: Red, yellow, and blue. Graphics: **#61** - Speed King. Maker: **Maruya**, Japan. Toy marks: YA (Maruya). Box marks: YA (Maruya). Box text: *Sparking Speed King*.
Scarcity: 5. Fine to Excellent (C6-C8): $175-$275, Mint: (C10): $375

1960s Ford Lotus open-wheel style Racer with 2-speed gear shift, vibrating and lighted engine, and steerable front wheels. **16 in** (41 cm). **Battery operated.** Known colors: Red, white, and gold. Graphics: **#78** - Gold Leaf - Team Lotus - Lotus Ford. Maker: **Asahi/Junior**, Japan. Toy marks: Junior.
Scarcity: 5. Fine to Excellent (C6-C8): $300-$400, Mint: (C10): $500

1960s Midget open-wheel style Racer with tin driver and side exhaust pipes (back car in photo). Radius rods lithographed on body. **7 in** (18 cm). **Friction.** Known colors: White and red. Graphics: **#63** - Champion - Midget Racer. Maker: **Yonezawa/Tomy**, Japan. Toy marks: Y (Yonezawa).
Notes: Same car design as Midget Racer by Yonezawa/Tomy sold as #3, 5, 6 or 8 (front car in photo).
Scarcity: 9. Fine to Excellent (C6-C8): $700-$1100, Mint: (C10): $1300

1960s Lotus Ford open-wheel style Racer with vinyl driver, lighted engine, and sound.. **16 in** (41 cm). **Battery operated.** Known colors: Red and blue; Green and yellow. Graphics: **#85** - Prestone - Lotus Ford. Maker: **Yonezawa**, Japan. Toy marks: Y (Yonezawa). Box marks: Y (Yonezawa). Box text: *Grand Prix Racer*.
Scarcity: 6. Fine to Excellent (C6-C8): $600-$700, Mint: (C10): $850

Single Seat Racers

1960s Ford Lotus open-wheel style Racer with detonating engine noise, steerable front wheels, and plastic engine and chassis. **11.5 in** (29 cm). **Battery operated**. Known colors: Red and yellow. Graphics: **#88** - Lotus. Maker: **Masudaya**, Japan. Toy marks: MT (Masudaya). Box marks: MT (Masudaya).
Scarcity: 4. Fine to Excellent (C6-C8): $125-$250, Mint: (C10): $350

1960s Mercedes Benz W-196 open-wheel style Racer. 13 in (33 cm). **Friction**. Known colors: Red. Graphics: Taifun **#100**. Maker: **Niedermeier**, Germany. Toy marks: PN (Niedermeier). Box marks: PN (Niedermeier). Box text: *Friction Racing Car Taifun*.
Scarcity: 4. Fine to Excellent (C6-C8): $250-$325, Mint: (C10): $400

1950s Open-wheel style Racer with tin driver, chrome side pipes, and radius rods. **18 in** (46 cm). **Friction**. Known colors: Cream and red. Graphics: **#98** - Agajanian Special, Troy Ruttman, Sanyo (tires). Maker: **Yonezawa**, Japan. Toy marks: Y (Yonezawa), ETC (Tomy). Box marks: Y (Yonezawa), ETC (Tomy). Box text: *Champions Racer*.
Notes: Agajanian graphics were not licensed and this version was replaced by the word "champion."
Scarcity: 9. Fine to Excellent (C6-C8): $1,200-$2,200, Mint: (C10): $4,000

1950s Atom Car open-wheel style Racer with tin driver. **16 in** (41 cm). **Friction**. Known colors: Green. Graphics: **#153** - Atom - Sports (hubcaps). Maker: **Yonezawa**, Japan. Toy marks: Y (Yonezawa). Box marks: Y (Yonezawa), KDP (Kyodo). Box text: *Atom Car*.
Notes: Rubber tire overlays are missing in this photo.
Scarcity: 7. Fine to Excellent (C6-C8): $1,200-$1,800, Mint: (C10): $2,500

1950s Open-wheel style Racer with tin driver, chrome side pipes, and radius rods. **18 in** (46 cm). **Friction**. Known colors: Cream and red. Graphics: **#98**, Champions Racer, Indianapolis Sanyo (tires). Maker: **Yonezawa**, Japan. Toy marks: Y (Yonezawa), ETC (Tomy). Box marks: Y (Yonezawa), ETC (Tomy). Box text: *Champions Racer*.
Scarcity: 8. Fine to Excellent (C6-C8): $1,000-$1,800, Mint: (C10): $2,600

1960s Open-wheel style Racer with vinyl driver head, lighted pistons, sound, and non stop action. **18 in** (46 cm). **Battery operated**. Known colors: Red. Graphics: **#301**. Maker: **Masudaya**, Japan. Toy marks: MT (Masudaya). Box marks: MT (Masudaya). Box text: *Champion Race Car*.
Scarcity: 6. Fine to Excellent (C6-C8): $400-$500, Mint: (C10): $600

(Not pictured) **1960s Mercedes open-wheel style Racer** with adjustable font wheels and engine noise. **6 in** (15 cm). **Friction**. Known colors: Assorted. Graphics: **(assorted numbers)**. Maker: **Linemar**, Japan. Toy marks: Linemar (Marx). Box marks: Linemar (Marx). Box text: *Racer With Noise*.
Notes: Sold with or without plastic driver.
Scarcity: 3. Fine to Excellent (C6-C8): $90-$135, Mint: (C10): $185

Race Cars 217

1960s Jaguar Racer with tin driver, lighted engine and forward/reverse action. **8 in** (20 cm). **R/C battery operated**. Known colors: Copper. Graphics: Jaguar Cars Ltd - Coventry. Maker: **Aoshin**, Japan. Toy marks: ASC (Aoshin). Box marks: ASC (Aoshin), Royal. Box text: *Jaguar Champ O' Racer*.
Scarcity: 3. Fine to Excellent (C6-C8): $75-$125, Mint: (C10): $185

(Not pictured) **1950s Rocket open-wheel style Racer** with tin driver, plastic canopy, and rocket type body. **8.5 in** (22 cm). **Friction**. Known colors: Yellow and red. Graphics: Fire Wings. Maker: **Marusan**, Japan. Toy marks: SAN (Marusan). Box marks: SAN (Marusan). Box text: *Fire Wings*.
Scarcity: 7. Fine to Excellent (C6-C8): $175-$350, Mint: (C10): $500

(Not pictured) **1950s Atomic Drive Jet open-wheel style Racer** 8.5 in (22 cm). **Friction**. Known colors: Graphics: Atomic Drive Jet. Maker: **Sanei**, Japan. Toy marks: AAA (Sanei).
Scarcity: 3. Fine to Excellent (C6-C8): $125-$175, Mint: (C10): $250

(Not pictured) **1950s Mercedes Benz W 196 Silver Arrow Racer** with composition driver. **10.5 in** (27 cm). **Friction**. Known colors: Silver. Maker: **Neuhierl**, Germany. Toy marks: JNF (Neuhierl).
Notes: Also produced as windup and battery operated model.
Scarcity: 6. Fine to Excellent (C6-C8): $300-$500, Mint: (C10): $700

(Not pictured) **1960s Racer** with vinyl driver head and sparking action. Lithographed trim. **11 in** (28 cm). **Friction**. Known colors: White. Graphics: Esso - Shell - Caltex. Maker: **Aoshin**, Japan. Toy marks: ASC (Aoshin).
Scarcity: 4. Fine to Excellent (C6-C8): $150-$185, Mint: (C10): $235

1950s Open-wheel style Racer with tin driver. **11.5 in** (29 cm). **Battery operated**. Known colors: Silver and red. Graphics: Silver Panther - S.P.7. Maker: **Marusan**, Japan. Toy marks: SAN (Marusan). Box marks: SAN (Marusan).
Scarcity: 6. Fine to Excellent (C6-C8): $200-$300, Mint: (C10): $400

1960s Open-wheel style Racer with tin driver. **8.5 in** (22 cm). **Windup**. Known colors: Red. Graphics: Fire Bird. Maker: **Terai**, Japan. Toy marks: Daiya (Terai).
Scarcity: 6. Fine to Excellent (C6-C8): $275-$375, Mint: (C10): $475

(Not pictured) **1960s Open-wheel style Racer** with tin driver and rear mounted propeller. **8.5 in** (22 cm). **Friction**. Known colors: Red and yellow. Graphics: Prop Rod. Maker: **Unknown**, Japan. Toy marks: None. Box text: *Prop-Rod, Speed Spins Spills Thrills*.
Scarcity: 5. Fine to Excellent (C6-C8): $175-$250, Mint: (C10): $325

1930s Open-wheel style Racer with tin driver head and tin wheels. **13.75 in** (35 cm). **Windup**. Known colors: Red and silver. Maker: **General Metal Toys**, Canada. Toy marks: General Metal Toys.
Scarcity: 5. Fine to Excellent (C6-C8): $150-$250, Mint: (C10): $375

(Not pictured) **1960s Open-wheel style Racer** with built-in jack mechanism to change tires, two extra tires, forward/reverse, cockpit light and detachable remote control. **14.75 in** (37 cm). **Friction**. Known colors: Green. Graphics: Maker: **Shioji**, Japan. Toy marks: none (Japan). Box marks: SSS (Shioji).
Scarcity: 6. Fine to Excellent (C6-C8): $300-$500, Mint: (C10): $750

The Toy Companies and Their Marks

Many familiar toy company names are on the list of tin toy car manufacturers, but there are also many names that are not so familiar. This is particularly true for toys produced in Japan. The Japanese industry's practice of using sub-contract suppliers for major parts, manufacturing, and assembly, along with a complex network of toy exporters and toy importers, can create a very confusing picture. It is confusing because so many different trademarks ended up on the toy or the toy box.

To get the full picture, you need to know who generated the toy idea, who designed the toy, who owned the design or mechanical patent (if any), who marketed the toy, which factory actually produced the toy, who owned the tooling, which trading (export) company was involved, and which import company was involved. Since most of the Japanese toy companies are no longer in business, many times this information is almost impossible to figure out.

Patent research can be helpful in determining the source of a toy. Often companies that held a mechanical or design patent on a toy would include their trademark somewhere on the toy or box, even if it was marketed under a different name.

Trademark research can often identify a company and whether they were a manufacturer, designer, or wholesaler, but that does not always tell what role they played for a specific toy. A large number of major toy companies started as wholesalers and then became involved in more of the total process. The same was true for sub-contract factories that made toys for other companies. Often, they eventually started producing toys under their own name.

In Japan during the post-war period there were a small number of factories but many toy companies. An interesting fact is that in the 1950s, the three largest toy companies in Japan were Masudaya, Nomura, and Alps, however none of these three companies ever had their own factory!

The Importers

Some importers are mistakenly identified as toy companies due to the practice of including the importer's mark on the toy or box. Initially, many established importers would purchase and distribute smaller quantities of toy and other goods from many different countries. Some importers specialized in buying from certain countries like Germany or Japan. As their import volume grew, importers promised higher volume purchases if the toy companies would put the importer's name on the toy and produce it in exclusive variations. When the importers started making these private label arrangements, sometimes this was the only name seen on the toy or box. Prime examples of this are the US import companies such as Marx (Linemar), Cragstan, Rosko, and Frankonia. Each of these company's marks can be found on toys imported from Japan or other parts of the world. Often, the only differences between toys with different trademarks were things like color, graphic, or a special feature. In this book, we have identified which companies were importers and included their marks in the listing.

Eventually, large retailers such as Sears and F. W. Woolworth, began buying directly from the toy companies and bypassing the importers. Sometimes these retailers would put their name on the box.

The Marks

Each toy car description in this book includes the toy company name, if known, and the specific company marks found on the toy or the box it came with. In this section, you will find a listing of toy companies along with illustrations of their known trademarks. Each listing includes the commonly known name of the company, the formal name of the company (if known or applicable), and the company's location. If we were unable to determine the company associated with a trademark, it is listed as unknown but with the trademark still illustrated. For example:

1) If the toy maker is listed as Bandai or the toy or box mark says Bandai, look in the alphabetical listing for Bandai to see the mark or marks used by this company.

2) If the mark included initials but the company is unknown, the mark will be shown in the alphabetical listing by the initials

Many companies used more than one trademark over the years. Sometimes a new trademark was a variation of a previous mark and other times it represented a whole new identity campaign and corresponding logo. This is a very comprehensive list of marks found on tin toy cars, but we continue to look for new trademarks or company names. Please feel free to contact the authors through the publisher should you find an unlisted trademark or have additional information regarding the trademarks or the toys.

AA *Unknown* Greece 	**AHI** Azrak-Hamway Inc. New York, USA 

Alps Toy Alps Shoji Co. Ltd. Tokyo, Japan

Amar Toy Delhi, India

AN *Unknown* Japan

Aoki Ind., Ltd. *Aoki Shokai* Tokyo, Japan

Aoshin *Aoshin Shoten Co., Ltd.* Tokyo, Japan

Arnold *K. Arnold GmbH & Co.* Nürnberg, Germany

Asahi *Asahi Trading Co.* Japan

Asahi Toy Company, Ltd. *Asahi Gangu Seisakusho* Tokyo, Japan

Asakusa Toy Ltd. (aka A-ONE Ltd.) Tokyo, Japan

Asakusa Toys & Dolls Co., Ltd. *Asakusa Gangu Ningyo* Tokyo, Japan

Bandai *Bandai Co., Ltd* Tokyo, Japan

Bandai (Cont'd) *Bandai Co., Ltd* Tokyo, Japan

Bell Company Milan, Italy

-BELL-

Bing
Gebrüder Bing
Germany

Bonzo
Bonzo Industria Brasileira
Brazil

Brio
Brio Corporation
Sweden

BRIO

CIJ
Compagnie Industrielle du Jouets
France

Clover
Clover Toys
Korea

Cragstan Industries
Craig-Stanton-Elmaleh, Inc. (US Importer)
USA

Daishin
Daishin Kogyo
Japan

Daito
Daito Co., Ltd.
Tokyo, Japan

Distler
Johann Distler KG
Nürnberg, Germany

DISTLER

DUX
Markes & Co.
Lüdenscheid, Germany

DUX

Epoch
Epoch Co., Ltd
Tokyo, Japan

Estrela
Estrela Toys
Brazil

ET
Unknown
Japan

Ever New Toy
Ever New Toy & Co.
Japan

MADE IN JAPAN

Fifties
Fifties Inc.
Japan

Fifties **50's**

Flare
Flare Import Corporation (US Importer)
USA

Fleetline
K & O Models Inc.
California, USA

Frankonia
Frankonia Products, Inc. (US Importer)
New York, USA

Fukuda
Fukuda Seisakusho
Tokyo, Japan

Gakken Toy Hobby Co., Ltd.
Gakushu Kenkyusha
Japan

Gama
Georg Adam Mangold
Fürth, Germany

GBC
Greenman Brothers Co. (US Importer)
New York, USA

G.B.C

GEM
Jouets GEM
France

General Metal Toys Ltd.
Canada

GENERAL METAL TOYS LTD.

George G. Wagner Co.
(US Importer)
California, USA

Gescha
Gebrüder Schmid
Nürnberg, Germany

Gilbert
A.C Gilbert
Connecticut, USA

Gorgo
Gorgo Industria
Argentina

 GORGO

GÖSO
Götz & Sohn
Fürth, Germany

GÖSO

Günthermann
S. Günthermann
Nürnberg, Germany

Hadson
Hadson Trading Co. Ltd. (US Importer)
USA

Harely Importer
Importadora Harely Ca (Venezuela Importer)
Venezuela

HARELY

Harusame
Harusame Seisakusho
Japan

Hayashi Manufacturing
Hayashi Seisakusho
Japan

HOKU
Unknown
Japan

Hope
Unknown
Japan

HTC
*US importer's mark.
(Possibly Hillel Trading Co.)*
USA

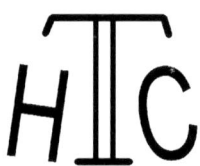

HUKI
Hubert Kienberger & Co.
Nürnberg, Germany

Ichida Co., Ltd.
Japan

Ichiko Manufacturing Co., Ltd
Ichiko Kogyo
Tokyo, Japan

Ichiko (Korea)
Korea

Ichimura Co., Ltd
Ichimura Shoten
Tokyo, Japan

Ingap
*Industria Nazionale Giocattoli
Automatica Padova*
Padova, Italy

IRCO
Unknown
Japan

Iwaya Corporation
Iwaya Seisakusho
Tokyo, Japan

I.Y. Metal Toys
Yamazaki Gangu
Japan

Joustra
France

Junior Company
Suda Kinzuku
Tokyo, Japan

KA
Unknown
Japan

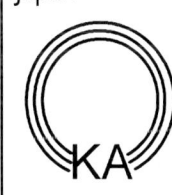

Kamiya
Kamiya Seisakusho
Japan

Kaname
Kaname Sangyo KK
Tokyo, Japan

Kanto
Kanto Toys Co., Ltd.
Tokyo, Japan

Kato Sairen/Nihon Boeki
Japan

Kellermann
Georg G. Kellermann and Company
Nürnberg, Germany

KK
Unknown
Japan

Koa Metal
Koa Kinzoku
Japan

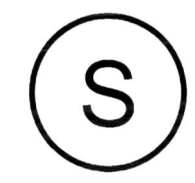

Kobayashi
Kobayashi Seisakusho
Japan

Kogure
Japan

Kohno, Kakuzo
Japan

Kokyu Trading Co., Ltd.
Kokyu Shokai
Tokyo, Japan

Komoda
Komoda Shoten Ltd.
Tokyo, Japan

Koshibe
Koshibe Shoten
Japan

Kosuge Toys Industrial Co., Ltd.
Kosuge Gangu Kenkyusho
Japan

Kosuge Toys Industrial Co., Ltd. (Cont'd)
Kosuge Gangu Kenkyusho
Japan

Kowa Kogyo
Japan

KS
Unknown
Japan

KT
Unknown
Japan

Kuramochi & Co., Ltd.
Tokyo, Japan

Kusama
Kusama Shoten
Japan

Kyodo
Kyodo Press K K
Japan

Kyoei Toy Co., Ltd.
Kyoei Gangu Co., Ltd.
Japan

Kyowa
Kyowa Gangu Seisakusho
Japan

Langcraft
Langfelder, Homma & Carroll, Inc.
New York, USA

Linemar
Japanese export office of Louis Marx, USA
Japan

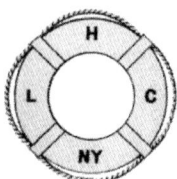

M
Unknown
Japan

Mansei Toys Co., Ltd
Tokyo, Japan

Marchesini Luigi Bologna
Bologna, Italy

Märklin
Gebrüder Märklin & Cie. GmbH
Goppingen, Germany

MÄRKLIN

Marusan Co. Ltd.
Marusan Shoten, Ltd.
Tokyo, Japan

Maruya Toys
Maruya Co., Ltd
Japan

Marx
Louis Marx & Co., Inc.
New York, USA

Masakiya Co.
Tokyo, Japan

Masuda
Masuda Press Tokyo
Tokyo, Japan

Masudaya Toys Co., Ltd.
Masudaya Saito Bokei
Tokyo, Japan

Masuya Toys Co., Ltd.
Masuya Gangu
Tokyo, Japan

Mattel, Inc.
California, USA

MEGO Corporation
New York, USA

Meiko
Meiko Shoji
Japan

Meiwa
Meiwa Kogyo Co. Ltd.
Tokyo, Japan

Memo
Mery Gutman
Paris, France

Metalma
Metalma Industria Brasileira
Brazil

Mettoy
Mettoy & Co. Ltd.
London, England

MHT
Unknown
Japan

M.H.T.

Michael Seidel
Nürnberg, Germany

Mitake Toy
Mitake Gangu Seisakusho
Japan

Mitomo
Mitomo Gangu
Japan

Mitsuhashi & Co., Ltd
Tokyo, Japan

Miura Toy Co.
Miura Shoji Co., Ltd.
Tokyo, Japan

Miyazawa Model Co.
Miyazawa Mokei Co. Ltd.
Japan

Mizuno
Nihon Alps Mizuno Seisakusho
Ueda City, Japan

Momoya Shoten
Japan

Mont-Blanc
Jouets Mont Blanc
France

MRK
Unknown
Tokyo, Japan

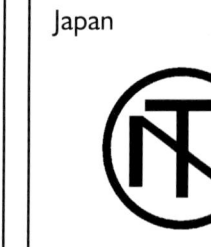

Nakamura Toy
Nakamura Gangu Seisakusho
Japan

Nemoto
Nemoto Shoten Co., Ltd.
Japan

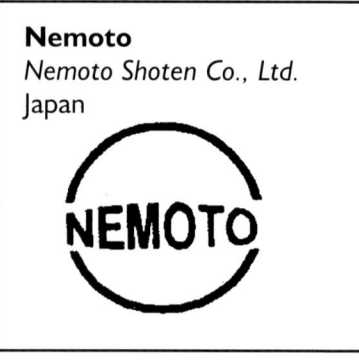

Neuhierl
Josef Neuhierl
Fürth, Germany

Niedermeier
Philipp Niedermeier
Nürnberg, Germany

Nihon Boeki/Kato Sairen
Japan

Nikko Toy
Nikko Gangu Kogyo
Japan

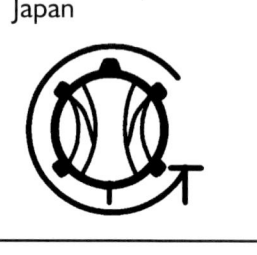

Nipon Goraku Shokai
Japanese export office of Cragstan
Tokyo, Japan

Nishimura
Nishimura Kiyosaburo Shoten
Tokyo, Japan

NK TOYS
Korea

Nomura
Nomura Toy Industrial Co., Ltd.
Tokyo, Japan

Ohta Kasaburo Co., Ltd.
Tokyo, Japan

Okuma
Okuma Seisakusho
Japan

Okyasu
Japan

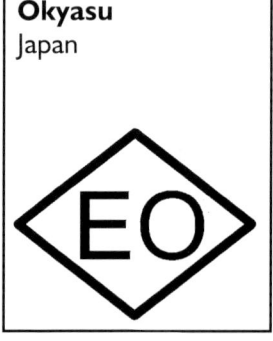

Oro
Oro Werke
Brandenburg, Germany

Paya Toys Corp.
*Paya Hermanos S.A.
Paya Coop S.C.L.
Clasicos Paya, S. Coop*
Ibi, Spain

Payva
Pascual y Valls
Spain

Plaything
Unknown
Japan

Poliumex
Mexico

Raja Toys Co.
India

Rico
Ibi, Spain

Roman
Juguetes Roma'n, S.A.
Alicante, Spain

Rosko
Rosko Steele Inc. (US importer)
New York, USA

Royal
Unknown
Japan

RS
Unknown
Japan

Safe Toy designation (not a company)
Adopted October 1971 by Japanese toy industry
Japan

Sanei Toy Company, Ltd.
Sanei Gangu Co., Ltd
Japan

Sankei
Sankei Gangu Kogyo
Tokyo, Japan

Sanko
Sanko Seisakusho
Japan

Sanshin
Sanshin Toys Co., Ltd.
Tokyo, Japan

Sanyo Toys Co., Ltd.
Sanyo Shoten Co., Ltd.
Japan

Sanyu
Japan

Sato
Sato Gangu Seisakusho
Japan

Sato Toys
Japan

Saxo
Argentina

Schuco
Schreyer & Co.
Nürnberg, Germany

Sears
Sears, Roebuck and Co.
Illinois, USA

Shimazaki
Japan

Shimazaki Toy
Shimazaki Gangu
Japan

Shinsei Kogyo
Shinsei Kogyo Kabash
Japan

Shinkosha Co., Ltd
Japan

Shinsei
Shinsei Kogyo Co., Ltd.
Japan

Shioji & Co., Ltd.
Shioji Shoten
Osaka, Japan

Showa
Showa Kogyo Co., Ltd
Japan

Shudo
Shudo Shoji
Japan

Sinsei Toys Industrial Co., Ltd.
Sinsei Kiki Kogyo
Japan

Siro
Siro Ferrari Company
Casalpusterlengo, Italy

Spesco
Japan

SSN
Unknown
Japan

ST
Unknown
Japan

Suda
Suda Kinzoku Seisakusho
Japan

Suzuki
Suzuki Gangu Seisakusho
Japan

Suzuki
Japan

Suzuki and Edwards Co., Ltd.
Tokyo, Japan

Swallow Toys Co., Ltd.
Tokyo, Japan

T
Unknown
Japan

Tada
Tada Seisakusho
Tokyo, Japan

Tagai
Tagai Shoten
Japan

Taguchi Toy Co.
Japan

Taico
Japan

Taiyo Kogyo Corporation
Taiyo
Japan

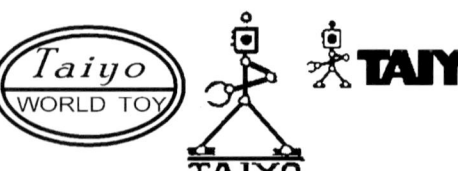

Takatoku Toys Co., Ltd.
Tokyo, Japan

Taniguchi Shoten Co., Ltd
Tokyo, Japan

Tatsuya
Tatsuya Shoten
Osaka, Japan

Telsada
Spain

Terai Toys Co., Ltd.
Terai Shoten
Tokyo, Japan

TET
Unknown
Japan

Tippco
Tipp and Company
Nürnberg, Germany

TKK
Unknown
Japan

Tohko Toy Co.
Japan

Tohnan
Japan

Tomy Co., Ltd.
Tomiyama Trading Co., Ltd.
Tokyo, Japan

Toplay, Ltd.
Tokyo Plaything Shokai
Tokyo, Japan

Toyo Plaything
Japan

Tsujimoto
Tsujimoto Shoji
Tokyo, Japan

Tsukuda Co., Ltd.
Tsukudaya Co., Ltd.
Tokyo, Japan

TT
Unknown
Japan

Tyco Industries, Inc.
USA

Ueno
Japan

Unknown
China

Unknown
China

Unknown
Osaka, Japan

Upton
Upton Machine Company
Michigan, USA

Usagiya Toys Co., Ltd.
Tokyo, Japan

Ventura Treviso
Treviso, Italy

Woolworth
F.W. Woolworth Company (Retailer)
New York, USA

F.W.W.

Wu Chou
Unknown
China

Yachio
Yachio Seisakusho
Japan

Yamada
Tokyo, Japan

Yamato Toys
Japan

Yamazaki Rubber Toy Co. Ltd
Yamazaki Gomu Seizo. Co. Ltd
Japan

Yanoman Corporation
Yanoman Shoten
Japan

Yoneya
Japan

Yonezawa Toys Co., Ltd.
Yonezawa Gangu
Tokyo, Japan

Yoshi
Yoshi Shoji
Japan

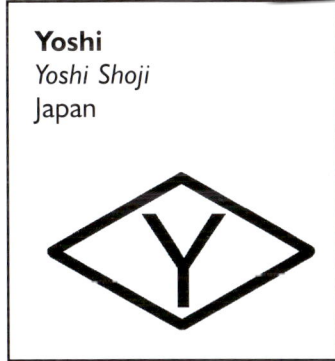

Yoshiya
Tokyo, Japan

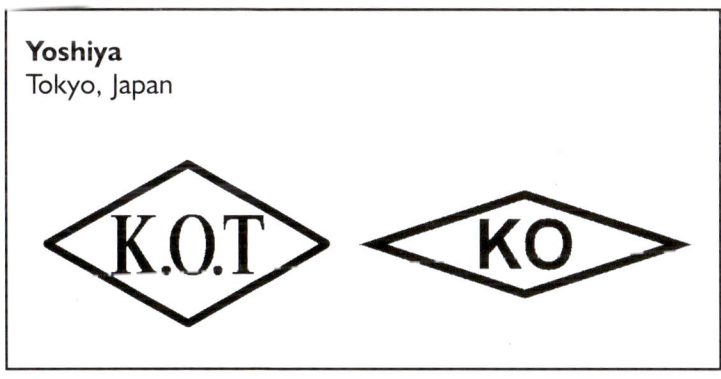

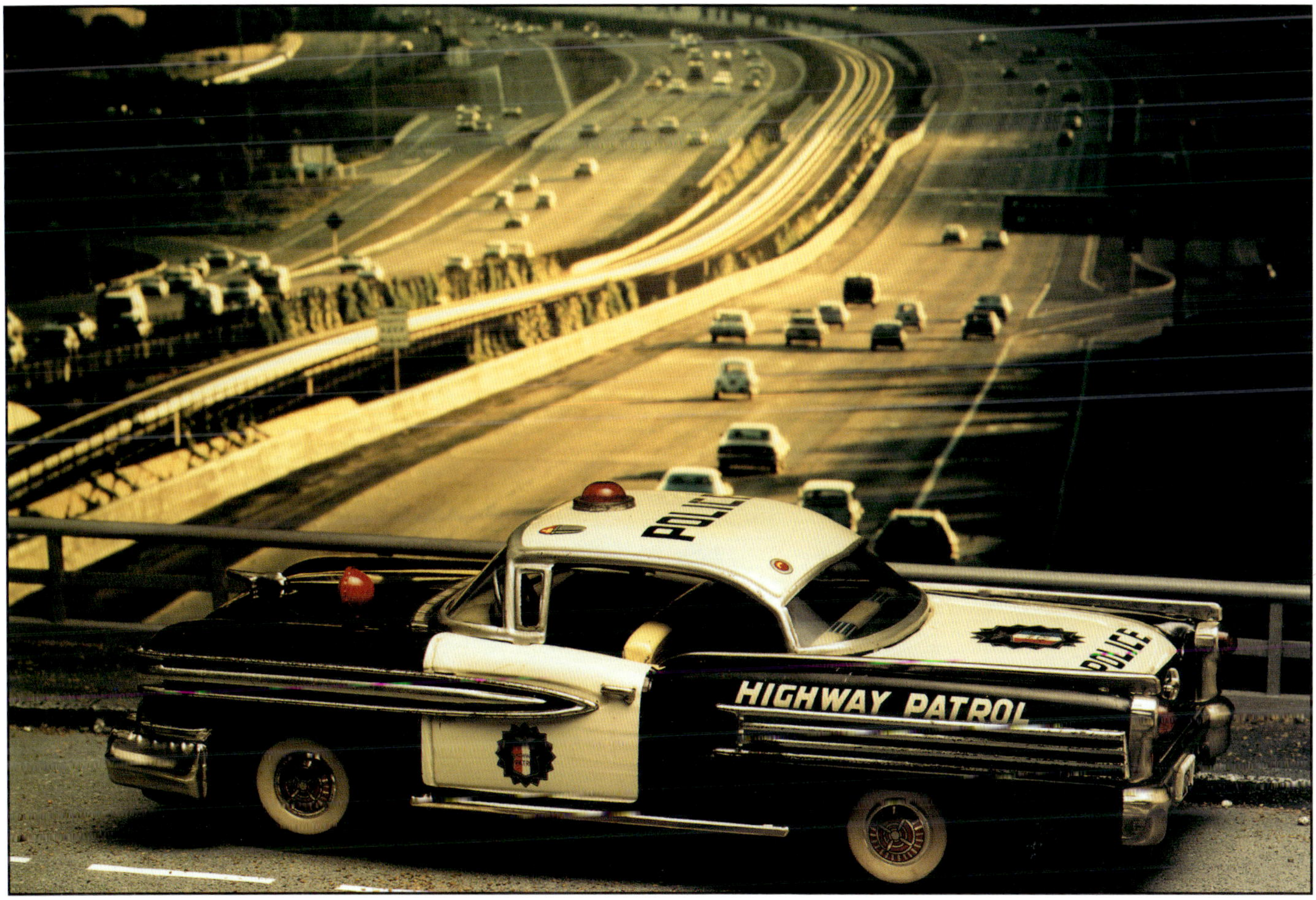

Photo by Tosh Wakabayashi

Bibliography

Barrett, Rex and Kathy. *Auction Catalogs*, 1988-2002.

Bolton, John. *Christmas Morning Auction Catalogs*, 1991-1999

Bossi, Marco. *Autohobby*. Ivrea, Italy: Priuli & Verlucca, Editori, 1974.

Broutin, Jacky. *Les Jouets Japanais*. Anamorphose, France 1982.

Burness, Tad. *Ultimate Car Spotter's Guide 1946-1969*. Iola, WI: Krause Publications, 1998.

Duellman, Elmer. *Elmer's Price Guide to Toys Volume 1*. Gas City, IN: L-W Book Sales, 1995.

Duellman, Elmer. *Elmer's Price Guide to Toys Volume 2*. Gas City, IN: L-W Book Sales, 1996.

Enoki, Noriaki. "We Love Toy!" Auction Catalogs 8-11, 2001-2002. Japan.

Flammang, James M. and Auto Editors of *Consumer Guide*. *100 Years Of The American Auto Millennium Edition*. Lincolnwood, IL: Publications International, Ltd., 1999.

Gallagher, William C. *Japanese Toys – Amusing Playthings From the Past*. Atglen, PA: Schiffer Publishing Ltd., 2000.

Japan Toy International Trade Fair Association. *1st Japan International Toy Fair Catalog*. 1962.

Japan Toys Museum Foundation, Shigeru Mozuka, Manager; Mitsuo Tsukuda, Owner and Founder. Tokyo, Japan.

Kaminaga, Eiji. COO, Marusan Toys, Ltd. Conversation with the authors. 2000-2003.

Kelley, Dale, Publisher. *Antique Toy World* magazine, Chicago, IL: Antique Toy World Publications, 2000-2003.

Kelley, Dale. *Collecting The Tin Toy Car 1950-1970*. Exton, PA: Schiffer Publishing Ltd., 1984.

Kitahara, Teruhisa. *T. Kitahara Collection Cars Tin Toy Dreams*. San Francisco, CA: Chronicle Books, 1985.

Kitahara, Teruhisa. *Teruhisa Kitahara Collection Tin Toy Box Graphic Arts* (in Japanese). Tokyo, Japan: Jitsugyo No Nihon Sya, Ltd., 1999.

Krim, Debby and Marty. New England Auction Gallery Catalogs.

Nakajima, Noburo. *Model Cars' Collection* (in Japanese). Tokyo, Japan: World Photo Press, 1998.

Machii, Mikio. Director, Iwaya Corporation. Conversations with the author. Tokyo, Japan 2000-2003.

O'Brien, Richard. "Japanese (Etc.) Tin Cars." Ron Smith, contributor. *Collecting Toys*. Florence, AL: Books Americana, 1997.

Pressland, David. *The Art of the Tin Toy*. Great Britain: New Cavendish Books, 1976

Ralston, Andrew. *Toy Cars of Japan and Hong Kong*. Atglen, PA: Schiffer Publishing Ltd., 2001.

Rampini, Paolo. *Enciclopedia Delle Auto-Giocattolo 1890-1940*. Milano, Italy: 1985.

Saito, Hank. Director, Masudaya Toys Co., Ltd. Conversations with the author. 2000-2003.

Smith, Herb and Barb. *Smith House Toys 1998 Price Guide*. Eliot, ME: Herb Smith, 1998.

Smith, Herb and Barb. *Smith House Toys Auction Catalogs*. 1998-2003.

Takayama, Toyoji. *Nostalgic Tin Toys Vol. 1, Commercial Cars*. Kyoto, Japan: Kyoto Shoin, 1989.

The Tin Toy Museum and collection of Toyoji Takayama, Kyoto, Japan.

Tin Toy Museum, Teruhisa Kitahara. Yokohama, Japan.

Toplay (T.P.S.) Ltd. *Catalogs, Illustration Drawings and Patent Drawings*.

Udagawa, Yoshio. Chairman of the Board, Toplay (T.P.S.) Ltd. Conversations with the author. Tokyo, Japan. 1998-1999.

Walter, Gerhard G. *Blechspielzeug im Wirtschaftswunder-Land* (in German). Ettlingen, Germany, 1996.

Walter, Gerhard G. *Tin Dream Machines*. Great Britain: New Cavendish Books Ltd., 1996.

Yamashita, Sumihiro. *Green Arrow Graffitti 23* (in Japanese), Tokyo, Japan: Green Arrow Graffitti.

9/29/05